TₑX and METAFONT

New Directions in Typesetting

T_EX and METAFONT
New Directions in Typesetting

Donald E. Knuth

Digital Press

American Mathematical Society

Printed in U.S.A.

1st Printing, December 1979
Documentation Number EY-BX003-DP-001

Knuth, Donald E
    T_EX and METAFONT, new directions in typesetting

    Includes index.
        1.   Computerized typesetting.   I.   Title.
Z253.3.K57   686.2'2544   79-25891
ISBN 0-932376-02-9

Cover illustration: the letter "S" as constructed by the Italian calligrapher Giovanbattista Palatino, circa 1550.

Foreword

Don Knuth's Tau Epsilon Chi (TeX) is potentially the most significant invention in typesetting in this century. It introduces a standard language for computer typography and in terms of importance could rank near the introduction of the Gutenberg press. The TeX system:

- understands typography from individual characters to page design;
- permits any typewriter, word processing system, computer-based editor, or TeX system editor to be used as an input device with a standard language;
- can typeset various formats and languages;
- is structured to be user-extendable to virtually all applications.

These improvements are benchmarks in typesetting and text creation. To date, computer-based typesetting systems have simply facilitated typesetting. Moreover, the proliferation of word processing systems makes possible the widespread direct transmission of text to typesetting without the intervening typesetting process—provided we use the standard language that TeX offers.

A direct link between text input and typesetting will permit a drastic restructuring of the journal- and book-publishing industry, allowing it to be oriented substantially more toward the author. Until now, even authors with word processing equipment have been unable to participate in the representation of their message in print. Prior to Gutenberg's invention, manuscripts were conceived and designed simultaneously, and often the author's hand shaped the entire final product. The results were beautiful and varied, in contrast to the manufacture of most modern books, which vary only in cover design. With TeX, moreover, not only can the author influence his own format and representation, but he also can produce more accurate material that can be rapidly mass-produced, shortening the time between idea and dissemination.

TeX is significant as a standard language because of the way it understands typography using a framework of boxes and glue in a hierarchical fashion so that any font, page layout, or other typesetting parameter can be set. This is in striking contrast to most typesetting systems, which are built with no generality. Finally, the input form is user-defined by means of a macroprocessor so that virtually any text can be input and can control the typography part of the program. It is this generality and segmentation of function that makes TEX significant.

This book is about much more than just the TEX system. The Gibbs Lecture presents the twin themes of how typography can help mathematics and how mathematics can help typography, and the material on METAFONT is intriguing and useful in its description of the use of mathematics in type design.

While the emphasis of TEX is on mathematics, the system is equally applicable to and will no doubt be used in many other domains. Don Knuth, in fact, shows us precisely how the system can humanize basic communications.

At Digital, we hope to use TEX immediately. I urge others to adopt and use it so that the language standard can be established.

C. Gordon Bell
Vice President of Engineering
Digital Equipment Corporation

Preface

Leonardo da Vinci made a sweeping statement in his notebooks: "Let no one who is not a mathematician read my works." In fact, he said it twice, so he probably meant it.

Fortunately, a lot of people failed to heed his injunction. It turns out that non-mathematicians are quite capable of dealing with mathematical concepts, when the description isn't beclouded with too much jargon. So I would like to reverse Leonardo's dictum and say, "Let everyone who is not a mathematician read my works." (Furthermore, mathematicians are invited too.)

Of course, every author likes to be read; but I have quoted Leonardo as a sort of apology for the fact that the first part of this book is the text of a talk that was addressed specifically to professional mathematicians. Two years ago I was deeply honored by an invitation to give the 1978 Gibbs Lecture, a lecture about applied mathematics that is delivered annually to the members of the American Mathematical Society. Since such prominent mathematicians as G. H. Hardy, Albert Einstein, and John von Neumann had previously been Gibbs lecturers, I wanted to say something that wasn't completely trivial, so I threw in some mathematics that was at least slightly sophisticated. The main point I wished to make, however, was that mathematical ideas need not be confined to the traditional areas of application and that I had found it especially exciting to bring mathematics to bear on the field of typography. I hope some of my excitement and the reasons for it will be understood by everybody concerned with written communication and the making of books of high quality.

This book is in three parts, each of which is intended to be reasonably self-contained. First comes the Gibbs Lecture, which gives an overview of the typographic research I have been doing. Then comes a complete description of the TEX typesetting system, a new system that seems to incorporate the "right" fundamental principles for computer-based composition in its notions of horizontal and vertical lists of boxes and glue. The last part is a similar description of METAFONT, a system for device-independent design of character shapes. Since the three parts are independent, each has separate page numbers, and the TEX and METAFONT descriptions have separate indexes.

My research on typography began only in 1977, so I can't claim that TEX and METAFONT are the best solutions to the problems they deal with. All I can say is that they have been applied to a great variety of typographic applications, and that the results look extremely promising. These initial successes have made it desirable to publish the present book as an interim report. In this way a larger community of people will be able to experiment with and criticize the ideas, even though TEX and METAFONT are in their infancy, and even though there hasn't yet been time for me to advance past the first draft of my designs for the fonts used or to typeset the material on a high-resolution phototypesetter.

I have been helped by so many people it is impossible to thank them all, so I must simply hit the highlights. In the first place, I want to thank the people at Digital Press for their encouragement to prepare this book and for the care with which they produced it. Second, I want to thank the American Mathematical Society for its unexpectedly strong endorsement of this work, and for the benefit of the experience and wisdom of several members of its editorial staff. Third, I wish to thank the National Science Foundation, the Office of Naval Research, and the IBM Corporation for supporting my research at Stanford. Fourth, I owe an enormous debt of gratitude to Leo Guibas and his associates at Xerox Research, who miraculously produced the camera-ready copy for Parts 2 and 3 of this book on experimental printing equipment. Fifth, I want to thank the hundreds of TEX users who have given me the benefit of their experiences. And above all, I wish to thank my wife, Jill, for her support and guidance.

D.E.K.
Stanford, California
August, 1979

Acknowledgments

D. E. Knuth: "Mathematical Typography." Copyright © 1979 by the American Mathematical Society. Reprinted with permission from the *Bulletin (New Series) of the American Mathematical Society*, March 1979, Vol. 1, No. 2, pp. 337–372. Josiah Willard Gibbs Lecture, given under the auspices of the American Mathematical Society, January 4, 1978; received by the editors February 10, 1978. This research was supported in part by the National Science Foundation grant MCS72-03752 A03, and by the Office of Naval Research contract N0014-76-C-0330.

D. E. Knuth: *TEX, a system for technical text*. Copyright © 1979 by the American Mathematical Society. Reprinted with permission. Originally published in June 1979 by the American Mathematical Society as a manual by the same title. The version that appears here is based on Stanford Artificial Intelligence Laboratory Memo AIM-317.3 / Computer Science Department Report No. STAN-CS-78-675, September 1979. This research was supported in part by the National Science Foundation grant MCS72-03752 A03, and by the Office of Naval Research contract N0014-76-C-0330. The author wishes to thank the many individuals who made helpful comments on the first drafts of the manual.

D. E. Knuth: *METAFONT, a system for alphabet design*. Copyright © 1979 by the American Mathematical Society. The version that appears here is based on Stanford Artificial Intelligence Laboratory Memo AIM-332 / Computer Science Department Report No. STAN-CS-79-762, September 1979. This research was supported in part by the National Science Foundation grant MCS72-03752 A03, and by the Office of Naval Research contract N0014-76-C-0330. The author wishes to thank the many individuals who made detailed comments on pre-preliminary drafts.

Digital Press gratefully acknowledges the support and cooperation of the American Mathematical Society.

Table of Contents

PART 1

Mathematical Typography

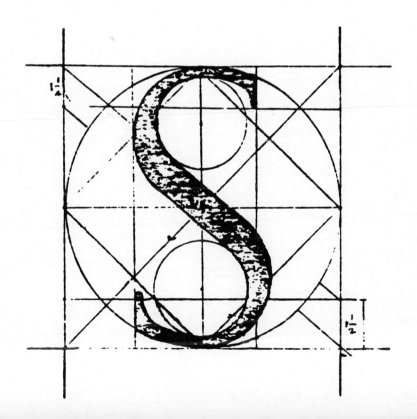

Mathematical Typography

Dedicated to George Pólya on his 90th birthday

ABSTRACT. Mathematics books and journals do not look as beautiful as they used to. It is not that their mathematical content is unsatisfactory, rather that the old and well-developed traditions of typesetting have become too expensive. Fortunately, it now appears that mathematics itself can be used to solve this problem.

A first step in the solution is to devise a method for unambiguously specifying mathematical manuscripts in such a way that they can easily be manipulated by machines. Such languages, when properly designed, can be learned quickly by authors and their typists, yet manuscripts in this form will lead directly to high quality plates for the printer with little or no human intervention.

A second step in the solution makes use of classical mathematics to design the shapes of the letters and symbols themselves. It is possible to give a rigorous definition of the exact shape of the letter "a", for example, in such a way that infinitely many styles (bold, extended, sans-serif, italic, etc.) are obtained from a single definition by changing only a few parameters. When the same is done for the other letters and symbols, we obtain a mathematical definition of type fonts, a definition that can be used on all machines both now and in the future. The main significance of this approach is that new symbols can readily be added in such a way that they are automatically consistent with the old ones.

Of course it is necessary that the mathematically-defined letters be beautiful according to traditional notions of aesthetics. Given a sequence of points in the plane, what is the most pleasing curve that connects them? This question leads to interesting mathematics, and one solution based on a novel family of spline curves has produced excellent fonts of type in the author's preliminary experiments. We may conclude that a mathematical approach to the design of alphabets does not eliminate the artists who have been doing the job for so many years; on the contrary, it gives them an exciting new medium to work with.

1

I will be speaking today about work in progress, instead of completed research; this was not my original intention when I chose the subject of this lecture, but the fact is I couldn't get my computer programs working in time. Fortunately it is just as well that I don't have a finished product to describe to you today, because research in mathematics is generally much more interesting while you're doing it than after it's all done. I will try therefore to convey in this lecture why I am so excited about the project on which I am currently working.

My talk will be in two parts, based on two different meanings of its title. First I will speak about mathematical typography in the sense of typography as the servant of mathematics: the goal here is to communicate mathematics effectively by making it possible to publish mathematical papers and books of high quality, without excessive cost. Then I will speak about mathematical typography in the sense of mathematics as the servant of typography: in this case we will see that mathematical ideas can make advances in the art of printing.

Preliminary examples. To set the stage for this discussion I would like to show you some examples by which you can "educate your eyes" to see mathematics as a printer might see it. These examples are taken from the *Transactions of the American Mathematical Society*, which began publication in 1900; by now over 230 volumes have been published. I took these volumes from the library shelves and divided them into equivalence classes based on what I could perceive to be different styles of printing: two volumes were placed into the same class if and only if they appeared to be printed in the same style. It turns out that twelve different styles can be distinguished, and it will be helpful for us to look at them briefly.

The first example (Figure 1a) comes from p. 2 of *Transactions* volume 1; I have shown only a small part of the page in order to encourage you to look at the individual letters and their positions rather than to read the mathematics. This typeface has an old-fashioned appearance, primarily because the upper case letters and the taller lower case ones like 'h' and 'k' are nearly twice as tall as the other lower case letters, and this is rarely seen nowadays. Notice the style of the italic letter 'x', the two strokes having a common segment in the middle. The subscripts and superscripts are set in rather small type.

This style was used in volumes 1 to 12 of the *Transactions*, and also in the first 21 pages of volume 13. Then page 22 of volume 13 introduced a more modern typeface (Figure 1b). In this example the subscripts are still in a very small font, and unfortunately the Greek α here is almost indistinguishable from an italic 'a'. Notice also that the printer has inserted more space before

(a)

$$\lambda = \pm \sqrt{\tfrac{1}{6} S} = \pm \sqrt{\tfrac{1}{6}(aa'a'')(aa'a'''}$$

there correspond two quadric forms each contain
rameters. So much HILBERT states. In order t
as known systems it will be convenient to use a
mental cubic, due to HESSE.*

Referred to an inflexional triangle, the equati

(3) $\qquad a_z^3 = x_1^3 + x_2^3 + x_3^3 + 6mx_1x_2$

All conic polars accordingly have the form :

(4) $\qquad a_y a_z^2 = (y_1 x_1^2 + y_2 x_2^2 + y_3 x_3^2) + 2m(y_1 x_2 x_3$

(b)

(5) $\qquad \varphi_a (x_1, \ x_2, \ \cdots, \ x_m : y_1, \ y_2, \ \cdots,$

in which the φ_a are polynomials in $y_1, y_2, \cdots,$
has been considered recently by W. D. MA
usual algebraic elimination theory to the p
$\Phi (x_1, \ x_2, \ \cdots, \ x_m : y_n)$ would be found fo
$\Phi (0, 0, \ \cdots, 0 : y_n)$ would be, say, of degree ρ.
theorem to $\Phi (x_1, \ x_2, \ \cdots, \ x_m : y_n)$, therefore,
degree ρ would appear. This is not in general t
is sought in this paper, as may readily be sho
The polynomials φ_a may have roots for which

(c)

I call this ineffective part of x_e *"innocuous"*
validate the fundamental proposition

$$[f(x_e') \neq f(x_e'')] = (x_e' \neq$$

which was proved above (P. 4) for effective val
ineffective part of x_e is innocuous is clear: it, *as*
that the variation of x_e does not take place in it

D. 3. But this consideration leads to the *defin*
of x. By this I mean the collection of values wl
i. e.,

(d)

six planes $y_i + y_k = 0$, each counted three tim
type $y_1 y_2 - y_3 y_4 = 0$, each counted twice.

We have seen that any point on the line $y_1 +$
image in (X) the whole line $X_1 + X_2 = 0$, X_3
in (y) meets the line in one point, its image s_9' co
the system s_9' has also the three lines of this tyl

12. **Algebraic procedure.** The plane co
and the vertex $(1, 0, 0, 0)$ has the equation

$$p_{31} x_2 + p_{42} x_3 + p_{23} x_4$$

Since (y) and (y') both satisfy this equation we

(e)

of systems of division algebras. The next syst
of order $p^2 q^2$ over F with the basal units $i^a j^b k^c$ (
with an irreducible equation of degree pq, three
rational functions $\theta(i)$ and $\psi(i)$ with coefficie
iterative $\theta^q(i)$ of $\theta(i)$ is i, and likewise $\psi^p(i) = i$
by

$$\theta^k[\psi^i(i)] = \psi^r[\theta^k(i)] \qquad (k = 0, 1, \cdots, q-1$$

The complete multiplication table of the un
associative law from

$$i^q = g, \qquad k^p = \gamma, \qquad kj = \alpha jk, \qquad ji =$$

(f)

$$z = e^{i\theta} z^0 \equiv (e^{i\theta} z_1^0, ..., e^{i\theta} z_n^0), \qquad 0 \leqq \theta \leqq 2\pi,$$

$\subset C^n$ is called a Reinhardt circular set if along w
$) \in E$ also the set

$$\{\bar{z} \,|\, |z_k| = |z_k^0|, \qquad k = 1, 2, ..., n\}$$

bounded closed subset of C^n, unisolvent with respec
The function $b(z)$ being defined and lower semic

$$h^{(\nu)} = \{h_1^{(\nu)}, ..., h_\nu^{(\nu)}\}, \qquad \nu_0 = C_{\nu + n - 1, n - 1}$$

FIGURE 1. A sequence of typographical styles
in the AMS *Transactions*: (a) vol **1** (1900), p. 2; (b)
vol **13** (1912), p. 135; (c) vol **23** (1922), p. 216; (d) vol
25 (1923), p. 10; (e) vol **28** (1926), p. 207; (f) vol **105**
(1962), p. 340;

and after parentheses than we are now accustomed to. During the next few years the spacing within formulas evolved gradually but the typefaces remained essentially the same up through volume 24: with one exception.

The exception was volume 23 in 1922 (Figure 1c), which in my opinion has the most pleasing appearance of all the *Transactions* volumes. This modern typeface is less condensed, making it more pleasant to read. The italic letters have changed in style too, not quite so happily—notice the '*x*', for example, which is not as nice as before—but by and large one has a favorable impression when paging through this volume. Such quality was not without its cost, however; according to a contemporary report in the AMS *Bulletin* [**45**, p. 100], the *Transactions* came out 18 months late at the time! Perhaps this is why the Society decided to seek yet another printer.

In order to appreciate the next change, let's look quickly at two excerpts from the *Bulletin* relating to the very first Gibbs Lecture (Figure 2). The preliminary announcement in 1923 appeared in the modern typeface used during that year, but the letter shapes in the report of the first lecture in 1924 were very cramped and stilted. The upper case letters in the title are about the same, but the lower case letters in the text are completely different.

This same style appeared in volume 25 of the *Transactions* (Figure 1d), which incidentally was set in Germany in order to reduce the cost of printing. Note that the boldface letters and the italic letters in this example are actually quite beautiful—and we're back to the good old style of '*x*' again—so the mathematical formulas looked great while the accompanying text was crowded. Fortunately only three volumes were published in this style.

A new era for the *Transactions* began in 1926, when its printing was taken over by the Collegiate Press in Menasha, Wisconsin. Volumes 28 through 104 were all done in the same style, covering 36 years from 1926 to 1961, inclusive, and this style (Figure 1e) was used also in the *American Mathematical Monthly*. In general the typefaces were quite satisfactory, but there was also a curious anomaly: Italic letters used in subscripts and superscripts of mathematical formulas were in a different style from those used on the main line! For example, notice the two k's in the first displayed formula of Figure 1e: the larger one has a loop, so it is topologically different from the smaller one. Similarly you can see that the p in k^p is quite different from the p in p^2. There are no x's in this example, but if you look at other pages you will find that the style of x that I like best appears only in subscripts and superscripts. I can't understand why this discrepancy was allowed to persist for so many years.

Another period of typographic turmoil for the *Transactions* began with volume 105 in 1962. This volume, which was typeset in Israel, introduced a switch to the Times Roman typeface (Figure 1f); an easy way to recognize the

(g)

$$0 = r_k x(\sum r_i \alpha_i) - (\sum r_i \alpha_i) x r_k = \sum_{i=1}^{k-1}$$

This element is of lower length. It follows there
$i = 1, \cdots, k$. Hence, (a) yields that $r_i = \lambda_i r_k$, λ_i
Now $r_k \neq 0$, by the minimality of k, and $\sum \lambda_i \alpha$
which we deduce that $\sum \lambda_i \alpha_i = 0$. But the α_i a
which is impossible since in particular $\lambda_k = 1$.

THEOREM 7. *Let R be a dense ring of linear t.*
F be a maximal commutative subfield D. If R_F
tion of finite rank over F, then R contains als

(h)

The set N_1 is nowhere dense in Z_1 and thus $N = \rho$
For each $\zeta \in Y - N$ we must prove that f_ζ satisfi
be the unique projection in $\{P_d \mid d \in D\}$ such that
the algebra $(E\mathscr{A}E) \cdot P_0$ is finite and homogeneou
onal abelian projections $E_1, E_2, \ldots, E_n$ such that
$(1 \leq j, k \leq n)$ be partial isometric operators in $(E\mathscr{A}$
  (1) $U_{jk} U_{lm} = \delta_{mj} U_{lk}$, where δ is the Kronecker d
  (2) $U_{jk}^* = U_{kj}$; and
  (3) $U_{jj} = E_j$,
for all $1 \leq j, k, l, m \leq n$. For each A in $(E\mathscr{A}E) \cdot P_0$, t
in $\mathscr{L}_1 P_0$ such that

(i)

The algebra P is nearly simple if and only if the
  (a) *N is spanned by $a, \cdots, a^{n-k-1}, b_1, \cdots$*
$i, j = 1, \cdots, k$.
  (b) *Either $n - k = $ char F with k even or n*

Proof. By Theorem 5.5, there are elements
$a, \cdots, a^{n-k-1}, b_1, \cdots, b_k$. Furthermore, $ab_i =$
for all i, j where each α_i, λ_{ij} is in F. From t
space of the space spanned by $a^{n-k-1}, b_1, \cdots,$
Assume P is nearly simple. Then there is
show that each b_i is in M. To do this, it is nec

(j)

:tions in GL(W) and $h_{\alpha\beta}$, $\alpha, \beta \in I$ as coordinate
ined by the respective bases chosen above. If α,
inction of $\wedge^p$ is the minor of $|g_{ij}|$ determined by
columns $\beta(1), \ldots, \beta(p)$. The coordinate ring of
$h_{\alpha\beta}$ together with $1/\det|h_{\alpha\beta}|$, while that of GL(W)
ogether with $1/\det|g_{ij}|$. The coordinate functions
, so to show $\wedge^p$ is a morphism it suffices to show
nial in g_{ij} and $1/\det|g_{ij}|$. For this, the following

haracter of GL(W) *is an integral power of the*

(k)

of Q, i.e.

$) = 0$ for every $x \in A$ for which $x(Q) = 0\}$.

or m_A is equivalent to the one induced by the
:

$\{|x(z)| : x \in A, \|x\| \leq 1$ and $x(w) = 0\}$.

present the open unit disk in the complex plane, $\mathbf{C}$,
t polydisk in n-dimensional complex space $\mathbf{C}^n$. T^n
oundary of D^n, i.e.

(l)

onverges pathwise to X^λ, and uniformly for $t \in$
for which X_i is the (last) minimum of Y^λ, let Y_i^λ
ilues of Y^λ, and T_i^λ the interjump times for Y^λ.
st an i such that $Y_i^\lambda = T_i^\lambda = \infty$. Notice that Y_Q^λ is
ud that as $\varepsilon \to 0$, Y_Q^λ converges to $I^\lambda = \inf_s X_s^\lambda$. Le
ts of $(-\infty, \infty)$. Then, for example, if $i \geq 1$

$-i \in B, Y_{Q+k}^\lambda - Y_Q^\lambda \in C, T_{Q+k}^\lambda \in D, N > Q > i\}$

$\in A, T_{l-i}^\lambda \in B, Y_{l+k}^\lambda - Y_l^\lambda \in C, T_{l+k}^\lambda \in D, N > Q$

FIGURE 1 [continued]: (g) vol **114** (1965), p. 216;
(h) vol **125** (1966), p. 38; (i) vol **169** (1972), p. 232; (j)
vol **179** (1973), p. 314; (k) vol **199** (1974), p. 370; (l)
vol **225** (1977), p. 372.

THE JOSIAH WILLARD GIBBS LECTURESHIP

The Council of the Society has sanctioned the establishment of an honorary lectureship to be known as the Josiah Willard Gibbs Lectureship. The lectures are to be of a popular nature on topics in mathematics or its applications, and are to be given by invitation under the auspices of the Society. They will be held annually or at such intervals as the Council may direct. It is expected that the first lecture will be delivered in New York City during the winter of 1923–24, and a committee has been authorized to inaugurate the lectures by choosing the first speaker and making the necessary arrangements.

R. G. D. RICHARDSON,
Secretary.

THE FIRST JOSIAH WILLARD GIBBS LECTURE

The first Josiah Willard Gibbs Lecture was delivered under the auspices of this Society on February 29, 1924, by Professor M. I. Pupin, of Columbia University, in the auditorium of the Engineering Societies' Building, New York City. A large and distinguished audience was present, including, besides members of the Society, many physicists, chemists, and engineers who had been invited to attend.

In introducing the speaker, President Veblen spoke as follows:

"In instituting the Willard Gibbs Lectures, the American Mathematical Society has recognized the dual character of mathematics. On the one hand, mathematics is one of the essential emanations of the human spirit,—a thing to be valued in and for itself, like art or poetry. Gibbs made

FIGURE 2. A time of transition. (Excerpts from the AMS Bulletin **29** (1923), p. 385; **30** (1924), p. 289.)

difference quickly is to look at the shading on the letter "o", since it now is somewhat slanted; in the previously used fonts this letter always was more symmetrical, as if it were drawn with a pen held horizontally, but in Times Roman it clearly has an oblique stress as if it were drawn by a right-handed penman. Note that the three k's are topologically the same in the displayed equation here; but for some reason the two subscript k's are of different sizes. Many of the Times Italic letters have a somewhat different style than readers of the *Transactions* had been accustomed to, and I personally think that this font tends to make formulas look more crowded. Actually the changeover to Times Roman and Times Italic wasn't complete; the italic letter g still had its familiar shape, perhaps because the new shape looked too strange to mathematicians.

Volumes 105 through 124 were all done in this style, except for a brief interruption: In volumes 114, 115, and 116 the shading on the o's was symmetrical and the k's had loops (Figure 1g). Another style was used for volumes 125–168 (Figure 1h): again Times Roman was the rule, even in the g's, except for subscripts and superscripts which were in the style I prefer; for example, compare the j's and k's. (These latter volumes were typeset in Great Britain.)

A greatly increased volume of publication, together with the rising salaries of skilled personnel, was making it prohibitively expensive to use traditional methods of typesetting, and the Society eventually had to resort to a fancy form of typewriter composition that could simply be photographed for printing. This unfortunate circumstance made volumes 169–198 of the *Transactions* look like Figure 1i, except for volumes 179, 185, 189, 192, 194, and 198, which were done in a far better (yet not wholly satisfactory) style that can be distinguished from Figure 1f by the italic g's. Figure 1j was composed on a computer using a system developed by Lowell Hawkinson and Richard McQuillin; this was one of the fruits of an AMS research project supported by the National Science Foundation [2], [3], [4], [5], [6].

Computer typesetting of mathematics was still somewhat premature at the time, however, and another kind of "cold copy" made its appearance in volumes 199 through 224—an "IBM Composer" was used, except for volumes 208 and 211 which reverted to the Varityper style of Figure 1i. The new alphabet was rather cramped in appearance, and some words were even more crowded than the others (see Figure 1k). At this point I regretfully stopped submitting papers to the American Mathematical Society, since the finished product was just too painful for me to look at. Similar fluctuations of typographical quality have appeared recently in all technical fields, especially in physics where the situation has gotten even worse. (The history of publication at the American Society of Civil Engineers has been discussed in an interesting and informative article by Paul A. Parisi [44].)

Fortunately things are now improving. Beginning with volume 225, which was published last year, the *Transactions* now looks like Figure 1l; like Figure 1j, it is computer composed, and the Times Roman typeface is now somewhat larger. I still don't care for this particular style of italic letters, and there are some bugs needing to be ironed out such as the overlap between lines shown in this example; but it is clear that the situation is getting better, and perhaps some day we will once again be able to approach the quality of volumes 23 and 24.

Computer-assisted composition. Perhaps the main reason that the situation is improving is the fact that computers are able to manipulate text and convert it into a form suitable for printing. Experimental systems of this kind have been in use since the early 1960s (cf. the book by Barnett [10]), and now they are beginning to come of age. Within another ten years or so, I expect that the typical typewriter will be replaced by a television screen attached to a keyboard and to a small computer. It will be easy to make changes to a manuscript, to replace all occurrences of one phrase by another and so on, and to transmit the manuscript either to the television screen, or to a printing device, or to another computer. Such systems are already in use by most newspapers, and new experimental systems for business offices actually will display the text in a variety of fonts [26]. It won't be long before these machines change the traditional methods of manuscript preparation in universities and technical laboratories.

Mathematical typesetting adds an extra level of complication, of course. Printers refer to mathematics as "penalty copy", and one of America's foremost typographers T. L. De Vinne wrote that "[even] under the most favorable conditions algebra will be troublesome." [17, p. 171.] The problem used to be that the two-dimensional formulas required complicated positioning of individual metal pieces of type; but now this problem reduces to a much simpler one, namely that two-dimensional formulas need to be represented as a one-dimensional sequence of instructions for transmission to the computer.

One-dimensional languages for mathematical formulas are now familiar in programming languages such as FORTRAN, but a somewhat different approach is needed when all the complexities of typesetting are considered. In order to show you the flavor of languages for mathematical typesetting, I will briefly describe the three reasonably successful systems known to me. The first, which I will call Type C, is typical of the commercially available systems now used to typeset mathematical journals (cf. [12]). The second, which I will

Formula	Type C	Type B	Type T
$\dfrac{1}{2}$	$f1$s2$t	1 over 2	1 \over 2
θ^2	*gq"2	theta sup 2	\theta↑2
$\sqrt{f(x_i)}$	$rf(x'i)$t	sqrt{f(x sub i)}	\sqrt{f(x↓i)}

FIGURE 3. Three ways to describe a formula.

call Type B, was developed at Bell Telephone Laboratories and has been used to prepare several books and articles including the article that introduced the system [27]. The third, which I will call Type T, is the one I am presently developing as part of the system I call TEX [29].[1]

Figure 3 shows how three simple formulas would be expressed in these three languages. The Type C language uses $f . . . $s . . . $t for fractions, *g for "the next character is Greek", q for the Greek letter theta, " for superscripts, $r . . . $t for square roots and ' for subscripts. The Type B language is more mnemonic, using "over", "theta", "sup", "sqrt", and "sub" together with braces for grouping when necessary. The Type T language is similar but it does not make use of "reserved words"; a special character \ is used before any nonstandard text. This means that spaces can be ignored, while they need to be inserted in just the right places in the Type B language; for example, the space after the "i" is important in the example shown, otherwise $f(x_i)$ would become $f(x_i$ according to the Type B rules. Another reason for the \ delimiter in Type T is that it becomes unnecessary to match each text item against a stored dictionary, and it is possible to use "sup" to mean supremum instead of superscript. The special symbols \ { } ↑ ↓ in Type T can be changed to any other characters if desired; although these five symbols don't appear on conventional typewriters, they are common on computer terminal keyboards.

---

[1] This has no connection with a similarly-named system recently announced by Honeywell Information Systems, or with another one developed by Digital Research. In my language, the T, E, and X are Greek letters and TEX is pronounced "tech", following the Greek words for art and technology.

Incidentally, computer typesetting brings us some good news: It is now quite easy to represent square roots in the traditional manner with radical signs and vincula, so we won't have to write $x^{1/2}$ when we don't want to.[2]

None of these languages makes it possible to *read* complex formulas as easily as in the two-dimensional form, but experience shows that it is not difficult for untrained personnel to learn how to type them. According to [12], "Within a few hours (a few days at most) a typist with no math or typesetting background can be taught to input even the most complex equations." And the Type B authors [27] report that "the learning time is short. A few minutes gives the general flavor, and typing a page or two of a paper generally uncovers most of the misconceptions about how it works." Thus it will be feasible for both typists and mathematicians to prepare papers in such a language, without investing a great deal of effort in learning the system. The only real difficulties arise when preparing tables that involve tricky alignments.

Once such systems become widespread, authors will be able to prepare their papers and see exactly how they will look when printed. Everyone who writes mathematical papers knows that his intentions are often misunderstood by the printer, and corrections to the galley proofs have a nontrivial probability of introducing further errors. Thus, in the words of three early users of the Bell Labs' system, "the moral seems clear. If you let others do your typesetting, then there will be errors beyond your control; if you do your own, then you have only yourself to blame." [1] Personally, I can't adequately describe how wonderful it feels when I now make a change to the manuscript of my book, as it is stored in the Stanford computer, since I *know* that the change is immediately in effect; it never will go through any middlemen who might misunderstand my intention.

Perhaps some day a typesetting language will become standardized to the point where papers can be submitted to the American Mathematical Society from computer to computer via telephone lines. Galley proofs will not be necessary, but referees and/or copy editors could send suggested changes to the author, and he could insert these into the manuscript, again via telephone.

Of course I am hoping that if any language becomes standard it will be my TEX language. Well . . . perhaps I am biased, and I know that TEX provides only small refinements over what is available in other systems. Yet several dozen small refinements add up to something that is important to me, and I think such refinements might prove important to other people as well. Therefore I'd like to spend the next few minutes explaining more about TEX.

---

[2] (ADDED IN PROOF). I was pleased to find that this announcement was greeted with an enthusiastic round of applause when I delivered the lecture.

The TeX input language. TeX must deal with "ordinary" text as well as mathematics, and it is designed as a unified system in which the mathematical features blend in with the word-processing routines instead of being "tacked on" to a conventional typesetting language. The main idea of TeX is to construct what I call *boxes*. A character of type by itself is a box, as is a solid black rectangle; and we use such "atoms" to construct more complex boxes analogous to "molecules", by forming horizontal or vertical lists of boxes. The final pages of text are boxes made out of lists of boxes made out of lists of boxes, and so on down to the individual characters and black rectangles, which are not decomposed further. For example, a typical page of a book is a box formed from vertical lists of boxes representing lines of type, and these lines of type are boxes formed from a horizontal list of boxes representing individual letters. A mathematical formula breaks down into boxes in a natural way; for example, the numerator and denominator of a fraction are boxes, and so is the bar line between them (since it is a thin but solid black rectangle). The elements of a rectangular matrix are boxes, and so on.

The individual boxes of a horizontal list or a vertical list are separated by a special kind of elastic mortar that I call "glue". The glue between two boxes has three component parts (x, y, z) expressed in units of length:

the *space* component, x, is the ideal or normal space desired between these boxes;

the *stretch* component, y, is the amount of extra space that is tolerable;

the *shrink* component, z, is the amount of space that may be removed if necessary.

Suppose the list contains $n + 1$ boxes $B_0, B_1, \ldots, B_n$ separated by n globs of glue having specifications $(x_1, y_1, z_1), \ldots, (x_n, y_n, z_n)$. When this list is made into a box, we *set the glue* according to the desired final size of the box. If the final size is to be larger than we would obtain with the normal spacing $x_1 + \cdots + x_n$, we increase the space proportional to the y's so that the actual space between boxes is

$$x_1 + ty_1, \ldots, x_n + ty_n$$

for some appropriate $t > 0$. On the other hand if the desired final size must be smaller, we decrease the space to

$$x_1 - tz_1, \ldots, x_n - tz_n,$$

in proportion to the individual shrinkages z_i. In the latter case t is not allowed to become greater than 1; the glue will never be smaller than $x - z$, although it might occasionally become greater than $x + y$. Once the glue has been set, the box is rigid and never changes its size again.

Consider, for example, a normal line of text, which is a list of individual character boxes. The glue between letters of a word will have $x = y = z = 0$, say, meaning that this word always has the letters butting against each other; but the glue between words might have x equal to the width of the letter 'e', and $y = x$, and $z = \frac{1}{2}x$, meaning that the space between words might expand or shrink. The spaces after punctuation marks like periods and commas might be allowed to stretch at a faster rate but to shrink more slowly.

An important special case of this glue concept occurs when we have "infinite" stretchability. Suppose the x and z components are zero, but the y component is extremely large, say y is one mile long. If such an element of glue is placed at the left of a list of boxes, the effect will be to put essentially all of the expansion at the left, therefore the boxes will be right-justified so that the right edge will be flush with the margin. Similarly if we place such infinitely stretchable glue at both ends of the list, the effect will be to center the line. These common typographic operations therefore turn out to be simple special cases of the general idea of variable glue, and the computer can do its job more elegantly since it is dealing with fewer primitives. Incidentally you will notice from this example that glue is allowed to appear at the ends of a list, not just between boxes; actually it is also possible to have glue next to glue, and boxes next to boxes, so that a list of boxes really is a list of boxes and glue mixed in any fashion whatever. I didn't mention this before, because for some reason it seems easier to explain the idea first in the case when boxes alternate with glue.

The same principles apply to vertical lists. For example, the glue that appears above and below a displayed equation will tend to be stretchable and shrinkable, but the glue between lines of text will be calculated so that adjacent base lines will be uniformly spaced when possible. You can imagine how the concept of glue allows you to do special tricks like backspacing (by letting x be negative), in a natural manner.

Line division. One of the more interesting things a system like TEX has to do is to divide up a paragraph into individual lines so that each line is about the right length. The traditional way to do this, which is still used on today's computer typesetting systems, is to make the best possible line division you can whenever you come to the right margin, but once this line has been output you never reconsider it—you start the next line with no memory of what has come before. Actually it often happens that one could do better by moving a short word down from one line to the next, but the problem is that you don't know what the rest of the paragraph will be like when you have only looked at one line's worth.

The TₑX system will introduce a new approach to the problem of line division, in which the end of a paragraph *does* influence the way the first lines are broken; this will result in more even spacing and fewer hyphenated words. Here is how it works: First we convert the line division problem to a precisely-defined mathematical problem by using TₑX's glue to introduce the concept of "badness". When a horizontal list of boxes has a certain natural width w (based on the width of its boxes and the space components of its glue), and a certain stretchability y (the sum of the stretch components) and a certain shrinkability z (the sum of the shrinkages), the *badness* of setting the glue to make a box of width W is defined to be $1 + 100t^3$ in our previous notation; more precisely, it is

$$1, \qquad\qquad\qquad \text{if } W = w,$$

$$1 + 100 \left(\frac{W - w}{y} \right)^3, \quad \text{if } W > w,$$

$$1 + 100 \left(\frac{w - W}{z} \right)^3, \quad \text{if } w - z \leq W < w,$$

$$\text{infinite}, \qquad\qquad \text{if } W < w - z.$$

Thus if the desired width W is near the natural width w, or if there is a lot of stretchability and shrinkability, the badness rating is very small; but if W is much greater than w and there isn't much ability to stretch, we have a lot of badness. Furthermore we add *penalty points* to the badness rating if the line ends at a comparatively undesirable place; for example, when a word needs to be hyphenated, the badness goes up by 50, and an even worse penalty is paid if we have to break up mathematical formulas.

The line division problem may now be stated as follows. "Given the text of a paragraph and the set of all allowable places to break it between lines, find breakpoints that minimize the sum of the squares of the badnesses of the resulting lines." This definition is quite arbitrary, of course, but it seems to work. Preliminary experiments show that the same choice of breakpoints is almost always found when simply minimizing the sum of the individual badnesses rather than the sum of their squares, but it seems wise to minimize the sum of squares as a precautionary measure since this will also tend to minimize the maximum badness.

Just stating the line division problem in mathematical terms doesn't solve it, of course; we need to have a good way to find the desired breakpoints. If there are n permissible places to break (including all spaces between words and all possible hyphenations), there are 2^n possible ways to divide up the paragraph, and we would never have time to look at them all. Fortunately there is a technique that can be used to reduce the number of computational steps to order n^2 instead of 2^n; this is a special case of what Richard Bellman calls "dynamic programming." Let $f(j)$ be the minimum sum of badness squares for all ways to divide the initial text of the paragraph up to breakpoint j, including a break at j, and let $b(i, j)$ be the badness of a line that runs from breakpoint i to breakpoint j. Let breakpoint 0 denote the beginning of the paragraph; and let breakpoint $n + 1$ be the end of the paragraph, with infinitely expandable glue inserted just before this final breakpoint. Then

$$f(0) = 0;$$
$$f(j) = \min_{0 \le i < j} (f(i) + b(i,j)^2), \quad \text{for } 1 \le j \le n + 1.$$

The computation of $f(1), \ldots, f(n + 1)$ can be done in order n^2 steps, and $f(n + 1)$ will be the minimum possible sum of badnesses squared. By remembering the values of i at which the minima occurred for each j, we can find breakpoints that give the best line divisions, as desired.

In practice we need not test extremely unlikely breakpoints; for example, there is rarely any reason to hyphenate the very first word of a paragraph. Thus it turns out that this dynamic programming method can be further improved to an algorithm whose running time is almost always of order n instead of n^2, and comparatively few hyphenations will need to be tried. Incidentally, the problem of hyphenation itself leads to some interesting mathematical questions, but I don't have time to discuss them today. (Cf. [41] and the references in that paper.)

The idea of badness ratings applies in the vertical dimension as well as in the horizontal; in this case we want to avoid breaking columns or pages in a bad manner. For example, penalty points are given for splitting a paragraph between pages after a hyphenation, or for dividing it in such a way that only one of its lines—a so-called "widow" line—appears on a page. The placement of illustrations, tables, and footnotes is also facilitated by formulating appropriate rules of placement in terms of badness.

There is more to TEX, including for example some facilities for handling the rather intricate layouts often needed to typeset tables without having to calculate column widths; but I think I have described the most important principles of its organization. During the next few months I plan to write the computer programs for TEX in such a way that each algorithm is clearly explained and so that the system can be implemented on many different computers without great difficulty; then I intend to publish the programs in a book so that everyone who wants to can use them.

Entr'acte. I said at the beginning that this talk would be in two parts, discussing both the ways that typography can help mathematics and that mathematics can help typography. So far we have seen a little of both, but the mathematics has been comparatively trivial. In the remainder of my lecture I would like to discuss what I believe is a much more significant application of mathematics to typography, namely to the specification of the letter shapes themselves. A more accurate way to describe the two parts of my lecture would be to say that the first part was about TEX, a system that takes manuscripts and converts them into specifications about where to put each character on each page; and the second part will be about another system I'm working on called METAFONT, which generates the characters themselves, for use in the inkier parts of the printing business.

Before I get into the second part of my lecture I need to discuss recent developments in printing technology. The most reliable way to print mathematics books of high quality during the past several decades has been to use the monotype process[3], which casts characters in hot lead, together with hand operations for complex built-up formulas. When I watched this process being applied to my own books several years ago, I was surprised to learn that the lead type was used to print only *one* copy; the master copy was then photographed, and the real printing took place from the photographic plates. This somewhat awkward sequence of steps was justified because it was the best way known to give good results. During the 1960s, however, hot lead type was replaced for many purposes by devices like the Photon machine used to prepare the printed programs for today's lecture; in this case the process is entirely photographical, since the letter shapes are stored as small negatives on a rotating disk, and the plates needed for printing are obtained by exposing the film after transforming the characters into the proper size and position with mirrors and lenses (cf. [10]). Such machines are limited by slow speed and the difficulties of adding new characters.

"Third-generation" typesetting equipment. More recent machines, such as the one used to prepare the current volumes of the *Transactions*, have replaced these "analog" processes by a "digital" one. The new idea is to divide the page or the photographic negative into millions of tiny rectangles, like a piece of graph paper or like a television screen but with a much higher resolu-

---

[3] Actually the Monotype Corporation now manufactures digital photosetting equipment as well as the traditional 'monotype' machines.

tion of about 1000 lines per inch. For each of the tiny "pixels" in such a raster pattern—there are about a million square pixels in every square inch—the typesetting machine decides whether it is to be black or white, and the black ones are exposed on the photographic plate by using a very precisely controlled electron beam or laser beam. Since these machines have few moving parts and require little or no mechanical motion, they can operate at very high speeds even though they are exposing only a tiny bit of the film at any time.

Stating this another way, the new printing equipment essentially treats each page of a book as a huge matrix of 0's and 1's, with ink to be placed in the positions that are 1 while the 0 positions are to be left blank. It's like the flashcards at a football stadium, although on a much grander scale. The total job of a system like TeX now becomes one of converting an author's manuscript into a gigantic matrix of binary digits or "bits."

The first question we must ask, of course, is, "What happens to the quality?" Clearly a television picture is no match for a photograph, and the digital typesetting machines would be quite unsatisfactory if their output looked inferior to the results obtained with metal type. In matters like this, I have to confess being somewhat of a stickler and a perfectionist; for example, I refuse to eat margarine instead of butter, and I have never heard an electronic organ that sounds even remotely as beautiful as a pipe organ. Therefore I was quite skeptical about digital typography, until I saw an actual sample of what was done on a high quality machine and held it under a magnifying glass: It was impossible to tell that the letters were generated with a discrete raster! The reason for this is not that our eyes can't distinguish more than 1000 points per inch; in appropriate circumstances they can. The reason is that particles of *ink* can't distinguish such fine details—you can't print the edge of an ink line that zigzags 1000 times on the diagonal of a square inch, the ink will round off the edges. In fact the critical number seems to be more like 500 than 1000. Thus the physical properties of ink cause it to appear as if there were no raster at all.

It now seems clear that discrete raster-based printing devices will soon make the other machines obsolete for nearly all publishing activity. Thus in future days the fact that Gutenberg and others invented movable type will not be especially relevant; it will merely be a curious historical fact that influenced history for only about 500 years. The ultimately relevant thing will be mathematics: the mathematics of matrices of 0's and 1's!

Semiphilosophical remarks. I have to tell the next part of the story from my personal point of view. As a combinatorial mathematician, I really identify with matrices of 0's and 1's, so when I learned last spring about such printing machines it was impossible for me to continue what I was doing; I just had to take time off to explore the possibilities of the new equipment. My motivation was also increased by the degradation of quality I had been observing in technical journals; and furthermore the publishers of my books on computer programming had tried valiantly but unsuccessfully to produce the second edition of volume 2 in the style of the first edition without using the rapidly-disappearing hot lead process. It appeared that my books would soon have to look as bad as the journals! When I saw that these problems could all be solved by appropriate computer programming, I couldn't resist trying to find a solution by myself.

One of the most important factors in my motivation was the knowledge that the problem would be solved once and for all, if I could find a purely mathematical way to define the letter shapes and convert them to discrete raster patterns. Even though new printing methods are bound to be devised in the future, possibly even before I finish volume seven of the books I'm writing, any new machines are almost certain to be based on a high precision raster; and although the precision of the raster may change, the letter shapes can stay the same forever, once they are defined in a machine-independent form. My goal was therefore to give a precise description of the shapes of all the symbols I would need.

I looked at the way fonts of type are being digitized at several places in different parts of the world; it is basically done by taking existing fonts and copying them using sophisticated camera equipment and computer programs, together with manual editing. But this seemed instinctively wrong to me, partly because the sophisticated equipment wasn't readily available in our laboratory at Stanford, and partly because the copying of copyrighted fonts is of questionable legality, but mostly because I felt that the whole idea of making a copy was not penetrating to the heart of the problem. It reminded me of the anecdote I had once heard about slide rules in Japan. According to this story, the first slide rule ever brought to the Orient had a black speck of dirt on it; so for many years all Japanese slide rules had a useless black spot in the same position! The story is probably apocryphal, but the point is that we should copy the substance rather than the form. I felt that the right question to ask would not be "How should this font of type be copied?" but rather: "If the great type designers of the past were alive today, how would they design fonts for the new equipment?" I didn't expect to be capable of finding the exact answer to this question, of course, but I did feel that it would lead me in the right direction, so I began to read about the history of type design.

Well, this is a most fascinating subject, but I can't talk much about it in a limited time. Two of the first things I read were autobiographical notes by two well-known 20th century type designers, Hermann Zapf [51] and Frederic W. Goudy [20], and I was especially interested by some of Zapf's remarks:

> With the beginning of the 'sixties . . . I was stimulated by this new field [photocomposing] . . . The type-designer—or better, let us start calling him the alphabet designer—will have to see his task and his responsibility more than before in the coordination of the tradition in the development of letterforms with the practical purpose and the needs of the advanced equipment of today . . . . The new photocomposing systems using cathode-ray tubes (CRT) or digital storage for the alphabet bring with them some absolutely new technical problems, many more than did the past . . . [51, p. 71].

I have the impression that Goudy would not have been so sympathetic to the new-fangled equipment, yet his book also gave helpful ideas.

Mathematical type design. Fortunately the Stanford Library has a wonderful collection of books about printing, and I had the chance to read many rather rare source materials. I learned to my surprise that the idea of defining letters mathematically is by no means new, it goes back to the fifteenth century and it became rather highly developed in the early part of the sixteenth. This was the time when there were Renaissance men who combined mathematics with the real world, and in particular there was an interest in constructing capital letters with ruler and compass. The first person to do this was apparently Felice Feliciano, about 1460, whose handwritten manuscript in the Vatican Library was published 500 years later [19]. Feliciano was an excellent calligrapher who wanted to put the principles of calligraphy on a sound mathematical foundation. Several other fifteen-century authors made similar experiments ([8] gives a critical summary of these early developments), but the most notable work of this kind appeared in the early sixteenth century.

The Italian mathematician Luca Pacioli, who had previously written the most influential book on algebra at the time (one of the first algebra books ever published), included an appendix on alphabets in his *De Divina Proportione*, a book about geometry and the "golden section" that appeared in 1509. Another notable Italian work on the subject was published by Francesco Torniello in 1517 [48], [33]; Figure 4 illustrates the letter *B* as constructed by Pacioli, Torniello, and by Giovanbattista Palatino [43]. Palatino was one of the best calligraphers of the century, and he did this work about 1550. Similar work appeared in Germany and France; the German book was probably the most famous and influential, it was Albrecht Dürer's *Underweysung der Messung* [18], a manual of instruction in geometry for Renaissance painters. The French book was also rather popular, it was *Champ Fleury* by Geofroy Tory [49], the

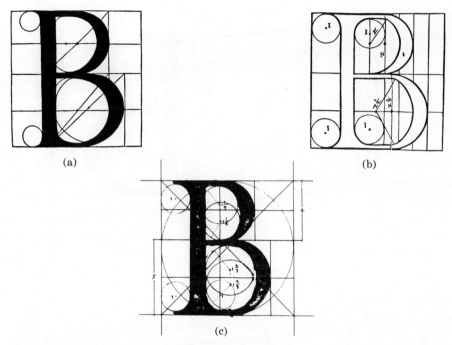

(a)

(b)

(c)

FIGURE 4. Sixteenth century ruler-and-compass constructions for the letter B by (a) Pacioli [**42**], (b) Torniello [**48**], and (c) Palatino [**43**].

first royal printer of France and the man who introduced accented letters into French typography. Figure 5 shows Tory's two suggestions for the letter B. Of all these books I much prefer Torniello's, since he was the only one who stated the constructions clearly and unambiguously.

Apparently nobody carried this work further to lower case letters, numerals, or italic letters and other symbols, until more than 100 years later when Joseph Moxon made a detailed study of some beautiful letters designed in Holland [**38**]. The ultimate in refinement of this mathematical approach took place shortly afterwards when Louis XIV of France commissioned the creation of a Royal Alphabet. A commission of artists and typographers worked on Louis's project for more than ten years beginning about 1690, and they made elaborate constructions such as those shown in Figure 6 [**24**].

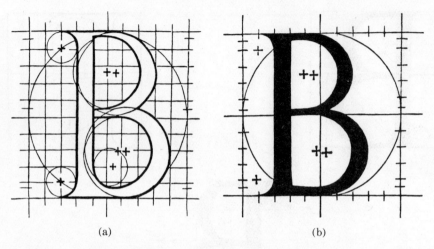

(a)   (b)

FIGURE 5. Two more B's, by Tory [**49**].

Thus it is clear that the mathematical definition of letter forms has a long history. However, I must also report near-universal agreement among today's scholars of typography that those efforts were a failure. At worst, the ruler-and-compass letters have been called "ugly" and at best they are said to be "deprived of calligraphic grace" [**8**]. The French designs were not really followed faithfully by Phillipe Grandjean who actually cut Louis XIV's type, nor by anybody else to date, and F. W. Goudy's reaction to this was: "God be praised!" [**20**, p. 139]. Such strictly geometric letter forms were in fact criticized already in the sixteenth century by Giovan Cresci, a noted scribe at the Vatican Library and the Sistine Chapel. Here is what Cresci wrote in 1560:

> I have come to the conclusion that if Euclid, the prince of geometry, returned to this world of ours, he would never find that the curves of the letters could be constructed by means of circles made with compasses. [**16**].

Well, Cresci was right. But fortunately there have been a few advances in mathematics during the last 400 years, and we now have some other tricks up our sleeves besides straight lines and circles. In fact, it is now possible to prescribe formulas that match the nuances of the best type designers; and

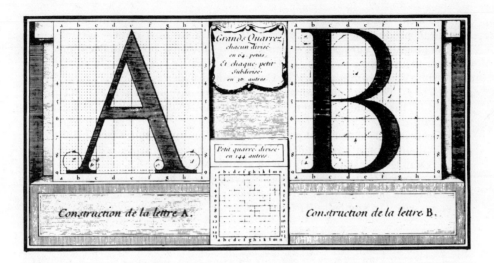

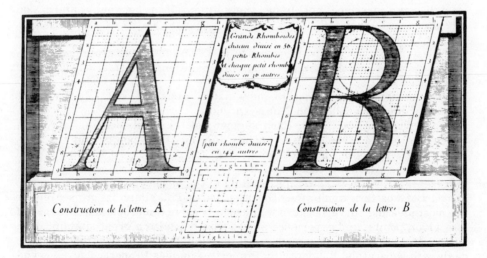

FIGURE 6. Roman and italic letters designed for Louis XIV of France [24].

perhaps a talented designer working with appropriate mathematical tools will be able to produce something even better than we now have.

Defining good curves. Let's consider the following mathematical problem: Given n points $z_1, z_2, \ldots, z_n$ in the plane, what is the most pleasing closed curve that goes through them in the specified order $z_1, z_2, \ldots, z_n$ and then returns to z_1? To avoid degenerate situations we may assume that n is equal to 4 or more. This problem is essentially like the dot-to-dot puzzles that we give to young children.

Of course it is not a well-posed mathematical problem, since I didn't say what it means for a curve to be "most pleasing". Let's first postulate some axioms that the most pleasing curve should satisfy.

PROPERTY 1 (INVARIANCE). If the given points are rotated, translated, or expanded, the most pleasing curve will be rotated, translated, or expanded in the same way. [In symbols: $MPC(az_1 + b, \ldots, az_n + b) = aMPC(z_1, \ldots, z_n) + b$.]

PROPERTY 2 (SYMMETRY). Cyclic permutation of the given points does not change the solution. [$MPC(z_1, z_2, \ldots, z_n) = MPC(z_2, \ldots, z_n, z_1)$.]

PROPERTY 3 (EXTENSIONALITY). Adding a new point that is already on the most pleasing curve does not change the solution. [If z is between z_k and z_{k+1} on $MPC(z_1, \ldots, z_n)$ then $MPC(z_1, \ldots, z_k, z, z_{k+1}, \ldots, z_n) = MPC(z_1, \ldots, z_k, z_{k+1}, \ldots, z_n)$.]

These properties are rather easy to justify on intuitive grounds. For example, the extensionality property says that additional information won't lead to a poorer solution.

The next property is not so immediately apparent, but I believe it is important for the application I have in mind.

PROPERTY 4 (LOCALITY). Each segment of the most pleasing curve between two of the given points depends only on those points and the ones immediately preceding and following. [$MPC(z_1, z_2, \ldots, z_n)$ is composed of $MPC(z_n, z_1, z_2, z_3)$ from z_1 to z_2, then $MPC(z_1, z_2, z_3, z_4)$ from z_2 to $z_3, \ldots$, then $MPC(z_{n-1}, z_n, z_1, z_2)$ from z_n to z_1.] According to the locality property, changes to one part of a pattern won't affect the other parts. This simplifies our search for the most pleasing curve, because we need only solve the problem in the case of four given points; and experience shows that it is also a great simplification when letters are being designed, since individual portions of strokes can be dealt with separately. Incidentally, Property 4 implies Property 2 (cyclic symmetry).

One way to satisfy all four of these properties is simply to let the most pleasing curve consist of straight line segments. But this doesn't seem adequately pleasing, so we add another postulate:

PROPERTY 5 (SMOOTHNESS). There are no sharp corners in the most pleasing curve. [$MPC(z_1, \ldots, z_n)$ is differentiable, under some parameterization.]

In other words, there is a unique tangent at every point of the curve.

The extensionality, locality, and smoothness properties taken together imply, in fact, that *the direction of the tangent at z_k depends only on z_{k-1}, z_k and z_{k+1}.* For this tangent appears in two curves, the one from z_{k-1} to z_k and the one from z_k to z_{k+1}, hence we know that it depends only on $(z_{k-2}, z_{k-1}, z_k, z_{k+1})$ and that it depends only on $(z_{k-1}, z_k, z_{k+1}, z_{k+2})$. By the extensionality property, we can assume that n is at least 5, so z_{k-2} is different from z_{k+2} and the tangent must be independent of them both. We have actually used only a very weak form of extensionality in this argument.

If we apply the full strength of the extensionality postulate, we obtain a much stronger consequence, which is quite unfortunate: *There is no good way to satisfy Properties 1–5!* For example, suppose we add one more axiom, which is almost necessary in any reasonable definition of pleasing curves:

PROPERTY 6 (ROUNDNESS). If z_1, z_2, z_3, z_4 are consecutive points of a circle, the most pleasing curve through them is that circle.

This property together with our previous observation about the tangent depending only on three points completely determines the tangent at each of our given points; namely, the tangent at z_k is the tangent to the circle that passes through z_{k-1}, z_k, and z_{k+1}. (Let's ignore for the moment the possibility that these three points lie on a straight line.) Now the extensionality property says that if z is any point between z_1 and z_2 on the most pleasing curve for z_1, $\ldots, z_n$, we know the tangent direction at z, as long as z is not on the line from z_1 to z_2. But there is a unique curve starting at any z off this line and having the specified tangents at each of its points, namely the arc of the circle from z to z_2 passing through z_1: No matter where you start, off the straight line, there is only one curve having the correct tangents. It follows that the tangent at z_2 depends only on z_1, z_2, and the tangent at z_1, and this is impossible.

The above argument proves that there is no way to satisfy Properties 3, 4, 5, and 6. A similar argument would show the impossibility for any reasonable replacement for Property 6, since the tangents determined for all z between z_1 and z_2 will define a vector field in which there are unique curves through essentially all of the points z, yet a two-parameter family of curves is required between z_1 and z_2 in order to allow sufficient flexibility in the derivatives there.

So we have to give up one of these properties. The locality property is the most suspicious one, but I mentioned before that I didn't want to give it up; therefore the extensionality property has to go. This means that if we take the most pleasing curve through $z_1, \ldots, z_n$ and if we specify a further point z actually on this curve between z_{k-1} and z_k, where the tangent at z is not the same as the tangent to the circle from z_{k-1} to z to z_k, then the "most pleasing" curve through these $n + 1$ points will be different. A possible virtue is that we are encouraged not to specify too many points; a possible drawback is that we may not be able to get the curves we want.

A practical approximation. Returning to the question of type design, our goal is to specify a few points z_k and to have a mathematical formula that defines a pleasant curve through these points; such curves will be used to define the shape of the character we are designing. Ideally it should also be easy to compute the curves. I decided to use cubic equations

$$z(t) = \alpha_0 + \alpha_1 t + \alpha_2 t^2 + \alpha_3 t^3$$

where $\alpha_0, \alpha_1, \alpha_2, \alpha_3$ are complex numbers and t is a real parameter. The curves I am dealing with are *cubic splines*, namely piecewise cubic equations, since a different cubic will be used in each interval between two of the given points; however, the way I am determining the coefficients of these cubics is different from any of the methods known to me, in my limited experience with the vast literature about splines. Perhaps my way to choose the coefficients is more awkward than the usual ones; but I have obtained good results with it, so I'm not ashamed to reveal the curious way I proceeded.

In the first place, I decided that the cubic equation between z_1 and z_2 should be determined completely by z_1 and z_2 and the directions of the tangents at z_1 and z_2. We have already seen that these tangents are essentially predetermined if Properties 4, 5, and 6 are to be valid, and I have also found frequent occasion in type design when it was desirable to specify that a certain tangent was to be made horizontal or vertical. Thus, my method of computing a nice curve through a given sequence of points is first to compute the tangent directions at each point, then to compute the cubics in each interval based solely on the endpoints of that interval and on the desired tangents there. By rotation and translation and scaling, according to Property 1, we can assume that the problem is to go in the complex plane from 0 to 1, with given directions at the endpoints. The most general cubic equation that does this is

$$z(t) = 3t^2 - 2t^3 + re^{i\theta}t(1 - t)^2 - se^{-i\varphi}t^2(1 - t),$$

and it remains to determine positive numbers r and s as appropriate functions of θ and φ.

In the second place, I realized that it was impossible to satisfy Property 6 with cubic splines, because you can't draw a circle as a cubic function of t. But I wanted to be able to get curves that were as near to being circles as possible, whenever four consecutive data points lay on a circle; the curves should preferably be indistinguishable from circles as far as the human eye is concerned. Therefore when $\theta = \varphi$ I decided to choose $r = s$ in such a way that $z(\tfrac{1}{2})$ was precisely on the relevant circle, hoping that the curve between 0 and $\tfrac{1}{2}$ and between $\tfrac{1}{2}$ and 1 wouldn't veer too far away. Well, this turned out to work extremely well: A little calculation, done with the help of a computer,[4] showed that the maximum deviation from a true circle occurs at the point $t = (3 \pm \sqrt{3})/6$, and the relative error is negligibly small. For example, if we take four points equally spaced at distance 1 from some center, the spline curve defined by these points in the above manner stays between distance 1 and distance $71/54 - 2\sqrt{2/9} < 1.00055$ from the center, an error of less than one part in a thousand. If there are 8 points, the maximum error is less than 4 parts per million; and if there are n points, the maximum error goes to zero as $1/n^6$.

(Changing the notation slightly, let

$$z(t) = 1 + (e^{i\theta} - 1)(3t^2 - 2t^3) + 4it(1 - t)(1 - t - e^{i\theta}t)\left(\sin\frac{\theta}{2}\right)\bigg/\left(1 + \cos\frac{\theta}{2}\right)$$

and $f(t) = |z(t)|^2$. Then

$$f'(t) = 8\left(\sin^2\frac{\theta}{2}\right)\left[\frac{\cos\dfrac{\theta}{2} - 1}{\cos\dfrac{\theta}{2} + 1}\right]^2 (t - 1)t\,(2t - 1)(6t^2 - 6t + 1)$$

and

$$\max_{0\le t\le 1} |z(t)| = \left|z\left(\frac{3 - \sqrt{3}}{6}\right)\right| = 1 + \frac{\theta^6}{55296} + \frac{\theta^{10}}{106168320} + \cdots,$$

while $\min_{0\le t\le 1}|z(t)| = z(0) = z(\tfrac{1}{2}) = z(1) = 1$. The "two-point circle" has $\max|z(t)| = \sqrt{28/27} = 1.01835$, while the three-point circle has $\max|z(t)| = \sqrt{325/324} = 1.001542$, and the eight-point circle has $\max|z(t)| = 1.0000042455$.)

Another case when a natural way to choose r and s suggests itself is when $\theta + \varphi = 90°$; then the curve $z(t)$ should be nearly the same as an ellipse having the endpoints on its axes. (This boils down to requiring that $(3t^2 - 2t^3 + (r/\cos\theta)t(1 - t)^2)^2 + (3t^2 - 2t^3 - (s/\cos\varphi)t^2(1 - t) - 1)^2$ be approximately equal to 1.) So far therefore I knew that I wanted

---

[4] Thanks are due to the developers of the computer algebra system called MACSYMA at MIT, and to the ARPA network which makes this system available for research work.

$$r = \frac{2}{1 + \cos\theta}, \qquad\qquad s = \frac{2}{1 + \cos\varphi} \qquad\qquad \text{when } \theta = \varphi;$$

$$r = \frac{2\cos\theta}{(1 + \cos 45°)(\cos 45°)}, \qquad s = \frac{2\cos\varphi}{(1 + \cos 45°)(\cos 45°)} \qquad \text{when } \theta + \varphi = 90°.$$

So I tried the formulas

$$r = \frac{2\cos\theta}{\left(1 + \cos\dfrac{\theta + \varphi}{2}\right)\left(\cos\dfrac{\theta + \varphi}{2}\right)}, \qquad s = \frac{2\cos\varphi}{\left(1 + \cos\dfrac{\theta + \varphi}{2}\right)\left(\cos\dfrac{\theta + \varphi}{2}\right)},$$

which fit both cases. However, this didn't give satisfactory results, especially when $\theta + \varphi$ approached 180°. My second attempt was

$$r = \left| \frac{2\sin\varphi}{\left(1 + \cos\dfrac{\theta + \varphi}{2}\right)\sin\dfrac{\theta + \varphi}{2}} \right|, \qquad s = \left| \frac{2\sin\theta}{\left(1 + \cos\dfrac{\theta + \varphi}{2}\right)\sin\dfrac{\theta + \varphi}{2}} \right|,$$

and this has worked very well. Figure 7 shows the spline curves that result from the above approach when $\varphi = 60°$ and when θ varies from 0° to 120° in 5° steps.

It can be proved that if θ and φ are nonnegative and less than 180°, the cubic curve $z(t)$ I have defined will never cross the straight lines at angles θ and φ that meet the endpoints 0 and 1 respectively. This is a valuable property in type design, since it can be used to guarantee that the curve won't get out of bounds. However, I found that it also led to unsatisfactory curves when one of θ or φ was very small and the other was not, since this meant that the curve $z(t)$ would be very close to a straight line yet it would enter that line from outside at a rather sharp angle. In fact, the angle θ is not infrequently zero, and this forces a straight line and a sharp corner at the right endpoint. Therefore I changed the formulas by making sure that both r and s are always $\frac{1}{2}$ or greater unless special exceptions are made; furthermore I never let r or s exceed 4. Figure 8 shows the spline curves obtained under the same conditions as Figure 7, but with s set to $\frac{1}{2}$ if the above formula calls for any smaller value.

Using these techniques we obtain a system for drawing reasonably nice curves, if not the most pleasing ones, and it is especially good at circles. If the method gives the wrong tangent direction at some point, you can control this by specifying the correct direction explicitly.

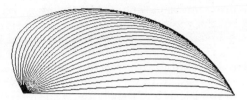

FIGURE 7. Spline curves with $\theta = 0°\,(5°)\,120°$ and $\phi = 60°$.

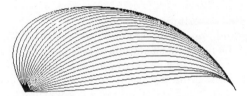

FIGURE 8. Same as Figure 7 but adjusted so that $r' = \max(\tfrac{1}{2}, r)$, $s' = \max(\tfrac{1}{2}, s)$.

Application to type design. Now let's take a closer look at what can be drawn with a mathematical system like this. I suppose the natural thing to show you would be the letters A to Z; but since this is a mathematical talk, let's consider the digits 0 to 9 instead. (See Figure 9.) Incidentally, the way I have

0123456789

FIGURE 9. Digits 0 to 9 drawn by the prototype METAFONT programs. (Further refinements to these characters will be made before the font has its final form.)

arranged these numerals illustrates a fundamental distinction between a mathematician and a printer: the mathematician puts 0 next to the 1, but the printer always puts it next to the 9.

Most of these digits are drawn by using another idea taken from the history of typography, namely to imitate the calligrapher who uses pen and ink. Consider first the numeral '3', for example. The computer program that drew this symbol in Figure 9 can be paraphrased as follows. "First draw a dot whose left boundary is $\frac{1}{6}$ of the way from the left edge to the right edge of the type and whose bottom boundary is $\frac{3}{4}$ of the way from the top to the bottom of the desired final shape. Then take a hairline pen and, starting at the left of the dot, draw the upward arc of an ellipse; after reaching the top, the pen begins to grow in width, and it proceeds downward in another ellipse in such a way that the maximum width occurs on the axis of the ellipse, with the right edge of the pen $\frac{5}{9}$ of the way from the left edge to the right edge of the type. Then the pen width begins to decrease to its original size again as the pen traverses another ellipse taking it down to a position 48% of the way from the top to the bottom of the desired final shape. . . ."

Notice that instead of describing the boundary of the character, as the renaissance geometers did, my METAFONT system describes the curve traveled by the *center* of the *pen*, and the shape of this pen is allowed to vary as the pen moves. The main advantage of this approach is that the same definition readily yields a family of infinitely many related fonts of type, each font being internally consistent. The change in pen size is governed by cubic splines in a manner analogous to the motion of the pen's center. In order to define the 20 or so different type fonts used in various places in my books, I need for the most part to use only three kinds of pens, namely (i) a circular pen, used for example to draw dots and at the base of the numeral '7'; (ii) a horizontal pen, whose shape is an ellipse, the width being variable but the height being constantly equal to the height of a hairline pen—such a pen is used most of the time, and in particular to draw all of the numeral '3' except for the dots; (iii) a vertical pen, analogous to the horizontal one, used for example to draw the strokes at the bottom of the '2' and at the top of the '5' and the '7'. For the fonts I am using, it was not necessary to use an oblique pen (i.e., an ellipse that is tilted on its side) except to make the tilde accent for Spanish n's; but to produce fonts of type analogous to Times Roman, an oblique pen would of course be used. If this system were to be extended to Chinese and Japanese characters, I think it might be best to add another degree of freedom to the pen's motion, allowing an elliptical pen shape to rotate as well as to change its width.

The digit '4' shows another aspect of the METAFONT system. Although this character is fairly simple, consisting entirely of straight lines, notice that the thick line has to be cut off at an angle at the top. In order to do this, there are *erasers* as well as pens. First the computer draws a thick line all the way from top to bottom, like the upper case letter 'I', then it takes an eraser that erases everything to its left and comes down the diagonal stroke, then it takes a hairline pen and finishes the diagonal stroke. Such an eraser is used also at the top of the '1' and the bottom of the '2', etc.

Sometimes a simple spline seems to be inadequate to describe the proper growth of pen width, so in a few cases I had to resort to describing the left and right edges of the pen as separate curves, to be filled in afterwards. This occurs for example in the main stroke of the numeral '2', whose edges are defined by two splines having a specified tangent at the bottom and having vertical slope at the right of the curve.

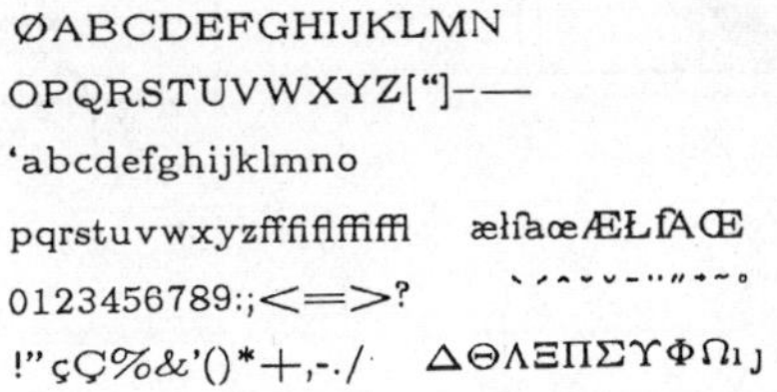

FIGURE 10. A font of 128 characters defined by METAFONT with standard pen settings. (The accent characters will be appropriately raised and centered over other letters when used by T_EX.)

With these techniques I found that it was possible to define a decent-looking complete font, containing a total of 128 characters, in about two months, although it will still be necessary of course to do fine tuning when more trial pages are typeset. (See Figure 10.) The most difficult symbol by far, at least for me, was the letter S (and the numeral 8, which uses the same procedure); in fact I spent three days and nights without sleep, trying to make the S look right, before I got it. At one point I even felt it would be easier to rewrite all my books without using any S's! After the first day of discouraging trials, I showed the meager results I had to my wife, and she said, "Why don't you make it S-shaped?"

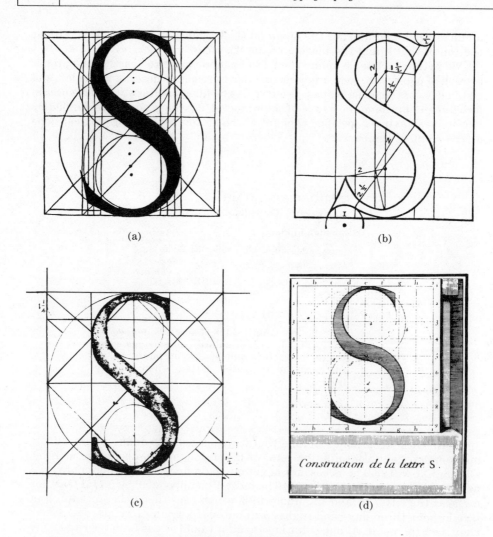

FIGURE 11. The letter S as defined by (a) Pacioli
[42]; (b) Torniello [48]; (c) Palatino [43]; (d)
French commission under Jaugeon [24].

Figure 11 shows how this problem was solved by Pacioli, Torniello, Palatino, and the French academicians; but the letter doesn't look like a modern S. Furthermore I think the engraver of the French S cheated a little in rounding off some lines near the middle—perhaps he used a French curve. With my wife's assistance, I finally came up with a satisfactory solution, somewhat like those used in the sixteenth century but generalized to ellipses. Each boundary of each arc of my S curve is composed of an ellipse and a straight line, determined by (i) the locations of the beginning and ending points, (ii) the slope of the straight line, and (iii) the desired left extremity of the curve. It took me three hours to derive the necessary formulas, and I think Newton and Leibniz would have enjoyed working on this problem. Figure 12 shows various trial S's drawn by this scheme with different slopes; I hope you prefer the middle one, since it is the one I am actually using.

SSSSSS

FIGURE 12. Different S's obtained by varying the slope in the middle. (This shows $\frac{1}{2}$, $\frac{2}{3}$, $\frac{3}{4}$, 1, $\frac{4}{3}$, $\frac{3}{2}$, and 2 times the "correct" slope.)

Families of fonts. To extend the METAFONT system, one essentially writes a computer program for the description of each character, in a special language intended for describing pen and eraser strokes. My colleague R. W. Gosper has observed that this is the opposite of *Sesame Street*: Instead of "This program was brought to you by the letter S" we have "This letter S was brought to you by a program." There are about 20 parameters to the program, telling how big a hairline pen is, how wide it should be when drawing straight or curved stem lines, and specifying the sizes and proportions of various parts of the letters (the x-height, the heights of ascenders and descenders, the set width, the length of serifs, and so forth). By changing these parameters, we obtain infinitely many different styles of type, yet all of them are related and they seem to blend harmoniously with each other.

For example, Figure 13 shows some of the possibilities. In Figure 13a we have a conventional "modern" font in the tradition of Bodoni and Bell and "Scotch Roman". Then Figure 13b shows a corresponding boldface, in which the hairlines are slightly larger and the stem lines are substantially wider. By

(a) Mathematical Typography

(b) **Mathematical Typography**

(c) Mathematical Typography

(d) **Mathematical Typography**

(e) Mathematical Typography

(f) *Mathematical Typography*

(g) MATHEMATICAL TYPOGRAPHY

(h) MATHematical TYPOgraphy

(i) Mathematical Typography

FIGURE 13. Different styles of type obtained by varying the parameters to METAFONT: (a) Computer modern roman; (b) Computer modern bold; (c) Computer modern sans serif; (d) Computer modern sans serif bold; (e) Computer modern typewriter; (f) Computer modern slanted roman; (g) Computer modern roman with small caps; (h) Computer modern roman with small caps and "small lower case"; (i) Computer modern funny.

making the hairlines and stem lines both the same size, and setting the serif length to zero, we obtain a sans-serif font as shown in Figure 13c. All of these examples are produced with the same programs defining the letter shapes; only the parameters are being varied. Actually the particular font shown in Figure 13c will have a different style of g, because the descenders are especially short in this font, but I have shown this "g" in order to illustrate the parametric variations. Figure 13d shows a boldface sans-serif style in which the pen has an oval shape wider than it is tall; I find this style especially pleasing, particularly because it came out by accident—I designed the programs only so that two or three different fonts would look right, all the others are free bonuses, and I had no idea that this one would be so nice.

With a suitable setting of the parameters, we can even imitate a typewriter with its fixed width letters, as shown in Figure 13e. There is also a provision to slant the letters as in Figure 13f; here the pen position is varied, but the actual shape of the pen is not being slanted, so circles remain circles.

Another setting of the parameters leads to caps and small caps as shown in Figure 13g; small caps are drawn with the pens and heights ordinarily used for lower case letters, but controlled by the programs for upper case letters. Figure 13h shows something printers have never seen before: that is what happens when you draw lower case letters in the small caps style, and we might call it "small lower case". It actually turns out to be one of the most pleasing fonts of all, except that the dots are too large.

Finally, Figure 13i illustrates the variations you can get by giving weirder settings to the parameters.

When I was an assistant professor at Caltech, the math department secretaries used to send occasional "crank" visitors to my office, and I recall one time when a man came to ask if anybody had calculated the value of π "out to the end" yet. I tried to explain to him that π had been proved irrational, but this didn't seem to sink in, so finally I showed him a table of π to 100,000 decimals and told him that the expansion hadn't ended yet. I wish I could have had my typography system ready at that time, so that I could have shown him Figure 14!

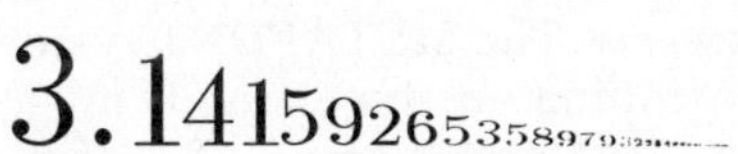

$$3.1415926535897932846\ldots$$

FIGURE 14. Variation in height, width, and pen size.

Figure 14 illustrates another principle of type design, namely that different sizes of type in the same style are not simply obtained from each other by optical transformations. The heights and widths and pen stroke sizes change at different rates, and a good typographer will design each size of type individually. I'm not claiming that Figure 14 shows the best way for the proportions to vary; it will take further experimentation before I have a good idea of what is desirable. The point I wish to make is that the alteration of type sizes for subscripts and so on is not as simple as it might seem at first, but a system like METAFONT will be able to vary the parameters quite readily; and visual experiments on different parameter settings can be carried out quickly. It used to take months for a type designer to make his drawings and have them converted to metal molds before he could see any proofs. One of the results was that there simply wasn't time to give proper attention to all the mathematical symbols and Greek letters, etc., as well as to the more common symbols, so a printer of mathematics had to make do with a hodge-podge of available characters in different sizes. (For example, he was often obliged to use different styles of letters in subscript positions, as we have seen.) Under the approach I am recommending, we automatically get consistency of all the symbols whenever the parameters change.

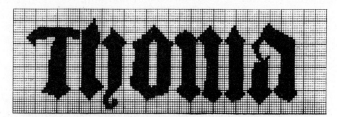

FIGURE 15. Lettering equivalent to this raster pattern appears in a Norwegian tapestry from Gildeskaal old church, woven about 1500 [22, p. 116].

From continuous to discrete. The METAFONT system must not only define the characters in the continuum on the plane, it must also express them in terms of a discrete raster. Such squaring off of letters on graph paper has a long history, going back far before the invention of computers or television; for example, we all can remember seeing cross-stitch embroidery samplers from the nineteenth century. The same idea on a finer scale has been used in tapestries for many centuries: In our own home library, my wife found the example of Figure 15 which was woven in the northern part of Norway about 1500; this shows the name of St. Thomas in a style imitating contemporary calligraphy. Examples that antedate the printing press can surely be found elsewhere.

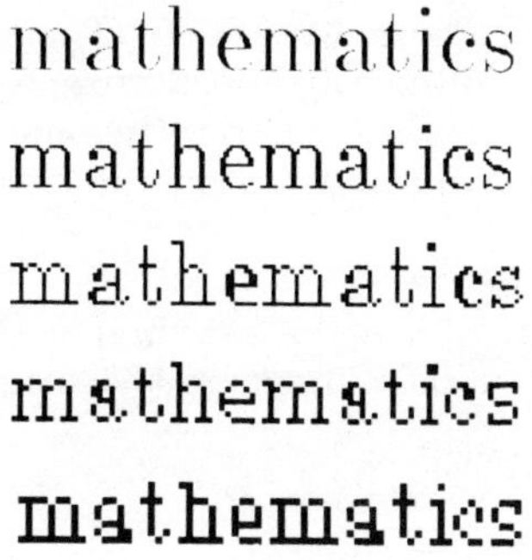

mathematics

mathematics

mathematics

mathematics

mathematics

FIGURE 16. Adjusting the letters to coarser rasters.

Figure 16 shows how METAFONT might produce the same letters from the same parameters but with different degrees of resolution in the raster. This digitization process itself is considerably more difficult than it may seem at first, and some nontrivial mathematical concepts were needed before I could obtain satisfactory results. In the first place, it is not sufficient merely to draw or to imagine drawing the character with infinite precision and then to "round" it by blacking in all the squares on graph paper that are sufficiently dark in the true image. One of the reasons this fails is that the three stem lines of the m, for instance, might be located in different relative positions with respect to the grid, so that the first stroke might round to three units wide (say) and the second might round to four. This would be quite unsatisfactory, as the eye quickly picks up such a variation in thickness, but it is avoided by METAFONT since the pen itself is first digitized and then the same digitized pen is used for all three strokes. Another problem is that those three strokes should be equally spaced; it would look bad if there were seven units between the first two and eight units between the last two, so the program for 'm' needs to round its points in such a way that this doesn't happen.

The process of digitizing the pen is not trivial either. Suppose, for example, we want a circular pen that is 2 raster units wide; the appropriate pen is clearly a 2 × 2 square, which is the closest to a circle that we can come at this low degree of resolution. Now notice that we can't *center* a 2 × 2 square on any particular square, since none of the four squares is at its center; the same problem arises whenever we have to deal with a pen having even dimensions. One way to resolve this would be to insist on working only with odd numbers, but this would be far too limiting; so METAFONT uses a special rounding rule for the position of the pen's center. In general, suppose the pen is an ellipse of integer width w and integer height h; then if the pen is to be positioned at the real coordinates (x, y), its actual position on the discrete grid is taken to be

$$(\lfloor x - \delta(w) \rfloor , \lfloor y - \delta(h) \rfloor) .$$

where $\lfloor x \rfloor$ denotes the greatest integer less than or equal to x, and $\delta(\text{even}) = \frac{1}{2}$, $\delta(\text{odd}) = 0$. The pen itself, if positioned at the origin, would consist of all integers (x, y) that satisfy

$$\left(\frac{2(x - \delta(w))}{w} \right)^2 + \left(\frac{2(y - \delta(h))}{h} \right)^2 \leq 1 + \max \left(\frac{2\delta(w)}{w}, \frac{2\delta(h)}{h} \right)^2 .$$

This formula—which incidentally is not the first one I tried—ensures that the discrete pen will indeed be w units wide and h units high, when w and h are positive integers. Figure 17 shows the pens obtained for small w and h.

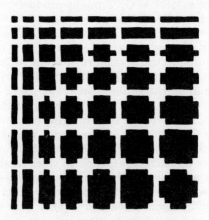

FIGURE 17. Discrete "elliptical" pens of small integer width and height.

Still another problem appears when we want curved lines to look right. Figure 18(a) shows a semicircle of radius 10 units, drawn with a pen of height 1 and width 3, when the right boundary of the pen falls exactly at an integer point; the pen sticks out terribly in one place. On the other hand if this right boundary falls just shy of an integer point, we get the curve in Figure 18(b), which looks too flat. The ideal occurs in Figure 18(c), when the right boundary occurs exactly midway between integers. Therefore the METAFONT programs adjust the location of curves to the raster before actually drawing the curves, forcing the favorable situation of Figure 18(c); the actual shape of each letter changes slightly in order to adapt that letter to the desired raster size in a pleasant way.

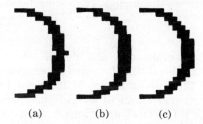

(a)　　　　(b)　　　　(c)

FIGURE 18. Difficulties of rounding an arc properly. (Three circles of radius 10 drawn with a 1×3 pen.)

There is yet another problem, which arises when the pen is growing in such a way that the edges of the curve it traces would be monotonic if the pen were drawn to infinite precision, yet the independent rounding of pen location and pen width causes this monotonicity to disappear. The problem arises only rarely, but when it does happen the eye immediately notices it. Consider, for example, the completely linear situation in Figure 19, where each decrease by one unit in y is accompanied by an increase of .3 units in x and an increase of .2 units in the pen width w; the intended pen height is constant and very small, but in the discrete case the pen height is taken to be 1. The lightly shaded portion of Figure 19 shows the true shape intended, but the darker squares show that the digitized form yields a nonmonotonic left boundary. META-FONT compensates for this sort of problem by keeping track of the desired boundaries when the pen width is varying, plotting the two boundaries independently. In other words, the idea of rounding the pen location and the width

Pen width and location	Rounded width and location
(3.5, 0.5,10.5)	(3, 0,10)
(3.7, 0.8, 9.5)	(3, 0, 9)
(3.9, 1.1, 8.5)	(3, 1, 8)
(4.1, 1.4, 7.5)	(4, 0, 7)
(4.3, 1.7, 6.5)	(4, 1, 6)
(4.5, 2.0, 5.5)	(4, 1, 5)
(4.7, 2.3, 4.5)	(4, 1, 4)
(4.9, 2.6, 3.5)	(4, 2, 3)
(5.1, 2.9, 2.5)	(5, 2, 2)
(5.3, 3.2, 1.5)	(5, 3, 1)
(5.5, 3.5, 0.5)	(5, 3, 0)

FIGURE 19. Failure of monotonicity due to independent rounding. (Rounding takes (w, x, y) into $(\lfloor w \rfloor, \lfloor x - \delta(\lfloor w \rfloor) \rfloor, \lfloor y \rfloor)$.)

independently is sometimes effectively abandoned.

The final digitization problem that I needed to resolve was to make the left half of an "0" look like the mirror image of its right half, to make a left parenthesis look like the mirror image of a right parenthesis, and so on. This was done by having the METAFONT programs in such cases choose a center point that was either exactly at an integer or an integer plus $\frac{1}{2}$, and to introduce rounding rules depending on pen motion in such a way that symmetry is guaranteed.

Alternative approaches. As I have said, I believe the METAFONT system is successful as a way to define letters and other symbols, but probably even better procedures can be devised with further research. Some of the limitations of my cubic splines are indicated in Figure 20. Part (a) of that illustration shows a five-pointed star and the word "mathematics" in an approximation to my own handwriting, done with straight line segments so that you can see exactly what the data points are that I fed to my spline routine. Part (b) shows the way my handwriting might look when I get older; it was obtained by simply setting $r = s = 2$ in all the spline segments, therefore making clear what tangent angles are prescribed by the system. Part (c) is somewhat more disciplined, it was obtained by putting $r = s = \frac{1}{2}$ everywhere. Figure 20(d) is like Figure 20(c) but drawn with a combined pen-and-eraser. Such a combination can lead to interesting effects, and the star here is my belated contribution to America's bicentennial.

When the general formulas for cubic splines are used as I explained above, we get Figure 20(e) in which the star has become a very good approximation to a circle (as I said it would). In this illustration the pen is thicker and has a slightly oblique stress. Although my handwriting is inherently unbeautiful, there are still some kinks in Figure 20(e) that could probably be ironed out if a different approach were taken.

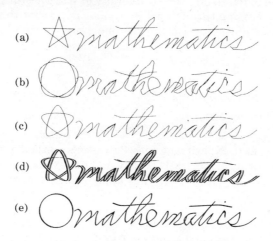

(a)

(b)

(c)

(d)

(e)

FIGURE 20. Examples of the cubic splines applied to sloppy handwriting.

The most interesting alternative from a mathematical standpoint seems to be to find a curve of given length that minimizes *the integral of the square of the curvature* with respect to arc length. This integral is proportional to the strain energy in a mechanical spline (in other words, a thin slat or beam) of the given length, going through the given points, so it seems to be an appropriate quantity to minimize. E. H. Lee and G. E. Forsythe [31] have reviewed early work on this variational problem, and shown that it is equivalent to having the spline at equilibrium with forces applied only at the given points of support. The Norwegian mathematician Even Mehlum [36] has shown that if we specify a fixed arc length between consecutive points, the optimum curve will have linearly changing curvature of the form $ax + by + c$ at point (x, y), and he has suggested choosing the constants by taking $b/a = (y_2 - y_1)/(x_2 - x_1)$ between (x_1, y_1) and (x_2, y_2), and requiring that slope and curvature be continuous across endpoints. Such an approach seems to require considerably more computation than the cubic splines recommended here, but it may lead to better curves, e.g. satisfying the extensionality property.

Another interesting approach to curve-drawing, which may be especially useful for simulating handwriting, is a "filtering" method suggested to me recently by Michael S. Paterson of the University of Warwick (unpublished). To get a smooth curve passing through points z_k, assuming that these points are about equally spaced on the desired curve, one simply writes

$$z(t) = \sum_k (-1)^k z_k f(t - k) \bigg/ \sum_k (-1)^k f(t - k)$$

where $f(t)$ is an odd function of order t^{-1} as $t \to 0$, decreasing rapidly away from zero; e.g.,

$$f(t) = \operatorname{csch} t = 2/(e^t - e^{-t}).$$

I have not had time yet to experiment with Paterson's method or to attempt to harness it for the drawing of letters. It is easy to see that the derivative $z'(z_k) = f(1)(z_{k+1} - z_{k-1}) - f(2)(z_{k+2} - z_{k-2}) + \cdots$ lies approximately in the direction of $z_{k+1} - z_{k-1}$.

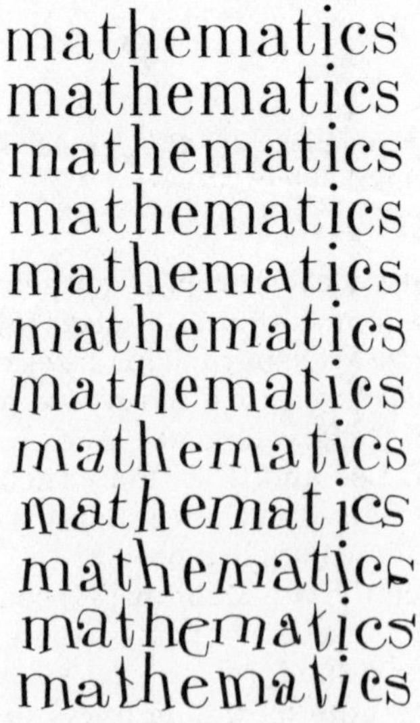

FIGURE 21. Increasingly random pen positions; $\sigma = 0, 1, \ldots$.

Randomization. In conclusion, I'd like to report on a little experiment that I did with random numbers. One might complain that the letters I have designed are too perfect, too much like a computer, so they lack "character." In order to counteract this, we can build a certain amount of randomness into the choices of where to put the pen when drawing each letter, and Figure 21 shows what happens. The coordinates of key pen positions were chosen independently with a normal distribution and with increasing standard deviation, so that the third example has twice as much standard deviation as the second, the fourth has three times as much, and so on. Note that the two m's on each line (except the first) are different, and so are the a's and the t's, since each letter is randomly drawn.

After the deviation gets sufficiently large the results become somewhat ludicrous; and I don't want people to say that I ended this lecture by making a travesty of mathematics. So let us conclude by looking at Figure 22, which shows what is obtained in various fonts when the degree of randomness is somewhat controlled. I think it can be said that the letters in this final example have a warmth and charm which makes it hard to believe that they were really generated by a computer following strict mathematical rules. Perhaps the reason that the printing of mathematics looked so nice in the good old days was that the fonts of type were imperfect and inconsistent.

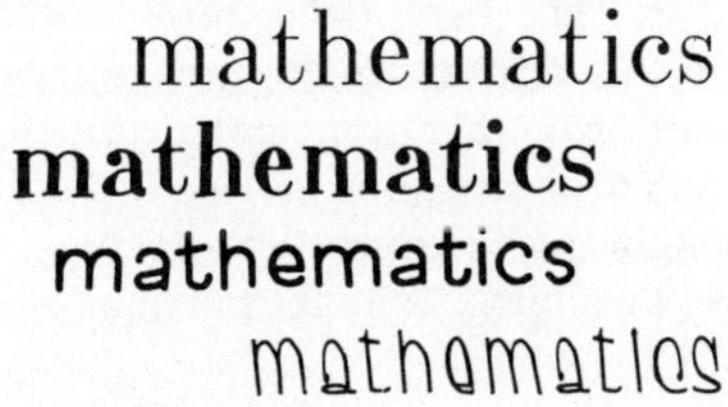

mathematics

mathematics

mathematics

mathematics

FIGURE 22. A bit of randomness introduced into various styles of type.

Summary. I'd like to summarize now by pointing out the moral of this long story. My experiences during the last few months vividly illustrate the fact that there are plenty of good mathematical problems still waiting to be solved, almost everywhere you look—especially in areas of life where mathematics has rarely been applied before. Mathematicians can provide solutions to these problems, receiving a double payoff—namely the pleasure of working out the mathematics, together with words of appreciation from the people who can use the solutions. So let's go forth and apply mathematics in new ways.

Acknowledgments. I would like to thank my wife Jill for the many important suggestions she made to me during critical stages of this research; also Leo Guibas and Lyle Ramshaw for the help they provided in making illustrations at Xerox Palo Alto Research Laboratories; also Lester Earnest, Michael Fischer, Frank Liang, Tom Lyche, Albert Meyer, Michael Paterson, Michael Plass, Bob Sproull, Jean E. Taylor, and Hans Wolf, for helpful ideas and stimulating discussions and correspondence about this topic; also Gordon L. Walker, for verifying my conjectures about the printing history of the *Transactions* and for providing me with additional background information; also Professor Dirk Siefkes for his help in acquiring Figures 4(c) and 11(c), and the Kunstbibliothek Berlin der Staatlichen Museen Preussischer Kulturbesitz for permission to publish them; and to André Jammes for permission to publish Figures 6 and 11(d).

Bibliography. The references below include several articles not referenced in the main text, namely a discussion of publishing at the American Institute of Physics [37]; some experiments in typesetting physics journals with the Bell Labs system [32], [7]; computer aids for technical magazine layout and editing, together with a brief proposal for a standard typesetting language [11]; reports about early computer programs for character generation and mathematics composition [23], [30], [34], [35], [40], [46]; a description of the mathematics a traditional printer needs to know [9]; three standard references on the typesetting of mathematics [14], [47], [50]; some fonts of type and special characters designed by the American Mathematical Society [39]; a recent and highly significant approach to mathematical definition of traditional type faces based on conic sections and on one-dimensional splines [15]; a proposal for a new way to control the spacing between letters based on somewhat mathematical principles [28]; and two purely mathematical papers inspired by typography [13], [21].

I recently learned of another paper about the problem of drawing "most pleasing curves" subject to the locality property: R. C. Johnson, *Interpolation by Local Space Curves*, Journal of Computational and Applied Math. **3** (1977) pp. 79–84. Johnson uses quintic splines in order to obtain continuous curvature at the transition points.

References

1. A. V. Aho, S. C. Johnson, and J. D. Ullman, *Typesetting by ACM considered harmful*, Communications of the ACM **18** (1975), 740.

2. American Mathematical Society, *Development of the Photon for efficient mathematical composition*, Final report (May 10, 1965), National Science Foundation grant G-21913; NTIS number PB168627.

3. American Mathematical Society, *Development of computer aids for tape-control of photocomposing machines*, Report No. 2 (July 1967), *Extension of the system of preparing a computer-processed tape to include the setting of multiple line equations*, National Science Foundation grant GN-533; NTIS number PB175939.

4. American Mathematical Society, *Development of computer aids for tape-control of photocomposing machines*, Final report, Section B (August 1968), *A system for computer-processed tape composition to include the setting of multiple line equations*, National Science Foundation grant GN-533; NTIS number PB179418.

5. American Mathematical Society, *Development of computer aids for tape-control of photocomposing machines*, Final report, Section C (January 1969), *Implementation, hardware, and other systems*, National Science Foundation grant GN-533; NTIS number PB182088.

6. American Mathematical Society, *To complete the study of computer aids for tape-control of composing machines by developing an operating system*, Final report, no. AMATHS-CAIDS-71-0 (April 1971), National Science Foundation grant GN-690; NTIS number PB200892.

7. American Physical Society, *APS tests computer system for publishing operations*, Physics Today **30**, 12 (December 1977), 75.

8. Donald M. Anderson, *Cresci and his capital alphabets*, Visible Language **4** (1971), 331–352.

9. J. Woodard Auble, *Arithmetic for printers*, second ed., Peoria, Ill., Bennett, 1954.

10. Michael P. Barnett, *Computer typesetting*: *Experiments and prospects*, Cambridge, Mass., M.I.T. Press, 1965.

11. Robert W. Bemer and A. Richard Shriver, *Integrating computer text processing with photocomposition*, IEEE Trans. on Prof. Commun. PC-16 (1973), 92–96. This article is reprinted with another typeface and page layout in Robert W. Bemer, *The role of a computer in the publication of a primary journal*, Proc. AFIPS Nat. Comput. Conf. 42, Part II (1973), M16-M20.

12. Peter J. Boehm, *Software and hardware considerations for a technical typesetting system*, IEEE Trans. on Prof. Commun. PC-19 (1976), 15–19.

13. J. A. Bondy, *The 'graph theory' of the Greek alphabet*, Graph Theory and Applications, Y. Alavi et al., eds., Berlin, Springer-Verlag, 1972, pp. 43–54.

14. Theodore William Chaundy, Percy Reginald Barrett, and Charles Batey, *The printing of mathematics*, Oxford, Oxford Univ. Press, 1954.

15. P. J. M. Coueignoux, *Generation of roman printed fonts*, Ph.D. thesis, Dept. of Electrical Engineering, M.I.T., June, 1975.

16. Giovanni Francesco Cresci Milanese, *Essemplare de piv sorti lettere*, Rome, 1560. Also edited and translated by Arthur Sidney Osley, London, 1968.

17. T. L. De Vinne, *The practice of typography*: *Modern methods of book composition*, New York, Oswald, 1914.

18. Albrecht Dürer, *Underweysung der Messung mit dem Zirckel und Richtscheyt*, Nuremberg, 1525. An English translation of the section on alphabets has been published as Albrecht Dürer, *Of the just shaping of letters*, R. T. Nichol, trans., Dover, 1965.

19. Felice Feliciano Veronese. *Alphabetum romanum*, Giovanni Mardersteig, ed., Verona, Officina Bodoni, 1960.

20. Frederic W. Goudy, *Typologia: Studies in type design and type making with comments on the invention of typography, the first types, legibility and fine printing*, Berkeley, Calif., Univ. of California Press, 1940.

21. F. Harary, *Typographs*, Visible Language **7** (1973), 199–208.

22. Roar Hauglid, Randi Asker, Helen Engelstad, and Gunvor Traetteberg, *Native art of Norway*, Oslo, Dreyer, 1965.

23. A. V. Hershey, *Calligraphy for computers*, NWL Report No. 2101, Dahlgren, Va., U. S. Naval Weapons Laboratory, August 1967; NTIS number AD662398.

24. André Jammes, *La réforme de la typographie royale sous Louis XIV*, Paris, Paul Jammes, 1961.

25. Paul E. Justus, *There is more to typesetting than setting type*, IEEE Trans. on Prof. Commun. PC-15 (1972), 13–16.

26. Alan C. Kay, *Microelectronics and the personal computer*, Scientific American **237**, 3, September 1977, 230–244.

27. Brian W. Kernighan and Lorinda L. Cherry, *A system for typesetting mathematics*, Communications of the ACM **18** (1975), 151–157.

28. David Kindersley, *Optical letter spacing for new printing systems*, London, Wynkyn de Worde Society, 1976.

29. Donald E. Knuth, *Tau Epsilon Chi, a system for technical text*, Stanford Computer Science report CS675, September, 1978. [Reprinted with corrections as Part 2 of the present book.]

30. Dorothy K. Korbuly, *A new approach to coding displayed mathematics for photocomposition*, IEEE Trans. on Prof. Commun. PC-18 (1975), 283–287.

31. E. H. Lee and G. E. Forsythe, *Variational study of nonlinear splines*, SIAM Rev. **15** (1973), 120–133.

32. M. E. Lesk and B. W. Kernighan, *Computer typesetting of technical journals on* UNIX, Computing Science Tech. Report 44, Murray Hill, N. J., Bell Laboratories, June, 1976.

33. Giovanni Mardersteig, *The alphabet of Francesco Torniello (1517) da Novara*, Verona, Officina Bodoni, 1971.

34. M. V. Mathews and Joan E. Miller, *Computer editing, typesetting, and image generation*, Proc. AFIPS Fall Joint Computer Conf. **27** (1965), 389–398.

35. M. V. Mathews, Carol Lochbaum and Judith A. Moss, *Three fonts of computer drawn letters*, Communications of the ACM **10** (1967), 627–630.

36. Even Mehlum, *Nonlinear splines*, Computer Aided Geometric Design, Robert E. Barnhill and Richard F. Riesenfeld, eds., New York, Academic Press, 1974, pp. 173–207.

37. A. W. Kenneth Metzner, *Multiple use and other benefits of computerized publishing*, IEEE Trans. on Prof. Commun. PC-18 (1975), 274–278.

38. Joseph Moxon, *Regulae trium ordinum literarum typographicarum, or the rules of the three orders of print letters: viz. the (roman, italick, english) capitals and*

small; Shewing how they are compounded of Geometrick Figures, and mostly made by Rule and Compass, London, Joseph Moxon, 1676.

39. Phoebe J. Murdock, *New alphabets and symbols for typesetting mathematics*, Scholarly Publishing 8 (1976), 44–53. Reprinted in Notices Amer. Math. Soc. 24 (1977), 63–67.

40. Nicholas Negroponte, *Raster scan approaches to computer graphics*, Computers and Graphics 2 (1977), 179–193.

41. Wolfgang A. Ocker, *A program to hyphenate English words*, IEEE Trans. on Prof. Commun. PC-18 (1975), 78–84.

42. Luca Pacioli, *Divina Proportione, Opera a tutti glingegni perspicaci e curiosi necessaria Ove ciascun studioso di Philosophia, Propectiva, Pictura, Sculptura: Architecturo: Musice: altre Mathematice: suavissima: sottile: e admirable et doctrina consequira: e delectarassi: con varie questione de secretissima scientia* (Venice, 1509).

43. Giovanbattista Palatino Cittadino Romano, *Libro primo del le lettere maiuscole antiche romane* (unpublished), Berlin Kunstbibliothek, MS. OS5280. Some of the individual pages are dated 1543, 1546, 1549, 1574, or 1575. See James Wardrop, *Civis romanus sum: Giovanbattista Palatino and his circle*, Signature, n.s. 14 (1952), 3–39.

44. Paul A. Parisi, *Composition innovations of the American Society of Civil Engineers*, IEEE Trans. on Prof. Commun. PC-18 (1975), 244–273.

45. R. G. D. Richardson, *The twenty-ninth annual meeting of the Society*, Bull. Amer. Math. Soc. 29 (1923), 97–116. (See also vol. 28 (1922) pp. 234–235, 378 for comments on the special *Transactions* volume, and pp. 2–3 of vol. 28 for discussion of deficits due to increased cost of printing.)

46. Glenn E. Roudabush, Charles R. T. Bacon, R. Bruce Briggs, James A. Fierst, Dale W. Isner and Hiroshi A. Noguni, *The left hand of scholarship: Computer experiments with recorded text as a communication media*, Proc. AFIPS Fall Joint Computer Conf. 27 (1965), 399–411.

47. Ellen E. Swanson, *Mathematics into type*, Amer. Math. Soc., Providence, R. I., 1971.

48. Francesco Torniello, *Opera del modo de fare le littere maiuscuole antique*, Milan, Italy, 1517.

49. Geofroy Tory, *Champ fleury*, Paris, 1529. Also translated into English and annotated by George B. Ives, New York, Grolier Club, 1927.

50. Karel Wick, *Rules for typesetting mathematics*, translated by V. Boublik and M. Hejlová, The Hague, Mouton, 1965.

51. Hermann Zapf, *About alphabets: some marginal notes on type design*, Cambridge, Mass. M.I.T. Press, 1970.

PART 2

TEX
a system for technical text

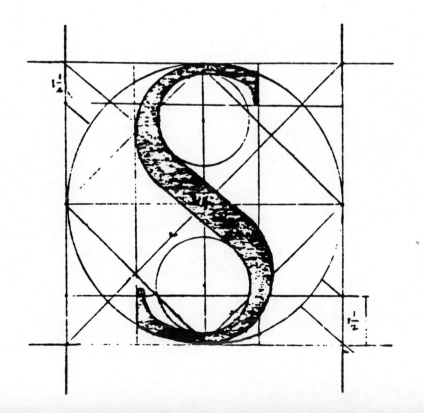

TAU EPSILON CHI
a system for technical text

G ENTLE READER: This is a handbook about TEX, a new typesetting system intended for the creation of beautiful books—and especially for books that contain a lot of mathematics. By preparing a manuscript in TEX format, you will be telling a computer exactly how the manuscript is to be transformed into pages whose typographic quality is comparable to that of the world's finest printers; yet you won't need to do much more work than would be involved if you were simply typing the manuscript on an ordinary typewriter. In fact, your total work will probably be significantly less, if you consider the time it ordinarily takes to revise a typewritten manuscript, since computer text files are so easy to change and to reprocess. (If such claims sound too good to be true, keep in mind that they were made by TEX's designer, on a day when TEX happened to be working, so the statements may be biased; but read on anyway.)

This manual is intended for people who have never used TEX before, as well as for experienced TEX hackers. In other words, it's the only manual there is. Everything you need to know about TEX is explained here somewhere, and so are a lot of things that most users don't need to know. If you are preparing a simple manuscript, you won't need to know much about TEX at all; on the other hand, some things that go into the printing of technical books are inherently difficult, and if you wish to achieve more complex effects you will want to penetrate into some of TEX's darker corners. In order to make it possible for many types of users

1

to read this manual effectively, a special symbol is used to designate material
that is for wizards only: When the symbol

appears at the beginning of a paragraph, it warns of a "dangerous bend" in
the train of thought; don't read the paragraph unless you need to. Brave and
experienced drivers at the controls of TEX will gradually enter more and more of
these hazardous areas, but for most applications the details won't matter.

All that you really need to know before reading on is how to get a file of text
into your computer using a standard editing program; this manual explains what
that file ought to look like so that TEX will understand it, but basic computer
usage is not explained here. Some previous experience with technical typing will
be quite helpful if you plan to do heavily mathematical work with TEX, although
it is not absolutely necessary. TEX will do most of the necessary formatting of
equations automatically; but users with more experience will be able to obtain
better results, since there are so many ways to deal with formulas.

Computer system manuals usually make dull reading, but take heart: This
one contains JOKES every once in a while, so you might actually enjoy reading it.
(However, most of the jokes can only be appreciated properly if you understand
a technical point that is being made—so read *carefully*.)

Another somewhat unique characteristic of this manual is that it doesn't
always tell the truth. When informally introducing certain TEX concepts, general
rules will be stated, but later you will find that they aren't strictly true. The
author feels that this technique of deliberate lying will actually make it easier
for you to learn the concepts; once you learn a simple but false rule, it will not
be hard to supplement that rule with its exceptions.

In order to help you internalize what you're reading, occasional EXERCISES are
sprinkled through this manual. It is generally intended that every reader should
try every exercise, except for exercises that appear in the "dangerous bend" areas.
If you can't solve a problem, you can always look at the answers at the end of
the manual. But please, try first to solve it by yourself; then you'll learn more
and you'll learn faster. Furthermore, if you think you do know the answer to an
exercise, you should turn to Appendix A and check it out just to make sure.

CONTENTS

<1> The name of the game

English words like "technology" stem from a Greek root beginning with the letters $\tau\epsilon\chi\ldots$; and this same Greek word means *art* as well as technology. Hence the name TEX, which is an upper-case form of $\tau\epsilon\chi$.

Insiders pronounce the χ of TEX as a Greek chi, not as an "x", so that TEX rhymes with the word blecchhh. It's the "ch" sound in Scottish words like *loch* or German words like *ach*; it's a Spanish "j" and a Russian "kh". When you say it properly to your computer, the terminal may become slightly moist.

The purpose of this pronunciation exercise is to remind you that TEX is primarily concerned with high-quality technical manuscripts: its emphasis is on art and technology, as in the underlying Greek word. If you merely want to produce passably good quality—something acceptable and basically readable but not really beautiful—a simpler system will usually suffice. With TEX the goal is to produce the *finest* quality; this requires more attention to detail, but fortunately it is not that much harder to go this extra distance, and you can take special pride in the finished product.

On the other hand you might find it more comfortable to pronounce TEX as a Texan would and to shrug off all this high-falutin' nonsense about beauty and quality. Go ahead and do what you want, the computer won't mind.

<2> Book printing versus ordinary typing

When you first started using a computer terminal, you probably had to adjust to the difference between the digit "1" and the lower case letter "l". When you take the next step to the level of typography that is common in book publishing, a few more adjustments of the same kind need to be made.

In the first place, there are two kinds of quotation marks in books, but only one kind on the typewriter. Even on your computer terminal, which has more characters than an ordinary typewriter, you probably have only a non-oriented double-quote mark ("), because the standard "ascii" code for computers was not invented with book publishing in mind. However, your terminal probably does have two flavors of single-quote marks, namely ' and ', which you can get by typing ` and '. The second of these is useful also as an apostrophe.

To produce double-quote marks with TEX, you simply type two single-quote marks of the appropriate kind. For example, to produce an output like

"I understand."

(including the quotation marks) you would type

``I understand.´´

on your terminal.

A typewriter-like style of type will be used throughout this manual to indicate TEX constructions you might type on your terminal, so that the symbols actually typed are readily distinguishable from the output TEX would produce and from the comments in the manual itself. Here are the symbols to be used in the examples:

```
ABCDEFGHIJKLMNOPQRSTUVWXYZ
abcdefghijklmnopqrstuvwxyz
0123456789"#$%&@*+-=,.:;?!
()<>≤≥[]{}`´→↑↓←\|/⊗≠∞
```

If these are not all on your computer terminal, do not despair; TEX can make do with the ones you have. One additional symbol

⊔

is also used to stand for a *blank space*, in case it is important to emphasize that a blank space is typed; without such a symbol you would have difficulty seeing the invisible parts of certain examples.

Another important distinction between book printing and ordinary typing is the use of dashes, hyphens, and minus signs. In good math books, these symbols are all different; in fact there are usually at least four different symbols in use:

a hyphen (-);
an en-dash (–);
an em-dash (—);
a minus sign (−).

Hyphens are used for compound words like "daughter-in-law" and "X-rated". En-dashes are used for number ranges like "pages 13–34" and also in contexts like "exercise 1.2.6–52". Em-dashes are used for punctuation in sentences—they are what we often call simply dashes. And minus signs are used in formulas. A conscientious user of TEX will be careful to distinguish these four usages, and here is how to do it:

> for a hyphen, type a hyphen (-);
> for an en-dash, type two hyphens (--);
> for an em-dash, type three hyphens (---);
> for a minus sign, type a hyphen in mathematics mode ($-$).

(Mathematics mode occurs between dollar signs; it is discussed later, so you needn't worry about it now.)

If you look closely at most well-printed books, you will find that certain combinations of letters are treated as a unit. For example, this is true of the "f" and the "i" of "find". Such combinations are called *ligatures*, and professional typesetters have traditionally been trained to watch for letter pairs such as ff, fi, fl, ffi, and ffl. (It's somewhat surprising how often these combinations appear.) Fortunately you do *not* have to concern yourself with ligatures, since TEX is perfectly capable of handling such things by itself. In fact, TEX will also look for combinations of adjacent letters (like "A" next to "V") that ought to be moved closer together for better appearance; this is called *kerning*.

To summarize this chapter: When using TEX for straight copy, you type the copy as on an ordinary typewriter, except that you need to be careful about quotation marks, the number 1, and various kinds of hyphens/dashes. TEX will take care of other niceties like ligatures and kerning.

In case you need to type quotes within quotes, for example a single quote followed by a double quote, you can't simply type ´´´ because TEX will interpret this as "' (namely, double-quote followed by single-quote). If you have already read Chapter 5, you might expect that the solution will be to use grouping—namely, to type something like {´}´´. But it turns out that this doesn't produce the desired result, because there is usually more space following a double quote than there is following a single quote: What you get is ''', which is indeed a single quote followed by a double quote (if you look at it closely enough), but it looks almost like three equally-spaced single quotes. On the other hand, you certainly won't want to type ´␣´´, because this space is much too large—just as large as the space between words—and TEX might even start a new line at such a space when making up a paragraph! There are at least two ways to solve the problem, both of which involve more complicated features of TEX that we shall study later. First, if you have a definition such as

```
\def\2{\hbox to 2pt{}}
```

in the format of your manuscript, you can type `´\2´´`. This definition puts 2 points of blank space between the quotes, so the result is '"; you could, of course, vary the amount of space, or define another control sequence besides \2 for this purpose. Second, you could use the idea of "thin space" in math formulas: namely, if you type `´$\,$´´` the result will be '".

> ▷Exercise 2.1: OK, now you know how to produce "' and '"; how do you get "'
> and '"?

<3> Controlling TEX

Your keyboard has very few keys compared to the large number of symbols you may want to specify. In order to make a limited keyboard sufficiently versatile, one of the characters you can type is reserved for special use, and it is called the *escape character*. Whenever you want to type something that controls the format of your manuscript, or something that doesn't use the keyboard in the ordinary way, you type the escape character followed by an indication of what you want to do.

You get to choose your own escape character. It can be any typeable symbol, preferably some character found in a reasonably convenient location on your keyboard, yet it should be a symbol that is rarely (if ever) used in the manuscript you are typing. For our purposes in this manual, the "backslash" character "\" will be used as the escape in all the examples. You may wish to adopt backslash as your personal escape symbol, but TEX doesn't have any character built in for this purpose. In fact, TEX always takes *the first nonblank character* you give it and assumes that it is to be your escape character.

Note: Some computer terminals have a key marked "ESC", but that is *not* your escape character! It is a key that sends a special message to the operating system, so don't confuse it with what this manual calls "escape".

Immediately after typing "\" (i.e., immediately after an escape character) you type a coded command telling TEX what you have in mind. Such commands are called *control sequences*. For example, you might type

```
\input ms
```

which (as we will see later) causes TEX to begin reading a file called "ms.TEX";
the string of characters "\input" is a control sequence. Here's another example:

```
George P\´olya and Gabor Szeg\"o.
```

TEX converts this to "George Pólya and Gabor Szegö." There are two control
sequences, \´ and \", in this example, and they are used to indicate the special
accents.

Control sequences come in two flavors. The first kind, like \input, consists
of the escape character followed by one or more letters, followed by a space or by
something besides a letter. (TEX has to know where the control sequence ends,
so you have to put a space after a control sequence if the following character is a
letter; for example, if you type "\inputms", TEX will interpret this as a control
sequence with seven letters.) The second variety of control sequence, like \´,
consists of the escape character followed by a single *nonletter*. In this case you
don't need a space to separate the control sequence from a letter that follows,
since control sequences of the second kind always have a single symbol after the
escape.

When a space comes after a control sequence (of either kind), it is ignored
by TEX; i.e., it is not considered to be a "real" space belonging to the manuscript
being typeset. Thus, the example above could have been typed as

```
George P\´ olya and Gabor Szeg\" o.
```

TEX will treat both examples the same way; it *always* discards spaces after control
sequences.

So the question arises, what do you do if you actually *want* a space to appear
after a control sequence? We will see later that TEX treats two or more consecutive
spaces as a single space, so the answer is *not* going to be "type two spaces." The
correct answer is to type "escape space", namely

(the escape character followed by a blank space); TEX will treat this as a space not to be ignored. Note that escape-space is a control sequence of the second kind, since there is a single nonletter (␣) following the escape character. According to the rules, further spaces immediately following \␣ will be ignored, but if you want to enter, say, three consecutive spaces into a manuscript you can type "\␣\␣\␣". Incidentally, typists are often taught to put two spaces at the ends of sentences; but we will see later that TEX has its own way to produce extra space in such cases. Thus you needn't be consistent in the number of spaces you type.

It is usually unnecessary for you to use "escape space", since control sequences aren't often needed at the ends of words. But here's an example that might shed some light on the matter: This manual itself has been typeset by TEX, and one of the things that occurs fairly often is the tricky logo "TEX", which requires backspacing and lowering the E. We will see below that it is possible for any user to define new control sequences to stand as abbreviations of commonly occurring constructions; and at the beginning of this manual, a special definition was made so that the control sequence

                                \TEX

would produce the instructions necessary to typeset "TEX". When a phrase like "TEX ignores spaces after control sequences." is to be typeset, the manuscript renders it as follows:

        \TEX\ ignores spaces after control sequences.

Notice the extra \ following \TEX; this produces the escape-space that is necessary because TEX ignores spaces after control sequences. Without this extra \, the result would have been

        TEXignores spaces after control sequences.

Consider also what happens if \TEX is not followed by a space, as in

        the logo ``\TEX´´.

It would be permissible to put a blank space after the X, but not an escape character; if the manuscript were changed to read

        the logo ``\TEX\´´

the result would be curious indeed—can you guess it? Answer: The \´ would be a control sequence denoting an acute accent, as in our P\´olya example above; the effect would therefore be to put an accent over the next nonblank character, which as it happens is a single-quote mark. In other words, the result would be

the logo "T_EX´"

because the ligature that changes ´´ into " is not recognized.

▶Exercise 3.1: State two ways to specify the French word "mathématique". Can you guess how the word "centimètre" should be specified?

TEX understands almost 300 control sequences as part of its standard built-in vocabulary, and all of these are explained in this manual somewhere. Fortunately you won't have too much trouble learning them, since the vast majority are simply the names of special characters used in mathematical formulas. For example, the control sequences \Ascr, \Bscr, ..., \Zscr stand for the upper case script letters $\mathcal{A}, \mathcal{B}, \ldots, \mathcal{Z}$; and you can type "\aleph" to get $\aleph$, "\doteq" to get $\doteq$, "\oplus" to get $\oplus$, "\←" to get $\Leftarrow$, etc.

As mentioned above, TEX can be taught to understand other control sequences besides those in its primitive vocabulary. For example, "\TEX" is not one of the standard control sequences; it had to be defined specially for producing this manual. In general there will be special control sequences that define the *style* of a book or a series of books: they will be used at the beginning of chapters, or to handle special formats such as might be used in a bibliography, etc. Such style-defining control sequences are usually defined once and for all by TEXperts skilled in the lore of control-sequence definition, and novice TEX users don't have to worry about the job of defining any new control sequences; the only problem is to learn how to use somebody else's definitions. (The person who designs a TEX style is obliged to write a supplement to this manual explaining how to use his or her control sequences.)

In this manual we shall frequently refer to a so-called "basic TEX style" consisting of the definitions in Appendix B, since these basic definitions have proved to be useful for common one-shot jobs; and since they probably also will be included as a part of more elaborate styles. Appendix E contains an example of a more elaborate style, namely the definitions used to typeset D. E. Knuth's series of books on *The Art of Computer Programming*. There's no need for you to look at these appendices now, they are included only for reference purposes.

The main point of these remarks, as far as novice TEX users are concerned, is that it is indeed possible to define nonstandard TEX control sequences, but it can be tricky. You can safely rely on the standard control sequences, and on the basic extensions defined in Appendix B (which will be explained later in this manual), until you become an experienced TEXnical typist.

Those of you who wish to define control sequences should know that TEX has further rules about them, namely that many different spellings of the same control sequence may be possible. This fact allows TEX to handle control sequences quite efficiently; and TEX's usefulness is not seriously affected, because new control sequences aren't needed very often. A control sequence of the first kind (i.e., one consisting of letters only) may involve both upper case and lower case letters, but the distinction between cases is ignored after the first letter. Thus \TEX could also be typed "\TEx" or "\TeX" or "\Tex"—each of these four has the same meaning and the same effect. But "\tex" would *not* be the same, because there *is* a case distinction on the first letter. (Typing "\gamma" results in γ, but "\Gamma" or "\GAMMA" results in Γ.)

Another rule takes over when there are seven or more letters after the escape: all letters after the seventh are replaced by "x", and then groups of eight letters are removed if necessary until at most 14 letters are left. Thus \underline is the same as \underlixx; and it is also the same as \underlinedsymbols or any other control sequence that starts with \u followed by n or N, then d or D, then e or E, then r or R, then l or L, then i or I, then 2 or 10 or 18 or 26 or $\cdots$ letters. But \underline is not the same as \underlines, because these two control sequences don't have the same length modulo 8.

As a consequence of these rules, there are 128 essentially distinct control sequences of length two—namely, escape followed by any 7-bit character, whether a letter or not. There are 52×26 essentially distinct control sequences of length three, because there are $26 + 26 = 52$ choices for the first letter following the escape and 26 different choices for the second letter; there are $52 \times 26 \times 26$ essentially distinct control sequences of length four, $52 \times 26 \times 26 \times 26$ of length five, $52 \times 26 \times 26 \times 26 \times 26$ of length six, $52 \times 26 \times 26 \times 26 \times 26 \times 26$ of length seven. There are $52 \times 26 \times 26 \times 26 \times 26 \times 26 \times 26$ essentially distinct control sequences of length 8 plus a multiple of 8, and the same number holds for length 9 plus a multiple of 8, ..., length 15 plus a multiple of 8. Thus the total number of distinct control sequences available is exactly

$$128 + 52 \cdot 26 + 52 \cdot 26^2 + 52 \cdot 26^3 + 52 \cdot 26^4 + 52 \cdot 26^5 + 8 \cdot 52 \cdot 26^6 = 129151507704;$$

that should be enough. Even though TEX accepts alternative spellings, you should be consistent in each manuscript, since some implementations of TEX may not be exactly the same in this respect.

Nonprinting control characters like ⟨carriage-return⟩ might follow an escape character, and these lead to distinct control sequences according to the rules. Initially TEX is set up to treat \⟨tab⟩ and \⟨line-feed⟩ and \⟨vertical-tab⟩ and \⟨form-feed⟩ and \⟨carriage-return⟩ the same as \␣ (escape space); it is recommended that none of these six control sequences be redefined.

<4> Fonts of type

Occasionally you will want to change from one typeface to another, for example if you wish to be bold or to *emphasize* something. TEX deals with sets of 128 characters called "fonts" of type, and the control sequence \: is used to select a particular font. If, for example, fonts n, b, and s have been predefined to represent normal, bold, and slanted styles of type, you might specify the last few words of the first sentence of this paragraph in the following way:

```
to be \:b bold \:n or to \:s emphasize \:n something.
```

(Blank spaces after font codes like b are ignored by TEX just like the spaces after control sequences; furthermore, since a font code is always of length 1, you don't need a space after it. Thus, \:bbold would be treated the same as \:␣b␣␣bold. It is probably best to type a space after the font codes, even though you don't really need one, for the sake of readability.)

You probably will never* use the \: sequence yourself, since the predesigned format you are using usually includes special control sequences that give symbolic names to the fonts. For example, the "basic TEX format" in Appendix B defines three control sequences for this purpose.

```
\rm switches to the normal "Roman" typeface:  Roman
\sl switches to a slanted typeface:           Slanted
\bf switches to a boldface style:             Bold
```

With such a system, you can type the above example as

```
to be \bf bold \rm or to \sl emphasize \rm something.
```

_____

*Well..., hardly ever.

The advantage of such control sequences is that you can use the same abbreviations \rm, \sl, \bf in any size of type, although different font codes are actually used for different sizes. For example, fonts a, n, q might be the normal, slanted, and bold fonts in a standard "10-point" size of type, while c, p, s might be the corresponding fonts in a smaller "8-point" size. It would be difficult to remember how the codes change in different sizes. So the *Art of Computer Programming* book design in Appendix E allows you to say

```
\tenpoint
```

whenever you are beginning to type material that belongs in 10-point size, after which \rm will be equivalent to \:a, and \sl will be equivalent to \:n, etc. Now if you switch to 8-point size (in a footnote, say) the instruction

```
\eightpoint
```

(which appears in the \footnote format) will cause \sl to be equivalent to \:p. All you need to remember is the abbreviations \rm, \sl, and \bf regardless of what type size you are using.

There actually is a better way yet to handle the above example, using TEX's "grouping" feature, which we shall discuss in the next chapter. With this feature you would type

```
to be {\bf bold} or to {\sl emphasize} something.
```

As we will see, switching fonts within { and } does not affect the fonts outside, so you don't need to say explicitly that you are returning to \rm in this scheme. Thus, you can pretty much forget about the other ways we have been discussing for font switching; it's best to use grouping.

When you do use the \: instruction to change fonts, here are the rules you need to know. TEX can handle up to 32 different fonts in any particular job (counting different sizes of the same style). These 32 fonts are distinguished by the least significant five bits of the 7-bit ascii character code you type following "\:"; if you don't understand what this means, use the following code names for your fonts:

Internal font number	TEX font code	Internal font number	TEX font code	Internal font number	TEX font code	Internal font number	TEX font code
1	@ or `	9	H or h	17	P or p	25	X or x
2	A or a	10	I or i	18	Q or q	26	Y or y
3	B or b	11	J or j	19	R or r	27	Z or z
4	C or c	12	K or k	20	S or s	28	[or ;
5	D or d	13	L or l	21	T or t	29	< or ≤
6	E or e	14	M or m	22	U or u	30	] or =
7	F or f	15	N or n	23	V or v	31	> or ↑
8	G or g	16	O or o	24	W or w	32	? or ←

You never refer to a font by its number, always by its code. Code A is treated the same as a, etc.; but a wise typist will consistently use the same codes in any particular manuscript, because later TEXs may allow more than 32 fonts.

Of course TEX can make use of hundreds of different fonts in different jobs. The 32-font restriction applies only within a particular job, because TEX doesn't want to keep the details about more than $32 \times 128 = 4096$ characters in its memory at once; there isn't enough room. Thus the internal font codes will refer, in general, to different "real" fonts. The first time you use a font code, you must *define* it by giving the full name of the font in the system's collection. For example, when the basic TEX format in Appendix B says

$$\backslash : a = cmr10$$

this selects font code a and defines it to be the system's font "cmr10", an abbreviation for "Computer Modern Roman 10 point". The rule for defining a font is that the font code (a in this example) must be followed immediately by "=" or "←" (not a space) when it first appears, and this must be followed immediately by the system name of the font file; then comes a blank space to denote the end of the font file name.

Once a font code is defined, it can never be redefined again. Thus if you type, say, "\:a=cmr10" when font code a has already been defined, the characters "=cmr10" will be treated as part of your manuscript, and they will dutifully be set into type (in font a). It's best to define all your fonts in format specifications at the very beginning of your input.

When you change fonts within a line, TEX will line the letters up according to their "baselines." For example, suppose that font codes a, b, c, d, e, f refer respectively to 10-point, 9-point, 8-point, 7-point, 6-point, and 5-point roman fonts; then if you type

```
\:a smaller \:b and smaller \:c and smaller
\:d and smaller \:e and smaller \:f and smaller \:a
```

the result is smaller and smaller and smaller and smaller and smaller and smaller. Of course this is something authors don't do very often at the moment, because printers can't do such things easily with traditional lead types. Perhaps poets who wish to speak in a still small voice will cause future books to make use of frequent font variations, but nowadays it's only an occasional font freak (like the author of this manual) who likes it. One should not get too carried away by the prospect of font switching unless there is good reason.

▶Exercise 4.1: Explain how to type the bibliographic reference "Ulrich Dieter, *Journal für die reine und angewandte Mathematik* **201** (1959), 37–70."

<5> Grouping

Every once in a while it is necessary to treat part of a manuscript as a unit, so you need to indicate in some fashion where that part begins and ends. For this purpose TEX gives special interpretation to two "grouping characters" (just as it treats the escape character in a special way). We shall assume in this manual that { and } are the grouping characters, although any other typeable characters may be reserved for this function.

We saw one example of grouping in the previous chapter, where it was pointed out that font changes inside a group do not affect the fonts in force outside. This gives the effect of what computer scientists call "block structure." Another example of grouping occurs when you are using certain control sequences; for example, if you want to center something on a line you can type

```
\ctrline{This information will be centered.}
```

using the control sequence \ctrline defined in basic TEX format (Appendix B).

Grouping is used in quite a few of TEX's more complex instructions, although it is largely unnecessary in simple manuscripts. Here's an example of a slightly more complex case, the definition of a new control sequence \rm as mentioned in the previous chapter:

$$\def\rm{\:a}$$

This means that control sequence \rm is henceforth to be replaced in the input by the control sequence \: followed by a. One can also have *groups within groups*, e.g.,

$$\def\tenpoint{\def\rm{\:a}\def\sl{\:n}\def\bf{\:q}}$$

which means that the control sequence \tenpoint is henceforth to be replaced in the input by

$$\def\rm{\:a}\def\sl{\:n}\def\bf{\:q}$$

and these, in turn, describe replacements for the control sequences \rm, \sl, and \bf. If you are a novice TEX user, you will probably not be using \def yourself to define control sequences; the point of this example is merely to demonstrate that groups can indeed arise within groups.

⚠ Groups within groups will happen only in rather complicated situations, but in such cases it is extremely important that you don't leave out a { or a }, lest TEX get hopelessly confused. For example, the \output routine in Appendix E has as many as five levels of groups within groups within ...; although each level is fairly simple by itself, the total cumulative effect can boggle the mind, so the author had to try three times before getting the {'s and }'s right. In such situations there is a handy rule for figuring out which { goes with which }, and whether or not you have forgotten any braces. Start with a mental count of zero, and go from left to right in your TEX input. When you get to a {, add one to the count, and write the resulting number lightly above the {. When you get to a }, write the current count lightly above it and *then* subtract one from the count. For example,

```
               1   2   2   2   3   3   3   3   2   2   2   1
            ...{...{...}...{...{...}...{...}...}...{...}...}...
Current count: 0   1   2   1   2   3   2   3   2   1   2   1   0
```

If the input is properly grouped, your count will return to zero, and it will never become less than zero. The { corresponding to any particular } is the nearest preceding { having the same number as the }. (You need not apply this procedure to the entire input manuscript, just to any part that is supposed to be understood as a unit. For example, you can apply this procedure to the right-hand side of any definition that uses \def.)

Suppose that you had typed

> `\ctrline{This information will be {\sl centered}.}`

Then you would have gotten

> This information will be *centered*.

Now suppose that you type

> `\ctrline{This information will be {centered}.}`

What do you think will happen? Answer: you will get

> This information will be centered.

The result looks just as if those innermost braces had not appeared at all, because you haven't used the grouping to change fonts or anything. TEX doesn't mind if you want to waste your time making groups for no reason.

Actually there is a reason why you might want to use grouping without font changes, etc., namely when you want to make sure that spacing comes out right. In Chapter 3 we discussed the control sequence \TEX that the author of this manual has used to get the logo "TEX", and we observed that the space after \TEX is ignored since \TEX is a control sequence. Thus it was apparently necessary to type "\TEX\␣" when there was supposed to be a space following "TEX", but it was a mistake to type "\TEX\" when the next character was to be a punctuation mark or something else besides a space. Well, in *all* cases it would be correct to type

> `{\TEX}`

whether or not the following character is a space, because the } stops TEX from looking for the optional space after \TEX. This might come in handy when you're using a text editor (e.g., when replacing all occurrences of a particular word by a control sequence). Another thing you could do is type

> `\TEX{}`

using an *empty* group for the same purpose: the {} here is a group of no characters, so it produces no output, but it does have the effect of shutting off TEX's scan for blanks.

▸Exercise 5.1: Suppose you want to specify two hyphens in a row; you can't type "--" because TEX will read that as an en-dash, so what can you do?

When TEX starts any job, all characters are alike; there is no escape character, and there are no grouping characters. TEX automatically makes the first nonblank input character the escape, but if a manuscript is going to use grouping, the grouping characters must be "turned on." The basic format in Appendix B does this, and you can do it yourself in the following way: Type "\chcode⟨number⟩←1" for the left delimiter and "\chcode⟨number⟩←2" for the right delimiter, where ⟨number⟩ is the numeric value of the 7-bit code for the desired character. For example, "{" and "}" have the respective codes ´173 and ´176 at Stanford—this is a local deviation from some ascii codes at other places—so the instructions

\chcode´173←1 \chcode´176←2

appear among the basic format definitions in Appendix B. (Numbers beginning with ´ are in octal notation, cf. Chapter 8.) It is possible to have several characters simultaneously serving as group delimiters, simply by using \chcode to specify each of them.

Font changes are not the only things that "stay inside" a group without affecting the text outside. This same localization applies to any control sequences defined within the group (except those using \gdef in place of \def); to glue-spacing parameters such as those set by \baselineskip and \tabskip; to TEX control parameters such as those set by \trace and \jpar; and to the character interpretations set by \chcode. But localization does *not* apply to definitions of \output routines, or to the size parameters set by \hsize, \vsize, \parindent, \maxdepth, and \topbaseline. Furthermore, if you type "{\:a=cmr10}", the "cmr10" part of this font definition still is irrevocably tied to code a.

▶Exercise 5.2: Would \def\rm{{\:a}} have the same effect as the definition \def\rm{\:a}? (The only difference is an extra level of grouping.)

▶Exercise 5.3: Suppose \chcode´74←1 \chcode´76←2 appears near the beginning of a group that begins with {; these specifications instruct TEX to treat < and > as group delimiters. According to the rules above, the characters < and > will revert to their previous meaning when the group ends; but should the group end with } or with >?

<6> Running TEX

The best way to learn how to do something is to do it, and the best way to learn how to use TEX is to use it. Thus, it's high time for you to sit down at a computer terminal and interact with the TEX system, trying things out to see what happens. Here are some small but complete examples suggested for your first encounter. The examples are presented in terms of the Stanford WAITS system; slightly different conventions may be in use at other installations.

Caution: This chapter is rather a long one. Why don't you stop reading now, and come back to this tomorrow?

OK, let's suppose that you're rested and excited about having a trial run of TEX. Step-by-step instructions for using it appear in this chapter. First do this: Go to the lab where the graphic output device is, since you will be wanting to see the output that you get—it won't really be satisfactory to generate new copy with TEX from a remote location. Then log in; and when the operating system types "." at you, type back

```
r tex
```

(followed by ⟨carriage-return⟩). This causes TEX to start up, and when it is ready it will type "∗". Now type

```
\input basic
```

and ⟨carriage-return⟩; this causes the basic TEX format of Appendix B to be read into the system. TEX will type

```
(basic.TEX 1 2 3 4)
```

on your terminal as it is processing this material, meaning that it has read pages 1, 2, 3, and 4 of this file. Then it types "∗", waiting for more input. At this point the \rm font has been selected, which is the "normal" cmr10 font, and TEX is ready to accept an input manuscript using the basic conventions.

Now type several more lines, each followed by ⟨carriage-return⟩:

```
\hsize 2 in
\vskip 1 in
\ctrline{MY STORY}
\vskip 36 pt
\ctrline{\sl by A. U. Thor}
```

```
\vskip 2.54 cm
Once upon a time, in a distant
galaxy called \error \"O\"o\c c,
there lived a computer
named R. J. Drofnats. \par
Mr. Drofnats---or ``R. J.,'' as
he preferred to be called---
was lousy at typesetting, but he
had other nice qualities. For
example, he gave error messages
when a typist forgot to end a paragraph
properly. \end
\par\vfill\end
```

This example is a bit long, and more than a bit silly, but it's no trick for a good typist like you and it will give you some worthwhile experience, so please do it. For your own good.

Incidentally, the example introduces a few more features that you might as well learn as you are typing, so it's probably best for you to type a line, then read the explanation that appears below, then type the next line and so on.

The instruction "\hsize 2 in" says that rather narrow lines will be set, only 2 inches wide. (On a low-resolution device like the XGP currently used at Stanford, "2 in" really means about 2.6 inches, because TEX expects that its output on such devices will be used only for proofreading, or that the output will be reduced to about 77% of its physical size before actual printing. The 10-point type cmr10 will actually appear to be essentially the same size as 13-point type in books; in other words, you should expect to see output "larger than life.")

The instruction "\vskip 1 in" means a *vertical skip* of one inch. (Really 1.3 inches, on an XGP or VERSATEC, but from now on we won't mention this expansion.) Then the instruction "\ctrline{MY STORY}" causes a line of type that says "MY STORY" to be centered in the 2-inch column. (Recall from Chapter 5 that TEX's basic formats, which we loaded by typing "\input basic", include this \ctrline and grouping facility for centering things.)

The instruction "\vskip 36 pt" is another vertical skip, this time by the amount 36 points—which is a printer's measure slightly less than half an inch. Book measurements have traditionally been specified in units of picas and points, and TEX does not want to shake printers up too badly, so it allows a variety of different units of length to be specified.

The instruction "\ctrline{\sl by A. U. Thor}" makes another centered line, this time in the slanted 10-point font (because of the \sl). This \sl is inside a group, so it doesn't affect the type style being used elsewhere.

You can probably guess what "\vskip 2.54 cm" means; or aren't you ready for the metric system yet? It turns out that 2.54 centimeters is exactly one inch.

The next line begins the straight text, which is what you will be typing most of the time; don't be dismayed by the messy spacing instructions like \vskip that you have been typing so far. Something messy like that is expected at the beginning of a manuscript, but it doesn't last long. When TEX begins to read the words

```
Once upon a time, in a distant
```

it starts up a new paragraph. Now comes the good news, if you haven't used computer typesetting before: You don't have to worry about where to break lines in the paragraph, TEX will do that for you. You can type long lines or short lines, it doesn't matter; *every time you hit ⟨carriage-return⟩ it is essentially the same as typing a space.* When TEX has read the entire paragraph, it will try to break up the text so that each line of output, except the last, contains about the same amount of copy; and it will hyphenate words if necessary (but only as a last resort).

After you type in the next input line,

```
galaxy called \error \"O\"o\c c,
```

something new will happen: TEX will type back an error message, saying

```
! Undefined control sequence.
(*) galaxy called \error
                         \"O\"o\c c,
    ↑
```

What does this mean? It means, as you might guess, that an undefined control sequence was found in the input. TEX shows how far it has read your input by displaying it in two lines; the first line shows what has been read before the error was detected (namely "galaxy␣called␣\error␣") and the next line shows what TEX hasn't looked at yet but will see next. So it is plain that "\error" is the culprit; it is a control sequence that hasn't been defined. After an error message, all is not lost, you have several options:

(1) Type ⟨line-feed⟩. This will cause future error messages to be printed on your terminal as usual, but TEX will always proceed immediately without waiting for your response. It is a fast, but somewhat dangerous, way to proceed.

(2) Type "x" or "X". This will cause TEX to stop right then and there, but you will be able to print any pages that have been completed.

(3) Type "e" or "E". This will terminate TEX and activate the system editor, allowing you to edit the input file that TEX is currently reading. (Don't do this unless there is such a file.)

(4) Type "i" or "I". This will cause TEX to prompt you (with "*") for text to be *inserted* at the current place in the input; TEX will go on to read this new text before looking at what it ordinarily would have read next. You can often use this option to fix up the error. For example, if you have misspelled a control sequence, you can simply insert the correct spelling. (The ⟨carriage-return⟩ that you type after an insertion does not count as a space in the inserted text.)

(5) Type ⟨carriage-return⟩. This is what you should do now. It causes TEX to resume its processing.

(6) Type a number (1 to 9). TEX will delete this many tokens from the input that it ordinarily would have read next, and then it will come back asking you to choose one of these options again. (A "token" is a single character or a control sequence. In certain rare circumstances TEX will not carry out the deletions, but you probably will never run into such cases.)

(7) Type "?" or anything else. Then TEX will refresh your memory about options (1) to (6), and will wait again for you to exercise one of these options.

If you respond by ⟨carriage-return⟩ or ⟨line-feed⟩ or "i" or "I", TEX tries to recover from the error as best it can before carrying on. For example, TEX simply ignores an undefined control sequence like \error. If the error message is

$$\texttt{! Missing \} inserted.}$$

TEX has inserted a } which it has reason to believe was missing. Chapter 27 discusses error messages and appropriate recovery procedures in further detail.

OK, you were supposed to type this line containing an \error so that you could experience the way TEX sometimes complains at you. Similar incidents will probably happen again, since TEX is constantly on the lookout for mistakes. The program tries to be a helpful and constructive critic, to catch errors before they lead to catastrophes. But sometimes, like all programs, it really doesn't understand what's going on, so you have to humor it a bit.

On the remainder of the \error line you will note the strange concoction

```
\"O\"o\c c
```

and you already know that \" stands for an umlaut accent. The \c stands for a "cedilla" accent, so you will get

Ööç

as the name of that distant galaxy.

The next two lines are very simple, except that we haven't encountered \par before. This is one of the ways to end a paragraph. (Another way is to have a completely blank line. A third way is to come to the end of a file-page in an input file.)

The following lines of the example are also quite straightforward; they provide a review of the conventions we discussed long ago for dashes and quotation marks.

But when you type "\end" in the position shown, you will get another error message. The \end instruction is the normal way to stop TEX, but it has to occur at a proper time: not in mid-paragraph. The error message you get this time is

```
! You can't do that in horizontal mode.
```

As we will see later, TEX gets into various "modes," and it is in "horizontal mode" when it is making a paragraph. If you try to do something that is incompatible with the current mode, you will get this sort of error message. The proper response here is, once again, to hit ⟨carriage-return⟩; TEX will resume and forget that you said \end when you shouldn't.

The final line of the example says \par (to end the paragraph and get you out of horizontal mode), then it says

```
\vfill
```

(which means vertical fill—it will insert as much space as necessary to fill up the current page), then it says

```
\end
```

and now TEX will end its processing gracefully. An "xspool" command will appear on your terminal; just hit ⟨carriage-return⟩ and the XGP will print your output. (At least, this is what will happen if you are at Stanford using the WAITS system.)

The output corresponding to the above example will not be shown in this manual; you'll have to do the experiment personally in order to see what happens.

At this point you might also like to look at the file called ERRORS.TMP on your area, since it records the error messages that TEX typed back at you. Say "type errors.tmp" to the operating system.

▶Exercise 6.1: If you had typed the second line of the story as

```
galaxy called \"O\"o\cc,
```

TEX would have issued an error message saying that the control sequence \cc is undefined. What is the best way to recover from this error?

That was Experiment Number 1, and you're ready for Experiment Number 2—after which you will be nearly ready to go on to the preparation of large manuscripts.

For Experiment 2, *prepare a file* called STORY.TEX that contains all the lines of the above example from "\vskip 1 in" to "\par\vfill\end" inclusive; but change the last line to

```
\par\vfill\eject
```

instead. (The \eject instruction is something like \end; it ends a page, but not the whole job.) Note that the line that specifies \hsize is to be omitted from your STORY file; the reason is that we are going to try typesetting the same story with a variety of column widths.

Start TEX again (r tex), and \input basic again. But now type

```
\hsize 4 in
\input story
```

and see what happens. Guess what: T_EX is now going to set 4-inch columns, and it is going to read your STORY.TEX file.

Again it is going to hiccup on the undefined control sequence \error. This time try typing "e", so you can see how to get right to the system file editor from T_EX in case your file is messed up. Delete the offending \error from the file, then start T_EX off from scratch again.

Now try typing several instructions on the same line:

```
\input basic\hsize 4in\input story
```

If you don't put a blank space after the c of basic here, you'll get an error message (a file name should be followed by a blank space), but in this case it's safe to hit ⟨carriage-return⟩ and continue. (T_EX is just warning you that something may have been amiss; the rule is that a space should be there, but it will be inserted if you proceed. From now on, always leave a space after file names, to avoid any hassle.)

Soon T_EX will be reading your story file again—and it will hang up on the \end error. Instead of removing this error, just type ⟨line-feed⟩ since you know it is harmless to bypass this error.

When T_EX asks for more input, type the following lines, one at a time:

```
\hsize 3in \input story
\hsize 1.5in \input story
\jpar 1000 \input story
\ragged 1000 \input story
\hsize 1 in \input story
\end
```

The results will be somewhat interesting, so try it!

If you have followed instructions, your output will consist of six pages; the first page has MY STORY set 4 inches wide, the next has it set 3 inches wide, then come three pages where it is set $1\frac{1}{2}$ inches wide, and a final page where T_EX tries to make 1-inch columns. Since 1-inch columns of 10-point type allow only about 15 characters per line, the last four pages put quite a strain on T_EX's ability to break paragraphs up into attractive lines.

When T_EX fails to find a good way to handle a paragraph, there usually *is* no good way (except that T_EX doesn't know how to hyphenate all words). In such cases the symptom is that T_EX reports an "overfull box," and lines that are too long will appear in the output. You probably noticed such a complaint about overfull boxes when TEX was first trying to set the story with 1.5 inch columns. (If you didn't notice it on your terminal, look at `errors.tmp` to refresh your memory.) Several lines on page 3 of your output will be more than 1.5 inches long—they are "overfull" and stick out like sore thumbs.

There are two remedies for overfull boxes: You can either rewrite the text of the manuscript to avoid the problem (in fact, careful authors often do just that), or you can tell TEX to consider larger spaces acceptable. The instruction `\jpar 1000` essentially makes TEX look for more ways to break the paragraph, including those with larger spaces; so the fourth page of the output shows a solution of the problem without any overfull boxes.

The expandability of spaces is defined by the font, not by TEX. Standard TEX fonts like cmr10 have fairly tight restrictions on spacing, in accordance with the recommendations of contemporary typographers. These strict standards are appropriate for books, but not for newspapers, when more tolerance is needed. If you are setting a lot of material with narrow margins, it would be better to use a font with more variability in its spacing than to use a high setting of `\jpar`, since TEX has to work harder when `\jpar` is large (it considers more possibilities). Chapter 14 explains more about `\jpar`.

The instruction `\ragged 1000` causes paragraphs to be set with a "ragged right margin"—i.e., the lines are broken as usual, but spaces between words don't stretch or shrink very much. Chapter 14 tells more about `\raggedness`.

When `\hsize` was one inch in the above experiment, TEX again came up with an overfull box, even when `\jpar` was quite large. The reason is that TEX doesn't know how to hyphenate "Drofnats", the second word of the second paragraph. To remedy this, replace "`Drofnats`" by "`Drof\-nats`" in both places where it occurs in your `story` file, and try setting the story with

```
\hsize 1 in \jpar 1000 \ragged 0  .
```

You'll see that the output is now quite reasonable, considering the extremely narrow column width. The control sequence `\-` means a *discretionary hyphen*, namely a legal place to hyphenate the word if TEX needs to.

At this point you might want to play around with TEX a bit before you read further. Try different stories, different measurements, and so on. One experiment particularly recommended is to type

```
\ctrline{MY \ERROR STORY}
```

after basic has been \input. This produces a somewhat more elaborate error
message with which you should become acquainted, namely:

```
! Undefined control sequence.
<argument> MY \Error
                        STORY
... plus1000cm minus1000cm #1
                                \hskip 0pt plus1000cm minu...
(*) \ctrline{MY \ERROR STORY}
```

The reason for all this is that \ctrline is not a built-in TEX instruction, it is
a control sequence defined in the basic format. Thus TEX did not detect any
mistake when it read "{MY \ERROR STORY}", it simply absorbed this group
and passed the text "MY \ERROR STORY" as an argument to the \ctrline
definition. According to Appendix B, \ctrline gets expanded into the text

```
\hbox to size{\hskip0pt plus1000cm minus1000cm
              #1\hskip0pt plus1000cm minus1000cm}
```

where the argument gets inserted in place of the "#1". (You don't have to understand exactly what this means, just believe that it is a way to center something
on a line.) A fragment of this expansion is shown in the error message, preceded
and followed by "..." to indicate that there was more to the expansion TEX
was reading. The error message shows that TEX had read the expansion up to
the point "#1", because \hskip etc. appears on the next line. Furthermore the
error message shows that TEX was reading the argument, and the last thing it
read was the control sequence "\Error". (You actually typed "\ERRUR", but
upper case and lower case are not distinguished by TEX after the first letter of a
control sequence.)

The point is that when you make an error within a routine controlled by a
defined control sequence like \ctrline, the error message will show everything
TEX knows about what it was reading; the display occurs in groups of two lines
per level of reading, where the first line shows what TEX has read at this level
and the second line shows what is yet to be read. Somewhere in there you should
be able to spot the problem, the thing TEX wasn't expecting.

  Careful study of the 1.5-inch example shows that TEX does not automatically break
lines just before a dash, although it does do so just *after* one. Some printers will
start new lines with dashes; if you really want to do this you can type "\penalty 0"
just before each dash. For example, "Drofnats\penalty 0---".

<7> How TEX reads what you type

While studying the example in the previous chapter, we observed that an input manuscript is expressed in terms of "lines" ending with ⟨carriage-return⟩s, but these lines of input are essentially independent of the lines of output that will appear on the finished pages. Thus you can stop typing a line of input at any convenient place. A few other related rules have also been mentioned:

- A ⟨carriage-return⟩ is like a space.
- Two spaces in a row count as one space.
- A blank line denotes end of paragraph.

Strictly speaking, these rules are contradictory: A blank line is obtained by typing ⟨carriage-return⟩ twice in a row, and this is different from typing two spaces in a row. So now let's see what the *real* rules are. The purpose of this chapter is to study the very first stage in the transition from input to output.

In the first place, it's wise to have a precise idea of what your keyboard sends to the machine. There are 128 characters that TEX might encounter at each step in a file or in a line of text typed directly on your terminal. These 128 characters are classified into 13 categories numbered 0 to 12:

Category code	Meaning	
0	Escape character	(\ in this manual)
1	Beginning of group	({ in this manual)
2	End of group	(} in this manual)
3	Begin or end math	($ in this manual)
4	Alignment tab	(⊗ in this manual)
5	End of line	(⟨carriage-return⟩ and % in this manual)
6	Parameter	(# in this manual)
7	Superscript	(↑ in this manual)
8	Subscript	(↓ in this manual)
9	Ignored character	
10	Space	
11	Letter	(A, ..., Z and a, ..., z)
12	Other character	

It's not necessary for you to learn these code numbers; the point is only that TEX responds to 13 different types of characters. At first this manual led you to

believe that there were just two types—the escape character and the others—
and more recently you were told about two more types, the grouping symbols
like { and }. Now you know that there are really 13. This is the whole truth of
the matter; no more types remain to be revealed.

Actually no characters are defined to be of types 0 to 8 when TEX begins,
except that ⟨carriage-return⟩ and ⟨form-feed⟩ are type 5. But if you are using a
predefined format (like almost everybody does) you will be told which characters
have special significance. For example, if you are using the basic package of
Appendix B you need to know that the nine characters

$$\backslash \quad \{ \quad \} \quad \$ \quad \otimes \quad \% \quad \# \quad \uparrow \quad \downarrow$$

cannot be used as ordinary characters in your text; they have special meaning.
(If you really need any of these symbols as part of what you're typing, e.g., if you
need a $ to represent dollars, there is a way out—this will be explained later. A
list of control sequences for special symbols appears in Appendix F.)

When TEX is reading a line of text from a file, or a line of text that you
entered directly on your terminal, it is in one of three "states":

State N	Beginning a new line
State M	Middle of a line
State S	Skipping blanks

At the beginning it's in state N, but most of the time it's in state M, and after
a control sequence or a space it's in state S. Incidentally, "states" are different
from the "modes" mentioned in Chapter 6; the current $state$ refers to TEX's eyes
and mouth as they take in characters of new text, but the current $mode$ refers
to the condition of TEX's gastro-intestinal tract. Modes are discussed further in
Chapter 13.

You hardly ever need to worry about what state TEX is in, but you may
want to understand the rules just in case TEX does something unexpected to your
input file. In general, it is nice to understand who you are talking to.

Furthermore, if you faithfully carried out the experiment in the previous
chapter you will probably have noticed that there was an unwanted space after
the dash in "called---"; the ⟨carriage-return⟩ after this dash got changed into
a space that doesn't belong there. This error was purposely put into the example

because the author of this manual feels that we learn best by making mistakes. But now let's look closely into TEX's reading rules so that such mistakes will be unlearned in the future.

Fortunately the rules are not complicated or surprising; you could probably write them down yourself:

If in state N (new line) and TEX sees

    a) an escape character (type 0), TEX scans the entire control sequence, then digests it (i.e., sends the control sequence to the guts of TEX where it will be processed appropriately) and goes to state S.

    b) an end-of-line character (type 5), TEX throws away any other information that might remain on the current line, then digests a "\par" instruction (paragraph end) and remains in state N.

    c) an ignored character or a space (types 9,10), TEX passes it by, remaining in state N.

    d) anything else (types 1,2,3,4,6,7,8,11,12), TEX digests it and goes to state M.

In summary, when TEX is beginning a line, it skips blanks, and if it gets to the end of the line without seeing anything it considers that a paragraph has ended.

If in state M (middle of line) and TEX sees

    a) an escape character (type 0), TEX scans the entire control sequence, then digests it and goes to state S.

    b) an end-of-line character (type 5), TEX throws away any other information that might remain on the current line, then digests a blank space and goes to state N.

    c) an ignored character (type 9), TEX passes it by, remaining in state M.

    d) a space (type 10), TEX digests a blank space and goes to state S.

    e) anything else (types 1,2,3,4,6,7,8,11,12), TEX digests it and remains in state M.

In summary, when TEX is in the middle of a line, it digests what it sees, but converts one or more blank spaces into a single blank space, and also treats the end of line as a blank space.

If in state S (skipping blanks) and TEX sees

a) an escape character (type 0), TEX scans the entire control sequence, then digests it, remaining in state S.

b) an end-of-line character (type 5), TEX throws away any other information that might remain on the current line, then switches to state N.

c) an ignored character or a space (types 9,10), TEX passes it by, remaining in state S.

d) anything else (types 1,2,3,4,6,7,8,11,12), TEX digests it and goes to state M.

In summary, when TEX is skipping blanks, it ignores blanks and doesn't treat the end of a line as a blank space.

So those are the rules. Only three major consequences deserve special emphasis here:

First, a ⟨carriage-return⟩ always counts as a space, even when it follows a hyphen. If you want to end a line with a ⟨carriage-return⟩ but no space, you can do this by typing the control sequence "\!" just before the ⟨carriage-return⟩. For example, the 7th-last line of MY STORY in Chapter 6 should really have been typed as follows:

```
he preferred to be called---\!
```

A second consequence of the rules, if you are using the basic format of Appendix B, is that the % sign is treated as an end-of-line mark equivalent to a ⟨carriage-return⟩. This is useful for putting comments into the manuscript. For example, you might include a copyright notice for legal protection; or you might say

```
% Figure 5 belongs here;
```

or you might say

```
% This } is supposed to match the { of "\ctrline{".
```

Anything that you might want to remember but not to print can be included after a %, because TEX will never look at the rest of the line.

A third consequence of the rules is that you should indicate the end of a paragraph either explicitly, by using the control sequence \par; or implicitly, by having an entirely blank line. (The end of a file page also counts as a blank line, because of the way files of text are conventionally represented in the computer.) In the latter case, TEX has always read a space before it came to the end of the paragraph, because it digested a space at the end of the line before the blank line. In the former case, you may or may not have typed a space before you typed "\par". Fortunately, there's nothing to worry about; the result is the same in either case, because TEX's paragraph processor discards the final item of a paragraph when it is a space.

If you have several blank lines in a row, TEX digests a "\par" instruction for each one, according to the rules. But this doesn't show up in the output, because empty paragraphs are discarded.

▶Exercise 7.1: If a line isn't entirely blank, but the first nonblank character on the line is %, does this signify end-of-paragraph?

When TEX first starts up, the 128 possible characters are initially interpreted as follows. Characters "A" to "Z" (ascii codes ´101 to ´132) and "a" to "z" (ascii codes ´141 to ´172) are type 11 (letters). The characters ⟨null⟩, ⟨line-feed⟩, ⟨vertical-tab⟩, ⟨alt-mode⟩, and ⟨delete⟩ (ascii codes 0, ´12, ´13, ´175, and ´177 at Stanford) are type 9 (ignored). The characters ⟨tab⟩ and ⟨ ⟩ (ascii codes ´11 and ´40) are type 10 (spaces). The characters ⟨form-feed⟩ and ⟨carriage-return⟩ (ascii codes ´14 and ´15) are type 5 (end of line). All other characters are type 12 (other). The first non-space input by TEX is defined to be the escape character used in error messages, and it is set to type 0 (escape). You can use \chcode to change the type code of any character, and it is possible to have several characters each defined to be of type 0 or any other type. The instruction

$$\text{\chcode}\langle number_1\rangle\leftarrow\langle number_2\rangle$$

(where ⟨number₁⟩ is between 0 and 127 and ⟨number₂⟩ is between 0 and 12) causes the character whose 7-bit code is ⟨number₁⟩ to be regarded as type ⟨number₂⟩ for the duration of the current group, unless its type is changed again by another \chcode. For example, if for some reason you want TEX to treat the letter "a" as a non-letter, you could say

$$\text{\chcode}´141\leftarrow12 \ .$$

But this would probably not be useful because, e.g., "\par" would no longer be a control sequence; it would be read as "\p" followed by "a" followed by "r".

We will see later that spaces are sometimes ignored after *other* things besides control sequences, since there are various TEX constructions that look better if spaces or end-of-line follow them. For convenient reference, here is a list of all cases in which TEX will ignore a space, even though most of these constructions haven't been explained yet in the manual:

- After a space or end-of-line character.

- After a control sequence.

- After the } that ends a \def or \if or \ifeven or \else or \noalign or \output or \mark.

- Between $ signs, when TEX is in math mode.

- After the $$ that ends a display.

- After a file name or an already-defined font code or a unit of measure or the words "to" or "par" or "size" in box specifications.

- Before or after a ⟨number⟩ or the sign preceding a ⟨number⟩.

- After a paragraph, or in general whenever TEX is in vertical mode or restricted vertical mode.

TEX goes into reading state S only as shown in the detailed reading rules above. When it ignores spaces at other times, e.g. after a unit of measure, the spaces it ignores are actually "digested" spaces; the processing routine calls on TEX's input mechanism to continue reading until a non-space is digested. This is a fine point, because it hardly ever makes a difference; but here is a case where it matters: Suppose you make the definition "\def\space{⊔}". Then if you type "\space\space", TEX will digest two spaces; these spaces would not be ignored after a space or end of line or control sequence, because of TEX's reading rules, but they would be ignored in the other cases listed above, because of TEX's digestive processes. On the other hand \⊔ (control space) is treated differently: it always means an explicit space and it is never ignored in any of the above cases except the last (in vertical mode). Sometimes TEX will ignore only one digested space, but at other times it will ignore as many as are fed to it; if you really need to know which cases fall into each category, you can find out by experiment.

<8> The characters you type

A lot of different keyboards are used with TEX, but few keyboards can produce 128 different symbols. Furthermore, as we have seen, some of the characters that you *can* type on your keyboard are reserved for special purposes like escaping and grouping. Yet when we studied fonts it was pointed out that there are 128 characters per font. So how can you refer to the characters that aren't on your keyboard, or that have been pre-empted for formatting?

One answer is to use control sequences. For example, the `basic` format of Appendix B, which defines % to be an end-of-line symbol so that you can use it for comments, also defines the control sequence \% to mean a per-cent sign.

To get access to any character whatsoever, you can type

$$\text{\char}\langle\text{number}\rangle$$

where ⟨number⟩ is any number from 0 to 127 (optionally followed by a space), and you will get the corresponding character from the current font. For example, the letter "b" is character number 98, so you could typeset the word `bubble` by typing

$$\text{\char98u\char98\char98le}$$

if the b-key on your typewriter is out of order. (Of course you need the \, c, h, a, and r keys to type "\char", so let's hope they are always working.)

Character numbers are usually given in *octal notation* in reference books (i.e., using the radix-8 number system). A ⟨number⟩ in TEX's language can be preceded by a ´, in which case it is understood as octal. For example, the octal code for "b" is *142**, so

$$\text{\char´142}$$

is equivalent to \char98. In octal notation, character numbers run from ´0 to ´177.

Formally speaking, a ⟨number⟩ in a TEX manuscript is any number of spaces followed by an optional "´" followed by any number of digits followed by an optional space. Or it can be any number of spaces followed by "\count⟨digit⟩" followed by an optional space; in the latter case the specified counter is used (cf. Chapter 23).

You can't use \char in the middle of a control sequence, though. If you type

$$\text{\\char´142}$$

---

*The author of this manual likes to use italic digits to denote octal numbers, instead of using the ´ symbol, when octal numbers appear in printed books.

TEX reads this as the control sequence \\ followed by c, h, a, etc., not as the control sequence \b.

Actually you will hardly ever have to use \char yourself, since the characters you want will probably be available as predefined control sequences; \char is just a last resort in case you really need it (and it is also indispensible for the designers of book formats).

Since TEX is intended to be useful on many different kinds of keyboards, it does not assume that you can type very many of the exotic characters. For example, if your keyboard has an α on it (Greek lower case alpha)—this is character code 2 at Stanford—you will be able to type "α" in a math formula and get an alpha. But if you don't have α on your keyboard, TEX understands the control sequence \alpha just as well.

Character code 2 in TEX's font cmr10 is not really an alpha; it is actually Θ, an upper case Greek theta! TEX doesn't want you to type "α" except in math formulas. When you are typing straight text with TEX's special fonts like cmr10, you should confine yourself to the symbols usually found on a typewriter and a few more that are listed in the next chapter. In fact, *every font you use might have a different way of assigning its symbols to the numbers 0 to 127*. Whoever designed the font should tell you what this encoding is. It's not even guaranteed that an "a" will yield an "a". Your keyboard converts what you type into codes between 0 and 127, and these codes will select the corresponding characters of the current font, but a font designer can put whatever symbol he or she wants into each position.

Furthermore, *different fonts might also have different ligatures*. It isn't true that -- will give you a dash in all fonts with TEX, nor that `` will become ", nor that ffl will become ffl. Each font designer decides what ligature combinations will appear in his or her font, and this person should tell you what they are. The seven ligatures

          ``   ´´   --   ---   ff   fi   fl   ffi   ffl

described in Chapter 2 are available in all the "standard" TEX roman and slanted fonts, but you should not assume that they are present in all fonts.

Similarly, accents like \ˇ and \" can't be used with all fonts; the accent characters have to be in certain positions within the font, and not all fonts have them.

If you want to use an accent on a nonstandard font (e.g., if you need a new accent for some newly discovered African dialect), suppose you have a font that includes this accent as character number ´20. Then you can type "\accent´20a" to get this accent over an "a", etc. In general, type

$$\accent\langle number\rangle\langle char\rangle$$

to get an accent over a character in the same font, or

$$\accent\langle number\rangle\backslash:\langle font\rangle\langle char\rangle$$

to get an accent over a character in a different font. You're not allowed to say things like "{\:b\accent´20}a", however; the character to be accented must immediately follow the accent except for font changes.

<9> TEX's standard roman fonts

When you are using a standard roman font (like cmr10, cmb10, cms10, or cmss10, which stand respectively for Computer Modern Roman, Bold, Slanted, or Sans-Serif, 10 points high), you need to know the information in this chapter.

These fonts are intended to contain nearly every symbol you will need for non-math text, including accents and special characters for use with foreign languages. When you are using such fonts you should confine yourself to typing the following symbols only:

the letters A to Z and a to z

the digits 0 to 9

the standard punctuation marks , : ; ! ? ( ) [ ] & ` ´ − * / .

You can also type + = < > and you will get the corresponding symbols, but this is not recommended because these symbols should be used only in mathematics mode (explained later). The result will look better in mathematics mode, because TEX will insert proper spacing. When you use the "−" and "/" it should not be for mathematics; do hyphens and slashes outside of math mode, but don't do subtractions and divisions.

Conspicuously absent from this list are the following symbols found on many keyboards:

$$\backslash \quad \{ \quad \} \quad \# \quad \$ \quad \% \quad \uparrow \quad \downarrow \quad " \quad @$$

Resist the temptation to type them. Also resist the temptation to type mathematical symbols like

$$| \quad \leftarrow \quad \alpha \quad \beta \quad \epsilon \quad \lambda \quad \pi \quad \forall \quad \exists \quad \infty$$

and so on, if your keyboard has them. Like + and =, they should be reserved for mathematics mode; but unlike + and =, they don't give the results you might expect, except in mathematics mode.

By using control sequences you can obtain the following special symbols needed in foreign languages:

Type	to get	
\ss	ß	(German letter ss)
\ae	æ	(Latin and Scandinavian ligature ae)
\AE	Æ	(Latin and Scandinavian ligature AE)
\oe	œ	(French ligature oe)
\OE	Œ	(French ligature OE)
\o	ø	(Scandinavian slashed o)
\O	Ø	(Scandinavian slashed O)

For example, if you want to specify "Æsop's Œuvres en français" you could type

```
\AE sop´s \OE uvres en fran\c cais  .
```

(Note the spaces after these control sequences. Another way to separate them from the surrounding text would be

```
{\AE}sop´s {\OE}uvres en fran{\c c}ais  ;
```

this looks a little nicer, perhaps, in the computer file, but it's harder to type.)

The following accents are available in standard roman fonts, shown here with the letter "o":

Type	to get	
\`o	ò	(accent grave)
\´o	ó	(accent aigu, acute accent)
\^ o	ô	(accent circonflexe, circumflex or "hat" accent)
\v o	ǒ	(Slavic háček accent, inverted circumflex)
\u o	ŏ	(breve, short vowel)
\=o	ō	(macron or bar, long vowel)
\"o	ö	(umlaut or double dot)
\H o	ő	(long Hungarian umlaut)
\b o	ō̬	(vector accent—used in mathematics)
\s o	õ	(tilde or squiggle)
\t oo	o͡o	(ties two letters together)
\a a	å	(Scandinavian a with circle)
\l l	ł	(Polish crossed l)
\c c	ç	(cedilla accent)

The last three of these examples are shown with other letters instead of "o" because they are somewhat special; the Scandinavian accent is shown over an "a" since "ŏ" isn't a Scandinavian letter. Similarly, the \l accent is specifically designed for the letter "l". Cedillas are usually associated with the letter "c" (although it is true that "ǫ" appears in Navajo).

Spaces are obligatory where shown in these examples. But the space can be omitted after the accent codes \`, \´, \=, and \", since they don't involve letters.

Within a font, accents are designed to appear at the right height for letters like "o"; but TEX will raise an accent if it is applied to a tall letter. For example, the result of "\"O" is "Ö". This simple rule almost always works all right, but sometimes it fails; for example, an upper case A with the circle accent traditionally has the circle touching the A (Å), at least in Scandinavian books, while "\a A" yields "Å". (Both of these forms are used by modern American printers to denote angstrom units, but Å is preferable.) The \l doesn't work with a capital L either; "\l L" yields "Ł". An even more conspicuous failure of TEX's rule occurs if you try to put a cedilla on an upper case "C" by typing "\c C"; TEX will raise the cedilla to give "Ç"! (See below for how to handle these anomalous cases.)

When the letters "i" and "j" are accented, it is traditional to omit the dots they contain. Therefore standard roman fonts contain the dotless letters

$$\imath \quad \text{and} \quad \jmath$$

which you can obtain by typing "\i" and "\j", respectively. For example, to obtain "mīnŭs" you would type "m\=\i n\u us".

▶Exercise 9.1: Explain what to type in order to get the sentence

Commentarii Academæ Petropolitanæ is now *Doklady Akademiiā Nauk SSSR.*

▶Exercise 9.2: How would you specify the names Øystein Ore, ĪŪri ĪAnov, Ja'far al-Khowârizmî, and Władyisław Süßman?

The character to be accented must immediately follow the accent, except for the fact that you are allowed to change fonts in between; see the remarks at the close of the previous chapter. TₑX adjusts for the slantedness of characters when placing accents, including the possibility that the accent comes from a font with a different slant than the character being accented. For example, if you type

```
\´e \´E \sl\´e \´E \rm\´\sl e \rm\´\sl E \´\rm e \sl\´\rm E
```

using basic format, the result will be

$$é\ É\ é\ É\ é\ É\ é\ É.$$

The fonts are designed so that the anomalous cases of "bad accents" mentioned above can be handled as follows, using the \spose (superpose) control sequence of basic format: To get

$$Å\ \ Ç\ \ Ł$$

type respectively

```
\spose{\raise 1.667pt\hbox{\char´27}}A
\spose{\char´30}C
\spose{\raise 2.5pt\hbox{\char´31}}L
```

(This is for 10-point sizes; the amounts to raise the accents must be adjusted proportionately when working with other sizes. For example, "\raise 1.667pt" would become "\raise 1.5pt" in 9-point type.)

A complete list of the 128 symbols in TₑX's standard roman fonts appears in Appendix F. But everything a typist needs to know about them has already been explained; it's not necessary for you to know the numeric character codes.

<10> Dimensions

The example program used in the trial runs of Chapter 6 involved mysterious TEX instructions like "\vskip 2.54cm". Now it is time to reveal part of this mystery, by explaining what units of measure TEX understands.

"Points" and "picas" are printers' traditional basic units of measure, so TEX understands points and picas. TEX also understands inches and certain metric units, but it converts everything internally to points. Each unit of measure is given a two-letter abbreviation; here is a complete list of the units TEX knows about:

pt   point
pc   pica (one pica equals 12 points)
in   inch (one point equals 0.01383700 inches)
cm   centimeter (one inch equals 2.5400 centimeters)
mm   millimeter (one centimeter equals 10 millimeters)
dd   Didot point (one centimeter equals 26.600 Didot points)
em   One "quad" of space in the current font (see Chapter 18)

When you want to express some physical dimension to TEX, type it as

⟨optional sign⟩⟨number⟩⟨unit of measure⟩

or

⟨optional sign⟩⟨number⟩.⟨number⟩⟨unit of measure⟩

(and in the second case your ⟨number⟩s had better not be in octal notation or TEX will get confused). An ⟨optional sign⟩ is either a "+" or a "−" or nothing at all.

For example, here are some typical lengths:

3 in
29 pc
−0.013837in
+ 42.1 dd
0 mm

A plus sign is redundant, but some people like occasional redundancy.

Spaces are optional before and after numbers and after the units of measure, but you should not put spaces *within* a number or between the two letters in the unit of measure.

In a manual like this it is convenient to use "angle brackets" in abbreviations for various constructions like ⟨number⟩ and ⟨optional sign⟩. Henceforth in this manual we will use the term ⟨dimen⟩ to stand for any dimension expressed in the above form. For example,

$$\texttt{\textbackslash hsize}\langle\text{dimen}\rangle$$

will be the general way to define the page width TEX is supposed to use.

When a dimension is zero, you have to specify a unit of measure even though it is redundant. Don't just say "0", say "0pt" or "0in" or something.

Chapter 6 mentions that units of measure may be inflated artificially on some output devices. The following "rulers" have been typeset by TEX so that you can calibrate the output device used to produce the copy of the manual you are reading:

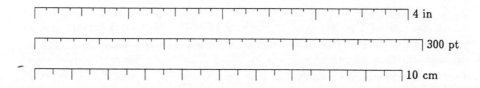

4 in

300 pt

10 cm

▶Exercise 10.1: (To be worked after you know about boxes and glue and have read Chapter 21.) Explain how to typeset a 10 cm ruler like this using TEX.

<11> Boxes

TEX makes complicated pages by starting with simple individual characters and putting them together in larger units, and putting these together in still larger units, and so on. Conceptually, it's a big paste-up job. The TEXnical terms used to describe such page construction are *boxes* and *glue*.

Boxes in TEX are two-dimensional things with a rectangular shape, having three associated measurements called *height*, *width*, and *depth*. Here is a picture of a typical box, showing its so-called reference point and baseline:

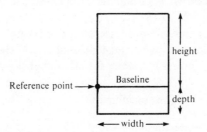

From TeX's viewpoint, a single character from a font is a box, one of the simplest kinds of boxes. The font designer has decided what the height, width, and depth of the character are, and what the symbol will look like when it is in the box; TeX just uses these dimensions to paste boxes together, and ultimately to determine the locations of the reference points for all characters on a page. In the cmr10 font, for example, the letter "h" has a height of 6.9444 points, a width of 5.5556 points, and a depth of zero; the letter "g" has a height of 4.4444 points, a width of 5 points, and a depth of 1.9444 points. Only certain special characters like parentheses have height plus depth actually equal to 10 points, although cmr10 is said to be a "10 point" font. The typist doesn't have to know these measurements, of course, but it is helpful for TeX's users to be aware of the sort of information TeX deals with.

The character shape need not fit inside the boundaries of the box. For example, some characters that are used to build up larger symbols like square-root signs intentionally protrude a little bit, so that they overlap properly with the rest of the symbol. Slanted letters frequently extend a little to the right of the box, as if the box were skewed right at the top and left at the bottom, keeping its baseline fixed. For example, compare the letter "q" in cmr10 and cms10 fonts:

In both cases TeX thinks the box is 5 points wide, so both letters get exactly the same treatment. TeX doesn't know exactly where the ink will go—only the font designer knows this. But the slanted letters will be spaced properly in spite of TEX's lack of knowledge, because the baselines will match up.

Actually the font designer also tells TEX one other thing, the so-called *italic correction*: A number is specified for each character, telling roughly how far that character extends to the right of its box boundary. For example, the italic correction for "q" in cmr10 is zero, but in cms10 it is 0.2083 points. If you type the control sequence

$$\backslash/$$

following a character, TEX will effectively increase the width of that character by the italic correction. It's a good idea to use \/ when shifting from slanted to unslanted fonts without intervening spaces, for example when a slanted word is immediately followed by an unslanted right parenthesis or semicolon. The author typed

```
the so-called {\sl italic correction\/}:
```

when specifying the first sentence of the paragraph you are now reading. Of course, there's no need to make the italic correction when a slanted letter is followed by an unslanted period or comma.

Another simple kind of box TEX deals with might be called a "black box," a rectangle like "█" that is to be entirely filled with ink at printing time. You can specify any height, width, and depth you like for such boxes—but they had better not have too much area or the printer might get upset. (Printers generally prefer white space to black space.)

Usually these black boxes are made very skinny, so that they appear as horizontal lines or vertical lines. Printers traditionally call such lines "horizontal rules" and "vertical rules," so the terms TEX uses to stand for black boxes are \hrule and \vrule. We will discuss the use of rule boxes in greater detail later.

Everything on a page that has been typeset by TEX is made up of simple character boxes or rule boxes, pasted together in combination. TEX pastes boxes together in two ways, either *horizontally* or *vertically*. When TEX builds a horizontal list of boxes, it lines them up so that their reference points appear in the same horizontal row; therefore the baselines of adjacent characters will match up as they should. Similarly, when TEX builds a vertical list of boxes, it lines them up so that their reference points appear in the same vertical column.

There is also a provision for lowering or raising the reference points of individual boxes in a horizontal list. This has been used, for example, to lower the

"E" in "TEX". Similarly, there is a way to move the reference points of boxes to the left or to the right in a vertical list. This is used, for example, when centering an accent over a letter, since an accented letter like É is essentially a box made from a vertical list containing the two character boxes "´" and "E".

When a big box has been made from a horizontal list of smaller boxes, the baseline of the big box is the common baseline of the smaller boxes. (More precisely, it's the common baseline they would share if they hadn't been raised or lowered.) The height and depth of the big box are determined by the maximum distances that the smaller boxes reach above and below the baseline, respectively; any raising and lowering of the smaller boxes is taken into account during this calculation. The width of the big box is determined by whatever TEX operation was used to create that box, as explained in the next chapter.

When a big box has been made from a vertical list of smaller boxes, its reference point is the reference point of the last (lowest) box in the list (but ignoring left or right shifts). The depth of the big box is therefore equal to the depth of this last smaller box. The width of the big box is determined by the maximum distance that the smaller boxes reach to the right of the reference point; any left or right shifting of the smaller boxes is taken into account during this calculation. (Note that if any of the smaller boxes have been shifted left, they will protrude past the left boundary of the big box.) The height of the big box is determined by whatever TEX operation was used to create that box, as explained in the next chapter.

A page of text like the one you're reading is itself a box, in TEX's view: It is a largish box made from a vertical list of smaller boxes representing the lines of text. Each line of text, in turn, is a box made from a horizontal list of boxes representing the individual characters. In more complicated situations, involving mathematical formulas and/or complex tables, you can have boxes within boxes within boxes ... to any level. But even these complicated situations arise from horizontal or vertical lists of boxes pasted together in a simple way, so all that you and TEX have to worry about is one list of boxes at a time. In fact, when you're typing straight text, you hardly have to think about boxes at all, since TEX will automatically take responsibility for assembling the character boxes into words and the words into lines and the lines into pages. You only need to be aware of the box concept when you want to do something out of the ordinary, like centering a heading or providing extra space, etc.

The height, width, or depth of a box might be negative, in which case it is a "shadow box" that is somewhat hard to draw. You might be able to think of some tricky things to do with such boxes; TEX just lines things up and adds up dimensions as if everything were positive or zero. Thus, for example, if a font designer specified a character with negative width, it would act like a backspace. When forming a box from a horizontal list, however, TEX sets the height and depth to zero if they turn out to be negative, so only the width can be negative. Similarly, only the height and depth of a box formed from a vertical list can be negative. Negative dimensions are not allowed in rule boxes.

<12> Glue

But there's more to the story than just boxes: there's also some magic mortar called *glue* that TEX uses to paste boxes together. For example, there is a little space between the lines of text in this manual; it has been calculated so that the baselines of consecutive lines within a paragraph are exactly 12 points apart. And there is space between words too; such space is not an "empty" box, it is part of the glue between boxes. This glue can stretch or shrink so that the right margin of each page comes out looking straight.

When TEX makes a large box from a horizontal or vertical list of smaller boxes, there often is glue between the smaller boxes. Glue has three attributes, namely its natural *space*, its ability to *stretch*, and its ability to *shrink*.

In order to understand how this works, consider the following example of four boxes in a horizontal list separated by three globs of glue:

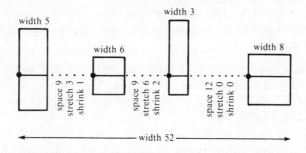

The first glue element has 9 units of space, 3 of stretch, and 1 of shrink; the next one also has 9 units of space, but 6 units of stretch and 2 of shrink; the last one has 12 units of space, but it is unable to stretch or to shrink, so it will remain 12 units of space no matter what.

The total width of boxes and glue in this example, considering only the space components of the glue, is $5 + 9 + 6 + 9 + 3 + 12 + 8 = 52$ units. This is called the *natural width* of the horizontal list; it's the preferred way to paste the boxes together. Suppose, however, that TEX is told to make the horizontal list into a box that is 58 units wide; then the glue has to stretch by 6 units. Well, there are $3 + 6 + 0 = 9$ units of stretchability present, so TEX multiplies each unit of stretchability by 6/9 in order to obtain the extra 6 units needed. Thus, the first glob of glue becomes $9 + (6/9) \times 3 = 11$ units wide, the next becomes $9 + (6/9) \times 6 = 13$ units wide, the last remains 12 units wide, and we obtain the desired box looking like this:

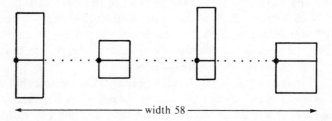

On the other hand, if TEX is supposed to make a box 51 units wide from the given list, it is necessary for the glue to shrink by a total of one unit. There are three units of shrinkability present, so the first glob of glue would shrink by 1/3 and the second by 2/3.

The process of determining glue thickness when a box is being made from a horizontal or vertical list is called *setting the glue*. Once glue has been set, it becomes rigid—it won't stretch or shrink any more, and the resulting box is essentially indecomposable.

Glue will never shrink more than its stated shrinkability. The first glob of glue above, for example, will never be allowed to become narrower than 8 units wide, and TEX will never shrink the given horizontal list to make its total width less than 49 units. But glue is allowed to stretch arbitrarily far, whenever it has a positive stretch component.

▶Exercise 12.1: How wide would the glue globs be if the horizontal list in the illustrations were to be made 100 units wide?

⚠ TEX is somewhat reluctant to stretch glue more than its stated stretchability, as we shall see later when we discuss the "badness" of particular glue settings. Therefore if you are trying to decide how big to make each aspect of the glue in some layout, the rules are: (a) The natural glue space should be the amount of space that looks best. (b) The glue stretch should be the maximum amount of space that can be added to the natural spacing before the layout begins to look bad. (c) The glue shrink should be the maximum amount of space that can be subtracted from the natural spacing before the layout begins to look bad.

In most cases the designer of a book layout will have specified all the kinds of glue that are to be used, so a typist will not need to decide how big any glue attributes should be. For example, the *Art of Computer Programming* layout in Appendix E includes the definition of three control sequences \xskip, \yskip, and \yyskip. A typist for those books will insert \xskip within a paragraph in certain places where a little extra stretchability is appropriate; and \yskip is inserted between paragraphs when the paragraphs discuss somewhat different topics. Even more space is inserted before and after theorems and algorithms, etc.; this is called \yyskip because it is twice as much glue as \yskip. (The same three control sequences have been used when preparing this manual. For example, "\xskip" appears in the paragraph preceding this one, just before "(a)", "(b)", and "(c)"; and "\yyskip" is used before and after every "dangerous bend" paragraph like the next one.)

⚠ To specify glue in a horizontal list of boxes, without using a predefined format like \xskip, type "\hskip⟨dimen⟩ plus⟨dimen⟩ minus⟨dimen⟩". The "plus⟨dimen⟩" and "minus⟨dimen⟩" specify stretch and shrink components. They are optional; and if left out, the corresponding glue component has length zero. The space component, however, must always be given, even when it is zero; and if zero, you must remember to type "0pt", not just "0". If you are omitting the shrink component, the next characters of your text had better not be "minus". If you are omitting both stretch and shrink components, the next characters of your text had better not be "plus". Similar remarks apply to the specification of glue in vertical lists; the only difference is that you type "\vskip" instead of "\hskip".

There is one aspect of glue that a careful typist will want to be aware of, namely that TEX automatically increases the stretchability (and decreases the shrinkability) after punctuation marks. The reason for this is that it's usually better to put more space after a period than between two ordinary words, when spreading a line out to reach the desired margins. Consider, for example, the following sentences from a classic kindergarten pre-primer:

```
``Oh, oh!´´ cried Baby Sally. Dick and Jane laughed.
```

If TEX sets this at its natural width, all the spaces will be the same:

"Oh, oh!" cried Baby Sally. Dick and Jane laughed.

But if the line needs to be expanded by 5 points, 10 points, 15 points, or more, TEX will set it as

"Oh, oh!" cried Baby Sally. Dick and Jane laughed.

"Oh, oh!" cried Baby Sally. Dick and Jane laughed.

"Oh, oh!" cried Baby Sally. Dick and Jane laughed.

"Oh, oh!" cried Baby Sally. Dick and Jane laughed.

and so on. There is no glue between adjacent letters, so individual words will always look the same. The glue after the comma stretches at 1.25 times the rate of the glue between adjacent words; the glue after the period and after the !´´ stretches at 3 times the rate. Furthermore if TEX had to shrink this line to its minimum width, the result would be

"Oh, oh!" cried Baby Sally. Dick and Jane laughed.

The glue after a comma shrinks only 80 per cent as much as ordinary inter-word glue, and after a period or exclamation point it shrinks by only one third as much.

The exact rule TEX uses at a space is this: Each font tells TEX what glue to use for spaces when that font is active. When starting to process a horizontal list, TEX sets an internal variable called the "space factor" to 1. When appending a character to a horizontal list, the space factor is changed to 3 if the character is a period, question mark, or exclamation point (as determined by its ascii code); it is changed to 2 if the character is a colon, to 1.5 if a semicolon, to 1.25 if a comma. The space factor is left unchanged if the character being appended is a) or] or ' or "; and it is reset to 1 whenever any other character or math formula or non-character box is appended. Furthermore, the space factor remains unchanged when appending a character immediately following an upper case letter. (The reason for this is to avoid treating the period specially when it merely follows an initial, like the periods in "P. A. M. Dirac".) When a space is encountered, the glue space is taken from the current font glue space specification; the stretch and shrink are obtained by respectively multiplying and dividing the font glue stretch and shrink specifications by the space factor.

The only trouble with this rule is that it fails when a period isn't really a period ... like when it is used (as in this sentence) to make an "ellipsis" of three dots, or when it is used after abbreviations. If, for example, you are typing a bibliographic reference to *Proc. Amer. Math. Soc.*, you don't want the glue after these periods to be any different from the ordinary inter-word glue. The best way to handle this is to use "escape space" after a non-sentence-ending period, e.g., to type

```
Proc.\ Amer.\ Math.\ Soc.
```

This works because the space in "\␣" always has the unmodified inter-word glue of the current font. Granted that this input looks a bit ugly, it does give the best-looking output. It's one of those things we occasionally have to do when dealing with a computer that tries to be smart.

▷Exercise 12.2: How can you defeat the rule the other way, for sentences like "... launched by NASA."?

Incidentally, if you try to specify "..." by typing three periods in a row, you get "..."—the dots are too close together. The best way to handle this is to go into *mathematics* mode, using the \ldots control sequence defined in basic TEX format. For example, if you type

```
Hmmm $\ldots$ I wonder why?
```

the result is "Hmmm ... I wonder why?" The reason this works is that math formulas are exempt from normal text spacing rules. Chapter 17 has more to say about \ldots and related topics.

One of the interesting things that happens when glue stretches and shrinks at different rates is that there might be glue with essentially *infinite* stretchability. For example, consider again the four boxes we had above, with the same glue as before except that the glue in the middle has stretchability 999997 (nearly one million) instead of 6. Now the total stretchability is one million; and when the line has to grow, almost all of the additional space will get put into the middle glue. If, for example, a box of width 58 is desired, the first glue expands from 9 to 9.000018 units, the middle glue from 9 to 14.999982 units, and of course the last glue remains exactly 12 units thick. For all practical purposes, the spacing has gone from 9, 9, 12 to 9, 15, 12.

If such infinitely stretchable glue is placed at the left of a row of boxes, the effect is to *right justify* them, i.e., to move them over to the rightmost boundary of the constructed box. And if you take *two* globs of infinitely stretchable glue, putting one at the left and one at the right, the effect is to *center* the list of boxes within a larger box. This in fact is how the \ctrline instruction works: it places infinite glue at both ends, then makes a box of width \hsize. [Actually the stretchability is 1000 cm, namely 10 meters (about 33 feet); that isn't infinite, but it's close enough.]

The glue actually used in the definition of \ctrline is \hskip 0pt plus 1000cm minus 1000cm; in other words, *both* stretch and shrink components are essentially infinite. The reason is that if you try to center something that is bigger than the actual \hsize, it will be centered but will extend into the margins; the glue at left and right will shrink from 0 to something *negative*. Like box dimensions, glue components can be negative, and this is occasionally useful for things like backspacing.

"Infinite" glue can be specified in a horizontal list by typing "\hfill", or in a vertical list by typing "\vfill". An \hfill instruction is equivalent to \hskip 0pt plus 10000000000pt (that's ten *billion* points), and \vfill is equivalent to \vskipping by the same amounts. We have already seen a typical use of \vfill in the example of Chapter 6.

<13> Modes

Just as people get into different moods, TEX gets into different "modes." (Except that TEX is more predictable than people.) There are six modes:

- Vertical mode. [Building the vertical list used to make the pages of output.]
- Restricted vertical mode. [Building a vertical list for a box within a page.]
- Horizontal mode. [Building the horizontal list used to make the next paragraph for the output pages.]
- Restricted horizontal mode. [Building a horizontal list for a box within a page.]
- Math mode. [Building a mathematical formula to be placed in a horizontal list.]

- Display math mode. [Building a mathematical formula to be placed on a line by itself, temporarily interrupting the current paragraph.]

In simple situations, you don't need to be aware of what mode TeX is in, because it just does the right thing. But when you get an error message that says "You can't do that in horizontal mode", a knowledge of modes helps explain why TeX thinks you goofed.

Basically TeX is in one of the vertical modes when it is preparing a list of boxes and glue that will be placed vertically on top of one another; it's in one of the horizontal modes when it is preparing a list of boxes and glue that will be strung out horizontally next to each other with baselines aligned; and it's in one of the math modes when it is reading a math formula.

A play-by-play account of a typical TeX job should make the mode idea clear: At the beginning, TeX is in vertical mode, ready to construct pages. If you specify glue or a box when TeX is in vertical mode, the glue or the box gets placed on the current page below what has already been specified. For example, the \vskip instructions in the sample run we discussed in Chapter 6 contributed vertical glue to the page; and the \ctrline{MY STORY} instruction contributed a box to the page. While building the \ctrline box, TeX went temporarily into restricted horizontal mode, but returned to vertical mode after setting the glue in that box.

Continuing with the example of Chapter 6, TeX switched into horizontal mode as soon as it read the "O" of "Once upon a time". Horizontal mode is the mode for making paragraphs. The entire paragraph up to the \par was input in horizontal mode; then it was divided into lines of the appropriate length, these lines were appended to the page (with appropriate glue between them), and TeX was back in vertical mode.

In general when TeX is in vertical mode, the first character of a new paragraph changes the mode to horizontal for the duration of a paragraph. If a begin-math character ($) appears when in horizontal mode, TeX plunges into math mode, processes the formula up until the closing $, then adds the text of this formula to the current paragraph and returns to horizontal mode. (Thus, in the "I wonder why?" example of the previous chapter, TeX would go into math mode temporarily while processing \ldots, treating the dots as a formula.)

However, if two consecutive begin-math characters appear in a paragraph ($$), TeX interrupts the paragraph where it is, contributes the paragraph-so-far to the page, then processes a math formula in display math mode, then contributes this formula to the current page, then returns to horizontal mode for more of the paragraph. (The formula to be displayed should end with $$.) For example, if you type

```
the number $$\pi \approx 3.1415926536$$ is important  ,
```

TEX goes into display math mode between the $$'s, and the output you get states that the number

$$\pi \approx 3.1415926536$$

is important.

TEX gets into restricted vertical mode when you ask it to construct a box from a vertical list of boxes (using \vbox or \valign) or when you do \topinsert or \botinsert. It gets into restricted horizontal mode when you ask it to construct a box from a horizontal list of boxes (using \hbox or \halign). Box construction is discussed in Chapter 21. Restricted modes are like the corresponding unrestricted ones except that you can't do certain things. For example, you can't say $$ in restricted horizontal mode, because you're not making a paragraph. You can't begin a paragraph in restricted vertical mode, etc. All the rules about what you can do in various modes are summarized in Chapters 24–26.

When handling simple manuscripts, TEX spends almost all of its time in horizontal mode (making paragraphs), with brief excursions into vertical mode (between paragraphs).

At the end of a job, you type "\end" at some point when TEX is in vertical mode; this causes TEX to finish any unfinished pages and stop. (Actually it is better to type "\vfill\end" in most cases, since \vfill inserts enough space to fill up the last page properly. Without the \vfill, TEX attempts to stretch out the lines it has accumulated for the last page, with the bottom line appearing at the bottom of the page; you probably don't want this.)

<14> How TEX breaks paragraphs into lines

When the end of a paragraph is encountered, TEX determines the "best" way to break it into lines. In this respect, TEX gives better results than most other typesetting systems, which produce each separate line of output before beginning the next, because the *final* words of a TEX paragraph can influence how the lines at the *beginning* are broken. TEX's new approach to this problem (based on "sophisticated computer science techniques"—whew!) requires only a little more computation than the traditional methods, and leads to significantly fewer cases in which words need to be hyphenated.

TEX does try to hyphenate words, but it uses a hyphenation only when there is no better alternative. The complete rules by which TEX hyphenates words are given in Appendix H. They are sufficiently simple that you could memorize them and apply them by hand if you wanted to, but there probably isn't any need for you to know them in detail. Basically TEX's approach to hyphenation is one of *extreme caution*: instead of trying to find all legitimate places where a hyphen could occur, TEX sticks to hyphenations that appear to be quite safe.

In view of TEX's improved line-breaking methods, this cautious approach to hyphenation is usually satisfactory; but every once in a while, like all automatic approaches to language processing, it fails. The reason for failure is generally that a rather long nonstandard word has occurred: TEX refuses to apply automatic hyphenation to a sequence of boxes unless that sequence

  a) consists entirely of lower case letters belonging to a single font; and

  b) is preceded immediately by glue (e.g., a space); and

  c) is followed immediately by glue or by a punctuation mark (something that doesn't set the "space factor" to 1, cf. Chapter 12).

One consequence of these conditions is that proper names and words containing accented letters will not be hyphenated, but such words tend to disobey the normal hyphenation rules anyway. Another consequence is that TEX won't mess around with words for which you have explicitly prescribed the hyphenation. And already-hyphenated compound words won't be broken up any further.

In spite of these apparently severe restrictions, experience shows that TEX works amazingly well in practice, except when the margins are extremely close together (small \hsize); and *nothing* works very well in that case. (A large dictionary, combined with TEX's line-breaking method, would do the best conceivable job; but for normal books and journals it isn't worthwhile for the computer to waste time referring to a large dictionary. TEX's program and tables for hyphenation require only about 3000 words of computer memory, so they place little burden on the overall processing.) When proofreading the output of TEX, the amount of additional work needed to correct missed hyphenations is quite negligible compared to the amount of work that proofreading already involves.

When you do find a word that TEX should have hyphenated but didn't, or when you find one of the extremely rare cases in which TEX inserts a hyphen in the wrong place, the remedy is to revise the manuscript, telling TEX how to hyphenate the offending word by inserting *discretionary hyphens*. The control sequence "\-" indicates a discretionary hyphen, namely a place where a word may be hyphenated if there is no better alternative.

For example, if you run into a situation where the French word *mathématique* must be hyphenated, you can type it as

```
math\-\´e\-ma\-tique   .
```

Another word TEX has trouble with is "onomatopoeia"; if necessary, type it in as

```
on\-o\-mat\-o\-poeia   .
```

(Or you could use the fancy "œ" ligature, cf. Chapter 9.) But don't bother to insert any discretionary hyphens until after TEX has failed to find a good way to break lines in some paragraph.

Before describing TEX's neat method for breaking a paragraph up into lines, we should discuss the rules for all legal breaks in a paragraph. Here they are: Outside of math formulas, you can break a paragraph

a) at glue, provided that the glue is immediately preceded by a character box or a constructed box (but not a rule box), or by the end of a math formula, or by a discretionary hyphen, or by an *insertion* (\topinsert or \botinsert, which are explained in Chapter 15).

b) where a \penalty has been specified in horizontal mode (see below), provided that the penalty is less than 1000.

c) at a discretionary hyphenation (with the hyphen included in the text, taken from the font that was current at the time the \- appeared), paying a penalty of 50.

d) where \eject has been specified (see below—this is a way to end a page at a particular place within a paragraph).

e) after "-" or any ligature that ends with "-" (thus, in standard roman fonts this means after "-", "--", or "---").

Inside math formulas, you can break

a) after a binary operation like "$+$" (paying a penalty of 95), or after a relation like "$=$" (paying a penalty of 50).

b) where a \penalty has been specified (see below), provided that the penalty is less than 1000.

c) at a "discretionary math hyphen" specified by "*" (this inserts a multiplication sign $\times$ into the formula), paying a penalty of 50.

d) where \eject has been specified.

Note that some breaks are "free" but others have an associated penalty. Penalties are used to indicate the relative desirability of certain breaks. Breaks at \eject are compulsory; all other breaks are optional. When a break occurs at glue or just before glue, this glue disappears.

TEX's procedure for line breaking is based on the notion of the "badness" of glue setting. This is a technical concept defined by a formula that assigns a badness of 100 to a box in which glue had to stretch or shrink to its total amount of stretchability or shrinkability, while the badness is near zero if the glue's stretchability or shrinkability is not very fully utilized. Furthermore the badness increases rapidly when glue is stretched to more than its stated limit; for example, the badness is 800 if the glue is stretched by twice its stretchability. Here is a precise way to calculate the badness, given that the total amount of glue stretch and shrink are y and z, respectively, and given that the box is supposed to grow by an amount x more than its natural width when the glue is set: Case 1, $x \geq 0$ (stretching). If $y < 10^{-4}$, replace y by 10^{-4}. Then the badness is $100(x/y)^3$. Case 2, $x < 0$ (shrinking). If $z < 10^{-4}$, replace z by 10^{-4}. Then the badness is $100|x/z|^3$ if $|x| \leq z$, otherwise it is ∞ (infinitely bad).

When breaking lines of a paragraph, TEX essentially considers all ways to break the lines so that no line will have badness B exceeding 200. Such breaks are called "feasible." Subject to this feasibility condition, TEX finds the best overall way to break, in the sense that the minimum total number of demerits occurs, where the demerits for each line of output are calculated as follows: If the penalty P for breaking at the end of this line is ≥ 0, the number of demerits is $(B + P + 1)^2$; if $P < 0$, the number is $(B + 1)^2 - P^2$. Furthermore an additional 3000 demerits are charged if two consecutive lines are being hyphenated or if the second-last line of the paragraph is hyphenated. A "dynamic programming" technique is used to find the breaks that lead to fewest total demerits. An attempt is made to hyphenate all words that meet the requirements mentioned earlier, whenever such words would straddle the end of line following some feasible break. The hyphenation algorithm of Appendix H is used to insert discretionary hyphens in all permissible places in such words. In practice the computation is quite fast, and only a few hyphenations need to be attempted, except in long paragraphs.

The current value of \hsize at the close of the paragraph is used to govern the width of each line, unless you specify "hanging" indentation. If you type "\hangindent ⟨dimen⟩ for ⟨number⟩", the specified dimension is supplied as an extra indentation on the first n lines of the paragraph, where n is the specified number. (That's how the second line of the paragraph you're reading was indented.) If you type "\hangindent ⟨dimen⟩ after ⟨number⟩", the specified dimension is supplied as an extra indentation on all but the first n lines of the paragraph. If you type just "\hangindent⟨dimen⟩", then "after 1" is assumed. If the specified dimension is negative, indentation occurs at the right margin instead of at the left.

TeX indents the first line of each paragraph by inserting an empty box of width \parindent at the beginning, unless you start the paragraph by typing the control sequence \noindent.

The number 200 used to determine feasibility can be changed to $100n$ for any integer $n \geq 1$ by typing "\jpar⟨number⟩", where n is the specified number. A large value of n will cause TeX to run more slowly, but it makes more line breaks feasible in cases where lines are so narrow that $n = 2$ finds no solutions.

The instruction \ragged⟨number⟩ specifies a degree of "raggedness" for the right-hand margins. If this number is r, the line width changes towards its natural width by the ratio $r/(100 + r)$. Thus, \ragged 0 (the normal setting) gives no raggedness; \ragged 100 causes the width of each line to be midway between \hsize and its natural width; and \ragged 1000000 almost completely suppresses any stretching or shrinking of the glue. Some people like to use this "ragged right margin" feature in order to make the output look less formal, as if it hadn't actually been typeset by an inhuman computer. (Some people also think that "ragged right" typesetting saves money. On traditional typesetting equipment, this was true, but computer typesetting has changed the situation completely: the most expensive part of the computation is now the breaking of lines, while the setting of glue costs almost nothing.)

The numbers 50, 3000, 95, and 50 used in the above rules for hyphenation penalties, consecutive-hyphenation demerits, binary-operation-break penalties, and relation-break penalties, can be changed by typing \chpar2←⟨number⟩, \chpar3←⟨number⟩, \chpar6←⟨number⟩, and \chpar7←⟨number⟩, respectively. Hyphenation penalties in force at the end of a paragraph are used throughout that paragraph; relation and operator penalties in force at the opening $ of a math formula are used throughout that formula.

To insert a penalty at a specified point in a paragraph, simply type "\penalty ⟨number⟩". Any penalty ≥ 1000 is equivalent to a penalty of ∞ (a non-permissible place to break); any penalty < 1000 implies that a break at the current place is permissible. The penalty may be zero or even negative, to indicate an especially desirable break location.

⚡ The control sequence \eject forces a break at the position where \eject occurs, and also causes TₑX to begin the next line on a new page. This gives you a way to remake page 100, say, without changing page 101, provided that it is possible to end the new page 100 at the same place where page 101 begins. Note that \eject will make the last line of the paragraph-so-far reach to the right-hand margin (if feasible); this is what some printers call a "quad middle" operation. It is quite different from what you would get if you simply typed "\par" at the spot that the revised page should end. TₑX's linebreaking algorithm is especially advantageous when handling \eject, because it has an apparent ability to "look ahead."

⚡ Additional vertical glue specified by \parskip is inserted just before each paragraph. This glue gets added to the normal interline glue.

<15> How TₑX makes lists of lines into pages

TₑX attempts to choose desirable places to stop making up one page and start another, and its technique for doing this usually works pretty well. But if you don't like the way a page is broken, you can force a page break in your favorite place by typing "\eject". An \eject command can occur in vertical mode (e.g., between paragraphs) or in horizontal mode (within a paragraph) or even in math mode; but you won't need to make much use of it.

⚡ TₑX groups things into pages in much the same way as it makes up paragraphs, except for the lookahead feature. Badness ratings and penalties are used to find the best place to break, but each page break is made once and for all when this "best" place is found—otherwise TₑX would have to remember the contents of so many pages, it would run out of memory space. Legal breaks between pages can occur

    a) at glue, provided that the glue is immediately preceded by a constructed box (but not a rule box). This includes the glue routinely inserted between lines, as explained below.

    b) where a \penalty has been specified in vertical mode, provided that the penalty is less than 1000. (Cf. Chapter 14.)

    c) after an insertion (arising from \topinsert or \botinsert, see below).

    d) where \eject is specified.

Breaks at \eject are compulsory; all other breaks are optional. When a break occurs at glue or just before glue, this glue disappears.

When boxes are appended to any vertical list (in particular, when they are appended to the current page), glue is automatically placed between them so that the distance between adjacent baselines tends to be the same. For example, the lines of 9-point text you are now reading have baselines 11 points apart. This implies that the glue between lines is not always the same, because more glue space is inserted under a line whose characters all stay above the baseline than under a line having characters that descend below it. Such interline glue is appended just before each box even when you have explicitly inserted glue yourself with \vskip or \vfill; any glue you specify is in addition to the interline glue.

Here is how interline glue gets figured: The book designer has specified two kinds of glue by using the operations \baselineskip ⟨glue⟩ and \lineskip ⟨glue⟩. Suppose the baselineskip glue has x units of space, y units of stretch, and z units of shrink. (In this paragraph TeX is using $x = 11$ points, $y = z = 0$, but y and z need not be zero.) Suppose we are appending a box of height h to a vertical list in which the previous box (ignoring glue) had depth d. Then the interline glue inserted just above the new box will have $x - h - d$ units of space, y units of stretch, and z units of shrink, whenever $x - h - d \geq 0$; but if $x - h - d < 0$, the interline glue will be the glue specified by \lineskip. For example, the basic TeX format in Appendix B says "\baselineskip 12 pt \lineskip 1 pt"; this means that baselines will normally be 12 points apart, but when this is impossible a space of 1 point will be inserted between adjacent boxes of a vertical list. *Exception:* Interline glue is not inserted before or after rule boxes, nor is it inserted before the first box or after the last box of a vertical list.

Contributions are made to the current page until the accumulated page height minus the accumulated glue shrinkability first exceeds the specified page size. (Page size is specified by the book designer using \vsize, see below.) At this point the break is made at whatever legal break in the page-so-far results in fewest badness-plus-penalty points $B + P$, where the badness B is defined as in Chapter 14 (except using vertical glue), and where the penalty P is zero unless explicitly specified or included by the paragraphing routine. The paragraphing routine inserts a penalty of 80 points just after the first line and just after the penultimate line of a multi-line paragraph, with an additional penalty of 50 points just after a line that ends with a hyphenation. This tends to avoid so-called "widows" (i.e., breaks that leave only one line of a paragraph on a page); for example, TeX breaks a four-line paragraph without 80 points of penalty only by breaking it into $2 + 2$ lines. A penalty of 500 points is charged for breaking pages just before a displayed equation. Furthermore there is a penalty of 80 for breaking after the first line of text that follows a display, unless the paragraph ends with such a line. (There is no penalty for breaking before the last line of text that precedes a display, since such a line is not considered to be a "widow.") Once the best break has been identified, the page is output, glue at the break is deleted, and everything remaining is contributed to the following page. (To change the numbers 80, 50, and 500 relating to widow-line, broken-line, and display-break penalties, you can use the \chpar instruction as explained in Chapter 24.)

The height of a page is the value of \vsize, and the depth in most cases is the depth of the bottom line on that page. Thus, if one page has 10-point type and the next has 9-point type, the baselines at the bottoms of both pages will be at the same place even though the descenders of 10-point letters go slightly further below the baseline than the descenders of 9-point letters do. However, the bottom line on a page is sometimes a constructed box whose depth is very large, and in such a case we want the baseline to be higher. TEX deals with the problem as follows: Whenever a box having depth greater than \maxdepth is contributed to the current page (where "\maxdepth⟨dimen⟩" has been specified by the book designer), the depth of the page-so-far is artificially decreased to \maxdepth, and the height of the page-so-far is correspondingly increased. (Interline glue calculation is not affected by this artificial adjustment, except possibly afterwards when the page is being dealt with as a completed box.) There is also another design parameter, "\topbaseline⟨dimen⟩", which is used to insert glue at the top of the page so that the baseline of the first box will be at least this distance from the top (if it isn't a rule box). All other glue is normally deleted at the top of each page; to put glue there, simply insert a \null box first. If several different values of \vsize, \maxdepth, or \topbaseline occur in the same TEX job, each page is governed by the values in force when the first item was contributed to that page.

A "floating-insertion" capability is built into TEX so that, among other things, illustrations can be placed at the top of the first subsequent page on which they fit, and footnotes can be placed at the bottom of the page on which the footnote reference appears. Here's how it works: You type "\topinsert{⟨vlist⟩}" or "\botinsert{⟨vlist⟩}", where ⟨vlist⟩ is a sequence of instructions that specifies a vertical list of boxes and glue. If such an insertion is made when TEX is in vertical mode, the specified vertical list will be contributed to the first page on which there is room for it. If such an insertion is made when TEX is in horizontal mode, the specified vertical list will be contributed to the same page on which the line containing the insertion appears. A \topinsert is contributed at the top, a \botinsert at the bottom. Glue specified by \topskip ⟨glue⟩ will be placed just below every \topinsert; glue specified by \botskip⟨glue⟩ will be placed just above every \botinsert.

You may be wondering how things like page numbers get attached to pages. Actually TEX has two levels of control: when a complete page has been built, this page is packaged as a box and another section of TEX input code comes into action. The designer has specified this other piece of code by writing "\output{...}", and we will discuss the details of \output routines in Chapter 23. For now, it should suffice to give just a small taste of what an \output routine looks like:

```
\output{\baselineskip 20pt
            \page\ctrline{\:a\count0}\advcount0}
```

This routine (which appears in Appendix B) takes the current page number, typeset in font a, and centers it on a new line below the contents of the current page; "\page" means the current page, "\count0" means the current page number, and "\advcount0" advances this number by 1. The baseline of the page number will be 20 points below the baseline of the page—assuming that \maxdepth has been set small enough that this is always possible. This setting of \baselineskip will be retracted at the end of the \output routine, according to the normal conventions of grouping; thus there will be no effect on TEX's page-building operations (which go on asynchronously).

<16> Typing math formulas

TEX was designed to handle complex mathematical formulas in such a way that most of them are easy to input. The basic idea is that a complicated formula is composed of less complicated formulas put together in a simple way, and these less complicated formulas are in turn made up of simple combinations of formulas that are even less complicated, and so on. Stating this another way, if you know how to type simple formulas and how to combine formulas into larger ones, you will be able to handle virtually any formula at all. So let's start with simple ones and work our way up.

The simplest formula is a single letter, like "x", or a single number, like "2". In order to enter these into a TEX text, you type "x" and "2", respectively. Note that all mathematical formulas are enclosed in special math brackets, and we are using $ as the math bracket in this manual, in accord with the basic TEX format defined in Appendix B. Note further that when you type "x" the "x" comes out in italic type, but when you type "2" the "2" comes out normally. In general, all characters on your keyboard have a special interpretation in math formulas, according to the normal conventions of mathematics printing. Letters now denote italic letters, while digits and punctuation denote roman digits and punctuation; a hyphen (–) now denotes a minus sign (—), which is almost the same as an em-dash but not quite (see Chapter 2). So if you forget one $ or type one $ too many, TEX will probably become thoroughly confused and you will probably get some sort of error message.

Formulas that have been typeset by a printer who is unaccustomed to doing mathematics usually look quite wrong to a mathematician, because a novice printer usually gets the spacing all wrong. In order to alleviate this problem, TEX does most of its own spacing in math formulas; and it *ignores* any spaces you type between $'s. For example, you can type "$ x$" and "$ 2 $" and they will mean the same thing as "x" and "2"; you can type "$(x + y)/(x - y)$" or "$(x+y) / (x-y)$", but both will result in "$(x + y)/(x - y)$". Thus, you are free to use blank spaces in any way you like. Of course, spaces are still used in the normal way to mark the end of control sequences, as explained in Chapter 7. In most circumstances TEX's spacing will be what a mathematician is accustomed to; but we will see in Chapter 18 that there are control sequences by which you can override TEX's spacing rules if you want.

One of the things mathematicians like to do is make their formulas look like Greek to the uninitiated. In TEX language you can type "$$\alpha, \beta, \gamma, \delta;$$" and you will get the first four Greek letters

$$\alpha, \beta, \gamma, \delta;$$

furthermore there are upper case Greek letters like "Γ", which you can get by typing either "Γ" or "$\GAMMA$". A few of the Greek letters deserve special attention: For example, lower case epsilon (ϵ) is quite different from the symbol used to denote membership in a set ($\in$); type "ϵ" for ϵ and "$\in$" for $\in$. Furthermore, three of the lower case Greek letters have variant forms on TEX's standard italic fonts; "(ϕ, θ, ω)" yields "(ϕ, θ, ω)" while "$(\varphi, \vartheta, \varomega)$" yields "$(\varphi, \vartheta, \varpi)$".

Besides Greek letters, there are a lot of funny symbols like "$\approx$" (which you get by typing "$\approx$") and "$\mapsto$" (which you get by typing "$\mapsto$"). A complete list of these control sequences and the characters they correspond to appears in Appendix F. The list even includes some non-mathematical symbols like

$$\S \quad \dagger \quad \ddagger \quad \P \quad © \quad \$ \quad £$$

which you can get by typing "$\section$", "$\dag$", "$\ddag$", "$\P$", "$\copyright$", "$\$$", and "$\sterling$", respectively; nearly all of the special symbols that you'll ever want are available in this way. Such control sequences are allowed only in math mode, i.e., between $'s, even when the corresponding symbols aren't traditionally considered to be mathematical, because they appear in the math fonts.

Now let's see how more complex formulas get built up from simple ones. In the first place, you can get superscripts and subscripts by using "↑" and "↓":

Type	and you get
`$x↑2$`	x^2
`$x↓2$`	x_2
`$2↑x$`	2^x
`$x↑2y↑2$`	x^2y^2
`$x ↑ 2y ↑ 2$`	x^2y^2
`$x↓2y↓2$`	x_2y_2
`$↓2F↓3$`	$_2F_3$

Note that ↑ and ↓ apply only to the next single character. If you want several things to be subscripted or superscripted, just enclose them in braces:

`$x↑{2y}$`	x^{2y}
`$2↑{2↑x}$`	2^{2^x}
`$2↑{2↑{2↑x}}$`	$2^{2^{2^x}}$
`$x↓{y↓2}$`	x_{y_2}
`$x↓{y↑2}$`	x_{y^2}

It is illegal to type "x↑y↑z" or "x↓y↓z" (TEX will complain of a "double superscript" or "double subscript"); you must type "x↑{y↑z}" or "{x↑y}↑z" or "x↑{yz}" in order to make your intention clear. (Some commonly-used languages for math typesetting treat x↑y↑z as x↑{y↑z} and others treat it as {x↑y}↑z or x↑{yz}; the ambiguous construction isn't needed much anyway, so TEX disallows it.)

A subscript or superscript following nothing (as in the "↓2F↓3" example above, where the ↓2 follows nothing) is taken to mean a subscript or superscript of an empty box. A subscript or superscript following a character applies to that character only, but when following a box it applies to that whole box; for example,

`$((x↑2)↑3)↑4$`	$((x^2)^3)^4$
`${({(x↑2)}↑3)}↑4$`	$((x^2)^3)^4$

In the first formula the ↑3 and ↑4 are superscripts on the right parentheses, but in the second formula they are superscripts on the formulas enclosed in braces.

You can have simultaneous subscripts and superscripts, and you can specify them in any order:

`$x↑2↓3$`	x_3^2
`$x↓3↑2$`	x_3^2
`$x↑{31415}↓{92}+\pi$`	$x_{92}^{31415} + \pi$
`$x↓{y↑a↓b}↑{z↓c↑d}$`	$x_{y_b^a}^{z_c^d}$

Note that simultaneous sub/superscripts are positioned over each other, aligned at the left.

The control sequence \prime stands for the character "$\prime$", which is used mostly in superscripts. Here's a typical example:

`$y↓1↑\prime+y↓2↑{\prime\prime\prime}$`	$y_1' + y_2'''$

Another way to get complex formulas from simple ones is to use the control sequences \sqrt, \underline, or \overline. These operations apply to the character or group that follows them:

`$\sqrt2$`	$\sqrt{2}$
`$\sqrt{x+2}$`	$\sqrt{x+2}$
`$\underline4$`	$\underline{4}$
`$\underline{\underline4}$`	$\underline{\underline{4}}$
`$x↑{\underline n}$`	$x^{\underline{n}}$
`$\overline{x↑3+\sqrt3}$`	$\overline{x^3 + \sqrt{3}}$

If you need cube roots (or n^{th} roots), TEX has no built-in mechanism for this. But you can insert a 3 (or n) over a square root sign by using Appendix B's control sequence \spose for superposition. Type

```
\spose{\raise⟨dimen⟩\hbox{\hskip⟨dimen⟩$\scriptscriptstyle⟨root⟩$}}
```

followed by \sqrt..., where you can figure out appropriate dimensions by fiddling around until the position looks right. (These dimensions depend on the size of the formula, the current size of type, and the size of the square root sign.) For example, "$\sqrt[3]{5}$" can be set with TEX's normal 10-point fonts by typing

```
$\spose{\raise5pt\hbox{\hskip2.5pt$\scriptscriptstyle3$}}\sqrt5$
```

Accents in math mode work something like \overline; you can accent a single character or a formula. (But the formula had better be short, since a tiny accent will be centered over the whole thing.) For example,

    $\=x+\overline x+\b x+\A x+\s x+\s{\s x}+\A{x+y}+e↑{\=x}$

produces $\bar x + \overline{x} + \b{x} + \hat x + \tilde x + \tilde{\tilde x} + x \hat{+} y + e^{\bar x}$.

▸Exercise 16.1: What would you type to get the following formulas?

$$2^{n+1} \qquad (n+1)^2 \qquad \sqrt{1-x^2} \qquad \overline{w+\bar z} \qquad p_1^{e_1} \qquad a_{b_{c_{d_e}}} \qquad h_n''(x)$$

▸Exercise 16.2: What's wrong with typing the following?

        If$ x = y$, then x is equal to $y.$

▸Exercise 16.3: Explain how to type the following sentence:

    Deleting an element from an n-tuple leaves an $(n-1)$-tuple.

<17> More about math

Another thing mathematicians like to do is make fractions—and they also like to build up symbols on top of each other, as in

$$\frac{1}{2} \quad \text{and} \quad \frac{n+1}{3} \quad \text{and} \quad \begin{bmatrix} n+1 \\ 3 \end{bmatrix} \quad \text{and} \quad \sum_{n=1}^{3} Z_n \ .$$

You can get these four formulas by typing "$$1\over 2$$" and "$$n+1\over 3$$" and "$$n+1\comb[]3$$" and "$$\sum↓{n=1}↑3 Z↓n$$"; we shall study the simple rules for such constructions in this chapter.

    First let's look at fractions, which use the "\over" notation. The control sequence \over applies to everything in the formula unless you enclose \over in a { } group; in the latter case it applies to everything in that group.

Type	and you get
`$$x+y↑2\over k+1$$`	$x + \dfrac{y^2}{k+1}$
`$$x+{y↑2\over k}+1$$`	$x + \dfrac{y^2}{k} + 1$
`$$x+{y↑2\over k+1}$$`	$x + \dfrac{y^2}{k+1}$
`$$x+y↑{2\over k+1}$$`	$x + y^{\frac{2}{k+1}}$

You aren't allowed to use \over twice in the same group; instead of typing a formula like "a \over b \over 2", you must specify what goes over what:

`$${a\over b}\over 2$$`	$\dfrac{\frac{a}{b}}{2}$
`$$a\over{b\over 2}$$`	$\dfrac{a}{\frac{b}{2}}$

Note that the letters get smaller when they are fractions-within-fractions, just as they get smaller when they are used as exponents. It's about time that we studied how TeX does this. Actually TeX has eight different styles in which it can treat formulas, namely

display style   (for formulas displayed on lines by themselves)
text style   (for formulas embedded in the text)
script style   (for formulas used as superscripts or subscripts)
scriptscript style   (for second-order superscripts or subscripts)

and four other styles that are almost the same except that exponents aren't raised quite so much. For brevity we shall refer to the eight styles as

$$D, \ T, \ S, \ SS, \ D', \ T', \ S', \ SS',$$

so that T is text style, D' is modified display style, etc. TeX also uses three sizes of type for mathematics, called text size, script size, and scriptscript size (t, s, and ss).

The normal way to typeset a formula with TeX is to enclose it in dollar signs `$...$`, which yields the formula in text style (style T), or to enclose it in double dollar signs `$$...$$`, which displays the formula in display style (style D). Once you know the style, you can determine the size of type TeX will use:

If a letter is in style	then it will be set in size
D, T, D', T'	t
S, S'	s
SS, SS'	ss

There is no "SSS" style or "sss" size; such tiny symbols would be even less readable than the ss ones. Therefore TeX stays with ss as its minimum size, as shown in the following chart:

In a formula of style	the superscript style is	and the subscript style is
D, T	S	S'
S, SS	SS	SS'
D', T'	S'	S'
S', SS'	SS'	SS'

For example, if `x↑{a↓b}` is in style D, then `{a↓b}` is in style S, and `b` is in style SS'.

So far we haven't seen any difference between styles D and T. Actually there is a slight difference in the positioning of exponents: you get x^2 in D style and x^2 in T style and x^2 in D' or T' style—do you see the difference? But there is a big distinction between D style and T style when it comes to fractions:

In a formula a\over β of style	the style of the numerator α is	and the style of the denominator β is
D	T	T'
T	S	S'
S, SS	SS	SS'
D'	T'	T'
T'	S'	S'
S', SS'	SS'	SS'

Thus if you type "$1\over2$" (in a text) you get $\frac{1}{2}$, namely style S over style S'; but if you type "$$1\over2$$" you get

$$\frac{1}{2}$$

(a displayed formula), which is style T over style T'.

When a fraction like $x+y\over z$ is put into the text of a paragraph, the letters are rather small and hard to read: $\frac{x+y}{z}$. So it is usually better to type the fraction in the mathematically equivalent way "$(x+y)/z$", which comes out "$(x + y)/z$". In other words, \over is useful mostly for displayed formulas or for numeric fractions.

While we're at it, we might as well finish the style rules: \underline does not change the style; \sqrt and \overline both change D to D', T to T', S to S', SS to SS', and leave D', T', S', SS' unchanged.

There's another operation "\atop", which is like \over except that it leaves out the fraction line:

$$x\atop y+2$$ $\qquad\qquad\frac{x}{y+2}$

The basic math definitions in Appendix B also define "\choose", which is like \atop but it encloses the result in parentheses:

$$n\choose k$$ $\qquad\qquad\binom{n}{k}$

This is a common notation for the so-called "binomial coefficient" that tells how many ways there are to choose k things out of n things; that's why the control sequence is called \choose.

You can't mix \over and \atop and \choose with each other. For example, "$$n \choose k \over 2$$" is illegal; you must use grouping, to get either "$${n \choose k} \over 2$$" or "$$n \choose {k \over 2}$$", i.e.,

$$\frac{\binom{n}{k}}{2} \quad \text{or} \quad \binom{n}{\frac{k}{2}} \quad.$$

The latter formula, incidentally, would look better as "`$$n \choose k/2$$`" or "`$$n \choose {1\over2}k$$`", yielding

$$\binom{n}{k/2} \qquad \text{or} \qquad \binom{n}{\frac{1}{2}k} \; .$$

Suppose you don't like the style TEX selects by its automatic style rules. Then you can specify the style you want by typing

`\dispstyle` or `\textstyle` or `\scriptstyle` or `\scriptscriptstyle`.

For example, if you want the $\binom{n}{k}$ to be larger in the formula `$${n\choose k}\over 2$$`, just type "`$$\dispstyle{n\choose k}\over 2$$`"; you will get

$$\frac{\binom{n}{k}}{2}$$

because the numerator of the formula is now "`\dispstyle{n\choose k}`". Here's another example (admittedly a rather silly one): `$$n+\scriptstyle n +\scriptscriptstyle n$$` gives

$$n + {\scriptstyle n + {\scriptscriptstyle n}} \; .$$

Note that the plus signs get smaller too, as the style changes; and there's no space around $+$ signs in script style.

▶Exercise 17.1: Explain how to specify the displayed formula

$$\binom{p}{2}x^2y^{p-2} - \frac{1}{1-x}\frac{1}{1-x^2} \; .$$

There are two other variants of `\over`, `\atop`, etc. First is "`\above⟨dimen⟩`", which is just like `\over` but the stated dimension specifies the exact thickness of the line rule. For example,

`$$\dispstyle{x\over y}\above 1pt\dispstyle{w\over z}$$`

will produce

$$\frac{\dfrac{x}{y}}{\dfrac{w}{z}}\ ;$$

this sort of thing was once customary in arithmetic textbooks, but nowadays it is rare (at least in pure mathematics). The second variant is a generalization of \choose: You can write "\comb⟨delim⟩⟨delim⟩", specifying any of the delimiters listed in Chapter 18; "\choose" is the same as "\comb()", and one of the examples at the beginning of this section used "\comb[]".

When you use \over, \atop, etc., the numerator and denominator are centered over each other. If you prefer to have the numerator or denominator at the left, follow it by "\hfill"; if you prefer to have it at the right, precede it by "\hfill". For example, the specification

```
$$1+{1\hfill\over\dispstyle a↓1+{1\hfill\over\dispstyle
     a↓2+{1\hfill\over\dispstyle a↓3+{1\over a↓4}}}}$$
```

yields

$$1+\cfrac{1}{a_1+\cfrac{1}{a_2+\cfrac{1}{a_3+\cfrac{1}{a_4}}}}$$

while without the \hfills you get

$$1+\cfrac{1}{a_1+\cfrac{1}{a_2+\cfrac{1}{a_3+\cfrac{1}{a_4}}}}\ .$$

Mathematicians often use the sign $\sum$ to stand for "summation" and the sign $\int$ to stand for "integration." If you're a typist but not a mathematician, all you need to remember is that \sum stands for $\sum$ and \int for $\int$; these abbreviations appear in Appendix F together with all the other symbols, in case you forget.

Symbols like $\sum$ and $\int$ (and a few others like $\bigcup$ and $\prod$ and $\oint$ and $\otimes$, all listed in Appendix F) are called *large operators*, and you type them just as you type ordinary symbols or letters. The difference is that TeX will choose a *larger* large operator in display style than it will in text style. For example,

`$\sum x↓n$`	yields	$\sum x_n$	(*T* style)
`$$\sum x↓n$$`	yields	$\sum x_n$	(*D* style).

Usually $\sum$ occurs with "limits," i.e., with formulas that are to appear below it or to the right. You type limits just the same as superscripts and subscripts: for example, if you want

$$\sum_{n=1}^{m}$$

you type either "`$$\sum↓{n=1}↑m$$`" or "`$$\sum↑m↓{n=1}$$`". According to the normal conventions of mathematics, TeX will change this to "$\sum_{n=1}^{m}$" if in text style rather than display style.

Integrations are slightly different from summations, in that the limits get set at the right even in display style:

`$\int↓{-∞}↑{+∞}$`	yields	$\int_{-\infty}^{+\infty}$	(*T* style)
`$$\int↓{-∞}↑{+∞}$$`	yields	$\int_{-\infty}^{+\infty}$	(*D* style).

Note further that the subscript is not directly below the superscript, in either style; again, this is a mathematical convention that TeX follows automatically (based on information stored with the fonts).

Some printers prefer to set limits above and below $\int$ signs; similarly, some prefer to set limits to the right of $\sum$ signs. You can change TeX's convention by simply typing "`\limitswitch`" after the large operator. For example,

`$$\int\limitswitch↓{-∞}↑{+∞}$$`	yields	$\int\limits_{-\infty}^{+\infty}$
`$$\sum\limitswitch↓{n=1}↑m$$`	yields	$\sum\limits_{n=1}^{m}$

If you have to put two or more rows of limits under a large operator, you can do this by using "\atop". For example, if you want the displayed formula

$$\sum_{\substack{0 \le i \le m \\ 0 < j < n}} P(i,j)$$

the correct way to type it is

```
$$\sum↓{\scriptstyle0≤i≤m\atop\scriptstyle0<j<n}P(i,j)$$
```

(perhaps with a few more spaces to make it look nicer in the manuscript file). Note that the instruction "\scriptstyle" was necessary here, twice—otherwise "$0 \le i \le m$" and "$0 < j < n$" would have been in scriptscript size, which is too small. This is one of the rare cases where TeX's automatic style rules need to be overruled.

▶Exercise 17.2: How would you type the displayed formula 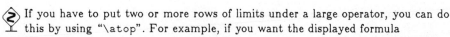 $\sum_{i=1}^{p} \sum_{j=1}^{q} \sum_{k=1}^{r} a_{ij} b_{jk} c_{ki}$?

▶Exercise 17.3: And how about $\sum_{\substack{1 \le i \le p \\ 1 \le j \le q \\ 1 \le k \le r}} a_{ij} b_{jk} c_{ki}$?

‹18› Fine points of mathematics typing

We have discussed most of the facilities needed to construct math formulas, but there are several more things a good mathematical typist will want to watch for.

1. Punctuation. When a formula is followed by a period, comma, semicolon, colon, question mark, exclamation point, etc., put the punctuation *after* the $, when the formula is in the text; but put the punctuation *before* the $$ when the formula is displayed. For example,

```
If $x<0$, we have shown that $$y=f(x).$$
```

The reason is that TeX's spacing rules within paragraphs work best when the punctuation marks are not considered part of the formulas.

Similarly, don't type something like this:

```
for $x = a, b$, or $c$.
```

It should be

```
for $x = a$, $b$, or $c$.
```

The reason is that TEX will always put a "thin space" between the comma and the b in $x = a, b$. This space will probably not be the same as the space TEX puts after the comma *after* the b, since the second comma is outside the formula; and such unequal spacing would look bad. When you type it right, the spacing will look good. Another reason for not typing "$x = a, b$" is that it inhibits the possibilities for breaking lines in a paragraph: TEX will never break at the space between the comma and the b because breaks after commas in formulas are usually wrong. For example, in the equation "$x = f(a, b)$" we certainly don't want to put "$x = f(a,$" on one line and "$b)$" on the next.

Thus, when typing formulas in the text of a paragraph, keep the math properly segregated: Don't take operators like — and = outside of the $'s, and keep commas inside the formula if they are truly part of the formula. But if a comma or period or other punctuation mark belongs linguistically to the sentence rather than to the formula, leave it outside the $'s.

2. Roman letters in formulas. The names of algebraic variables in formulas are usually italic or Greek letters, but common mathematical operators like "log" are always set in roman type. The best way to deal with such operators is to make use of the following control sequences (all of which are defined in the basic format of Appendix B):

\cos	\exp	\lim	\log	\sec
\cot	\gcd	\liminf	\max	\sin
\csc	\inf	\limsup	\min	\sup
\det	\lg	\ln	\Pr	\tan

The following examples show that such control sequences lead to roman type as desired:

Type	and you get
`$\sin2\theta=2\sin\theta\cos\theta$`	$\sin 2\theta = 2\sin\theta\cos\theta$
`$O(n\log n\log\log n).$`	$O(n\log n\log\log n)$
`$\exp(-x↑2)$`	$\exp(-x^2)$
`$$\max↓{1≤n≤m}\log↓2P↓n$$`	$\displaystyle\max_{1\le n\le m}\log_2 P_n$
`$$\lim↓{x→0}{\sin x\over x}=1$$`	$\displaystyle\lim_{x\to 0}\frac{\sin x}{x}=1$

In the second example, note that O is an upper case letter "oh", not a zero; a formula should usually have "O" instead of "0" when a left parenthesis follows. The fourth and fifth examples show that some of the special control sequences are treated by TEX as "large operators" with limits just like $\sum$; compare the different treatment of subscripts applied to `\max` and to `\log`.

⚋ Another way to get roman type into mathematical formulas is to include constructed boxes (cf. Chapter 21); such boxes are treated the same as single characters or subformulas. For example,

  `$\exp(x+\hbox{constant})$`   yields $\exp(x + \text{constant})$.

The fonts used inside such boxes are the same as the fonts used *outside* of the math brackets `$...$`; the characters do *not* change size when the style changes.

⚋ ▶Exercise 18.1: Explain how to type the phrase "n^{th} root", where "n^{th}" is treated as a mathematical formula with a superscript. The letters "th" should be in font d.

⚋ There is, of course, a way to specify characters that do change size with changing styles; you can do it with the `\char` command. We studied `\char` in Chapter 8, but `\char` works a little differently in math mode because math mode deals with up to ten fonts instead of just one font. TEX keeps three fonts for text size, three for script size, and three for scriptscript size, plus one font for oversize and variable-size characters. The three fonts of changing size are called rm, it, and sy fonts—short for roman, italic, and symbols, according to TEX's normal way of using these fonts; and the oversize font is called the ex font. (The rm and it fonts are essentially normal fonts like all other fonts TEX deals with, but each sy and ex font must have special control information stored with it, telling TEX how to do proper spacing of math formulas.

Thus, TEX is able to do math typesetting on virtually any style of font, provided that the font designer includes these parameters.) To specify which fonts you are using for mathematics, you type

```
\mathrm ⟨font⟩⟨font⟩⟨font⟩
\mathit ⟨font⟩⟨font⟩⟨font⟩
\mathsy ⟨font⟩⟨font⟩⟨font⟩
\mathex ⟨font⟩
```

before getting into math mode, where the rm, it, and sy fonts are specified in the order text size, script size, scriptscript size. For example, by typing "\mathit tpk" you are saying that TEX should use font t as the it font in text size math, font p as the it font in script size math, font k in scriptscript size math. If you don't use scriptscript size in your formulas, you must still specify a font, but you could say "\mathit tpp" or even "\mathit ttt". (When you specify a font letter for the first time you must follow it with the font file name, as described in Chapter 4; e.g., "\mathit t←cmi10 p←cmi7 p" would work. But it's best to declare all your fonts first, before specifying the ones to be used for math.) Now... about that "\char" operation in math mode: Although \char selects up to 128 characters in non-math modes, it selects up to 512 characters in math mode. Characters ´000 to ´177 are in the rm font of the current size, ´200 to ´377 are in the it font of the current size, ´400 to ´577 are in the sy font of the current size, and ´600 to ´777 are in the ex font. For example, the "dangerous bend" road symbol is in the ex font being used to typeset this user manual, and it is actually character number ´177 in this font, so it is referred to by typing "$\char´777$". The symbol ∞ is character number ´61 in TEX's standard symbol fonts; in math mode you can refer to it either as "\infty" or as "\char´461", or simply as "∞" if you happen to have this key on your keyboard.

TEX fonts used for variables ("it" fonts) have spacing appropriate for math formulas but not for italic text. You should use a different font for "italicized words" in the text. For example:

This sentence is in font cmi10, which is intended for formulas, not text.
This sentence is in font cmti10, which is intended for text, not formulas.

3. Large parentheses and other delimiters.
Since mathematical formulas can get horribly large, TEX has to have some way to make ever-larger symbols. For example, if you type

```
$$\sqrt{1+\sqrt{1+\sqrt{1+
        \sqrt{1+\sqrt{1+\sqrt{1+\sqrt{1+x}}}}}}}$$
```

the result shows a variety of available square-root signs:

$$\sqrt{1+\sqrt{1+\sqrt{1+\sqrt{1+\sqrt{1+\sqrt{1+\sqrt{1+x}}}}}}}$$

The three largest signs here are all essentially the same, except for a vertical segment "|" that gets repeated as often as necessary to reach the desired size; but the smaller signs are distinct characters found in TEX's math fonts.

A similar thing happens with parentheses and other so-called "delimiter" symbols. For example, here are the different sizes of parentheses that TEX might use in formulas:

$$\Bigg(\bigg(\Big(\big(((((((\cdots))))))\big)\Big)\bigg)\Bigg)$$

The three largest pairs are made with repeatable extensions, so they can become as large as necessary.

TEX chooses the correct size of square root sign by simply using the smallest size that will enclose the formula being \sqrted, but it does not use large parentheses or other delimiters unless you ask it to. If you want to enclose a formula in variable-size delimiters, type

$$\texttt{\textbackslash left}\langle\text{delim}_1\rangle \; \langle\text{formula}\rangle \; \texttt{\textbackslash right}\langle\text{delim}_2\rangle$$

where each ⟨delim⟩ is one of the following:

.	blank ( )		vertical line (|)
(	left parenthesis (( )	|	double vertical line (‖)
)	right parenthesis ( ))	\langle or <	left angle bracket (⟨)
[	left bracket ([ )	\rangle or >	right angle bracket (⟩)
]	right bracket ( ])	\lfloor	left floor bracket (⌊)
\{	left brace ({)	\rfloor	right floor bracket (⌋)
\}	right brace (})	\lceil	left ceiling bracket (⌈)
/	slash (/)	\rceil	right ceiling bracket (⌉)

For example, if you type "`$$1+ \left( 1\over1-x↑2 \right) ↑3$$`" you will get

$$1 + \left(\frac{1}{1 - x^2} \right)^3 \ .$$

Notice from this example that `\left` and `\right` have the effect of grouping just as { and } do: The "`\over`" operation does not apply to the "1+" or to the "↑3", and the "↑3" applies to the entire formula enclosed by `\left(` and `\right)`.

When you use `\left` and `\right` they must match each other, nesting like braces do in groups. You can't have `\left` in one formula and `\right` in another, nor can you type things like "`\left(...{...\right)...}`". This restriction makes sense, of course, but it is worth explicit mention here because you do *not* have to match parentheses and brackets, etc., when you are not using `\left` and `\right`: TEX will not complain if you input a formula like "`$[0,1)$`" or even "`$) ($`". (And it's a good thing TEX doesn't, for such unbalanced formulas occur surprisingly often in mathematics papers.) Even when you are using `\left` and `\right`, TEX doesn't look closely at the particular delimiters you happen to choose; thus, you can type strange things like "`\left)`" and/or "`\right(`" if you know what you're doing. Or even if you don't.

If you type "`\left.`" or "`\right.`", the corresponding delimiter is blank—not there. Why on earth would anybody want that, you may ask. Well, there are at least two reasons. One is to take care of situations like this:

$$|x| = \begin{cases} x, & \text{if } x \geq 0; \\ -x, & \text{if } x < 0. \end{cases}$$

The formula in this case could be typed as follows:

$$\verb|$$|x|=\left\{ ... \right.$$|$$

where "..." stands for a TEX box containing the text

$$\boxed{\begin{array}{ll} x, & \text{if } x \geq 0; \\ -x, & \text{if } x < 0. \end{array}}$$

Later in this chapter we shall discuss how you might specify such a box; just now we are simply trying to discuss the use of a blank delimiter.

The second example of a blank delimiter occurs when you want a variable-size slash; type either "\left/ ... \right." or "\left. ... \right/", whichever will make the correct size slash (i.e., a slash that is just big enough for the formula enclosed between \left and \right). For example, if you want to get the formula

$$\frac{a+1}{b} \left/ \frac{c+1}{d} \right.$$

you can type either "$$\left. a+1 \over b \right/ {c+1\over d}$$" or "$${a+1\over b} \left/ c+1 \over d \right.$$".

A third example, which occurs less often, is the problem of getting three large delimiters of the same size, as in a formula of the form "$[\,\alpha\mid\beta\,]$" where α and β are large formulas and, say, α is bigger than β. You can type

    \left.\left[α \right| β \right]

to handle this. Note that a construction like "\left(\left(... \right)\right)" will always produce double parentheses of the same size.

The size chosen by TeX when you use \left and \right is usually appropriate, but there is an important exception: When the \left and \right enclose a displayed $\sum$ or $\prod$, etc., with upper and/or lower limits, TeX will often make the delimiters much too large. For example, if you type

    $$\left(\sum↓{i=1}↑n A↓i \right)↑2$$

the result is

$$\left(\sum_{i=1}^{n} A_i \right)^2$$

(rather shocking). The reason is that TeX adds extra blank space above and below the limits so that they don't interfere with surrounding formulas; usually this is the right thing to do, except when large delimiters are involved. In fact, most math compositors prefer to let the limits on $\sum$'s protrude above or below any enclosing parentheses, so \left and \right aren't really the proper things to type anyway. What you should do is use control sequences such as \bigglp and

`\biggrp`, which are defined in the `basic` TEX format (Appendix B). When the above example is retyped in the form

$$\biggrp\ \backslash\texttt{bigglp}\ \backslash\texttt{sum↓\{i=1\}↑n A↓i}\ \backslash\texttt{biggrp↑2}$$

it will come out right:

$$\left(\sum_{i=1}^{n} A_i \right)^2 \ .$$

Incidentally, `basic` format also defines two other useful sizes of parentheses, for those occasions when you wish to control the size by yourself in a convenient manner: `\biglp` and `\bigrp` produce parentheses that are just a little bit bigger than normal ones, while `\biggglp` and `\bigggrp` produce really big ones. Here is a typical example of a formula that uses `\biglp` and `\bigrp`:

$$\bigl(x - s(x) \bigr)\bigl(y - s(y) \bigr).$$

▶Exercise 18.2: Explain exactly how to type this formula so that TEX would typeset it as shown.

Instead of using "bigg" delimiters, there is another way to get TEX to choose a more reasonable size with respect to displayed $\sum$'s with limits, namely to fool TEX into thinking that the formulas aren't as big as they really are. Using Appendix B, type "`\chop to ⟨dimen⟩{⟨formula⟩}`" to produce a box containing the specified formula in display style but with the depth of the box artificially assumed to be the specified dimension. The ⟨dimen⟩ must be in points (pt). For example,

```
\sqrt{\chop to 9pt{\sum↓{1≤k≤n}A↓k}}
```

yields

$$\sqrt{ \sum_{1 \le k \le n} A_k } \ .$$

You can also access other delimiters that might be present in your fonts by using the versatile \char command. We saw above that \char has an extended meaning in math mode; its meaning is even further extended when used to specify delimiters. Besides the options listed above, any ⟨delim⟩ can be "\char´c_1c_2" where c_1 and c_2 are three-digit octal codes; c_1 is the code for this delimiter in its smaller sizes (rm, it, or sy fonts) and c_2 is the code for this delimiter in the ex font. For example, it turns out that the left brace delimiter can be specified as \char´546610, since a normal size left brace is character ´146 in the sy font, and since all oversize left braces are reachable starting at character ´010 in the ex font. (Characters in an ex font are internally linked together in order of increasing size.) You should let c_1 or c_2 equal 000 if there is no corresponding character. TeX handles variable-size delimiters in the following way: If $c_1 \neq$ 000, the first step is to look at math character ´c_1 in the current size, then in any larger sizes. (For example, in script style TeX looks first at script size character ´c_1, then at the corresponding character in text size.) If $c_2 \neq$ 000, the next step is to look at all characters linked together in the ex font, starting at ´c_2, in increasing order of size. (This linked list might end with an extensible character.) The first character TeX sees that is large enough (i.e., $\geq$ the desired size) is chosen. Special note to those who have read this far: Standard ex fonts for TeX often contain the "left pretzel" and "right pretzel" delimiters that you can get by typing

                \left\char´000656   and   \right\char´000657,

respectively. Startle your friends by using these instead of parentheses around your big matrices, or try typing "$$\left\char´656\quad\vcenter{\hbox par 250pt{ ... several sentences of text ... }}\quad\right\char´657$$".

4. Spacing. Chapter 16 says that TeX does automatic spacing of math formulas so that they look right, and this is almost true, but occasionally you must give TeX some help. The number of possible math formulas is vast, and TeX's spacing rules are rather simple, so it is natural that exceptions should arise. Furthermore there are occasions when you need to specify the proper spacing between two formulas. Perhaps the most common example of this is a display containing a main formula and side conditions, like

$$F_n = F_{n-1} + F_{n-2}, \qquad n \geq 2.$$

You need to tell TeX how much space to put after the comma.

The traditional hot-metal technology for printing has led to some ingrained standards for situations like this, based on what printers call a "quad" of space. Since these standards seem to work well in practice, TeX makes it easy for you to continue the tradition. When you type "\quad", TeX converts this into an amount of space equal to a printer's quad, approximately the width of a capital M. (The em-dash discussed in Chapter 2 is usually one quad wide; and one quad in 10-point type is usually equal to 10 points. This is where the name "quad" comes from; it once meant a square piece of blank type. But of course a font designer is free to specify any sizes that he or she wants for the widths of quads, em-dashes, and M's.)

The abbreviation "\qquad" is defined in Appendix B to be the same as "\quad\quad", and this is the normal spacing for situations like the F_n example above. Thus, the recommended procedure is to type

```
$$ F↓n = F↓{n-1} + F↓{n-2}, \qquad n ≥ 2. $$
```

It is perhaps worth reiterating that TeX ignores all the spaces in math mode (except, of course, the space after "\qquad", which is needed to distinguish "\qquad n" from "\qquadn"); so the same result would be obtained if you were to type

```
$$F↓n=F↓{n-1}+F↓{n-2},\qquad n≥2.$$
```

Thus, all spacing that differs from the normal conventions has to be specified explicitly by control sequences such as \quad and \qquad.

Of course, \quad and \qquad are big chunks of space, more than the space between words in a sentence, so it is desirable to have much finer units. The basic elements of space that TeX deals with in math formulas are often called a "thin space" and a "thick space", defined respectively to be $\frac{1}{6}$ of a quad and $\frac{5}{18}$ of a quad. In order to get a feeling for these units, let's take a look at the F_n example again: thick spaces occur just before and after the $=$ sign, and also before and after the $\geq$ sign. A thin space is slightly smaller, yet quite noticeable; it's a thin space that makes the difference between "loglog" and "log log".

TeX has variable glue, as we discussed in Chapter 12, so spaces in TeX's math formulas actually can get a little thicker or thinner when a line is being stretched or squeezed. Here is a precise chart telling about all the different kinds of spaces that you can specify in math formulas:

Control sequence	Name	Spacing in styles D, T, D', T'			Spacing in styles S, SS, S', SS'
\,	Thin space	(1/6,	0,	0)	(1/6, 0, 0)
\␣	Control space	(2/9,	1/9,	2/9)	(1/6, 0, 0)
\>	Op space	(2/9,	1/9,	2/9)	(0, 0, 0)
\;	Thick space	(5/18,	5/18,	0)	(0, 0, 0)
\quad	Quad space	(1,	0,	0)	(1, 0, 0)
\≥	Conditional thin space	(1/6,	0,	0)	(0, 0, 0)
\!	Negative thin space	(−1/6,	0,	0)	(−1/6, 0, 0)
\?	Negative thick space	(−5/18,	−5/18,	0)	(0, 0, 0)
\<	Negative op space	(−2/9,	−1/9,	−2/9)	(0, 0, 0)
\≤	Negative \≥	(−1/6,	0,	0)	(0, 0, 0)

(Don't try to memorize this chart, just plan to use it for reference in case of need.) The spacing is given in units of quads; thus, for example, the entry "$(5/18, 5/18, 0)$" for a thick space in D style means that a thick space in displayed formulas is $\frac{5}{18}$ of a quad wide, with a stretchability of $\frac{5}{18}$ quad and a shrinkability of zero. Note that spacing is different in subscript or superscript styles: thick spaces disappear while thin spaces stay the same. This reflects the fact that no space surrounds $=$ signs in subscripts, but there still remains a space in "log log" when you type "\log\log" in a script style.

The control sequences in this table are allowed only in math mode, except that \quad is allowed also in horizontal mode. Actually \␣ and \! are used in horizontal mode too, but with a different meaning explained earlier. It is permissible to use \hskip explicitly in math mode, if you want to specify any nonstandard glue.

As mentioned earlier, you will probably not be using any of these spaces very much. You can probably get by with only an occasional \quad (or \qquad) and an occasional thin space.

In fact, there are probably only three occasions on which you should always remember to insert a thin space ("\, "):

a) Before the dx or dy or $d$whatever in formulas involving calculus. For example, type "$\int↓0↑∞e↑x\,dx$" to get "$\int_0^\infty e^x \, dx$"; type "$dx\,dy=r\,dr\, d\theta$" to get "$dx\,dy = r\,dr\,d\theta$". (But type "dy/dx".)

b) After square roots that happen to come too close to the following symbol. For example, "$O\biglp 1/\sqrt n\bigrp$" comes out as "$O\bigl(1/\sqrt{n}\bigr)$", but "`$O\biglp 1/\sqrt n\,\bigrp$`" yields "$O\!\left(1/\sqrt{n}\,\right)$". And it sometimes looks better to put a thin space after a square root to separate it visually from a symbol that follows: "$\sqrt{2}\,x$" is preferable to "$\sqrt{2}x$", so type "`$\sqrt2\,x$`" instead of "`$\sqrt2 x$`".

c) After an exclamation point (which stands for the "factorial" operation in a formula) when it is followed by a letter or number or left delimiter. For example, "`$(2n)!\over n!\,(n+1)!$`".

Other than this, you can usually rely on TEX's spacing until after you look at what comes out, and it shouldn't be necessary to insert optical spacing corrections except in rather rare circumstances. (One of these circumstances is a formula like "$\log n\,(\log\log n)^2$", where a thin space has been inserted just before the left parenthesis; TEX inserts no space before this parenthesis, because similar formulas like "$\log f(x)$" want no space there. Another case is a formula like "$n/\log n$", where a negative thin space has been inserted after the slash.)

Here are the rules TEX uses to govern spacing: The styles and sizes of all portions of a formula are determined as explained in Chapter 17. We may assume that the formula doesn't have the form "$\alpha\over\beta$" (or "$\alpha\atop\beta$", etc.), since numerators and denominators of such formulas are treated separately. We may also assume that all subformulas have been processed already (using the same rules) and replaced by boxes. (Subformulas include anything enclosed in { ... }, possibly combined with \sqrt, \underline, \overline, or \accent; subformulas also include anything enclosed in \left⟨delim₁⟩ ... \right⟨delim₂⟩, unless this turns out to be the entire formula. Subscripts and superscripts are attached to the appropriate boxes, and so any given formula can be reduced to a list of boxes to be placed next to each other; all that remains is to insert the appropriate spacing. The boxes are divided into seven categories:

• Ord box; e.g., an ordinary variable like x, or a subformula like \sqrt{x+y} that has already been converted into a box.

• Op box; e.g., a $\sum$ sign (together with its limits, if any), or an operator like \log that has already been converted into a box.

• Bin box; e.g., a binary operator like + or − or \times (but not /, which is treated as "Ord").

• Rel box; e.g., an = sign or a < sign or a ←.

• Open box; e.g., a left parenthesis or \left⟨delim⟩.

• Close box; e.g., a right parenthesis or \right⟨delim⟩.

• Punct box; a comma or semicolon (but not a period, which is treated as "Ord").

Every Bin box must be preceded by an Ord box or a Close box, and followed by an Ord or Op or Open box, otherwise Bins are reclassified as Ords, from left to right. (For example, in "$-\infty<x+y<+\infty$", only the $+$ of "$x+y$" is a Bin box; the $<$ signs are Rel boxes, and all other symbols are Ord boxes.) The following table now determines the spacing between pairs of adjacent boxes:

		Right box type					
		Ord	Op	Bin	Rel	Open	Close	Punct
	Ord	0	\,	\>	\;	0	0	0
	Op	\,	\,	*	\;	0	0	0
Left	Bin	\>	\>	*	*	\>	*	*
box	Rel	\;	\;	*	0	\;	0	0
type	Open	0	0	*	0	0	0	0
	Close	0	\,	\>	\;	0	0	0
	Punct	\≥	\≥	*	\;	\≥	\≥	\≥

Here "0" means no space is inserted; "\," is a thin space; and so on. Table entries marked "*" are never needed, because of the definition of Bin boxes.

 For example, consider the displayed formula

$$x+y=\max\{x,y\}+\min\{x,y\}$$,

which is transformed into the sequence of boxes

$$x \boxplus y = \boxed{\max} \{ x, y \} \boxplus \boxed{\min} \{ x, y \}$$

of respective types

Ord,Bin,Ord,Rel,Op,Open,Ord,Punct,Ord,Close,Bin,Op,Open,Ord,Punct,Ord,Close.

Inserting the appropriate spaces according to the table gives

Ord\>Bin\>Ord\;Rel\;Op Open Ord Punct\≥Ord Close
\>Bin\>Op Open Ord Punct\≥Ord Close

and the resulting formula is

$$x \boxplus y = \boxed{\max}\{x,y\} \boxplus \boxed{\min}\{x,y\}$$

i.e.,

$$x + y = \max\{x, y\} + \min\{x, y\} \quad .$$

This example doesn't involve subscripts or superscripts; but subscripts and superscripts merely get attached to boxes without changing the type of box. If you have inserted any spacing yourself by means of \quad or \, or \hskip or whatever, TEX's automatic spacing gets included in addition to what you specified. Similarly, if you have included \penalty or \eject or * in a math formula, this specification is ignored for purposes of calculating the automatic glue between components of formulas. For example, if you type "`$... =\penalty100 x ...$`", there is a Rel box ($=$) followed by a penalty specification (which tends to avoid breaking lines here) followed by an Ord box (x), so TEX inserts "\;" glue between the penalty and the Ord box.

You can make TEX think that a character or formula is Op or Bin or $\cdots$ or Punct by typing one of the instructions \mathop⟨atom⟩ or \mathbin⟨atom⟩ or \mathrel⟨atom⟩ or \mathopen⟨atom⟩ or \mathclose⟨atom⟩ or \mathpunct⟨atom⟩, where ⟨atom⟩ is either a single character (like x), or a control sequence denoting a mathematics character (like \gamma or \approx), or "\char⟨number⟩", or "{⟨formula⟩}". For example, "\mathopen|" denotes a vertical line (absolute value bracket) treated as an Open box; and

$$\mathop{\char´155\char´141\char´170}$$

stands for the roman letters "max" in a size that varies with the math style. Control sequences like \mathop are used mostly in definitions of other control sequences for common idioms; for example, "\max" is defined in Appendix B to be precisely the above sequence of symbols. Note that there's no special control sequence to make a box "ordinary"; you get an Ord box simply by enclosing a formula in braces. For example, if you type "{+}" in a formula, the plus sign will be treated as an ordinary character like x for purposes of spacing. Another way to get the effect of "{+}" is to type "\char´53", since characters entered with \char are considered ordinary.

5. Line breaking. When you have formulas in a paragraph, TEX may have to break them between lines; it's something like hyphenation, a necessary evil that is avoided unless the alternative is worse. Generally TEX will break a formula after a relation symbol like $=$ or $<$ or $\leftarrow$, or after a binary operation symbol like $+$ or $-$ or $\times$, if these are on the "outer level" of the formula (not enclosed in {...} and not part of an "\over" construction). For example, if you type

$$\text{\$f(x,y) = x↑2-y↑2 = (x+y)(x-y)\$}$$

in mid-paragraph, there's a chance that TEX will break after either of the = signs (it prefers this) or after the – or + or – (in an emergency). Note that there won't be a break after the comma in any case—commas after which breaks are desirable shouldn't ever appear between $'s. If you don't want to permit breaking in this example except after the = signs, you could type

$$\texttt{\$f(x,y) = \{x\char94 2-y\char94 2\} = \{(x+y)(x-y)\}\$}$$

But it isn't necessary to bother worrying about such things unless TEX actually does break a formula badly, since the chances of this are pretty slim.

There's a "discretionary hyphen" allowed in formulas, but it means multiplication: If you type "`$(x+y)\*(x-y)$`", TEX will treat the `\*` something like the way it treats `\-`; namely, a line break will be allowed at that place, with the hyphenation penalty. However, instead of inserting a hyphen, TEX will insert a $\times$ sign in the current size.

The penalty for breaking after a Rel box is 50, and the penalty for breaking after a Bin box is 95. These penalties can be changed either by typing "`\penalty⟨number⟩`" immediately after the box in question (thus changing the penalty in a particular case) or by using `\chpar` as explained in Chapter 14 (thus changing the penalties applied at *all* subsequent Rel and/or Bin boxes of math formulas enclosed in the current group).

6. Ellipses ("three dots"). Mathematical copy looks much nicer if you are careful about how "three dots" are typed in formulas and text. Although it looks fine to type "`...`" on a typewriter with fixed spacing, the result looks too crowded when you're using a printer's fonts:

$$\texttt{"\$x...y\$"} \qquad \text{results in} \qquad \text{"}x...y\text{",}$$

and such close spacing is undesirable except in subscripts or superscripts.

Furthermore there are two kinds of dots that can be used, one higher than the other; the best mathematical traditions distinguish between these. It is generally correct to produce formulas like

$$x_1 + \cdots + x_n \qquad \text{and} \qquad (x_1, \ldots, x_n),$$

but wrong to produce formulas like

$$x_1 + \ldots + x_n \qquad \text{and} \qquad (x_1, \cdots, x_n).$$

When using TEX with the basic control sequences in Appendix B, you can solve the "three dots" problem in a simple way, and everyone will be envious of the beautiful formulas you produce. There are five main control sequences:

\ldots	three low dots (...);
\cdots	three center dots ($\cdots$);
\ldotss	three low dots followed by a thin space;
\cdotss	three center dots followed by a thin space;
\ldotsm	three low dots preceded and followed by thin spaces.

Of these, "\cdots" and "\ldotss" are the most commonly used, as we shall see.

In general, it is best to use center dots between $+$ and $-$ signs, and also between $=$ signs or $\leq$ signs or $\leftarrow$ signs or other similar relational operations. Lower dots are used between commas and when things are juxtaposed with no signs at all. Here are the recommended rules for using the above control sequences:

a) Use \cdots between signs inside of a formula; use \cdotss just before punctuation at the end of a formula. Examples: "$x↓1=\cdots=x↓n=0$"; "the infinite sum $y↓1+y↓2+\cdotss$".". (The extra thin space in \cdotss will make the second example look better than if \cdots had simply been used.)

b) Use \ldotss before commas. Example:

```
The vector $(x↓1, \ldotss, x↓n)$ is composed
        of the components $x↓1$, $\ldotss$, $x↓n$.
```

This example deserves careful study. Note that the commas in the "vector" are part of the formula, but in the list of the components they are part of the sentence. Note also that you must be in math mode when using \ldotss.

c) Use \ldotsm in "multiplicative" contexts, i.e., when three dots are used with no surrounding operator sign. Examples:

```
$x↓1x↓2\ldotsm x↓n$;     $(1-x)(1-x↑2)\ldotsm(1-x↑k)$.
```

Exception: Type "$x↑1x↑2\ldotss x↑n$", because this formula when typeset ($x^1x^2\ldots x^n$) already has a "hole" at the baseline after x^2.

d) Use \ldots in those comparatively rare cases where you want three lower dots without a thin space before or after them. Example: "$(\ldots)$".

e) Use \cdotss between integral signs. Example:

$$\int↓0↑1\cdotss\int↓0↑1$$
$$f(x↓1,\ldotss,x↓n)\,dx↓1\ldotsm dx↓n.$$

f) Use "$\ldotss\,$." when a sentence ends with three lower dots. Example: "The periodic sequence 0, 1, 0, 1, 0, 1, $\ldotss\,$."

7. Handling vertical lines. Besides the "idioms" represented by \cdots and \ldotss, there are a few other situations that can be typeset more beautifully with a little care. A vertical line "|" and a double vertical line "||" are used for several different purposes in math formulas, and TeX will sometimes do a better job if you tell it what kind of a vertical line is meant. The following control sequences will help you in this task:

\leftv   vertical line used as a left parenthesis;
\rightv   vertical line used as a right parenthesis;
\relv   vertical line used as a relation.

For example, "$$\leftv +x \rightv = \leftv -x \rightv$$" specifies the displayed equation

$$|+x| = |-x|\ \ .$$

If this equation had been typed "$$|+x|=|-x|$$" the spacing would have been quite wrong, namely

$$|+x|=|-x|\ \ ,$$

because the |'s get the same spacing as ordinary variables like x when you haven't specified them to be \leftv or \rightv or \relv. Compare also the following two formulas:

$a|b$ $a|b$;
$a\relv b$ $a|b$.

There are three more control sequences \leftvv, \rightvv, and \relvv, which do the same for double vertical lines.

Appendix B defines two control sequences of use when specifying formulas like

$$\{\,x \mid x \geq 5\,\}\quad.$$

The best way to type this is "$$\leftset x \relv x\geq5 \rightset$$", because \leftset and \rightset introduce braces with spacing to match the spaces surrounding the \relv.

8. Number theory. To specify a formula like "$x \equiv y + 1 \pmod{p^2}$", type "$x\eqv y+1\mod{p↑2}$", using the control sequences \eqv and \mod defined in Appendix B. Note that you don't type the parentheses in this case; the control sequence provides them for you, with proper spacing and line-breaking conventions. (There is also a control sequence "\neqv" that produces the inequivalence symbol "$\not\equiv$".) To specify the formula

$$\gcd(m, n) = \gcd(n \bmod m, m)\quad,$$

type "$$\gcd(m,n)=\gcd(n\modop m, m)$$", using the control sequences \gcd and \modop. (Actually this latter formula would look slightly better if "\," were inserted after the second comma.)

9. Matrices. Now comes the fun part. Many different kinds of matrices are used in mathematics, and you can handle them in TEX by using the general alignment procedures we shall be studying in a later chapter. For now, let's consider only simple cases. Suppose you want to specify the formula

$$A = \begin{pmatrix} x - \lambda & 1 & 0 \\ 0 & x - \lambda & 1 \\ 0 & 0 & x - \lambda \end{pmatrix}\quad;$$

here's how to do it:

```
$$A=\left(\vcenter{
        \halign{$\ctr{#}$\quad
                ⊗$\ctr{#}$\quad
                ⊗$\ctr{#}$\cr
        x-\lambda⊗1⊗0\cr
        0⊗x-\lambda⊗1\cr
        0⊗0⊗x-\lambda\cr}}\right)$$
```

Explanation: We already know about "\left(" and "\right)", which make the big parentheses that go around the matrix. The \vcenter control sequence forms a box in restricted vertical mode, and centers that box vertically so that the middle of the box is the same height as a minus sign. The \halign control sequence is one of the things you can do in restricted vertical mode; it is a general operator for producing aligned tables. After "\halign{" and up to the first "\cr" is a mysterious ritual for specifying three columns of a matrix. (We will learn the rules of this later, let's take it on faith just now.) Then comes a specification of the three matrix rows, with tab marks "⊗" between columns, and with pseudo-carriage-returns "\cr" at the end of each row. (Here ⊗ is one of the special characters mentioned in Chapter 8, it is not the ⟨tab⟩ key on your keyboard; similarly, \cr is a control sequence, it is not ⟨carriage-return⟩. Furthermore \cr need not come at the end of a line; you can type several rows of a matrix on a single line of your TEX input manuscript.) After the final \cr comes the "}" to end "\halign{"; then comes the "}" to end "\vcenter{". Finally the "\right)" finishes off the formula.

If there were five columns instead of three, the \halign specification would be about the same, only longer; namely,

```
\halign{$\ctr{#}$\quad
     ⊗$\ctr{#}$\quad
     ⊗$\ctr{#}$\quad
     ⊗$\ctr{#}$\quad
     ⊗$\ctr{#}$\cr
```

followed by the individual rows. Here \ctr means that the corresponding column is to be centered; if you change it to \lft or \rt, the entries in the corresponding column will be set flush left or flush right, if they have different widths. When all matrix entries are numbers, it is usually better to use \rt than \ctr.

The \quads in the \halign ritual are used to specify the space between columns. If you want twice as much space you can replace \quad by \qquad.

Another way to specify the matrix equation in the above example is to use the \cpile control sequence of Appendix B for each column:

```
$$A=\left(\cpile{x-\lambda\cr 0\cr 0\cr}\quad
     \cpile{1\cr x-\lambda\cr 0\cr}\quad
     \cpile{0\cr 1\cr x-\lambda\cr}\right)$$
```

However, this use of \cpile is *not* recommended, because it doesn't work in general: Each column is being typeset independently as a separate \cpile, so the rows won't line up properly if some matrix entries are taller than others. It's best to use \halign as suggested above—those funny-looking column format specifications are scary only the first few times you encounter them; afterwards they are quite simple to use. On the other hand \cpile (and its cousins \lpile and \rpile, which produce left-justified and right-justified columns of formulas just as \cpile produces centered columns) can be handy in simple cases.

How about matrices involving \ldots? The following example should help you answer this question. Suppose you want to specify the matrix

$$\begin{pmatrix} a_{11} & a_{12} & \ldots & a_{1n} \\ a_{21} & a_{22} & \ldots & a_{2n} \\ \vdots & \vdots & & \vdots \\ a_{m1} & a_{m2} & \ldots & a_{mn} \end{pmatrix}.$$

One way to do it, using the "\vdots" control sequence of Appendix B, is

```
$$\left(\vcenter{\halign{$\ctr{#}\;$\!
            @$\ctr{#}\;$@$\ctr{#}\;$@$\ctr{#}$\cr
    a↓{11}@a↓{12}@\ldots@a↓{1n}\cr
    a↓{21}@a↓{22}@\ldots@a↓{2n}\cr
    \vdots@\vdots@ @\vdots\cr
    a↓{m1}@a↓{m2}@\ldots@a↓{mn}\cr}}\right)$$
```

Long ago in this chapter you were promised a solution to the problem of typing a displayed equation such as

$$|x| = \begin{cases} x, & \text{if } x \geq 0; \\ -x, & \text{if } x < 0. \end{cases}$$

Here it is, using \vcenter and \halign; see if you can understand it now:

```
$$\leftv x \rightv = \left\{\vcenter{
    \halign{\lft{$#$,}\qquad
            @if \lft{$#$}\cr
    x@x≥0;\cr -x@x<0.\cr}}\right.$$
```

Note that the commas and ifs are generated by the \halign specification; this trick isn't necessary, but it saves some typing. Another solution could be devised using \lpile, but (as in the discussion of matrices above) it is not recommended.

▶Exercise 18.3: Explain how to type

$$\frac{1}{2\pi} \int_{-\infty}^{\sqrt{y}} \left(\sum_{k=1}^{n} \sin^2 x_k(t) \right) \bigl(f(t) + g(t) \bigr) \, dt.$$

▶Exercise 18.4: Also explain how to type

$$\frac{(n_1 + n_2 + \cdots + n_m)!}{n_1! \, n_2! \ldots n_m!} = \binom{n_1 + n_2}{n_2} \binom{n_1 + n_2 + n_3}{n_3} \cdots \binom{n_1 + n_2 + \cdots + n_m}{n_m}.$$

▶Exercise 18.5: How can you get TEX to typeset the column vector $\begin{pmatrix} y_1 \\ \vdots \\ y_k \end{pmatrix}$?

▶Exercise 18.6: Using Appendix F to find the names of special characters, explain how to type

$$\mathcal{P}_{Lhj}(x) = \mathrm{Tr}\left[\frac{\partial F_{L^{-1}}}{\partial t_h} \chi(L) \mathcal{M}_{nj}(x) \right], \qquad \text{evaluated at } \chi(\Gamma) \bmod SL(n, \mathrm{C}).$$

▶Exercise 18.7: Define a control sequence \e for the "colon-equal" operator in computer science, so that a formula like "$x := 2 \times x + 1$" will be properly spaced after it has been typed "`$x\e2\times x+1$`".

<19> Displayed equations

By now you know how to type mathematical formulas so that TEX will handle them with supreme elegance; but there is one more aspect of the art of mathematical typing that we should discuss. Namely, displays.

As mentioned earlier, you can type "`$$⟨formula⟩$$`" to display a formula in flamboyant display style. Another thing you can do is type

$$⟨formula⟩\eqno⟨formula⟩$$;

this displays the first formula and also puts an equation number (the second formula) at the right-hand margin. For example,

`$$x↑2-y↑2 = (x+y)(x-y).\eqno(15)$$`

will produce this:

$$x^2 - y^2 = (x + y)(x - y). \eqno{(15)}$$

⚡ Here's what $$ and \eqno do, in more detail: The formula to be displayed is made into a box using display style (unless you override the style). If \eqno appears, the formula following it is made into a box using text style. When the combined width of these two boxes, plus one text size quad, exceeds the current line width, squeezing is attempted as follows: If the shrinkability of the formula to be displayed would allow it to fit, the formula is repackaged into a box that has just enough width; otherwise the formula is repackaged into a box having the current line width, and the equation number (if any) will be placed on a new line just below the formula box. The formula to be displayed is centered on the line, where this centering is independent of the width of the equation number, *unless* this would leave less space between the formula and the equation number than the width of the equation number itself; in the latter case, the formula is placed flush left on the line. Now TeX looks at the length of the previous line of the current paragraph: if this is short compared to the size of the displayed equation, vertical glue that the designer has specified by "\dispaskip⟨glue⟩" will be placed above the formula, and vertical glue specified by "\dispbskip⟨glue⟩" will be placed below. Otherwise vertical glue specified by "\dispskip⟨glue⟩" will be placed both above and below. (The glue below is, however, omitted if an equation number has to be dropped down to a separate line; this separate line takes the place of the glue that ordinarily would have appeared.)

⚡ Another thing you can type for displays, when you know what you're doing, is "$$\halign⟨spec⟩{⟨alignment⟩}$$". This is just like an ordinary \halign, except that the $$'s interrupt a paragraph and insert \dispskip glue above and below the aligned result. Note that \eqno cannot be used in this case, and no automatic centering is done. Page breaks might occur in the midst of such displays.

OK, the use of displayed formulas is very nice, but when you try typing a lot of manuscripts you will run into some displays that don't fit the simple pattern of a single formula with or without an equation number. Appendix B defines special control sequences that will cover most of the remaining cases:

1. **Two or more equations that should be aligned on = signs.** (The alignment can also be on other signs like ≤, etc.) For this case, type

$$\eqalign{⟨\text{left-hand side}_1⟩\&⟨\text{right-hand side}_1⟩\cr$$
$$⟨\text{left-hand side}_2⟩\&⟨\text{right-hand side}_2⟩\cr$$

$$\vdots$$

$$⟨\text{left-hand side}_n⟩\&⟨\text{right-hand side}_n⟩\cr}$$

with an optional \eqno⟨formula⟩ just before the closing "$$" and after the closing "\cr}". *N.B.: Don't forget to type the final \cr!* The relation symbols on which you are aligning should be the first symbols of the right-hand sides (not the last symbols of the left-hand sides). If \eqno appears, the equation number will be centered vertically in the display (or—if it doesn't fit—it will be dropped down to the line following the display, as mentioned earlier). For example, if you type

```
$$\eqalign{a↓1+b↓1w+c↓1w↑2⊗=\alpha+\beta;\cr
          b↓2x+c↓2x↑2⊗= 0.\cr}\eqno(30)$$
```

the result will be

$$a_1 + b_1 w + c_1 w^2 = \alpha + \beta;$$
$$b_2 x + c_2 x^2 = 0. \tag{30}$$

Note that the left-hand sides are right-justified and the right-hand sides are left-justified, so the = signs line up; the whole formula is also centered, and the equation number (30) is halfway between the lines.

Sometimes you may want more or less vertical space between the aligned equations. Type "\noalign{\vskip(glue)}" after any \cr, to insert a given amount of extra glue after any particular equation line. (You can even do this before the first equation and after the last one.)

In general, the result of \eqalign is a \vcentered box, so \eqalign can be used in a fashion analogous to \lpile or \cpile. Thus, it is possible to type such things as "$$\eqalign{...} \qquad \eqalign{...}$$", obtaining a display with two columns of aligned formulas.

2. Two or more equations that should be aligned, some of which have equation numbers. For this case you use \eqalignno, which is something like \eqalign, but each line now has the form

⟨left-hand side⟩⊗⟨right-hand side⟩⊗⟨equation number⟩\cr   .

For example,

```
$$\eqalignno{a↓1+b↓1w+c↓1w↑2⊗=\alpha+\beta;⊗(29)\cr
            b↓2x+c↓2x↑2⊗=0.⊗(30)\cr}$$
```

yields

$$a_1 + b_1 w + c_1 w^2 = \alpha + \beta; \tag{29}$$
$$b_2 x + c_2 x^2 = 0. \tag{30}$$

You can't use \eqno together with \eqalignno; the equation numbers now must appear as shown.

If the ⟨equation number⟩ of some line is blank, you can omit the ⊗ before it. Example:

```
$$\eqalignno{f(x)⊗=(x−1)(x+1)\cr
               ⊗=x↑2−1.⊗(31)\cr}$$
```

This will produce the following display:

$$\eqalign{f(x) &= (x-1)(x+1)\\ &= x^2 - 1.}\tag{31}$$

(Note the position of the equation number.)

⚠ You can use \noalign within \eqalignno to insert new lines of text. For example, "\noalign{\hbox{implies}}" will insert a line containing the word "implies" (at the left margin) between two aligned formulas.

3. A long equation that must be broken into two lines. You may want to type this as

```
$$\twoline{⟨first line⟩}{⟨glue⟩}{⟨second line⟩}$$   .
```

The formula's first line will be moved to the left so that it is one text size quad from the left margin, and its second line will be moved to the right so that it is one text size quad from the right margin. The specified glue will be inserted between these two lines in addition to the normal glue.

Another way to break a long equation is to use \eqalign with appropriate quads inserted at the beginning of the second line.

For example, here's an equation that is clearly too big to fit:

$$\sigma(2^{34} - 1, 2^{35}, 1) = -3 + (2^{34} - 1)/2^{35} + 2^{35}/(2^{34} - 1) + 7/2^{35}(2^{34} - 1) - \sigma(2^{35}, 2^{34} - 1, 1).$$

Let's break it just before the "$+7$". One way to do this is to type

```
$$\twoline{\sigma(2↑{34}−1,2↑{35},1)=−3+(2↑{34}−1)/
          2↑{35}+2↑{35}/(2↑{34}−1)}{2pt}{\null+7/2↑
          {35}(2↑{34}−1)−\sigma(2↑{35},2↑{34}−1,1).}$$
```

The two-line result will then be

$$\sigma(2^{34}-1, 2^{35}, 1) = -3 + (2^{34}-1)/2^{35} + 2^{35}/(2^{34}-1) \\ + 7/2^{35}(2^{34}-1) - \sigma(2^{35}, 2^{34}-1, 1).$$

The other alternative is to type

```
$$\eqalign{\sigma(2↑{34}-1,2↑{35},1)⊗=-3+(2↑{34}-1)/
          2↑{35}+2↑{35}/(2↑{34}-1)\cr
          ⊗\qquad\null+7/2↑{35}(2↑{34}-1)
          -\sigma(2↑{35},2↑{34}-1,1).\cr}$$
```

which yields

$$\sigma(2^{34}-1, 2^{35}, 1) = -3 + (2^{34}-1)/2^{35} + 2^{35}/(2^{34}-1) \\ + 7/2^{35}(2^{34}-1) - \sigma(2^{35}, 2^{34}-1, 1).$$

A couple of things should be explained and emphasized about this example: (a) The second line starts with "\null+7" instead of just "+7". The control sequence \null is defined in Appendix B to mean a box of size zero, containing nothing, and this may seem rather insignificant; but it makes a big difference to TEX, because a plus sign in the middle of a formula is followed by a space, but a plus sign that begins a formula is not. Thus, you should always remember to type "\null" when you are continuing a multi-line formula. (b) When you use \twoline, never hit ⟨carriage-return⟩ on your keyboard just after the } that follows the ⟨first line⟩, or just after the } that follows the ⟨glue⟩; this ⟨carriage-return⟩ makes TEX think a space was intended, and \twoline won't work correctly. (You'll probably get some inscrutable error message like "\halign in display math mode must be followed by $$.")

Breaking of long displayed formulas into several lines is an art; TEX never attempts to do it, because no set of rules is really adequate. The author of a mathematical manuscript should really decide how all such formulas should break, since the break position depends on subtle factors of mathematical exposition. Furthermore, different publishers tend to have different styles for line breaks. But several rules of thumb can be stated, since they seem to reflect the best mathematical practice:

a) Although formulas within a paragraph always break *after* binary operations and relations, displayed formulas always break *before* binary operations and relations. Thus, we didn't end the first line of the above example with "`(2↑{34}-1)+\null`", we ended it with "`(2↑{34}-1)`" and began the second line with "`\null+7`".

b) The `\twoline` form is generally preferable for equations with a long left-hand side; then the break usually comes just before the $=$ sign.

c) When an equation is broken before a binary operation, the second line should start at least two quads to the right of where the innermost subformula containing that binary operation begins on the first line. For example, if you wish to break

$$\verb|$$\sum↓{1≤k≤n}\left((⟨formula₁⟩+⟨formula₂⟩\right)$$|$$

at the plus sign between ⟨formula₁⟩ and ⟨formula₂⟩, it is almost mandatory to have the plus sign on the second line appear somewhat to the right of the large left parenthesis corresponding to "`\left(`". [Note further that your uses of `\left` and `\right` must balance in both parts of the broken formula. You could type, for instance,

```
\eqalign{\sum↓{1≤k≤n}⊗\left((⟨formula₁⟩\right.\cr
                    ⊗\qquad\left.\null+⟨formula₂⟩\right)$$
```

provided that ⟨formula₁⟩ and ⟨formula₂⟩ are both of the same height and depth so that the `\left(` on the first line will turn out to be the same size as the `\right)` on the second. But in such cases it's simpler and safer to use, e.g., `\bigglp` and `\biggrp` instead of `\left(` and `\right).]

‹20› Definitions (also called macros)

You can often save time typing math formulas by defining control sequences as abbreviations for constructions that occur frequently in a particular manuscript. For example, if some manuscript frequently refers to the vector "$(x_1, \ldots, x_n)$", you can type

```
\def\xvec{(x↓1,\ldotss,x↓n)}
```

and `\xvec` will henceforth be an abbreviation for "$(x_1,\ldots,x_n)$". Formulas like

$$\sum_{(x_1,\ldots,x_n)\neq(0,\ldots,0)} \big(f(x_1,\ldots,x_n)+g(x_1,\ldots,x_n)\big)$$

can then be typed simply as

```
$$\sum_{\xvec\neq(0,\ldotss,0)}\biglp f\xvec+g\xvec\bigrp$$  .
```

TeX's definition facility is what a designer uses to define all the standard formats, so Appendices B and E contain many illustrations of the use of `\def`. For example, `\eqalign` and `\eqalignno` are both defined in Appendix B. Defined control sequences can be followed by arguments, so we shall study the general rules for such definitions in this chapter. It's a good idea for you to look at Appendix B now.

The general form is "`\def`⟨controlseq⟩⟨parameter text⟩{⟨result text⟩}", followed by an optional space, where the ⟨parameter text⟩ contains no { or }, and where all occurrences of { and } in the ⟨result text⟩ are properly nested in groups. Furthermore the # symbol (or whatever symbol is being used to stand for parameters, cf. Chapter 7) has a special significance: In the ⟨parameter text⟩, the first appearance of # must be followed by 1, the next by 2, and so on; up to nine #'s are allowed. In the ⟨result text⟩ each # must be followed by a digit that appeared after # in the ⟨parameter text⟩, or else the # should be followed by another #. The latter case stands for insertion of a single # in the result of any use of the definition; the former case stands for insertion of the corresponding argument.

For example, let's consider a "random" definition that doesn't do anything useful except that it does exhibit TeX's rules. The definition

```
\def\cs AB#1#2CD\$E#3 {#3{ab#1}#1 c\x ###2}
```

says that the control sequence `\cs` is to have a parameter text consisting of ten tokens

A,   B,   #1,   #2,   C,   D,   \$,   E,   #3,   ⊔,

and a result text consisting of twelve tokens

#3,   {,   a,   b,   #1,   },   #1,   ⊔,   c,   \x,   #,   #2.

Henceforth when TeX reads the control sequence `\cs` it expects that the next two input tokens will be A and B (otherwise you will get the error message "Use of \cs doesn't match its definition"); then comes argument #1, then argument #2, then C, then D, then \$, then E, then argument #3, and finally a space. (It is customary to use the word "argument" to mean the string of tokens that gets substituted for a parameter; parameters appear in a definition, and arguments appear when that definition is used.)

How does TEX determine where an argument stops, you ask. Answer: If a parameter is followed in the definition by another token, the corresponding argument is the shortest (possibly empty) sequence of tokens with properly nested {...} groups that is followed in the input by this particular token. Otherwise the corresponding argument is the shortest *nonempty* sequence of tokens with properly nested {...} groups; namely, it is the next token, unless the token is {, when the argument is an entire group. In any case, if the argument found in this way has the form "{⟨balanced tokens⟩}", where ⟨balanced tokens⟩ stands for a sequence of tokens that is properly nested with respect to { and }, the outermost { and } enclosing this argument are removed. For example, let's continue with \cs as defined above, and suppose that the subsequent input contains

\cs AB{\Look}ABCD\$ E{And }{look} F.

Argument #1 will be the token \Look, since #1 is immediately followed by #2 in the definition, and since {\Look} is the shortest acceptable sequence of tokens following "\cs AB". Argument #2 will be the two tokens "AB", since it is to be followed by "C". Argument #3 will be the twelve tokens "{And }{look}", since it is to be followed by a space. Note that the exterior { and } are not removed from #3 as they were from #1, since that would leave an unnested string "And }{look". Note also that the space following "\$" is ignored since it isn't really a space (it follows a control sequence). The net effect then, after substituting arguments for parameters in the result text, will be that TEX's input will essentially become

{And }{look}{ab\Look}\Look⊔c\x#ABF.

The space ⊔ here *will* be digested, even though it follows the control sequence \Look, because it was part of the defined result text. The "F." here comes from the yet-unscanned input.

Definitions are not "expanded" (i.e., replaced by the result text) when they occur in a \def or an argument. Thus \Look and \$ and \x are treated as single tokens in the example above, even though \Look has presumably been defined elsewhere. If ⊗ or \cr occurs without being enclosed in {...}, in a definition or an argument in the midst of an alignment, TEX assumes that this ⊗ or \cr belongs to the alignment and not to the definition or argument.

If you have difficulty understanding why some \def doesn't work as you expected, try running your program with \trace´355 (see Chapter 27).

The effect of \def lasts only until the control sequence is redefined or until the end of the group containing that \def. But there is another control sequence \gdef that makes a "global" definition, i.e., it defines a control sequence valid in all groups unless redefined. The \gdef instruction is especially useful in connection within \output routines, as explained in Chapter 23.

▷Exercise 20.1: The example definition of \cs includes a ## in its result text, but the way ## is actually used in that example is rather pointless. Give an example of a definition where ## serves a useful purpose.

<21> Making boxes

In Chapters 11 and 12 we discussed the idea of boxes and glue; now it is time to study the various facilities TEX has for making various kinds of boxes. In most cases, you can get by with boxes that TEX manufactures automatically with its paragraph builder, page builder, and math formula processor; but if you want to do nonstandard things, you have the option of making boxes by yourself.

To make a rule box, type "\hrule" in vertical mode or "\vrule" in horizontal mode, followed if desired by any or all of the specifications "width⟨dimen⟩", "height⟨dimen⟩", "depth⟨dimen⟩", in any order. For example, you can type "\vrule height 4pt width 3pt depth 2pt" in the middle of a paragraph, and you will get the black box "▮". The dimensions you specify should not be negative. If you leave any dimensions unspecified, you get the following by default:

	\hrule	\vrule
width	*	0.4 pt
height	0.4 pt	*
depth	0.0 pt	*

(Here "*" means that the rule will extend to the boundary of the smallest enclosing box.)

To make a box from a horizontal list of boxes, type "\hbox{⟨hlist⟩}", where ⟨hlist⟩ specifies the list of boxes in restricted horizontal mode. For example, "\hbox{This is not a box}" makes the box

This is not a box

(in spite of what it says). The boundary lines in this illustration aren't typeset, of course; they merely indicate the box's actual extent, as determined by the rules of Chapters 11 and 12.

Similarly, the instruction "\vbox{⟨vlist⟩}" makes a box from a *vertical* list of boxes. If you type

```
\vbox{\hbox{T}\hbox{h}\hbox{i}\hbox{s}
        \hbox{ }\hbox{b}\hbox{o}\hbox{x}}
```

you will get this box:

Automatic baseline adjustment is done on vertical lists, as explained in Chapter 15. The following example shows what happens if the baseline adjustment is varied:

```
\vbox{\def\\#1{\hbox{#1}}
        \baselineskip-1pt
        \lineskip 3pt
        \\T\\h\\i\\s
        \\{ }\\b\\o\\x}
```

Note that a specially defined control sequence \\ saves a lot of typing in this example.

▶Exercise 21.1: When the author of this manual first prepared the above example, he wrote "\baselineskip 0pt" instead of "\baselineskip-1pt". Why didn't this work?

▶Exercise 21.2: How would you change the above example so that the letters are *centered* with respect to each other, instead of being placed flush left?

The phrase "list of boxes" in the above discussion really means a list of boxes and glue. But if \hbox and \vbox are used in the simple manner stated, the glue does not stretch or shrink. When you want the glue to do its thing, type "\hbox to ⟨dimen⟩{⟨hlist⟩}" and you will get a box of the specified width; or type "\vbox to ⟨dimen⟩{⟨vlist⟩}" and you will get a box of the specified height. (The depth of a \vboxed box is always the depth of the last box in the vertical list, except that it is zero when glue follows the last box.) You may also type "\hbox to size{⟨hlist⟩}" or "\vbox to size{⟨vlist⟩}"; this means that the ⟨dimen⟩ is to be the most recently specified \hsize or \vsize, respectively. Finally, there's a further option of typing "\hbox expand ⟨dimen⟩{⟨hlist⟩}" or "\vbox expand ⟨dimen⟩{⟨vlist⟩}"; these expand the box to its natural width or height plus the (possibly negative) amount specified.

You can also get the effect of paragraphing and line-breaking with `\hbox`, in the following way: If you give the instruction "`\hbox par ⟨dimen⟩`", TEX will use its paragraph line-breaking routine to convert the horizontal list into one or more lines of the specified width. In this case the `\hbox` will actually result in a box formed from a *vertical* list of horizontal lists of the desired width. The boxed paragraph that you get is not indented.

> For example, the box that you are now reading was made by typing "`\hbox par 156pt{For example, the box ... five lines.}`" and TEX broke it into five lines.

If you specify hanging indentation with such a boxed paragraph, it applies to the box and not to the paragraph (if any) containing the box. For example,

`\hbox par 200pt{\hangindent 10 pt ⟨ text ⟩ }`

will put the specified text into a box 200 points wide, where all lines after the first are indented by 10 points at the left. However, all other parameters affecting the setting of the boxed paragraph (the baseline skip, raggedness, etc.) should be set up *before* the `\hbox par`.

You can save a constructed box for later use by typing "`\save⟨digit⟩⟨box⟩`, where ⟨digit⟩ is 0 or 1 or ⋯ or 9 and ⟨box⟩ specifies a box. For example, "`\save3\hbox {The formula ``$x+y$´´.}`" will save away the box

$$\boxed{\text{The formula ``} x + y \text{''.}}$$

(Note that math formulas are allowed in ⟨hlist⟩s; but displays are not.) Later you can use this saved box by typing "`\box⟨digit⟩`". The `\save` and `\box` instructions are useful for constructing rather complex layouts like those in a newspaper page. Caution: You can use a saved box only once; after you type "`\box3`" the contents of box 3 becomes null. If you type "`\save3\box2`" the effect is to move box 2 to box 3 and then to make box 2 empty.

> ▶Exercise 21.3: Define a control sequence `\boxit` so that "`\boxit{⟨box⟩}`" yields the given box surrounded by 3 points of space and ruled lines on all four sides. For example, this exercise has been typeset by telling TEX to `\boxit{\boxit{\box4}}`, where box 4 was created by typing "`\save4\hbox par 300pt{\exno 21.3: Define ...}`".

To raise or lower a constructed box in a horizontal list, or in a math formula, precede it by "\raise⟨dimen⟩" or "\lower⟨dimen⟩". For example, the \TEX control sequence that prints the TₑX logo in this manual is defined by

```
\def\TEX{\hbox{\:aT\hskip-2pt\lower1.94pt\hbox{E}\hskip-2pt X}}
```

Similarly, you can move a constructed box left or right in a vertical list if you type "\moveleft⟨dimen⟩" or "\moveright⟨dimen⟩" just before its description. The control sequences \vcenter and \vtop are also useful for box positioning (see Chapter 26).

There is also a way to repeat a box as many times as necessary to fill up some given space; this is what printers call "leaders." The general construction is "\leaders⟨box or rule⟩⟨glue⟩", where ⟨box or rule⟩ is any box or rule specified by \hbox or \vbox or \box or \page or \hrule or \vrule, and where ⟨glue⟩ is specified by \hskip or \hfill in horizontal mode, \vskip or \vfill in vertical mode. TₑX treats the glue in the normal way, possibly stretching it or shrinking it; but then instead of leaving the resulting space blank, TₑX places the contents of the box there, as many times as it will fit, subject to the condition that the reference point of each box will be congruent to some fixed number, modulo the box's width (in horizontal leaders) or modulo the box's height plus depth (in vertical leaders). This "congruence" means that leaders in different places will line up with each other. For example,

```
\def\lead{\leaders\hbox to 10pt{\hfill.\hfill}\hfill}
\hbox to size{Alpha\lead Omega}
\hbox to size{The Beginning\lead The Ending}
```

will produce the following two lines:

Alpha . . . . Omega
The Beginning . . . . The Ending

(Here "\hbox to 10pt{\hfill.\hfill}" specifies a box 10 points wide, with a period in its center; the control sequence \lead then causes this box to be replicated when filling another box.) When a rule is used as a leader, it completely fills the glue space; for example, if we had made the definition "\def\lead{\leaders\hrule\hfill}", the two lines would have come out looking this way instead:

Alpha_____Omega
The Beginning_____The Ending

Leaders can be used in an interesting way to construct variable-width braces in the horizontal direction. TEX's math extension font cmathx (used with basic format) contains four characters that allow you to typeset such braces in the following way. First make the definitions

```
\def\bracex{\leaders\hrule height 1.5pt \hfill}
\def\dnbrace{$\char´772$\bracex$\char´775
          \char´774$\bracex$\char´773$}
\def\upbrace{$\char´774$\bracex$\char´773
          \char´772$\bracex$\char´775$}
```

Then

```
\hbox to 100pt{\dnbrace}
\hbox to 200pt{\upbrace}
```

will produce

This is occasionally useful in connection with math formulas.

▶Exercise 21.4: How do you think the author of this manual made asterisks fill the rest of the current page? [*Hint:* The asterisk used (in font cmr10) has a height of 7.5 points.]

<22> Alignment

A novice TEX user can prepare manuscripts that involve mathematical formulas but no complicated tables; but a TEX Master can prepare complicated tables using \halign or \valign. In this chapter, if you're ready for it, you can learn to be a TEX Master. (And the next chapter—which talks about the design of \output routines—will enable you to become a Grandmaster.)

For simplicity, let's consider \halign first; \valign is similar, and it is used much more rarely. If you type

$$\halign \text{ to } \langle dimen \rangle \{\langle alignment\ preamble \rangle \backslash cr \langle alignment\ entries \rangle \}$$

in vertical mode or restricted vertical mode, you append a list of aligned boxes that are each ⟨dimen⟩ units wide to the current vertical list; these boxes are formed from the ⟨alignment entries⟩ by using the specifications in the ⟨alignment preamble⟩. We've already seen examples of alignment in Chapter 18, where \halign was used to construct matrices. In general, the preamble tells how to format individual vertical columns whose entries are going to be assembled into horizontal rows of the specified width. Before we get into any details of the alignment, let's observe straightaway that "\halign to ⟨dimen⟩" can be changed to "\halign to size" if the ⟨dimen⟩ is to be the current \hsize; it can be shortened to simply "\halign" if the minimum size (without shrinking) is desired, or replaced by "\halign expand ⟨dimen⟩" if the boxes should be stretched to a given amount in addition to this minimum size. In other words, \halign has the same four options as \hbox.

The ⟨alignment preamble⟩ consists of one or more ⟨format⟩ specifications separated by ⊗'s. Each ⟨format⟩ specification is a sequence of tokens that is properly nested with respect to {...} groups and contains exactly one "#". For example, the ⟨alignment preamble⟩ suggested for three-column matrices in Chapter 18 was

$$\texttt{\$\textbackslash ctr\{\#\}\$\textbackslash quad⊗\$\textbackslash ctr\{\#\}\$\textbackslash quad⊗\$\textbackslash ctr\{\#\}\$}\quad.$$

A ⟨format⟩ is essentially a simple \def with one parameter; the idea is to replace the # by whatever alignment entry is typed in that column position. For example, if the ⟨alignment entries⟩ following this preamble are

$$\texttt{x↓1⊗x↓2⊗x↓3\textbackslash cr\ \ y↓1⊗y↓2⊗y↓3\textbackslash cr}$$

then there will be two rows of the matrix obtained by substituting these entries in the preamble, namely

$$\texttt{\$\textbackslash ctr\{x↓1\}\$\textbackslash quad} \qquad \texttt{\$\textbackslash ctr\{x↓2\}\$\textbackslash quad} \qquad \texttt{\$\textbackslash ctr\{x↓3\}\$}$$
$$\texttt{\$\textbackslash ctr\{y↓1\}\$\textbackslash quad} \qquad \texttt{\$\textbackslash ctr\{y↓2\}\$\textbackslash quad} \qquad \texttt{\$\textbackslash ctr\{y↓3\}\$}$$

The ⟨alignment entries⟩ consist of zero or more ⟨row⟩s; and a ⟨row⟩ is one or more entries separated by ⊗'s and followed by \cr. In general if the preamble contains n ⟨format⟩s

$$\langle u_1\rangle\#\langle v_1\rangle \quad \otimes \quad \langle u_2\rangle\#\langle v_2\rangle \quad \otimes \ \cdots \ \otimes \quad \langle u_n\rangle\#\langle v_n\rangle$$

and if there are m rows each containing n entries

$$
\begin{array}{ccccccccc}
\langle x_{11}\rangle & \otimes & \langle x_{12}\rangle & \otimes \cdots \otimes & \langle x_{1n}\rangle & \cr \\
\langle x_{21}\rangle & \otimes & \langle x_{22}\rangle & \otimes \cdots \otimes & \langle x_{2n}\rangle & \cr \\
\vdots & & \vdots & & \vdots & \\
\langle x_{m1}\rangle & \otimes & \langle x_{m2}\rangle & \otimes \cdots \otimes & \langle x_{mn}\rangle & \cr
\end{array}
$$

we will obtain mn fleshed-out entries

$$
\begin{array}{cccc}
\langle u_1\rangle\langle x_{11}\rangle\langle v_1\rangle & \langle u_2\rangle\langle x_{12}\rangle\langle v_2\rangle & \cdots & \langle u_n\rangle\langle x_{1n}\rangle\langle v_n\rangle \\
\langle u_1\rangle\langle x_{21}\rangle\langle v_1\rangle & \langle u_2\rangle\langle x_{22}\rangle\langle v_2\rangle & \cdots & \langle u_n\rangle\langle x_{2n}\rangle\langle v_n\rangle \\
\vdots & \vdots & & \vdots \\
\langle u_1\rangle\langle x_{m1}\rangle\langle v_1\rangle & \langle u_2\rangle\langle x_{m2}\rangle\langle v_2\rangle & \cdots & \langle u_n\rangle\langle x_{mn}\rangle\langle v_n\rangle
\end{array}
$$

by repeatedly copying the preamble format information.

Now here's what TeX does with the mn fleshed-out entries: The natural width of each entry \hbox{⟨u_j⟩⟨x_{ij}⟩⟨v_j⟩} is determined; and the *maximum* natural width is computed in each column. Suppose that w_j is the maximum natural width in the jth column; then each fleshed-out entry in that column is replaced by the box "\hbox to w_j{⟨u_j⟩⟨x_{ij}⟩⟨v_j⟩}". Thus, all entries in a particular column now have the same width. Finally these boxes are welded together to make the m rows, by inserting $n+1$ elements of glue in each row (before the first box, between boxes, and after the last box). The glue to use in this welding process has previously been specified by "\tabskip⟨glue⟩". The m row boxes are finally appended to the current vertical list.

If you don't understand what was said so far, look back at the matrix example and reread the above until you understand. Because there are also some refinements that we shall now discuss. (a) After any \cr you can type "\noalign{⟨vlist⟩}", and this ⟨vlist⟩ will simply appear in its place among the aligned row boxes. The ⟨vlist⟩ in this case usually contains vertical glue, penalty specifications, or horizontal rules; but it might contain anything that is allowed in restricted vertical mode, even another \halign. (b) If some row has fewer than n entries, i.e., if the \cr of some row occurs before there have been $n-1$ ⊗'s, all remaining columns of the row are set to null boxes regardless of their format. (This is not necessarily the same as "\hbox{$\langle u_j \rangle \langle v_j \rangle$}"; the preamble formats are simply ignored.) (c) If you specify \tabskip$\langle$glue$\rangle$ in the preamble, the $n+1$ globs of glue that weld together the final row boxes will be different, so you can get different spacing between columns. Here's how it works: The glue placed before column 1 is the \tabskip glue in effect when the \halign control sequence itself appears; the glue that replaces a ⊗ or \cr is the \tabskip glue in effect when that ⊗ or \cr appears in the preamble.

Warning: Any spaces you type in the $\langle$format$\rangle$s of the preamble will be taken seriously! Don't start a new line after a ⊗ unless you intend a corresponding space to be there in every column. (You may, of course, start a new line after \cr without inserting an unwanted space, or you can type "⊗\!" and go to a new line.) The same applies to spaces in the aligned entries; *always be extra careful with your use of spaces inside* \halign.

Another warning: Don't use a construction like "$\$#\$$" in your $\langle$format$\rangle$s if the corresponding column entries might be null. Otherwise TEX will scan "$\$\$$" and think display math is intended, and this probably will lead to hopeless confusion. (The matrix example above has "$\ctr\{#\}$" instead of "\ctr{$\$#\$$}" for precisely this reason. Another safe possibility would be "\ctr{$\$#\ \$$}".)

You can have \halign or \valign within \halign or \valign (for example, matrices within aligned equations). In order to allow this, TEX insists that { and } be balanced in alignment entries, so that it is possible to distinguish which level of alignment corresponds to a given ⊗ or \cr. Consider, for example, the extremely simple alignment

$$\text{\halign\{\ctr\{#\}\cr}$$
$$\langle\text{entry}\rangle\text{\cr\}} \quad .$$

When TEX begins to scan the alignment entry, it scans the string of tokens "\ctr{ $\langle$entry$\rangle$}\cr}..."; and the appearance of "\ctr" causes TEX to look for \ctr's argument. This argument begins with "{", so the scanning continues until the matching "}". However, when the \cr is encountered after $\langle$entry$\rangle$, TEX is supposed to insert the matching "}" from the preamble. If $\langle$entry$\rangle$ itself contains a use of \halign, there will be \cr's in the middle of $\langle$entry$\rangle$; so TEX doesn't simply look for the first \cr. Instead it ignores the tokens ⊗ and \cr until finding one that is not enclosed in braces, thereby correctly determining the argument to \ctr.

Defined control sequences in the preamble are not usually expanded until the alignment entries are being processed. However, a control sequence following "\tabskip$\langle$glue$\rangle$" in the preamble might be expanded, since a $\langle$glue$\rangle$ specification might involve control sequences. For example, "\tabskip 0pt \ctr{#}" will effectively be expanded by TEX to "`\tabskip 0pt \hfill # \hfill`" while the preamble is being scanned, because TEX won't know (when it gets to "`\ctr`") whether or not the expansion of this control sequence will begin with "`plus 1pt`" or some other continuation of the glue specification.

In the rest of this chapter we shall discuss two worked-out examples. First suppose that we want to typeset three pairs of displayed formulas whose $=$ signs are to be aligned, such as

$$
\begin{aligned}
V_i &= v_i - q_i v_j, & X_i &= x_i - q_i x_j, & U_i &= u_i, && \text{for } i \neq j; \\
V_j &= v_j, & X_j &= x_j, & U_j &= u_j + \textstyle\sum_{i \neq j} q_i u_i.
\end{aligned}
\tag{13}
$$

We could do this with three `\eqalign`'s, but let's not, since our current goal is to learn more about the general `\halign` construction. One solution is to type

```
$$\vcenter{\halign{⟨alignment preamble⟩\cr
V↓i⊗v↓i-q↓iv↓j,⊗X↓i⊗x↓i-q↓ix↓j,⊗U↓i⊗u↓i,\qquad\hbox{for }i≠j;\cr
V↓j⊗v↓j,⊗X↓j⊗x↓j,⊗U↓j⊗u↓j+\sum↓{i≠j}q↓iu↓i.\cr}}\eqno(13)$$
```

with some suitable alignment preamble. (It sometimes helps to figure out how you want to type the alignment entries before you design the preamble; there's a tradeoff between ease of typing the entries and ease of constructing the preamble.) One suitable preamble is

```
$\rt{#}$⊗\lft{$\null=#$}\qquad
⊗$\rt{#}$⊗\lft{$\null=#$}\qquad
⊗$\rt{#}$⊗\lft{$\null=#$}
```

Note the `\null`s here: they ensure proper spacing before the $=$ signs, because the equations are being broken into two parts. Study this example carefully and you'll soon see how to make useful alignments.

▶Exercise 22.1: What would happen if "`\vcenter`" were replaced by "`\vbox`" in the above example?

If we didn't have to include an equation number like "(13)", the `\vcenter` could have been omitted; but then there would have been a possible page break between the two equations, and the equations would not have been centered on the line. (The only effect of the $$'s in "`$$\halign{...}$$`" is to insert `\dispskip` glue above and below the alignment.) One way to prevent a page break would be to insert "`\noalign{\penalty 1000}`" between the lines. And one way to center the equations would be to vary the tabskip glue, as in the definition of `\eqalignno` in Appendix B. But it is much easier to use `\vcenter`.

The second example is slightly more complex, but once you master it you will have little or no trouble with other tables. Suppose you want to specify this:

AT&T Common Stock		
Year	Price	Dividend
1971	41–54	$2.60
2	41–54	2.70
3	46–55	2.87
4	40–53	3.24
5	45–52	3.40
6	51–59	.95*

*(first quarter only)

including all those horizontal and vertical lines. The table is to be 150 points wide. Here is one way to do it, letting the tabskip glue expand to give the column widths (so that, for example, the "Price" column will turn out to be exactly one en-dash-width wider than the "Year" column):

```
$$\vbox{\tabskip 0pt
\def\|{\vrule height 9.25pt depth 3pt}
\def\.{\hskip-10pt plus 10000000000pt}
\hrule
\hbox to 150pt{\|\.AT&T Common Stock\.\|}
\hrule
\halign to 150pt{#\tabskip 0pt plus 100pt
⊗\hfill#⊗#⊗\ctr{#}⊗#⊗\hfill#⊗#\tabskip 0pt\cr
\|⊗\.Year\.\hfill⊗\|⊗\.Price\.⊗\|⊗\.Dividend\.\hfill⊗\|\cr
\noalign{\hrule}
\|⊗1971⊗\|⊗41--54⊗\|⊗$\$$2.60⊗\|\cr\noalign{\hrule}
\|⊗2⊗\|⊗41--54⊗\|⊗2.70⊗\|\cr\noalign{\hrule}
\|⊗3⊗\|⊗46--55⊗\|⊗2.87⊗\|\cr\noalign{\hrule}
\|⊗4⊗\|⊗40--53⊗\|⊗3.24⊗\|\cr\noalign{\hrule}
\|⊗5⊗\|⊗45--52⊗\|⊗3.40⊗\|\cr\noalign{\hrule}
\|⊗6⊗\|⊗51--59⊗\|⊗.95\spose*⊗\|\cr\noalign{\hrule}}
\vskip 3pt
\hbox{*(first quarter only)}}$$
```

 Here is an explanation of this rather long sequence of commands: The control sequence "\|" is defined to be a vertical rule that guarantees appropriate spacing of baselines between individual rows. (TEX doesn't use \baselineskip and \lineskip before or after horizontal rules.) The alignment is defined in such a way that the \tabskip glue is zero at the left and right of the alignment, but it is "0pt plus 100pt" between columns; this glue will therefore expand to make the columns equally spaced. There are seven (not three) columns, since the vertical rules are considered to be columns. The preamble has just "#" for the columns that are to be vertical rules; the "Year" column and "Dividend" column both have format "\hfill#", causing them to be right-justified, while the "Price" column has format "\ctr{#}". The top row of the table appears before the \halign, since it does not have to be aligned with the other rows. In the second row of the table, an extra "\hfill" has been typed after "Year" and "Dividend", to compensate for the fact that the columns are being right-justified yet the titles are supposed to be centered. The special control sequence "\." is also placed around these title words; this is somewhat tricky. It has the effect of telling TEX to ignore the width of the title words when computing the column widths. The asterisk in the final row of the table is preceded by "\spose" in order to make it zero-width, otherwise the decimal points wouldn't line up properly.

 Another way to get vertical and horizontal rules into tables is to typeset without them, then back up (using negative glue) and insert them.

 The control sequence \valign is analogous to \halign, but with rows and columns changing rôles. In this case \cr marks the bottom of a column. The boxes in each row will line up as if their reference points were at the bottom; in other words, their depth is effectively set to zero by modifying their height.

<23> Output routines

We discussed TEX's page-building technique in Chapter 15. Constructed pages will be output directly, if the book design you are using has not specified any special \output routine. But usually a designer will have given special instructions that attach page numbers, headings, and so on. Even the basic format in Appendix B has a simple \output routine, described at the end of Chapter 15.

Complex \output specifications use the most arcane features of TEX, so it usually takes a designer three or four trials before he or she gets them right. Thus, you'll want to skip the rest of this chapter when you're first learning the TEX language. But—like alignments—\output routines soon lose their mystery after you have some experience with them.

When you type "\output{(output list)}", the specified output list is stored away for later use, without expanding any of its defined control sequences. Then, when TEX decides to output a page, the saved output list is effectively inserted into the input, wherever TEX happens to be reading the input at the time. The purpose of the output list is to construct a box from a vertical list, as if one had typed

$$\text{\vbox}\{(\text{output list})\};$$

this box is what gets output. The output routine might, however, produce a null box, if it saves away the current page in order to combine it with a later page.

This would be a good time for you to reread Chapter 15 if you don't recall TEX's mechanism for breaking pages. Since TEX looks ahead for a good place to break— it usually is well into page 109, say, before page 108 is output—some care is needed to synchronize this asynchronous mechanism. For example, if you want to put the current section title at the top of each page, the section title might have changed by the time that page is actually shipped off to the output routine, since TEX might be working on a new section before finding the most desirable break. An \output routine therefore needs some way of remembering past history. Such coordination is provided by so-called *marks*; when you're in vertical mode, you can type "\mark{(mark text)}". This causes the (mark text) to be invisibly attached to your current position in the vertical list that is being broken into pages. If defined control sequences appear in a (mark text), they are expanded at the time the mark appears, so that the \output routine will later be able to make use of values that were current.

The best way to think of this is probably to regard vertical mode as the mode in which you generate an arbitrarily long vertical list of boxes that somehow gets divided up into pages. The long vertical list may contain marks, and whenever you are outputting a page the \output routine will be able to make use of the most recent mark preceding the break at the bottom of the page (\botmark), the most recent mark preceding the break at the top of the page (\topmark), and the first mark on the page (\firstmark). For example, suppose your manuscript includes four instances of \mark, and suppose that the pages get broken in such a way that \mark{α} happens to fall on page 2, \mark{β} and \mark{γ} on page 4, and \mark{δ} on page 5. Then

On page	\topmark is	\firstmark is	\botmark is
1	null	null	null
2	null	α	α
3	α	α	α
4	α	β	γ
5	γ	δ	δ
6	δ	δ	δ

(When there is no mark, all three of these are equal.) The mark concept makes it possible to typeset things like dictionaries, where you want to indicate the current word-interval at the top of each page, if appropriate marks are inserted just before and after the space between entries.

TeX has four control sequences that you are allowed to use only in \output routines: (i) \page, which represents the box containing the current page being output; (ii) \topmark, which represents the top mark for the current page (the corresponding ⟨mark text⟩ is inserted into TeX's input at this point); (iii,iv) \botmark and \firstmark, which are analogous to \topmark. The \output routine should use \page exactly once each time a page is to be output, but it may use \topmark, \botmark, and \firstmark as often as desired.

There are several other control sequences of special interest in connection with output routines, even though they are allowed to appear almost anywhere in a TeX manuscript:

\setcount⟨digit⟩⟨optional sign⟩⟨number⟩ Sets one of ten "counters" to the specified number (possibly negative). For example, "\setcount2 53" sets counter number 2 equal to 53.

\count⟨digit⟩ The current value of the specified "counter" is inserted into the input. If this number is zero, the result is the single digit "0"; if positive, the result is expressed as a decimal integer without leading zeros; if negative, the result is expressed as a roman numeral with lower case letters. (For example, —18 yields "xviii", —19 yields "xix".) As mentioned in Chapter 8, \count⟨digit⟩ can also be used when TeX is expecting a ⟨number⟩; for example, "\setcount4\count2" sets counter number 4 equal to the current contents of counter number 2.

\advcount⟨digit⟩ The specified "counter" is increased by 1 if it is zero or positive, decreased by 1 if it is negative. (Thus, its magnitude increases by 1, but it retains the same sign.)

\ifeven⟨digit⟩{⟨true text⟩}\else{⟨false text⟩} If the specified "counter" is even, the ⟨true text⟩ is input and the ⟨false text⟩ is ignored; if odd, the ⟨true text⟩ is ignored and the ⟨false text⟩ is input.

\if ⟨char₁⟩⟨char₂⟩{⟨true text⟩}\else{⟨false text⟩} If the input ⟨char₁⟩ is equal to the input ⟨char₂⟩, the ⟨true text⟩ is input and the ⟨false text⟩ is ignored; if not, the ⟨true text⟩ is ignored and the ⟨false text⟩ is input.

Typical uses of \if have ⟨char₁⟩ constant, while ⟨char₂⟩ is specified by a control sequence that has been defined elsewhere. For example, you might type

```
\def \firsttime{T}
```

at the beginning of a chapter; then

$$\if T\firsttime\{\gdef\firsttime\{F\}\}\else\{\alpha\}$$

will do α every time except the first, in each chapter. (Note that \gdef must be used here instead of \def, otherwise the new definition of \firsttime would be rescinded immediately!)

Now let's look at some examples. First, suppose you want your output pages to be numbered consecutively, with a number in font c centered at the bottom of each page. Suppose further that you want a running title in font b to be centered at the top of each page, except on the first page of each chapter. Each page (not counting margins) is to be $4\frac{1}{2}$ inches wide and $7\frac{1}{2}$ inches tall; but the pages output by TeX's page builder will have a height of $6\frac{1}{2}$ inches and a maximum depth of $\frac{1}{16}$ inch, so that you can put the running title in a half-inch strip at the top of each page, and you can put the current page number in a $\frac{7}{16}$- to $\frac{1}{2}$-inch strip at the bottom. Let's assume that font z is a big bold font suitable for chapter titles. Then the \output might be designed as follows:

```
\hsize4.5in\vsize6.5in\maxdepth.0625in  % inner page dimensions
\gdef\tpage{F}                   % \tpage will be T for title pages
\def\chapterbegin#1. #2{    % control sequence for new chapters
  \vfill\eject   % finish previous chapter and begin a new page
  \gdef\tpage{T}          % first page of chapter is a title page
  \vskip .5in              % extra space above chapter title
  \ctrline{\:z Chapter #1.}         % first line of title
  \vskip .25in             % extra space between title lines
  \ctrline{\:z #2}                  % second line of title
  \vskip .5in       % space between title and first paragraph
  \mark{#2}       % insert a mark containing the running title
  \noindent         % first paragraph will not be indented
  \tenpoint\!}          % and it will use 10-point type fonts

\output{\vbox to 7.5in{        % begin output of 7.5-inch page
   \baselineskip0pt\lineskip0pt      % turn off interline glue
   \if T\tpage{                      % test if title page
     \gdef\tpage{F}\vskip.5in} % no running head on title page
   \else{\vbox to.15in{\vfill  % fill space above running head
      \hbox to 4.5in{\hfill\:b\topmark\hfill}} % running head
    \vskip .35in} % space between running head and inner page
```

```
\page    % place the compiled inner page just below top strip
\vfill          % space between inner page and page number
\hbox to 4.5in{\hfill\:c\count0\hfill}}        % page number
\advcount0}   % increase page number, end the \output routine
```

With this setup one types, for example, "\chapterbegin 13. {UNLUCKY NUMBERS}" at the beginning of chapter number 13. Appendix E shows how the more elaborate page layout of *The Art of Computer Programming* can be handled.

▶Exercise 23.1: Why is it better for this \output routine to say "\hbox to 4.5in" than to say "\hbox to size"?

▶Exercise 23.2: How would you change the above \output routine so that pages will come out with the top line of non-title pages saying "⟨page number⟩——⟨running title⟩" on even-numbered pages and "⟨running title⟩——⟨page number⟩" on odd-numbered pages? (Leave the page number at the bottom of title pages.)

One more example should suffice to give the flavor of \output routines. Suppose you wish to typeset three-column format: three individual columns 6″ tall by $1\frac{1}{2}″$ wide are to appear on a $7″ \times 5″$ page, with vertical rules between the columns. The page number is to be placed in the upper left corner of even-numbered pages and in the upper right corner of odd-numbered pages. For this application you should use \hsize 1.5in and \vsize 6in; and, say, \maxdepth .2in. (Recall that \maxdepth is the maximum amount by which the depth of the bottom line on a page is allowed to overhang the \vsize.) The \output routine has to save the first two "pages" it receives, then it must spew out three at once. There are at least two ways to do the job:

Solution 1.
```
\output{\outa}
    \def\outa{\output{\outb}\save1\page}
    \def\outb{\output{\outc}\save2\page}
    \def\outc{\output{\outa}
      \vbox to 7in{\baselineskip0pt\lineskip0pt
        \vbox to 10pt{\vfill
          \hbox to 5in{\:b
            \ifeven0{\count0\hfill}\else{\hfill\count0}}}
        \vfill
        \hbox to 5in{\box1\hfill\vrule\hfill\box2
          \hfill\vrule\hfill\page}}
      \advcount0}
```

Solution 2. `\def\firstcol{T}`
```
\output{\if T\firstcol{\gdef\firstcol{F}
    \gdef\secondcol{T}\save1\page}
  \else{\if T\secondcol{\gdef\secondcol{F}
      \save2\page}
    \else{\gdef\firstcol{T}
      \vbox to 7in{...(as before)...}\advcount0}}}
```

Solution 1 is more elegant, but the switching mechanism of Solution 2 can be used in more complicated situations.

<24> Summary of vertical mode

Now here is a complete specification of everything you are allowed to type in vertical mode. This chapter and the following two are intended to be a concise and precise summary of what we have been discussing rather informally. Perhaps it will be a useful reference when you're stuck and wondering what TeX allows you to do.

Chapter 13 explains the general idea of vertical mode and restricted vertical mode. In both cases TeX is scanning a "⟨vlist⟩" and building a vertical list containing boxes and glue; this list might also contain other things like penalty and mark specifications. The vertical list is empty when TeX first enters vertical mode or restricted vertical mode, and it remains empty unless something is appended to it as explained in the rules below. For brevity the rules are stated for vertical mode; the same rules apply to restricted vertical mode unless the contrary is specifically stated.

When TeX is in vertical mode, its next action depends on what it sees next, according to the following possibilities:

- ⟨space⟩   Do nothing.

This notation means: If TeX is in vertical mode and you type a blank space, nothing happens and TeX stays in vertical mode. (The end of a line in an input file counts as a blank space, and so do certain other characters, as explained in Chapter 7.)

- \par   Do nothing.

End of paragraph is ignored in vertical mode. This applies also to the "end of paragraph" signal that TeX digests when you have blank lines in the input or at the end of a file page.

- ⟨unknown control sequence⟩   "! Undefined control sequence."

For example, if you type "\hbx" instead of "\hbox", and if \hbx hasn't been defined, you get an error message showing that \hbx has just been scanned. To recover you can type "i" (for insertion); then (when prompted by "*") type "\hbox" and ⟨carriage-return⟩, and TEX will resume as if the misspelling hadn't occurred.

- ⟨defined control sequence⟩   Macro call.

A control sequence that has been defined with \def or \gdef, for example a control sequence defined in a book format such as Appendix B or Appendix E, followed by its "arguments" (if any), will be replaced in the input as explained in Chapter 20.

- {   Begin a new group.

A new level of nomenclature begins, as explained in Chapter 5; a matching } should appear later. The matching } usually occurs in vertical mode, but it might occur in horizontal mode (in the midst of some paragraph). The beginning of a new group does not affect the current vertical list.

- }   End a group or an operation.

The matching { is identified, and all intervening \defs, \chcodes, \chpars, current font definitions, and glue parameter definitions are forgotten. If the matching { is the beginning of a group, TEX remains in vertical mode and the current vertical list is not affected. Otherwise TEX finishes whatever the { marked the beginning of, or you get an error message. The error messages are "Too many }´s", meaning that there was no matching {; or "Extra }", meaning that an unmatched right brace appears in the ⟨v_n⟩ list of some alignment preamble; or "Missing \cr inserted", meaning that the matching { was in "\valign⟨spec⟩{". In the former cases the } is ignored; in the latter case a \cr is inserted.

- \hrule⟨rule spec⟩   Append a horizontal rule.

The specified horizontal line is appended to the current vertical list. (See Chapter 21 for further details.) TEX remains in vertical mode.

- ⟨box⟩   Append a box.

Here ⟨box⟩ means one of the following:

\hbox⟨spec⟩{⟨hlist⟩}	box formed in restricted horizontal mode
\hbox par ⟨dimen⟩{⟨hlist⟩}	boxed paragraph in restricted horizontal mode
\vbox⟨spec⟩{⟨vlist⟩}	box formed in restricted vertical mode
\box⟨digit⟩	saved box (e.g., \box1 was saved by \save1)
\page	current page (allowed only in output routines)

And ⟨spec⟩ is one of the following:

to ⟨dimen⟩	desired width or height is specified
to size	width \hsize or height \vsize
⟨nothing⟩	use natural width or height
expand ⟨dimen⟩	augment natural width or height

(Chapters 21 and 23 give further details.) The specified box is appended to the current vertical list, with appropriate interline glue depending on \baselineskip and \lineskip inserted just before it, as described in Chapter 15. (After using \box or \page, that \box or \page becomes null, so it can't be used twice.) Then TeX resumes scanning in vertical mode.

- $\left\langle \begin{matrix} \texttt{\textbackslash moveleft} \\ \texttt{\textbackslash moveright} \end{matrix} \right\rangle \langle\text{dimen}\rangle\langle\text{box}\rangle$ Append a shifted box.

The specified box is appended to the current vertical list as described above, but its contents are shifted left or right by the specified amount. (The right edge of the shifted box is used in figuring the maximum width of the box ultimately constructed from the current vertical list; but if the left edge of the appended box extends to the left of the current reference point, it will stick out of the constructed box.)

- \save⟨digit⟩⟨box⟩   Save a box.

The specified box is stored away for possible later use by "\box⟨digit⟩". Then TeX resumes scanning in vertical mode, having made no change to its current vertical list.

- $\left\langle \begin{matrix} \texttt{\textbackslash vfill} \\ \texttt{\textbackslash vskip}\langle\text{glue}\rangle \end{matrix} \right\rangle$ Append glue.

The specified glue is appended to the current vertical list. (See Chapter 12 for details about glue.) TeX remains in vertical mode.

- $\texttt{\textbackslash leaders} \left\langle \begin{matrix} \langle\text{box}\rangle \\ \langle\text{rule}\rangle \end{matrix} \right\rangle \left\langle \begin{matrix} \texttt{\textbackslash vfill} \\ \texttt{\textbackslash vskip}\langle\text{glue}\rangle \end{matrix} \right\rangle$ Append leaders.

The specified leaders are appended to the current vertical list; this will have an effect like the specified glue except that the box or rule will be replicated in the resulting space (see Chapter 21). TeX remains in vertical mode.

- \noindent   Begin nonindented paragraph.

(Not allowed in restricted vertical mode.) The glue currently specified by \parskip is appended to the current vertical list. Then TeX switches from page building to paragraph building by going into horizontal mode: What you type from now on until the next \par will be assembled into a paragraph and appended to the current vertical list.

- $\left\langle \begin{matrix} \langle\text{char}\rangle \\ \langle\text{accent}\rangle \\ \$ \end{matrix} \right\rangle$ Begin indented paragraph.

(Not allowed in restricted vertical mode.) Here ⟨char⟩ stands for either ⟨letter⟩ or ⟨otherchar⟩ or ⟨nonmathletter⟩ or \char⟨number⟩, all of which are defined in Chapter 25. When any of these things occurs in vertical mode, TeX thinks it is time to start a paragraph. The operations described above for \noindent are performed; then an empty box whose width is the current value of \parindent is placed at the beginning of a horizontal list, which will become the next paragraph. Then processing continues as if the ⟨char⟩ or ⟨accent⟩ or $ had appeared in horizontal mode. See Chapter 25 for a description of what happens next. (Note that a paragraph won't start with a box; if you really want to start a paragraph with a box, enclose it in $'s.)

• \penalty⟨number⟩   Append a page break penalty.
(Has no effect in restricted vertical mode.) If the specified number is 1000 or more, page breaking is inhibited here; otherwise this number is added to the badness when deciding whether to break a page at this place. A negative penalty indicates a desirable place to break. (See Chapter 15.) TeX remains in vertical mode.

• \eject   Force a page break.
(Has no effect in restricted vertical mode.) A new page will start at this place in the current vertical list, no matter how "bad" it may be to break a page here. Two consecutive \ejects count as a single one. TeX remains in vertical mode.

• \mark{⟨mark text⟩}   Append a mark.
(Not allowed in restricted vertical mode.) The mark text is attached invisibly to the current vertical list, with its defined control sequences expanded. TeX remains in vertical mode.

• ⟨stored mark⟩   Insert the text of a stored mark.
(Here ⟨stored mark⟩ stands for one of the control sequences \topmark, \botmark, or \firstmark. These are allowed only in \output routines.) TeX inserts the specified mark text into its input; see Chapter 23.

• \x   Extension to TeX.
The control sequence \x allows special actions that might exist in some versions of TeX. (Such extensions are obtained by loading a separately compiled module with the TeX system; individual users might have their own special extension modules.)

• \halign⟨spec⟩{⟨alignment preamble⟩\cr⟨alignment entries⟩}   Append alignment.
A vertical list of aligned rows is constructed as explained in Chapter 22, and this list is appended to the current list. Interline glue will be calculated as if the aligned boxes had been appended one by one in the ordinary way.

• $\left\langle \begin{matrix} \otimes \\ \backslash\mathtt{cr} \end{matrix} \right\rangle$ Spurious alignment delimiter.
The symbols ⊗ and \cr are detected deep inside TeX's scanning mechanism when they occur at the proper nesting level of braces, because they cause TeX to start scanning a "⟨v_j⟩" as explained in Chapter 22. Therefore if these symbols appear in vertical mode, they are ignored, and you get the error message "There's no \halign or \valign going on."

- \ENDV   End of alignment entry.

An \ENDV instruction is inserted automatically by TEX at the end of each "$\langle v_j \rangle$" list of an alignment format. (You can't actually give this control sequence yourself; it only occurs implicitly.) If the alignment entry involves an unmatched {, you get the message "Missing } inserted." Otherwise TEX finishes processing this entry, by \vboxing the current vertical list, and appends the resulting box to the current column of the current \valign. (Interline glue is not used, but \tabskip glue will be inserted.) If the present \ENDV corresponds to an alignment entry that was followed by \cr, TEX looks at the next part of the input as follows: Blank spaces are ignored; "\noalign{⟨hlist⟩}" causes the ⟨hlist⟩ to be processed in restricted horizontal mode, and the resulting horizontal list is appended to the horizontal list of the current \valignment; "}" terminates the \valign; and anything else is assumed to begin the next column of the alignment, so $\langle u_1 \rangle$ is inserted into the input. On the other hand, if this \ENDV corresponds to an entry that was followed by ⊗, TEX inserts $\langle u_{j+1} \rangle$ into the input. In either case TEX remains in restricted vertical mode to process the new alignment entry, beginning with an empty vertical list.

- $\left\langle \begin{matrix} \texttt{\textbackslash topinsert} \\ \texttt{\textbackslash botinsert} \end{matrix} \right\rangle$ {⟨vlist⟩}   Floating insertion of a vertical list.

(Not allowed in restricted vertical mode.) TEX reads the specified ⟨vlist⟩ in restricted vertical mode and constructs the corresponding vertical list. This list will be inserted at the top or bottom of the next page on which it will fit, followed by \topskip glue or preceded by \botskip glue, respectively (see Chapter 15). If possible, two or more inserts will appear on the same page in first-in-first-out order. Note that stretchable or shrinkable glue in the vertical list is not set until the page is finally made up. After the specified list has been constructed and stored in a safe place, TEX resumes vertical mode where it left off.

- $\left\langle \begin{matrix} \texttt{\textbackslash def} \\ \texttt{\textbackslash gdef} \end{matrix} \right\rangle$ ⟨controlseq⟩⟨parameter text⟩{⟨result text⟩}   Define a control sequence.

The specified control sequence is defined as described in Chapter 20. TEX remains in vertical mode, and the current vertical list is not affected. You are not allowed to redefine certain control sequences like \: and \baselineskip, because TEX relies on these to control its operations at critical points. Definitions with \def disappear at the end of the current group; definitions with \gdef do not. It is best not to apply both \def and \gdef to the same control sequence in different parts of a manuscript.

- $\left\langle \begin{matrix} \texttt{\textbackslash :} \\ \texttt{\textbackslash mathex} \end{matrix} \right\rangle$ ⟨font⟩   Define the current font.

The specified font code is selected; "\:" selects the current font to be used in horizontal mode, as explained in Chapter 4, while "\mathex" selects the current ex font to be used in mathematics mode, as explained in Chapter 18. If this code is making its first appearance in the manuscript it must be followed by the font file name (see Chapter 4 and Appendix S) followed by a space. Current font code selections are "local" and will be forgotten at the end of the current group. TEX remains in vertical mode, and the current vertical list is not affected.

- $\left\langle\begin{matrix}\texttt{\textbackslash mathrm}\\\texttt{\textbackslash mathit}\\\texttt{\textbackslash mathsy}\end{matrix}\right\rangle$ ⟨font⟩⟨font⟩⟨font⟩   Define current math fonts.

The specified font codes are selected, providing up to three sizes of characters to be used in math formulas as explained in Chapter 18. If any font code is making its first appearance in the manuscript, it must be followed by the font file name (see Chapter 18 and Appendix S) followed by a space. Current font code selections are "local" and will be forgotten at the end of the current group. TEX remains in vertical mode, and the current vertical list is not affected.

- ⟨dimenparam⟩⟨dimen⟩   Set a dimension parameter.

Here ⟨dimenparam⟩ stands for one of the control sequences \hsize, \vsize, \maxdepth, \parindent, \topbaseline. The corresponding TEX parameter is set equal to the specified dimension; TEX remains in vertical mode, and the current vertical list is not affected. This assignment is "global," in the sense that it holds even after the end of a group. The initial default values of these five parameters are $(324, 504, 3, 0, 10)$ points, respectively.

- ⟨glueparam⟩⟨glue⟩   Define a glue parameter.

Here ⟨glueparam⟩ stands for one of the control sequences \lineskip, \baselineskip, \parskip, \dispskip, \dispaskip, \dispbskip, \topskip, \botskip, \tabskip. The corresponding TEX parameter is set equal to the specified glue; TEX remains in vertical mode, and the current vertical list is not affected. This assignment is "local," it will be forgotten at the end of the current group. The initial value for all these types of glue is zero.

- \chcode⟨number$_1$⟩←⟨number$_2$⟩   Define a character interpretation.

The character whose seven-bit code is ⟨number$_1$⟩ is subsequently treated as being of category ⟨number$_2$⟩, where the category codes are described in Chapter 7. This definition will be local to the current group. TEX remains in vertical mode, and the current vertical list is not affected.

- \chpar⟨number$_1$⟩←⟨number$_2$⟩   Define an integer parameter.

TEX's internal parameter ⟨number$_1$⟩ is set equal to ⟨number$_2$⟩. Here is a table of the internal parameters:

Number	Name	Default value	Reference
0	\trace	′345	Chapter 27
1	\jpar	2	Chapter 14
2	hyphenation	50	Chapter 14
3	doublehyphen	3000	Chapter 14
4	widowline	80	Chapter 15
5	brokenline	50	Chapter 15
6	binopbreak	95	Chapters 14 & 18
7	relbreak	50	Chapters 14 & 18
8	\ragged	0	Chapter 14
9	displaybreak	500	Chapter 15

This definition will be local to the current group. TEX remains in vertical mode, and the current vertical list is not affected.

- \hangindent⟨dimen⟩ $\left\{ \begin{matrix} \text{for } \langle\text{number}\rangle \\ \text{after } \langle\text{number}\rangle \\ \langle\text{nothing}\rangle \end{matrix} \right\}$ Set up hanging indentation.

This instruction causes a specified number of lines of the next paragraph to be indented either at the left margin or the right margin (see Chapter 14). TEX remains in vertical mode, and the current vertical list is not affected.

- \output{⟨vlist⟩}   Set the output routine.

The specified ⟨vlist⟩ is stored for later use when pages are output (see Chapter 23). TEX remains in vertical mode, and the current vertical list is not affected. This assignment is "global," it will hold even after the end of the current group.

- \setcount⟨digit⟩⟨optional sign⟩⟨number⟩   Set a specified counter.

One of ten counters, indicated by the specified digit, is set to the specified integer value (see Chapter 23). This assignment is "global," it is not rescinded at the end of a group. TEX remains in vertical mode, and the current vertical list is not affected.

- \advcount⟨digit⟩   Advance the specified counter.

The magnitude of the specified counter is increased by 1. TEX remains in vertical mode, and the current vertical list is not affected.

- \count⟨digit⟩   Insert the specified counter.

The specified counter is converted to characters (see Chapter 23) and inserted into the input; this will cause TEX to begin a new paragraph as explained earlier.

- $\left\langle \begin{array}{l} \texttt{\textbackslash ifeven}\langle\text{digit}\rangle \\ \texttt{\textbackslash if}\langle\text{char}_1\rangle\langle\text{char}_2\rangle \end{array} \right\rangle \texttt{\{}\langle\text{true text}\rangle\texttt{\}\textbackslash else\{}\langle\text{false text}\rangle\texttt{\}}$ Conditional text.

TEX reads either the true text or the false text, see Chapter 23.

- \input ⟨file name⟩⟨space⟩   Insert a file of text.

The specified file of characters is inserted into the input at this place. After the file has been read, TEX will resume input at the present position (unless \end occurred in that file).

- \end   Stop.

(Not allowed in restricted vertical mode.)   The current page is ejected, followed if necessary by pages containing leftover material, until there is nothing more to eject. Then if the last call on the output routine produced only a null box—for example, two out of three calls on the output routines at the end of Chapter 23 will do this—a page containing an empty box of size \hsize × \vsize is sent to the output routine, until either getting a nonnull output or until 25 consecutive null outputs have appeared. Then TEX terminates: the output files are tidied up, and a friendly warning message is issued if there is an unmatched "{" still waiting for its "}".

- \ddt   Print debugging data.

If bit 4 of the \trace parameter is 1, TEX prints out its current activities (the lists and pages it is currently building). Furthermore if bit ´40 of the \trace parameter is 1, TEX will stop, giving you the chance to insert text on-line. TEX remains in vertical mode, and the current vertical list is not affected.

- ⟨anything else⟩   "! You can't do that in vertical mode."

If anything not listed above appears in vertical mode, you get an error message. TEX ignores the token of input that broke the rules, and remains in vertical mode; the current vertical list is not affected.

<25> Summary of horizontal mode

Here is a complete specification of everything you are allowed to type in horizontal mode. This chapter and the adjacent two are intended to be a concise and precise summary of what we have been discussing rather informally. Perhaps it will be a useful reference when you're stuck and wondering what TEX allows you to do.

Chapter 13 explains the general idea of horizontal mode and restricted horizontal mode. In both cases TEX is scanning an "⟨hlist⟩" and building a horizontal list containing boxes and glue; this list might also contain other things like penalty and insertion specifications. The horizontal list is empty when TEX first enters horizontal mode or restricted horizontal mode, and it remains empty unless something is appended to it as explained in the rules below. For brevity the rules are stated for horizontal mode; the same rules apply to restricted horizontal mode unless the contrary is specifically stated.

When TEX is in horizontal mode, its next action depends on what it sees next, according to the following possibilities:

• ⟨unknown control sequence⟩   "! Undefined control sequence."

For example, if you type "r\Aole" instead of "r\A ole", and if \Aole hasn't been defined, you get an error message showing that \Aole has just been scanned. To recover you can type "i" (for insertion); then (when prompted by "*") type "\A ole" and ⟨carriage-return⟩, and TEX will resume as if the mistake hadn't occurred.

• ⟨defined control sequence⟩   Macro call.

A control sequence that has been defined with \def or \gdef, for example a control sequence defined in a book format such as Appendix B or Appendix E, followed by its "arguments" (if any), will be replaced in the input as explained in Chapter 20.

• {   Begin a new group.

A new level of nomenclature begins, as explained in Chapter 5; a matching } should appear later. The matching } usually occurs in horizontal mode, but it might occur in vertical mode (after the end of some paragraph). The beginning of a new group does not affect the current horizontal list.

• }   End a group or an operation.

The matching { is identified, and all intervening \defs, \chcodes, \chpars, font definitions, and glue parameter definitions are forgotten. If the matching { is the beginning of a group, TEX remains in horizontal mode and the current horizontal list is not affected. Otherwise TEX finishes whatever the { marked the beginning of, or you get an error message. The error messages are "Too many }'s", meaning that there was no matching {; or "Extra }", meaning that an unmatched right brace appears in the ⟨v_n⟩ list of some alignment preamble; or "Missing \cr inserted", meaning that the matching { was in "\halign⟨spec⟩{". In the former cases the } is ignored; in the latter case a \cr is inserted.

•
⟨ ⟨letter⟩
  ⟨nonmathletter⟩ ⟩   Append a character box.
  ⟨otherchar⟩

Here ⟨letter⟩ normally means any of the characters A...Z and a...z, and ⟨otherchar⟩ normally stands for any other character that has not been given a special meaning like the special meanings often assigned to $ and @ and ⟨carriage-return⟩, etc. However, \chcode can be used to reclassify any character, as explained in Chapter 7. A ⟨nonmathletter⟩ is one of the control sequences \ss, \ae, \AE, \oe, \OE, \o, \O, mentioned in Chapter 9. Each character has an associated 7-bit code that is used to select one of 128 characters from the current font. (If no current font has been defined, you lose: TEX will come to a grinding halt.) Information stored with the current font is now examined to see whether or not this character is the first of a ligature or kerned pair. If so, TEX looks at the next character; when a ligature is completed, the two characters are replaced by a new character (as specified in the font) and this new character might in turn be the first of another ligature or kerned pair. In any event, a character box is appended to the current horizontal list; and if a kerned pair is found, appropriate negative glue is appended next, in such a way that the line-breaking and hyphenation algorithms will not be confused. Furthermore if the character code is ´055 (the code for "–") or if a ligature ends with this particular code, a "\penalty.0" is automatically appended to the horizontal list. TEX remains in horizontal mode.

• \char⟨number⟩   Append a character box.

The ⟨number⟩ is reduced modulo 128, and TEX proceeds just as if an ⟨otherchar⟩ had just been scanned having this 7-bit code.

• ⟨accent⟩⟨accentee⟩   Append an accented character.

Here ⟨accent⟩ stands for one of the control sequences \`, \´, \A, \v, \u, \=, \", \H, \b, \s, \t, \a, \l, \c, discussed in Chapter 9, or for "\accent⟨number⟩"; and ⟨accentee⟩ stands for either ⟨letter⟩ or ⟨nonmathletter⟩ or ⟨otherchar⟩ or \char⟨number⟩, possibly preceded by a new font definition "\:⟨font⟩". The accent and accentee are made into character boxes, and the accent is superimposed on the accentee, moving the accent left or right if necessary so that it is centered (also taking into account the slantedness of the characters and their heights, based on information stored with the fonts). Furthermore the accent is raised or lowered in case the height of the accentee is different from the "xheight" of the accent's font (the height of lower case "x"). The width of the resulting box is the width of the accentee; this box is appended to the current horizontal list, and TEX remains in horizontal mode.

• ⟨⟨space⟩ / \⊔⟩   Append variable space glue.

Here ⟨space⟩ means either an explicit typed space or an implicit one obtained at the end of a typed line. (Consecutive spaces are treated as single spaces, and spaces are sometimes ignored, as explained in Chapter 7.) The current font specifies what sort of glue should be inserted between words of a paragraph when they are typeset in that font. The stretchability and shrinkability of this glue is modified by the "space factor," as explained in Chapter 12, except that no modification is made when "\⊔" has been typed. TEX appends the glue to its current horizontal list and remains in horizontal mode.

• \quad   Append one quad of space.

Space glue amounting to one quad in the current font is appended to the current horizontal list. TEX remains in horizontal mode.

- `\!`   Ignore space.

TEX looks at the next token of the input (expanding it if is a defined control sequence), and discards it if it is a ⟨space⟩. The current horizontal list is not affected, and TEX remains in horizontal mode.

- `\-`   Append discretionary hyphen.

A "discretionary" hyphen is appended to the current horizontal list. This means that the current place is a legal place to break a line, with a specified penalty for hyphenation (see Chapter 14). If the line actually breaks here, character number ´055 from the current font is inserted into the text, otherwise nothing is inserted. TEX remains in horizontal mode.

- `\/`   Append italic correction.

If the final entry on the current horizontal list is not a character box, you get an error message

        ! Italic correction must follow an explicit character.

Otherwise an empty box whose width is the italic correction for the corresponding character is appended to the current horizontal list. (This information is stored in the font with each character, except in "ex fonts"; don't try to use italic correction with a character from an ex font.) TEX remains in horizontal mode.

- `\vrule`⟨rule spec⟩   Append a vertical rule.

The specified vertical line is appended to the current horizontal list. (See Chapter 21 for further details.) TEX remains in horizontal mode.

- ⟨box⟩   Append a box.

Here ⟨box⟩ means one of the following:

`\hbox`⟨spec⟩`{`⟨hlist⟩`}`	box formed in restricted horizontal mode
`\hbox par` ⟨dimen⟩`{`⟨hlist⟩`}`	boxed paragraph in restricted horizontal mode
`\vbox`⟨spec⟩`{`⟨vlist⟩`}`	box formed in restricted vertical mode
`\box`⟨digit⟩	saved box (e.g., `\box1` was saved by `\save1`)
`\page`	current page (allowed only in output routines)

And ⟨spec⟩ is one of the following:

`to` ⟨dimen⟩	desired width or height is specified
`to size`	width `\hsize` or height `\vsize`
⟨nothing⟩	use natural width or height
`expand` ⟨dimen⟩	augment natural width or height

(Chapters 21 and 23 give further details.) The specified box is appended to the current horizontal list, and TEX resumes scanning in horizontal mode. (After using `\box` or `\page`, that `\box` or `\page` becomes null, so it can't be used twice.)

- $\left\langle \begin{matrix} \texttt{\textbackslash raise} \\ \texttt{\textbackslash lower} \end{matrix} \right\rangle \langle\text{dimen}\rangle\langle\text{box}\rangle$ Append a shifted box.

The specified box is appended to the current horizontal list as described above, but its contents are shifted up or down by the specified amount. (The top and bottom edges of the shifted box are used to compute the height and depth of the box ultimately constructed from the current horizontal list, as explained in Chapter 21.)

- $\texttt{\textbackslash save}\langle\text{digit}\rangle\langle\text{box}\rangle$ Save a box.

The specified box is stored away for possible later use by "$\texttt{\textbackslash box}\langle\text{digit}\rangle$". Then TEX resumes scanning in horizontal mode, having done nothing to its current horizontal list.

- $\left\langle \begin{matrix} \texttt{\textbackslash hfill} \\ \texttt{\textbackslash hskip}\langle\text{glue}\rangle \end{matrix} \right\rangle$ Append glue.

The specified glue is appended to the current horizontal list. (See Chapter 12 for details about glue.) TEX remains in horizontal mode.

- $\texttt{\textbackslash leaders}\left\langle \begin{matrix} \langle\text{box}\rangle \\ \langle\text{rule}\rangle \end{matrix} \right\rangle \left\langle \begin{matrix} \texttt{\textbackslash hfill} \\ \texttt{\textbackslash hskip}\langle\text{glue}\rangle \end{matrix} \right\rangle$ Append leaders.

The specified leaders are appended to the current horizontal list; this will have an effect like the specified glue except that the box or rule will be replicated in the resulting space (see Chapter 21). TEX remains in horizontal mode.

- $\texttt{\$}\langle\text{formula}\rangle\texttt{\$}$ Append a math formula.

The specified ⟨formula⟩ is scanned in math mode, as explained in Chapter 26. This results in a horizontal list, which is appended to the current horizontal list. Then TEX resumes scanning in horizontal mode. Mathematics fonts (the so-called rm and it and sy and ex fonts) must have been defined earlier.

- $\texttt{\textbackslash par}$ End of paragraph.

(Ignored in restricted horizontal mode.) If the current horizontal list is empty, nothing happens. Otherwise the current horizontal list is "justified" using TEX's line-breaking routine described in Chapter 14; the resulting vertical list is appended to the current vertical list of the page-builder, and TEX continues in vertical mode as described in Chapter 24.

- $\texttt{\$\$}\langle\text{display}\rangle\texttt{\$\$}$ Interrupt paragraph for display.

(Not allowed in restricted horizontal mode.) The current horizontal list is converted to a vertical list just as if a paragraph had ended, except that hanging indentation is not reset. Then the ⟨display⟩ is processed, as explained in Chapter 26, resulting in another vertical list that is given to the page-builder. (A displayed formula counts as either two or three lines, with respect to the line count in hanging indentation, depending on whether $\texttt{\textbackslash dispaskip}$ or $\texttt{\textbackslash dispskip}$ glue is appended above the formula, cf. Chapter 19.) Then TEX returns to horizontal mode, ignoring a space if it follows the closing "$$". At this point TEX's current horizontal list will be empty, so the paragraph will continue without indentation. Mathematics fonts (the so-called rm and it and sy and ex fonts) must have been defined earlier.

- \penalty⟨number⟩   Append a line break penalty.

If the specified number is 1000 or more, line breaking is inhibited here; otherwise this number is added to the badness when deciding whether to break a line at this place. A negative penalty indicates a desirable place to break. (See Chapter 15.) TEX remains in horizontal mode.

- \eject   Force a page and line break.

(Forces only a line break when in restricted horizontal mode.) A new line will start at this place in the current horizontal list, and a new page will start with this new line when it is appended to the page builder's current vertical list, no matter how "bad" it may be to break a page or line here. (See the discussion in Chapter 14.) TEX remains in horizontal mode.

- ⟨stored mark⟩   Insert the text of a stored mark.

(Here ⟨stored mark⟩ stands for one of the control sequences \topmark, \botmark, or \firstmark. These are allowed only in \output routines.) TEX inserts the specified mark text into its input; see Chapter 23.

- \x   Extension to TEX.

The control sequence \x allows special actions that might exist in some versions of TEX. (Such extensions are obtained by loading a separately compiled module with the TEX system; individual users might have their own special extension modules.)

- \valign⟨spec⟩{⟨alignment preamble⟩\cr⟨alignment entries⟩}   Append alignment.

A horizontal list of aligned columns is constructed as explained in Chapter 22, and this list is appended to the current horizontal list. Then TEX resumes scanning in horizontal mode.

- $\left\langle \begin{matrix} \otimes \\ \backslash\text{cr} \end{matrix} \right\rangle$ Spurious alignment delimiter.

The symbols ⊗ and \cr are detected deep inside TEX's scanning mechanism when they occur at the proper nesting level of braces, because they cause TEX to start scanning a "⟨v_j⟩" as explained in Chapter 22. Therefore if these symbols appear in horizontal mode, they are ignored, and you get the error message "There's no \halign or \valign going on."

- \ENDV   End of alignment entry.

An \ENDV instruction is inserted automatically by TEX at the end of each "⟨v_j⟩" list of an alignment format. (You can't actually give this control sequence yourself; it only occurs implicitly.) If the alignment entry involves an unmatched {, you get the message "Missing } inserted." Otherwise TEX finishes processing this entry, by \hboxing the current horizontal list, and appends the resulting box to the current row of the current \halign. (The \tabskip glue will also be inserted.) If the present \ENDV corresponds to an alignment entry that was followed by \cr, TEX looks at the next part of the input as follows: Blank spaces are ignored; "\noalign{⟨vlist⟩}" causes the ⟨vlist⟩ to be processed in restricted vertical mode, and the resulting vertical list is appended to the vertical list of the current \halignment; "}" terminates the \halign; and anything else is assumed to begin the next row of the alignment, so ⟨u₁⟩ is inserted into the input. On the other hand, if this \ENDV corresponds to an entry that was followed by ⊗, TEX inserts ⟨u_{j+1}⟩ into the input. In either case TEX remains in restricted horizontal mode to process the new alignment entry, beginning with an empty horizontal list.

- $\left\langle {\tt \backslash topinsert} \atop {\tt \backslash botinsert} \right\rangle${⟨vlist⟩}   Bound insertion of a vertical list.

(Not allowed in restricted horizontal mode.) TEX reads the specified ⟨vlist⟩ in restricted vertical mode and constructs the corresponding vertical list. This list will be inserted at the top or bottom of the same page on which the line containing the present place in the current horizontal list, followed by \topskip glue or preceded by \botskip glue, respectively. (See Chapter 15; this mechanism is intended primarily to accommodate illustrations and footnotes.) If necessary, two or more inserts will appear on the same page in first-in-first-out order. Note that stretchable or shrinkable glue in the vertical list is not set until the page is finally made up. After the specified list has been constructed and stored in a safe place, TEX resumes horizontal mode where it left off.

- $\left\langle {\tt \backslash def} \atop {\tt \backslash gdef} \right\rangle$ ⟨controlseq⟩⟨parameter text⟩{⟨result text⟩}   Define a control sequence.

The specified control sequence is defined as described in Chapter 20. A ⟨space⟩ following the definition will be ignored. TEX remains in horizontal mode, and the current horizontal list is not affected. You are not allowed to redefine certain control sequences like \: and \baselineskip, because TEX relies on these to control its operations at critical points. Definitions with \def disappear at the end of the current group; definitions with \gdef do not. It is best not to apply both \def and \gdef to the same control sequence in different parts of a manuscript.

- $\left\langle {\tt \backslash :} \atop {\tt \backslash mathex} \right\rangle$⟨font⟩   Define the current font.

The specified font code is selected; "\:" selects the current font to be used in horizontal mode, as explained in Chapter 4, while "\mathex" selects the current ex font to be used in mathematics mode, as explained in Chapter 18. If this code is making its first appearance in the manuscript it must be followed by the font file name (see Chapter 4 and Appendix S) followed by a space. Current font code selections are "local" and will be forgotten at the end of the current group. TEX remains in horizontal mode, and the current horizontal list is not affected.

- $\left\{\begin{array}{c}\backslash\text{mathrm}\\\backslash\text{mathit}\\\backslash\text{mathsy}\end{array}\right\}$⟨font⟩⟨font⟩⟨font⟩   Define current math fonts.

The specified font codes are selected, providing up to three sizes of characters to be used in math formulas as explained in Chapter 18. If any font code is making its first appearance in the manuscript, it must be followed by the font file name (see Chapter 18 and Appendix S) followed by a space. Current font code selections are "local" and will be forgotten at the end of the current group. TEX remains in horizontal mode, and the current horizontal list is not affected.

- ⟨dimenparam⟩⟨dimen⟩   Set a dimension parameter.

Here ⟨dimenparam⟩ stands for one of the control sequences \hsize, \vsize, \maxdepth, \parindent, \topbaseline. The corresponding TEX parameter is set equal to the specified dimension; TEX remains in horizontal mode, and the current horizontal list is not affected. This assignment is "global," in the sense that it holds even after the end of a group. The initial default values of these five parameters are $(324, 504, 3, 0, 10)$ points, respectively.

- ⟨glueparam⟩⟨glue⟩   Define a glue parameter.

Here ⟨glueparam⟩ stands for one of the control sequences \lineskip, \baselineskip, \parskip, \dispskip, \dispaskip, \dispbskip, \topskip, \botskip, \tabskip. The corresponding TEX parameter is set equal to the specified glue; TEX remains in horizontal mode, and the current horizontal list is not affected. This assignment is "local," it will be forgotten at the end of the current group. The initial value for all these types of glue is zero.

- \chcode⟨number$_1$⟩←⟨number$_2$⟩   Define a character interpretation.

The character whose seven-bit code is ⟨number$_1$⟩ is subsequently treated as being of category ⟨number$_2$⟩, where the category codes are described in Chapter 7. This definition will be local to the current group. TEX remains in horizontal mode, and the current horizontal list is not affected.

- \chpar⟨number$_1$⟩←⟨number$_2$⟩   Define an integer parameter.

TEX's internal parameter ⟨number$_1$⟩ is set equal to ⟨number$_2$⟩. Here is a table of the internal parameters:

Number	Name	Default value	Reference
0	\trace	´345	Chapter 27
1	\jpar	2	Chapter 14
2	hyphenation	50	Chapter 14
3	doublehyphen	3000	Chapter 14
4	widowline	80	Chapter 15
5	brokenline	50	Chapter 15
6	binopbreak	95	Chapters 14 & 18
7	relbreak	50	Chapters 14 & 18
8	\ragged	0	Chapter 14
9	displaybreak	500	Chapter 15

This definition will be local to the current group. TEX remains in horizontal mode, and the current horizontal list is not affected.

- \hangindent⟨dimen⟩$\left\{ \begin{array}{l} \text{for } \langle\text{number}\rangle \\ \text{after } \langle\text{number}\rangle \\ \langle\text{nothing}\rangle \end{array} \right\}$ Set up hanging indentation.

This instruction causes a specified number of lines of the next paragraph to be indented either at the left margin or the right margin (see Chapter 14). In restricted horizontal mode, this applies only to the paragraph being boxed, if any. TEX remains in horizontal mode, and the current horizontal list is not affected.

- \output{⟨vlist⟩}⟨optional space⟩   Set the output routine.

The specified ⟨vlist⟩ is stored for later use when pages are output (see Chapter 23). TEX remains in horizontal mode, and the current horizontal list is not affected. This assignment is "global," it will hold even after the end of the current group.

- \setcount⟨digit⟩⟨optional sign⟩⟨number⟩   Set a specified counter.

One of ten counters, indicated by the specified digit, is set to the specified integer value (see Chapter 23). This assignment is "global," it is not rescinded at the end of a group. TEX remains in horizontal mode, and the current horizontal list is not affected.

- \advcount⟨digit⟩   Advance the specified counter.

The magnitude of the specified counter is increased by 1. TEX remains in horizontal mode, and the current horizontal list is not affected.

- \count⟨digit⟩   Insert the specified counter.

The specified counter is converted to characters (see Chapter 23) and inserted into the input; TEX will read it in horizontal mode.

- $\left\langle \begin{array}{l} \texttt{\textbackslash ifeven}\langle\text{digit}\rangle \\ \texttt{\textbackslash if}\langle\text{char}_1\rangle\langle\text{char}_2\rangle \end{array} \right\rangle \texttt{\{}\langle\text{true text}\rangle\texttt{\}\textbackslash else\{}\langle\text{false text}\rangle\texttt{\}}$ Conditional text.

TEX reads either the true text or the false text, see Chapter 23. Spaces following the "{⟨true text⟩}" and "{⟨false text⟩}" are ignored.

- `\ddt`   Print debugging data.

If bit 4 of the `\trace` parameter is 1, TEX prints out its current activities (the lists and pages it is currently building). Furthermore if bit ´40 of the `\trace` parameter is 1, TEX will stop, giving you the chance to insert text on-line. TEX remains in horizontal mode, and the current horizontal list is not affected.

- ⟨anything else⟩   "`! You can't do that in horizontal mode.`"

If anything not listed above appears in horizontal mode, you get an error message. TEX ignores the token of input that broke the rules, and remains in horizontal mode; the current horizontal list is not affected.

<26> Summary of math mode

Here is a complete specification of everything you are allowed to type in math mode or display math mode. This chapter and the previous two are intended to be a concise and precise summary of what we have been discussing rather informally. Perhaps it will be a useful reference when you're stuck and wondering what TEX allows you to do.

Chapter 13 explains the general idea of math mode and display math mode. In both cases TEX is scanning an "⟨mlist⟩" and building a horizontal list containing boxes, glue, and line-breaking information. The ⟨mlist⟩ is called a ⟨display⟩ if it is scanned in display math mode, a ⟨formula⟩ if scanned in ordinary math mode. Mathematics processing actually takes place in two stages: first the entire formula (up to the end of math mode) is input and made into a "tree structure," then this tree is converted into the desired horizontal list. The reason for doing the job in two steps is that TEX's language makes it impossible in general to determine the style for setting formulas as the formulas are being read in (e.g., a subsequent "`\over`" might change everything). It is convenient, however, to describe the rules below as if TEX had clairvoyance, knowing what style to use as it reads the input. Please keep in mind that the correct style will be chosen for subformulas, according to the rules in Chapters 17 and 18, even though the following description makes that seem somewhat miraculous. For brevity the rules below are stated for math mode; the same rules apply to display math mode unless the contrary is specifically stated.

When TEX is in math mode, its next action depends on what it sees next, according to the following possibilities:

- ⟨space⟩   Do nothing.

This notation means: If TEX is in math mode and you type a blank space, nothing happens and TEX stays in math mode. (The end of a line in an input file counts as a blank space, and so do certain other characters, as explained in Chapter 7.)

- ⟨unknown control sequence⟩   "! Undefined control sequence."

For example, if you type "\alfa" instead of "\alpha", and if \alfa hasn't been defined, you get an error message showing that \alfa has just been scanned. To recover you can type "i" (for insertion); then (when prompted by "*") type "\alpha" and ⟨carriage-return⟩, and TEX will resume as if the mistake hadn't occurred.

- ⟨defined control sequence⟩   Macro call.

A control sequence that has been defined with \def or \gdef, for example a control sequence defined in a book format such as Appendix B or Appendix E, followed by its "arguments" (if any), will be replaced in the input as explained in Chapter 20.

- {⟨mlist⟩}   Append a subformula.

The ⟨mlist⟩ is processed in math mode and \hboxed into a box having its natural width. This box is then appended to the current list as an "Ord" box. Definitions inside the subformula are forgotten afterwards.

- \left⟨delim⟩⟨mlist⟩\right⟨delim⟩ Append a subformula with variable delimiters. The ⟨mlist⟩ is processed in math mode, and surrounded by delimiters of sufficient size to contain it, as explained in Chapter 18. The resulting list is \hboxed and appended to the current list as an "Ord" box. Definitions inside the subformula are forgotten afterwards.

- }   "Extra }."

The matching {, if any, lies outside the $ or \left that precedes the current ⟨mlist⟩, so an error message is issued and the } is ignored.

- \right   "Extra \right." or "Missing } inserted."

The matching \left, if any, lies outside the $ or { that preceded the current ⟨mlist⟩, so an error message is issued. TEX automatically inserts a "}" if it appears to be missing.

- $ "Missing \right. inserted." or "Missing } inserted."

The matching $, if any, lies outside the \left or { that preceded the current ⟨mlist⟩, so an error message is issued and TEX automatically inserts what it assumes was missing.

- $\left\langle \begin{matrix} \langle \text{letter} \rangle \\ \langle \text{mathchar} \rangle \\ \langle \text{otherchar} \rangle \end{matrix} \right\rangle$ Append a character box.

Here ⟨letter⟩ normally means any of the characters A...Z and a...z, and ⟨otherchar⟩ normally stands for any other character that has not been given a special meaning like the special meanings often assigned to $ and ⊗ and ⟨carriage-return⟩, etc. However, \chcode can be used to reclassify any character, as explained in Chapter 7. A ⟨mathchar⟩ is one of the many control sequences \alpha, \beta, etc. listed in Appendix F. Each ⟨mathchar⟩ has an associated 9-bit code that is used to select one of 512 characters from TEX's current math fonts in the desired size; each ⟨letter⟩ and ⟨otherchar⟩ also has an associated 9-bit code, determined from its 7-bit code by using a table in Appendix F. Each character also has an associated category (Ord or Op or Bin, etc.), as explained in Chapter 18 and Appendix F; these categories are used to determine spacing and line-breaking. The character box is appended to the current list and TEX continues scanning in math mode. (Note: The italic correction is included when computing the width of this box. However, it will be removed by TEX if this box has a subscript but no superscript; thus, subscripts will be closer to letters like "*P*". The spacing on TEX's math fonts is intended to make formulas look right when typeset by TEX's rules, so it is quite different from spacing that makes text look right; cf. the examples of fonts cmi10 and cmti10 in Chapter 18.)

- \char⟨number⟩   Append a character box.

The ⟨number⟩ is reduced modulo 512, and TEX proceeds just as if a ⟨mathchar⟩ of category Ord has just been scanned having this 9-bit code.

- ↑⟨atom⟩   Superscript the previous box.

(Here and in two rules that follow, an ⟨atom⟩ is either a single character (i.e., ⟨letter⟩ or ⟨mathchar⟩ or ⟨otherchar⟩ or \char⟨number⟩) or a subformula of the form "{⟨mlist⟩}". Atoms may be regarded as rigid boxes that will be combined to build up larger formulas.) If the last element of the current list is not a box, append a null box. Otherwise if the last box of the current list has already been superscripted, report a "Double superscript" error. Attach the box corresponding to the ⟨atom⟩ as the superscript of the last box of the current list.

- ↓⟨atom⟩   Subscript the previous box.

Subscripting is entirely analogous to superscripting.

- ⟨ ⟨mathcontrol⟩ / ⟨accent⟩ ⟩⟨atom⟩   Build up a formula.

Here ⟨mathcontrol⟩ stands for one of the nine control sequences \sqrt, \underline, \overline, \mathop, \mathbin, \mathrel, \mathopen, \mathclose, \mathpunct; and ⟨accent⟩ stands for one of the control sequences \`, \´, \A, \v, \u, \=, \", \H, \b, \s, \t, \a, \l, \c, discussed in Chapter 9, or for "\accent⟨number⟩". (The ⟨number⟩ in the latter case is reduced modulo 512.) Each of these does something to the box formed from the ⟨atom⟩: \sqrt inserts a variable-size radical sign in front of the box and a line over the box (and a little blank space above that line); \underline and \overline insert a line and a little blank space under or over the box; the control sequences \mathop, ..., \mathpunct are simply used to classify the box as type Op,

..., Punct, respectively; and an accent is centered over the box. (Accents in horizontal mode are corrected for slant, but in math mode they are simply centered; in both cases they are raised or lowered by the same amount when applied to the same letter.) The box resulting from the specified operation is appended to the current list, and TₑX continues in math mode.

- ⟨mathglue⟩   Append glue based on the current style.

Here ⟨mathglue⟩ means one of the control sequences \ , , \⊔, \>, \;, \quad, \≥, \!, \?, \<, \≤, described in Chapter 18. The corresponding glue is appended to the current list, and TₑX continues in math mode.

- $\left\langle \begin{array}{l} \texttt{\textbackslash hfill} \\ \texttt{\textbackslash hskip}\langle\text{glue}\rangle \end{array} \right\rangle$ Append explicit glue.

The specified glue is appended to the current list. (See Chapter 12 for details about glue, and see Chapter 17 for an example of \hfill used in the numerator of a formula.) TₑX remains in math mode.

- ⟨box⟩   Append a box.

Here ⟨box⟩ means one of the following:

\hbox⟨spec⟩{⟨hlist⟩}	box formed in restricted horizontal mode
\hbox par ⟨dimen⟩{⟨hlist⟩}	boxed paragraph in restricted horizontal mode
\vbox⟨spec⟩{⟨vlist⟩}	box formed in restricted vertical mode
\box⟨digit⟩	saved box (e.g., \box1 was saved by \save1)
\page	current page (allowed only in output routines)

And ⟨spec⟩ is one of the following:

to ⟨dimen⟩	desired width or height is specified
to size	width \hsize or height \vsize
⟨nothing⟩	use natural width or height
expand ⟨dimen⟩	augment natural width or height

(Chapters 21 and 23 give further details.) The specified box is appended to the current list as an Ord box, and TₑX resumes scanning in math mode. (After using \box or \page, that \box or \page becomes null, so it can't be used twice.)

- $\left\langle \begin{array}{l} \texttt{\textbackslash raise} \\ \texttt{\textbackslash lower} \end{array} \right\rangle$⟨dimen⟩⟨box⟩   Append a shifted box.

The specified box is appended to the current list as described above, but its contents are shifted up or down by the specified amount.

- \save⟨digit⟩⟨box⟩   Save a box.

The specified box is stored away for possible later use by "\box⟨digit⟩". Then TₑX resumes scanning in math mode, having made no change to its current list.

- `\*`   Append discretionary times sign.

A "discretionary" $\times$ is appended to the current list. This means that the current place is a legal place to break a line, with a specified penalty for hyphenation (see Chapter 14). If the line actually breaks here, character number ´402 from the current font is inserted into the text; otherwise nothing is inserted. TeX remains in math mode.

- `\limitswitch`   Change convention on displayed limits.

(Allowed only when the last item in the current list is an Op box; has an effect only when setting a formula in display style.) TeX's normal convention for typesetting the "limits" (i.e., the superscript and subscript) of an operator in display style is to center them above and below the Op box—unless that Op box is a single character in the current ex font having a nonzero "italic correction" in the font; in the latter case the subscripts and superscripts are normally set to the right as usual. But `\limitswitch` has the effect of reversing these conventions on the current operator: centering changes to placement at the right and vice versa. TeX remains in math mode.

- $\left\langle \begin{matrix} \texttt{\textbackslash over} \\ \texttt{\textbackslash above}\langle\texttt{dimen}\rangle \\ \texttt{\textbackslash atop} \end{matrix} \right\rangle$ Separate numerator from denominator.

If a numerator has previously been set aside for the current formula, give an error message

                  `! Ambiguous; you need another { and }.`

and ignore the input. Otherwise the current list is set aside to be the numerator, and the list after this point until the end of the formula will be the denominator. Afterwards the numerator will be centered over the denominator, essentially by inserting the glue "`\hskip 0pt plus 100000pt`" at the left and right of whichever one has less natural width and `\hbox`ing it to the width of the other. The fraction line inserted between them will be at the height of the "axis" of the overall formula (a position specified in the sy font of the appropriate size). The current ex font specifies a "default rule thickness" to be used for the ruled lines in `\sqrt`, `\underline`, and `\overline`; this same thickness is used for the fraction line in `\over`, while `\above` lets you specify any desired thickness. (See the examples in Chapter 17.) The thickness is zero for `\atop`, i.e., there is no fraction line at all; in this case, the positioning of numerator and denominator is somewhat different in order to take advantage of the extra flexibility. A little extra space is attached to the left and right of the formula after the numerator and denominator have been pasted together.

- `\comb`⟨delim⟩⟨delim⟩   Build a combinatorial formula.

This is like `\atop`, except that the specified delimiters are placed at the left and right of the formula after the numerator and denominator have been positioned. (In fact, "`\atop`" is precisely equivalent to "`\comb..`".) TeX chooses the size of the delimiters based only on the current style, regardless of the sizes of numerator and denominator.

- $\left\langle \begin{array}{c} \verb|\vcenter| \\ \verb|\vtop| \end{array} \right\rangle$ Append a centered or top-adjusted box.

The specified vertical list is constructed in restricted vertical mode, then it is \vboxed and the resulting box is moved up or down so that (\vcenter) it is centered vertically just as large delimiters are, or (\vtop) the baseline of the topmost box in the vertical list coincides with the baseline of the formula. Then TEX resumes its activities in math mode.

- \penalty⟨number⟩   Append a line break penalty.

(This has no effect in a subformula or a displayed formula.) If the specified number is 1000 or more, line breaking is inhibited here; otherwise this number is added to the badness when deciding whether to break a line at this place. A negative penalty indicates a desirable place to break. (See Chapter 15.) If this penalty is specified immediately following a Bin or Rel box, it overrides the penalty ordinarily placed there (see Chapter 18). TEX remains in math mode.

- \eject   Force a page and line break.

(This has no effect in a subformula or a displayed formula.) A new line will start at this place in the current horizontal list, and a new page will start with this new line when it is appended to the page builder's current vertical list, no matter how "bad" it may be to break a page or line here. (See the discussion in Chapter 14.) TEX remains in math mode.

- ⟨mathstyle⟩   Define the current style.

Here ⟨mathstyle⟩ stands for one of the control sequences \dispstyle, \textstyle, \scriptstyle, \scriptscriptstyle discussed in Chapter 17. The specified style will apply from this point on, until it is redefined or until the end of the current formula or subformula. TEX remains in math mode.

- \eqno   Separate a display from its equation number.

(Allowed only in display math mode.) The current list is converted to a displayed formula and saved away in a safe place; TEX now switches to non-display math mode. The subsequent ⟨mlist⟩ will become an equation number, placed at the right of the display as explained in Chapter 19.

- \x   Extension to TEX.

The control sequence \x allows special actions that might exist in some versions of TEX. (Such extensions are obtained by loading a separately compiled module with the TEX system; individual users might have their own special extension modules.)

- ⟨stored mark⟩   Insert the text of a stored mark.

(Here ⟨stored mark⟩ stands for one of the control sequences \topmark, \botmark, or \firstmark. These are allowed only in \output routines.) TEX inserts the specified mark text into its input; see Chapter 23.

- \halign⟨spec⟩{⟨alignment preamble⟩\cr⟨alignment entries⟩}　Append alignment. This is allowed only in display math mode, and only if there are no formulas being displayed outside of this alignment and no \eqno. The behavior is identical to \halign when it appears in vertical mode, except that \dispskip glue is appended above and below the resulting vertical list.

- $\left\langle \begin{matrix} \otimes \\ \texttt{\textbackslash cr} \end{matrix} \right\rangle$　Spurious alignment delimiter.

The symbols ⊗ and \cr are detected deep inside TEX's scanning mechanism when they occur at the proper nesting level of braces, because they cause TEX to start scanning a "⟨v_j⟩" as explained in Chapter 22. Therefore if these symbols appear in math mode, they are ignored, and you get the error message "There's no \halign or \valign going on."

- $\left\langle \begin{matrix} \texttt{\textbackslash ENDV} \\ \texttt{\textbackslash par} \end{matrix} \right\rangle$　"Missing $ inserted."

An \ENDV instruction is inserted automatically by TEX at the end of each "⟨v_j⟩" list of an alignment format. (You can't actually give this control sequence yourself; it only occurs implicitly.) A \par token occurs either implicitly, as a result of a blank line in the input, or explicitly. Neither case should happen in math mode, so TEX issues an error message and inserts a $ in an attempt to keep going.

- $\left\langle \begin{matrix} \texttt{\textbackslash def} \\ \texttt{\textbackslash gdef} \end{matrix} \right\rangle$⟨controlseq⟩⟨parameter text⟩{⟨result text⟩}　Define a control sequence.

The specified control sequence is defined as described in Chapter 20. TEX remains in math mode, and the current list is not affected. You are not allowed to redefine certain control sequences like \baselineskip and \:, since TEX relies on these to control its operations at critical points. Definitions with \def disappear at the end of the current formula or subformula; definitions with \gdef do not. It is best not to apply both \def and \gdef to the same control sequence in different parts of a manuscript.

- ⟨dimenparam⟩⟨dimen⟩　Set a dimension parameter.

Here ⟨dimenparam⟩ stands for one of the control sequences \hsize, \vsize, \maxdepth, \parindent, \topbaseline. The corresponding TEX parameter is set equal to the specified dimension; TEX remains in math mode, and the current list is not affected. This assignment is "global"—it holds even after the end of the current formula. The initial default values of these five parameters are $(324, 504, 3, 0, 10)$ points, respectively.

- ⟨glueparam⟩⟨glue⟩　Define a glue parameter.

Here ⟨glueparam⟩ stands for one of the control sequences \lineskip, \baselineskip, \parskip, \dispskip, \dispaskip, \dispbskip, \topskip, \botskip, \tabskip. The corresponding TEX parameter is set equal to the specified glue; TEX remains in math mode, and the current list is not affected. This assignment is "local," it will be forgotten at the end of the current formula or subformula; so this construction is of very limited utility in math mode. The initial value for all these types of glue is zero.

- \chcode$\langle$number$_1\rangle\leftarrow\langle$number$_2\rangle$ Define a character interpretation.

The character whose seven-bit code is $\langle$number$_1\rangle$ is subsequently treated as being of category $\langle$number$_2\rangle$, where the category codes are described in Chapter 7. This definition will be local to the current formula or subformula. TEX remains in math mode, and the current list is not affected.

- \chpar$\langle$number$_1\rangle\leftarrow\langle$number$_2\rangle$ Define an integer parameter.

TEX's internal parameter $\langle$number$_1\rangle$ is set equal to $\langle$number$_2\rangle$. See Chapter 25 for a table of the internal parameters. This definition will be local to the current formula or subformula, and any new settings of "binopbreak" and "relbreak" will disappear before TEX uses them in the present formula, so they are best defined *outside* of math mode. TEX remains in math mode, and the current list is not affected.

- \output{$\langle$vlist$\rangle$}$\langle$optional space$\rangle$ Set the output routine.

The specified $\langle$vlist$\rangle$ is stored for later use when pages are output (see Chapter 23). TEX remains in math mode, and the current list is not affected. This assignment is "global," it will hold even after the end of the current formula.

- \setcount$\langle$digit$\rangle\langle$optional sign$\rangle\langle$number$\rangle$ Set a specified counter.

One of ten counters, indicated by the specified digit, is set to the specified integer value (see Chapter 23). This assignment is "global," it is not rescinded at the end of the formula. TEX remains in math mode, and the current list is not affected.

- \advcount$\langle$digit$\rangle$ Advance the specified counter.

The magnitude of the specified counter is increased by 1. TEX remains in math mode, and the current list is not affected.

- \count$\langle$digit$\rangle$ Insert the specified counter.

The specified counter is converted to characters (see Chapter 23) and inserted into the input; TEX will read it in math mode.

- $\left\langle \begin{array}{l} \text{\textbackslash ifeven}\langle\text{digit}\rangle \\ \text{\textbackslash if}\langle\text{char}_1\rangle\langle\text{char}_2\rangle \end{array} \right\rangle$ {$\langle$true text$\rangle$}\else{$\langle$false text$\rangle$}   Conditional text.

TEX reads either the true text or the false text, see Chapter 23.

- \ddt   Print debugging data.

If bit 4 of the \trace parameter is 1, TEX prints out its current activities (the lists and pages it is currently building). Furthermore if bit ´40 of the \trace parameter is 1, TEX will stop, giving you the chance to insert text on-line. TEX remains in math mode, and the current list is not affected.

- ⟨anything else⟩   "! You can't do that in math mode."

If anything not listed above appears in math mode, you get an error message. TEX ignores the token of input that broke the rules, and remains in math mode; the current list is not affected.

<27> Recovery from errors

OK, everything you need to know about TEX has been explained—unless you happen to be fallible.

If you don't plan to make any errors, don't bother to read this chapter. Otherwise you might find it helpful to make use of some of the ways TEX tries to pinpoint bugs in your manuscript.

In the trial runs you did when reading Chapter 6, you learned the general form of error messages, and you also learned the various ways you can respond to TEX's complaints. With practice, you will be able to correct most errors "on line," as soon as TEX has detected them, by inserting and deleting a few things. On the other hand, some errors are more devastating than others; one error might cause some other perfectly valid construction to seem wrong. Furthermore, TEX doesn't always diagnose your errors correctly, since it is a rather simple-minded computer program that doesn't readily understand what you have in mind. (In other words, let's face it: TEX can get hopelessly confused.)

By looking at the input context that follows an error message, you can often tell what TEX will read next if you proceed by hitting ⟨carriage-return⟩. For example, look again at the error message discussed at the end of Chapter 6; it shows that TEX is about to read "STORY", then (since the <argument> will be finished) will come "\hskip 0pt" and so on. Here's another example:

```
! Missing { inserted.
<to be read again>
                        A
(*) \hbox A
            nother example.
```

In this case TEX has read the "A" and discovered that a "{" was missing. The missing left brace has been inserted and the "A" will be read again, followed by "nother example." If you understand what TEX has read and is going to read next, you will be able to make good use of the insertion and deletion options when error messages appear on your terminal, because you'll be able to make corrections before an error propagates.

Here is a complete list of the messages you might get from TEX, presented in alphabetic order for reference purposes. Each message is followed by a brief explanation of the problem, from TEX's viewpoint, and of any remedial action you might want to take. (See also Appendix I.)

! A box specification was supposed to be here.
TEX was expecting to see a ⟨box⟩ now, based on what it had recently seen (e.g., "\raise" or "\save" or "\leaders"), but what it now sees is not the beginning of a ⟨box⟩. (See Chapter 24 or 25 or 26 for the definition of a ⟨box⟩.) Proceed, and TEX will forget whatever led it to expect a ⟨box⟩.

! Ambiguous; you need another { and }.
You seem to be using \over or \atop or \above or \comb more than once in the same formula or subformula. Proceed, and the formula will appear as if the current \over (or whatever) weren't there.

! All mixed up, can't continue.
TEX is quitting, because it is confused about an alignment that has gone awry.

! Argument of ⟨control sequence⟩ can't begin with }.
The first character of some argument to the specified macro is }. Proceed, and this } will be ignored.

! Bad font link for large delimiter ⟨number⟩.
TEX is trying to make a variable-size delimiter, but either you gave it the wrong code number or the font information of the current ex font is messed up. Maybe the wrong ex font has been selected. Proceed, and the delimiter will be changed to "." (blank).

! Blank space should follow file name.
TEX usually continues to read a file name until seeing a blank space, so it may have incorporated part of your input text into the file name. Proceed and you might be lucky.

! Display math should end with $$.
TEX got to a $ in display math mode, and it wasn't followed by another $. If you simply have typed a single dollar sign instead of a double one, proceed and TEX will happily pretend there were two. Otherwise you're probably in deep trouble—

but don't give up yet. (Perhaps you didn't want TEX to get into display math mode at all; are you doing an alignment with "$#$" in some format, where the entry to be aligned is empty, contrary to the advice in Chapter 22?)

! Double subscript.

You can't apply ↓ twice to the same thing. Proceed, and the first subscript will be ignored.

! Double superscript.

You can't apply ↑ twice to the same thing. Proceed, and the first superscript will be ignored.

! \else required here.

TEX is processing conditional code initiated by \if or \ifeven, and the condition was false, so the ⟨true text⟩ has just been skipped over. But the next token was not \else; perhaps the ⟨true text⟩ contains improper grouping of braces. Proceed, and TEX will resume reading the input.

(\end occurred on level ⟨number⟩).

This message may appear on your terminal just before TEX signs off; it warns you that the stated number of {'s still is waiting to be matched.

! Extra ⟨something⟩.

There are several messages telling you that your input text contains something "extra"; for example, if your input contains a math formula like "$x}+y$", TEX will say that you have an extra "}". Proceed, and TEX will ignore what it claims is extra. (If you forget to type "\cr" in an alignment, you may get the message "Extra alignment tab", meaning that there are more tabs than specified in the preamble. Your alignment will probably be messed up and overfull boxes will appear; it's too bad.)

! First use of font must define it.

A font code has appeared for the first time in your manuscript, and it wasn't immediately followed by "=" or "←". (This is a rather serious error—always make it a habit to declare your fonts early in your manuscript.) Insert "=⟨font file name⟩⟨space⟩" and TEX will be able to continue.

! \halign in math mode must be preceded and followed by $$.

TEX has just scanned the "}" that completes an \halign in display math mode. You get this error if a nonempty formula preceded the \halign or if the current item of input isn't "$". Proceed, and TEX will continue in display math mode. (Strange things may happen.)

`! Illegal font code.`

You should always refer to fonts as suggested in Chapter 4; for example, you shouldn't type crazy things like "`\:\hbox`" unless you have redefined the control sequence `\hbox`. Insert the font code you intended, by first typing "`i`".

`! Illegal parameter number in definition of ⟨controlseq⟩.`

The result text of the stated definition contains an appearance of `#` that isn't followed by `#` or by the number of a parameter in the parameter text. Proceed, and TEX will assume that you meant to type "`##`".

`! Illegal unit of measure (pt inserted).`

TEX is scanning a ⟨dimen⟩ (see Chapter 10), but the ⟨number⟩ isn't followed by any of the two-letter codes TEX knows. Proceed, and TEX will assume that "pt" was there.

`! Improper code.`

You are attempting to use `\chcode` or `\chpar` with an improper ⟨number₁⟩. The operation is aborted, but you may proceed.

`! Input page ended while scanning def of ⟨controlseq⟩.`

The ⟨parameter text⟩ or the ⟨result text⟩ of a `\def`, or the ⟨mark list⟩ of a `\mark`, or the ⟨vlist⟩ of an `\output`, has extended beyond the current file page of the input file. This probably means that you forgot a "`}`" in some faraway part of the input manuscript, so it's probably a disaster. Insert a right brace if you want, and proceed if you dare.

`! Input page ended while scanning use of ⟨controlseq⟩.`

This message has been preceded by a "Runaway argument?" message that shows what TEX thinks is the beginning of an argument to a defined control sequence. For some reason, a file page in the input file has ended before the text of that argument has ended. This probably is a serious error, because it has presumably gone undetected for a while. You can try to insert something into the input that will terminate the runaway argument, but you most likely should start over, after fixing the argument so that it terminates where it should. (You probably left out a "`}`".)

`! Large delimiter ⟨number⟩ should be in mathex font.`

You are specifying a ⟨delim⟩ by a 9-bit code, but you should have specified either $c_2 = 0$ or $c_2 \geq$ ´600. Proceed, and the delimiter will be selected using c_1 only. (See Chapter 18 for the meaning of c_1 and c_2.)

`! Italic correction must follow an explicit character.`
The control sequence \/ is supposed to follow a character from some font, but your input tells TEX to apply an "italic correction" to something else. Perhaps you are using a defined control sequence that slants one of its arguments (e.g., \algbegin in Appendix E), where the argument ends with a math formula instead of a word. Proceed.

`! Limit switch must follow math operator.`
If the control sequence \limitswitch doesn't follow an Op box, it doesn't accomplish anything. Proceed.

`! Lookup failed on file ⟨filename⟩.`
TEX can't find the file you indicated. Type "i" and insert the correct file name (followed by a blank space and ⟨carriage-return⟩). But be careful: You get only one more chance to get the file name right, otherwise TEX will decide not to input *any* file just now.

`! Missing ⟨something⟩ inserted.`
This message can arise in lots of ways and it can name a variety of things that TEX sometimes thinks are missing. For example, if you type

$$\texttt{\\left(x+\{\\right)}$$

in math mode, TEX thinks (correctly) that there's a missing "}". (See Chapter 26.) *In general, when you get this message, TEX has already inserted what it says was missing—don't insert another one.* If TEX has guessed correctly, just proceed. Otherwise, it may be fun to try getting TEX back into synch; you might get the message "Missing } inserted" followed by one that says "Too many }´s", indicating a certain lack of logic on TEX's part.

`! Missing digit (0 to 9), 0 inserted.`
TEX was expecting to see a decimal digit following \box or \save, but it isn't there. Proceed; TEX has already inserted a "0".

`! OK.`
This isn't an error message. TEX is stopping because you asked it to (\ddt with \trace bit ´40 set).

`! Only one # allowed per tab.`
A ⟨format⟩ in an alignment preamble must have exactly one #, but you seem to have typed more than one. Proceed, and the extra # will be ignored.

`! Only single characters can be accented in horizontal mode.`
An ⟨accent⟩ has not been followed by a proper ⟨accentee⟩. Proceed, and the ⟨accent⟩ will be ignored.

`! \output routine didn't use \page.`
A page was assembled for output, but the \output routine didn't make use of it, so it is lost forever. Proceed.

`! Parameters must be numbered consecutively.`
You must say #1, #2, etc., in order, when designating parameters in the ⟨parameter text⟩ of a macro definition. When you get this message, TEX has already inserted the correct parameter number, so you may want to delete an incorrect one before proceeding.

`Overfull box, ...`
This is an information message, not an error message (i.e., TEX doesn't stop). The box whose contents are partially displayed is "overfull" because it doesn't have enough glue shrinkage to get down to the required size. Thus the box contents are too wide or too high by the specified amount; in your output you will probably see this box sticking out somewhere or overlapping another one, unless the excess is very small. Overfull boxes can arise from a variety of reasons, notably when there is no decent way to break the lines of certain paragraphs, or when a displayed equation is too wide to fit on a single line. You may want to settle for badly broken lines in a paragraph, by increasing the value of \jpar as discussed in Chapter 14; or you might be able to help by inserting discretionary hyphens, especially if there is a word that TEX doesn't try to hyphenate (e.g., "Inter\-change" in the first line of Appendix F). But in a high-quality job an overfull box usually means that the author should rewrite the text, eliminating the problem entirely.

`Runaway argument?`
This message is followed by the tokens of a macro argument that didn't end where you wanted it to. (See "`! Input page ended while scanning use of ...`" above.)

`! TEX capacity exceeded, sorry [⟨size⟩=⟨number⟩].`
This is a bad one. Somehow you have stretched TEX beyond its finite limits. The thing that overflowed is indicated in brackets, together with its numerical value in the TEX implementation you are using. The following table shows the internal

sizes that might have been exceeded:

alignsize	the number of simultaneous alignments;
fmemsize	the number of words of auxiliary font information;
hashsize	the number of different multiletter control sequences;
idlevs	logarithm of the number of levels of grouping;
memsize	memory used to store tokens and many other types of things;
nestsize	number of simultaneous partially-complete lists;
parsize	number of simultaneous partially-scanned arguments;
savesize	number of values to restore at end of group or formula;
stacksize	number of simultaneous levels of input;
stringsize	number of independent operations on typesetting device;
varsize	memory used to store boxes and many other types of things.

If your job is error-free, the remedy is to recompile the TeX system, increasing what overflowed. However, there's probably something you can do to your job that will make it run. Maybe you have specified an infinite macro-expansion; then it would cause overflow no matter how big you make TeX. If savesize has overflowed, you probably have started a group and forgot to finish it. (Every time you change fonts, say, inside a group, an entry is being saved, *unless* you are on level zero.) Or perhaps you are trying to specify a gigantic alignment that spans more than a page; TeX has to read all the way to the end of an alignment before outputting any of it, so this consumes huge amounts of memory space. (It's necessary to limit your alignments to reasonable size, by using a fixed format for the multipage cases.) As the message says, it is a sorry situation.

! There's no \halign or \valign going on.
Your input contains a ⊗ or a \cr that didn't get recognized as part of an alignment, perhaps because you didn't mean to type it, but most likely because some alignment entry doesn't have properly-balanced grouping. TeX has deleted the offending ⊗ or \cr; to recover, try to insert braces that balance the group, followed by the current token. For example, if your input was "{x⊗" up to this point, the "{" is hiding the "⊗"; type "i" and then insert "}⊗".

! This can't happen.
Something really unexpected has caused TeX to come to a screeching halt.

! This is allowed only in output routines.
The current input token will be ignored, since it specifies an operation not available except when TeX is running an \output routine (and TeX isn't).

! This dimension shouldn't be negative.
You were naughty and tried to specify a negative ⟨dimen⟩ where it isn't allowed.
Proceed, and the dimension will be assumed zero.

! Too many }'s.
You are not inside a group, so the "}" just scanned will be discarded when you
proceed.

! Too much stretch for proper line breaking.
This message usually occurs when you're doing something like "\hbox par
⟨dimen⟩{...}" and TEX's line-breaking procedure is trying to produce a boxed
paragraph as described in Chapter 21. In such cases, "\hfill" shouldn't be
used in the box; TEX will not break lines in a paragraph when the glue has more
than one million points of accumulated stretchability. (The reason for this is
that the computations are performed with limited-precision arithmetic, and the
spacing will come out looking bad if TEX tries to make precise measurements
after subtracting infinity from infinity.) Proceed, and you'll probably see how
bad it looks.

! Undefined control sequence.
TEX has encountered a control sequence it doesn't know; see Chapters 24, 25, or
26 for hints on how to fix this.

! Unknown delimiter.
The ⟨delim⟩ you have specified isn't one of those listed in Chapter 18. Proceed,
and TEX will use a blank delimiter.

! Use of ⟨controlseq⟩ doesn't match its definition.
You have typed something that doesn't follow the rules of the specified control
sequence. (For example, consider the control sequence \ansno of Appendix E.
If you type "\ansno 5.No.", you have forgotten the space that's required after
"5.".) TEX will proceed by assuming that the thing you typed was the thing
that was required; thus, in the above example, TEX will assume that the "N" is
a space, and your best strategy is to insert a new "N".

! Warning: Long input line has been broken.
Your input file contained a very long sequence of characters between consecutive
⟨carriage-return⟩s. TEX arbitrarily broke it after 150 characters.

! Whoa---you have to define a font first.
TEX has aborted your job, because it can't do what you asked it to do without
having some font selected as the "current font."

`! You can only define a control sequence.`
Your manuscript apparently contains \def or \gdef and the next thing wasn't
a control sequence. Proceed, and TEX forgets that the \def or \gdef occurred.
For example, if you typed "\def ansno" when you meant "\def\ansno", TEX
will read the "a" and complain; to recover, you should delete the next four tokens
(namely "nsno"), then insert "\def\ansno".

`! You can't do that in ⟨mode⟩.`
Your manuscript is trying to do something incompatible with TEX's current mode.
TEX will ignore the token it has just read; so the proper way to recover is usually
to insert something that takes TEX into the correct mode (e.g., "\par" will usually
go from horizontal mode to vertical mode, and "$" will usually go from math
mode to horizontal mode), followed by the current token again. For example,
suppose you have typed "\vskip .5 in" before ending a paragraph; TEX will
stop before it reads the ".5". To recover, type "i" for insertion, then type
"\par\vskip" and ⟨carriage-return⟩.

`! You can't redefine this control sequence,`
You have discovered one of TEX's reserved control sequences. The \def or \gdef
will be ignored if you proceed.

 ▶Exercise 27.1: What is the best way to recover from the following error?

```
! You can't do that in math mode.
\sl →\:
            n
p.3,l.307 $x+y is {\sl
                          not} zero.
```

 ▶Exercise 27.2: And what about this one?

```
! Illegal units of measure.
<to be read again>
                      p
<to be read again> p
                      {
(*) \hbox to 50p{Test}
```

You can get more information from TEX if you make use of its *tracing* capability. Type "\trace´*mmmnnnxy*" (using the control sequence \trace defined in Appendix B) to set up the combination of tracing facilities you want, according to the following cryptic encoding scheme:

mmm is an octal code for the number of items per list that will be shown when a box is displayed. (If *mmm* = 0, it is automatically changed to 5.)

nnn is an octal code for the number of levels deep that will be shown when a box is displayed.

x equals (1, if you want to see what replacements are being made in macros as they are expanded)

plus (2, if you want each line of your input files to be entered on your terminal before it is processed by TEX, giving you a chance to edit it first)

plus (4, if you want TEX to stop whenever the control sequence \ddt appears in the input).

y equals (1, if you want to be told about "overfull boxes")

plus (2, if you want to see the gory details about what is being typeset on each page before it is shipped to the \output routine)

plus (4, if you want to see TEX's current activities whenever the control sequence \ddt appears in the input).

The normal setting is \trace´345. Thus TEX normally shows boxes to depth 3, with up to 5 items per list; it stops and dumps on \ddt calls; and it shows overfull boxes. If you say "\trace0" you get *nothing*, while if you say "\trace´77777777" you probably get *too much*. Boxes are displayed when they are overfull, or when they are completed pages, or when they are in the list of current activities, but only if the current *x* or *y* setting calls for information about these boxes. The contents will appear on your terminal as well as on the "errors.tmp" file; and the format of this information is self-explanatory, once you understand it. You can, of course, change the combination of tracing facilities as many times as you want to, so that you aren't deluged with information when you don't want any.

Final hint: When working on a long manuscript, it's best to prepare only a few pages at a time. Set up a "galley" file and a "book" file, and enter your text on the galley file. (Put control information that sets up your basic format and fonts at the beginning of this file, so that you don't have to retype it each time.)

After the galleys come out looking right, you can append them to the book file; then you can run the book file through TEX once a week, or so, in order to see how the pages really fit together. For example, when the author prepared this manual, he did one chapter at a time; and Chapter 18 was split into three parts, because of its incredible length.

Final exhortation: GO FORTH now and create *masterpieces of the publishing art!*

<A> Answers to all the exercises

2.1: `` ` ` $\,$ ` `` or `` ` `\2` `` (but *not* `` ` ` ` ``); `` ` {}` ` `` or `{ ` }` `` , etc.

3.1: math\´ematique, math\´ ematique; centim\`etre.

4.1: Ulrich Dieter, {\sl Journal f\"ur die reine und angewandte Mathematik \bf 201} (1959), 37--70. (Note in particular the use of "--" to get an en-dash, did you remember that?)

5.1: Type "{-}-" or "-{-}" or "{-}{-}" or "-{}-", etc.

5.2: No—the first definition is pretty lousy because it accomplishes nothing! (When \rm appears in the subsequent text it will be replaced by {\:a}, but this font change immediately disappears because it's inside a group.)

5.3: It could end with any character that has been \chcoded to 2 at the time the group ends. After that point the effect of all \chcodes inside the group will be lost.

6.1: Type "i" (for insert). Then when TEX prompts you for more input, type "\c c"; this will be inserted at the current place in the input (the undefined \cc has already been discarded), and then TEX resumes reading the original line (i.e., it will then read the comma; you shouldn't insert another comma, since the comma wasn't in error).

7.1: Yes, if the format you are using (e.g., basic) has defined % to be an end-of-line character (type 5).

9.1: {\sl Commentarii Academ\ae\ Petropolitan\ae} is now {\sl Doklady Akademi\t\i a Nauk SSSR}.

9.2: \O ystein Ore, \t IUri \t IAnov, Ja`far al-Khow\A arizm\A\i, and W\l ladyis\l law S\"u\ss man.

10.1: Here is one of many possible solutions.

```
\def\1{\hbox to 5mm{\hfill\vrule depth 4pt}}
\def\2{\hbox to 5mm{\hfill\vrule depth 8pt}}
\vbox{\hrule\hbox{\vrule depth 8pt
    \1\2\1\2\1\2\1\2\1\2\1\2\1\2\1\2\1\2\1\2}}
```

12.1: 25, 41, and 12 units, respectively.

12.2: "`... launched by \hbox{NASA}.`"; or "`... launched by NASA\null.`"

16.1: `$2↑{n+1}$, $(n+1)↑2$, $\sqrt{1-x↑2}$, $\overline{w+\overline z}$,`
`$p↓1↑{e↓1}$, $a↓{b↓{c↓{d↓e}}}$, $h↓n↑{\prime\prime}(x)$.`

16.2: No space will be typeset after the "If". (Also, it would have been slightly better to end with "`$y$.`".)

16.3: `Deleting an element from an $n$-tuple leaves an $(n-1)$-tuple.`

17.1: `$${p \choose 2}x↑2 y↑{p-2} - {1 \over 1-x}{1 \over 1-x↑2}.$$`

17.2: `$$\sum↓{i=1}↑p\sum↓{j=1}↑q\sum↓{k=1}↑r a↓{ij}b↓{jk}c↓{ki}$$` .

17.3: `$$\sum↓{{\scriptstyle1≤i≤p\atop\scriptstyle1≤j≤q}\atop`
`\scriptstyle1≤k≤r}a↓{ij}b↓{jk}c↓{ki}$$` .

18.1: `$n↑{\hbox{\:d th}}$ root` .

18.2: `$$\biglp x-s(x)\bigrp\biglp y-s(y)\bigrp.$$` (Note that the period is included in this display.)

18.3: `$${1\over2\pi}\int↓{-∞}↑{\sqrt y}\bigglp\sum↓{k=1}↑n`
`\sin↑2x↓k(t)\biggrp\biglp f(t)+g(t)\bigrp\,dt.$$`

18.4: `$${(n↓1+n↓2+\cdots+n↓m)!\over n↓1!\,n↓2!\ldotsm n↓m!}=`
`{n↓1+n↓2\choose n↓2}{n↓1+n↓2+n↓3\choose n↓3}\ldotsm`
`{n↓1+n↓2+\cdots+n↓m\choose n↓m}.$$`

18.5: `$\left(\cpile{y↓1\cr\vdots\cr y↓k\cr}\right)$` .

18.6: `$$\Pscr↓{Lhj}(x)=\hbox{Tr}\left[{\partial F↓{L↑{-1}}\over`
`\partial t↓h}\chi(L)\Mscr↓{nj}(x)\right],\qquad\hbox{evaluated`
`at }\chi(\Gamma)\modop\hbox{\sl SL}(n,\hbox{\bf C}).$$`

(Here "`\hbox{\sl SL}`" gives slightly better spacing than simply *SL*, because it suppresses the italic correction on the *S*.)

18.7: `\def\e{\mathrel{{:}{=}}}` . (The braces prevent space between : and =, since they specify one-character subformulas that are converted into Ord boxes.) Another solution is `\def\e{\mathrel{\char´72\char´75}}` .

20.1: The `##` feature is indispensable when the result text of a definition contains *other* definitions. (We will see later that `##` is also useful for alignments; cf. the definitions of `\eqalign` and `eqalignno` in Appendix B.)

21.1: When a null box was placed on the vertical list below the "s" box, the `\lineskip` glue of 3 points was not inserted, because the `\baselineskip` distance of 0 points was not exceeded. Thus the interline glue was computed to be 0 points, and the blank line didn't show up.

21.2: `\vbox{\baselineskip-1pt\lineskip 3pt\halign{\ctr{#}\cr`
`T\cr h\cr i\cr s\cr \cr b\cr o\cr x\cr}}` .

21.3: `\def\boxit#1{\vbox{\hrule\hbox{\vrule\hskip 3pt`
`\vbox{\vskip 3pt #1 \vskip 3pt}\hskip 3pt\vrule}\hrule}}` .

21.4: `\leaders\chop to 0pt{\hbox to size{\hfill*\lower 3.75pt`
`\hbox{*}*\lower 3.75pt\hbox{*}*}}\vfill` . [For more interesting effects, try
`\leaders` *inside* of boxes used as leaders.]

22.1: The equation number "(13)" would appear on the bottom line instead of being centered vertically. (A box constructed by `\vbox` has the same baseline as the bottom box in the vertical list.)

23.1: Since the `\output` routine might occur at an unpredictable time, the value of `\hsize` may not be 4.5 inches. (On the other hand, if it is known that the manuscript never diddles with `\hsize`, the output routine will be more readable if `\ctrline` is used for the running title and page number lines.)

23.2: For example, you can replace it by the following:

```
\output{\vbox to 7.5in{\baselineskip0pt\lineskip0pt
    \if T\tpage{\vskip.5in}
    \else{\vbox to.15in{\vfill
        \def\lead{ \leaders\hrule\hfill\ }
        \hbox to 4.5in{\ifeven0{\:b\count0\lead\topmark}
          \else{\:b\topmark\lead\count0}}}
    \vskip .35in}
\page\vfill
\if T\tpage{\gdef\tpage{F}
  \hbox to 4.5in{\hfill\:c\count0\hfill}}
\else{}}\advcount0}   .
```

27.1: (A "$" was forgotten after the "y".) If you just insert a dollar sign now, the "{" will be unmatched in the math formula, so TEX will stop again after inserting a "}" before the "$" you just inserted; this will cause unbalance and possible embarrassment. The correct procedure is to insert "}$\{\:", then TEX will proceed almost as if the error hadn't happened.

27.2: TEX has already decided that "pt" was intended but missing from the input. If you simply proceed now, TEX will insert a "{" and give you another error message (after which you'll have to delete "p" and "{"). The correct procedure is to delete the "p" now (by typing "1"); then type ⟨carriage-return⟩. The error has been fully corrected (unless picas were meant instead of points).

\<B\> Basic TEX format

The following listing of file "basic.TEX" shows how to give TEX enough knowledge to do the "basic" things mentioned in the main text.

```
\chcode´173←1 \chcode´176←2 \chcode´44←3 \chcode´26←4
\chcode´45←5 \chcode´43←6 \chcode´136←7 \chcode 1←8

\def\%{\char´45 } % Note, the space after 45 is needed! (e.g.\%0)
\def\lft#1{#1\hfill}
\def\ctr#1{\hfill#1\hfill}
\def\rt#1{\hfill#1}

\def\rjustline#1{\hbox to size{
    \hskip0pt plus1000cm minus1000cm #1}}
\def\ctrline#1{\hbox to size{\hskip0pt plus1000cm minus1000cm
    #1\hskip0pt plus1000cm minus1000cm}}

\def\trace{\chpar0←} \def\jpar{\chpar1←} \def\ragged{\chpar8←}

\def\log{\mathop{\char´154\char´157\char´147}\limitswitch}
\def\lg{\mathop{\char´154\char´147}\limitswitch}
\def\ln{\mathop{\char´154\char´156}\limitswitch}
\def\lim{\mathop{\char´154\char´151\char´155}}
\def\limsup{\mathop{\char´154\char´151\char´155
    \,\char´163\char´165\char´160}}
\def\liminf{\mathop{\char´154\char´151\char´155
    \,\char´151\char´156\char´146}}
\def\sin{\mathop{\char´163\char´151\char´156}\limitswitch}
\def\cos{\mathop{\char´143\char´157\char´163}\limitswitch}
\def\tan{\mathop{\char´164\char´141\char´156}\limitswitch}
\def\cot{\mathop{\char´143\char´157\char´164}\limitswitch}
\def\sec{\mathop{\char´163\char´145\char´143}\limitswitch}
\def\csc{\mathop{\char´143\char´163\char´143}\limitswitch}
\def\max{\mathop{\char´155\char´141\char´170}}
\def\min{\mathop{\char´155\char´151\char´156}}
\def\sup{\mathop{\char´163\char´165\char´160}}
\def\inf{\mathop{\char´151\char´156\char´146}}
\def\det{\mathop{\char´144\char´145\char´164}}
\def\exp{\mathop{\char´145\char´170\char´160}\limitswitch}
\def\Pr{\mathop{\char´120\char´162}}
\def\gcd{\mathop{\char´147\char´143\char´144}}
\def\choose{\comb()}
```

```
\def\leftset{\mathopen{\{\,}}
\def\rightset{\mathclose{\,\}}}
\def\modop{\<\,\mathbin{\char´155\char´157\char´144}\penalty900\<\,}
\def\mod#1{\penalty0\;(\char´155\char´157\char´144\,\,#1)}
\def\eqv{\mathrel\char´421 }
\def\neqv{\mathrel{\not\eqv}}
\def\qquad{\quad\quad}
\def\ldots{{.\>.\>.}}
\def\cdots{{\char´401\>\char´401\>\char´401}}
\def\ldotss{{.\>.\>.\>}}
\def\cdotss{\cdots\>}
\def\ldotsm{{\>.\>.\>.\>}}
\def\vdots{\vbox{\baselineskip 4pt\vskip 6pt
    \hbox{.}\hbox{.}\hbox{.}}}
\def\eqalign#1{\vcenter{\halign{\hfill$\dispstyle{##}$\!
      @$\dispstyle{\null##}$\hfill\cr#1}}}
\def\eqalignno#1{\vbox{\tabskip0pt plus1000pt minus1000pt
    \halign to size{\hfill$\dispstyle{##}$\tabskip 0pt
      @$\dispstyle{\null##}$\hfill
      \tabskip0pt plus1000pt minus1000pt
      @$\hfill##$\tabskip 0pt\cr#1}}}
\def\cpile#1{\vcenter{\halign{$\hfill##\hfill$\cr#1}}}
\def\lpile#1{\vcenter{\halign{$##\hfill$\cr#1}}}
\def\rpile#1{\vcenter{\halign{$\hfill##$\cr#1}}}
\def\null{\hbox{}}
\def\twoline#1#2#3{\halign{\hbox to size{##}\cr$\quad\dispstyle
    {#1}$\hfill\cr\noalign{\penalty1000\vskip#2}
    \hfill$\dispstyle{#3}\quad$\cr}}
\def\chop to#1pt#2{\hbox{\lower#1pt\null\vbox{\hbox{\lower99pt
        \hbox{\raise99pt\hbox{$\dispstyle{#2}$}}}\vskip-99pt}}}
\def\spose#1{\hbox to 0pt{#1\hskip0pt minus10000000pt}}

\:@←cmathx
\:a←cmr10 \:d←cmr7 \:f←cmr5
\:g←cmi10 \:j←cmi7 \:l←cmi5
\:n←cms10
\:q←cmb10
\:u←cmsy10 \:x←cmsy7 \:z←cmsy5
\:?←cmti10
```

```
\def\rm{\:a} \def\sl{\:n} \def\bf{\:q} \def\it{\:?}
```

```
\parindent 20pt \maxdepth 2pt \topbaseline 10pt
\parskip 0pt plus 1 pt \baselineskip 12pt \lineskip 1pt
\dispskip 12pt plus 3pt minus 9pt
\dispaskip 0pt plus 3pt \dispbskip 7pt plus 3pt minus 4pt
```

```
\def\biglp{\mathopen{\vcenter{\hbox{\:@\char´0}}}}
\def\bigrp{\mathclose{\vcenter{\hbox{\:@\char´1}}}}
\def\bigglp{\mathopen{\vcenter{\hbox{\:@\char´22}}}}
\def\biggrp{\mathclose{\vcenter{\hbox{\:@\char´23}}}}
\def\biggglp{\mathopen{\vcenter{\hbox{\:@\char´40}}}}
\def\bigggrp{\mathclose{\vcenter{\hbox{\:@\char´41}}}}
```

```
\mathrm adf \mathit gjl \mathsy uxz \mathex @
```

```
\output{\baselineskip20pt\page\ctrline{\:a\count0}\advcount0}
\setcount0 1
```

```
\rm
\null\vskip-12pt % allow glue at top of first page
```

<E> Example of a book format

This appendix contains two parts: First comes a supplement to the TEX report, explaining the main conventions a typist uses when entering material from *The Art of Computer Programming* (*ACP*) into the system. Second is a listing of file acphdr.TEX, in which the precise format for those books is defined in terms of TEX control sequences. As you read the first part of this appendix, try to imagine that you yourself are a typist with the responsibility for inputting part of the manuscript for this series of books.

Several examples below are best understood if you have a copy of *ACP* handy; so why not go fetch your copy of Volume 1 now? (And if you have Volume 2, that will help even more.)

• Since this appendix must cover a wide range of topics in a reasonably short space, it is rather terse; please forgive the author for this. Every time you see "•" in this appendix, you're being hit with a new topic.

• Everything in Appendix B—the "basic" format that is explained throughout the user manual—is used also in *ACP*, except that the conventions for number theory are slightly different. (See Chapter 18, part 8, for a discussion of Appendix B's approach to number theory.) To typeset "$x \equiv 0$ (modulo pq)", type "$x \eqv 0 \modulo{pq}$"; and to typeset the operator "mod" you can use \mod instead of \modop. There also is one further control sequence defined for mathematics, namely \deg for the degree symbol: type "$45\deg$" to get "45°".

• The style of typical bibliographic references is "⟨author name⟩,␣{\sl⟨name of book or journal⟩␣\bf⟨volume number⟩}␣(⟨year⟩),␣⟨starting page⟩--⟨ending page⟩." For example,

```
M. R. Garey et.\ al., {\sl SIAM J. Appl.\
    Math.\ \bf34} (1978), 477--495.
```

Another example appears in the answer to exercise 4.1 (see Appendix A).

• Remember to type "\" after any abbreviation in which a lower case letter is followed by a period followed by a space, when this period is not the end of a sentence. Abbreviations aren't used very much in *ACP*, but they do occur frequently in bibliographic references (as in the example just given). Furthermore you should be on the lookout for the following commonly-used abbreviations:

```
Eq.\     Eqs.\     Fig.\     Figs.\     cf.\     ed.\     etc.\
```

The special abbreviations "A.D." and "B.C.", sometimes used in dates, are typed "{\:m A.D.}" and "{\:m B.C.}", respectively, in order to get them into the small caps font.

● Remember to type en-dashes, not only when giving page numbers in bibliographic references but also in constructions like the following:

```
exercise 3.1--6    Table 3.2.1.1--1    Fig.\ A--1
```

● Each major section of *ACP* starts on a new page. (A major section is a section whose number contains just one decimal point, for example "Section 3.2".) A separate computer file is maintained for each major section; for example, file v232.TEX contains Volume 2, Section 3.2. Such a file starts out with the following fixed information:

```
\input acphdr
\runninglefthead{⟨chapter title with all letters capitalized⟩}
\titlepage\tenpoint
\vfill
\ctrline{SECTION ⟨major section number⟩ OF
                    THE ART OF COMPUTER PROGRAMMING}
\ctrline{$\copyright$ ⟨year⟩
                    Addison--Wesley Publishing Company, Inc.}
\vfill
\runningrighthead{⟨section title with all letters capitalized⟩}
\section{⟨major section number⟩}
\eject\setcount0 ⟨starting page number⟩
\sectionbegin{⟨major section number⟩.␣⟨section title with all letters capitalized⟩}
```

For example, the last four lines of this introductory information have the following form on file v232.TEX:

```
\runningrighthead{GENERATING UNIFORM RANDOM NUMBERS}
\section{3.2}
\eject\setcount0 9
\sectionbegin{3.2. GENERATING UNIFORM RANDOM NUMBERS}
```

The beginning of a major section is a major event in *ACP*, so you are asked to type all of the above—no special control sequence has been made for it.*

One further piece of fanciness is used at the beginning of a major section: The first words of the opening sentence are typeset with capital letters from font \:c in place

---

*The beginning of a chapter is an even more major event; the format for such a gala occasion won't be described here, since the author will do the first page of each chapter by himself, just to keep his hand in.

of lower case letters. For example, the four lines that we have quoted from `v232.TEX` are immediately followed in that file by

```
I{\:cN THIS SECTION} we shall consider methods
```

(and the result when typeset looks like this: "IN THIS SECTION we shall consider methods").

- A <u>minor section</u> of *ACP* is one whose number contains two decimal points, for example "Section 4.2.2". Each minor section starts out with four special lines

```
\runningrighthead{⟨section title with all letters capitalized⟩}
\section{⟨minor section number⟩}
\sectionskip
\sectionbegin{⟨minor section number⟩.␣⟨section title partially capitalized⟩}
```

followed by the text of the first paragraph. "Partially capitalized" means that you capitalize only major words, as in the title of a book. For example:

```
\runningrighthead{ACCURACY OF FLOATING-POINT ARITHMETIC}
\section{4.2.2}
\sectionskip
\sectionbegin{4.2.2. Accuracy of Floating-Point Arithmetic}
Floating-point computation is by nature inexact, and ...
```

Thus, a minor section has much less fanfare, and there is no messing around with font `\:c`.

- A <u>diminished section</u> of *ACP* is one whose number contains three decimal points, for example "Section 1.2.11.1". This is typed just the same as a minor section, except that you omit the `\sectionskip`, you use `\dimsectionbegin` instead of `\sectionbegin`, and you capitalize only the first word of the section title. For example:

```
\runningrighthead{THE O-NOTATION}
\section{1.2.11.1}
\dimsectionbegin{\star 1.2.11.1. The $O$-notation}
A very convenient notation for dealing with ...
```

This example illustrates another thing: you type "`\star`" just after "`sectionbegin{`" when beginning a "starred" section or subsection. (TEX will then insert an asterisk in the left margin.) Such stars occur sometimes even in major sections.

- A <u>subsection</u> of *ACP* ranks lowest in the hierarchy. It is part of a section that is introduced by a bold-face subhead, but this subhead never gets into the running headline at the top of right-hand pages. You specify the beginning of a subsection simply by typing

```
\subsectionbegin{⟨subhead⟩}
```

followed by the opening paragraph of the subsection. Don't type a period after the subhead—TEX will typeset one anyway, it's part of the subsection format—and if you include another period there will be two! This is consistent with the titles of sections in general (see the examples above); you never put a period before the }.

Here are two examples of subsection format, taken from within sections 1.3.3 and 3.3.2 of *ACP*:

```
\subsectionbegin{Products of permutations}
We can ``multiply´´ two permutations together, ...

\subsectionbegin{E. Coupon collector's test}
This test is related to the poker test ...
```

- Special events like theorems and algorithms sometimes occur in the text of a section, and they have their own special format. Type

```
\algbegin ⟨name of algorithm or program⟩␣(⟨descriptive title⟩) .␣
```

at the beginning of an algorithm or program. For example (taken from pages 2 and 141 of Volume 1):

```
\algbegin Algorithm E (Euclid's algorithm) . Given two ...

\algbegin Program M (Find the maximum) . Register assignments: ...
```

Similarly, you type

```
\thbegin ⟨name of theorem or lemma or corollary⟩ .␣
```

at the beginning of a theorem or lemma or corollary. The text of a theorem or lemma or corollary is set in *slanted* type, with any embedded math formulas set off by $'s as usual (so that italic letters will be distinguishable from slanted ones). For example,

```
\thbegin Corollary P. {\sl If a $[0,1)$ sequence is
$k$-distributed, it satisfies the permutation test of
order $k$, in the sense of Eq.\ $(10)$ .}
```

Be sure to remember the final } that turns off the \sl, otherwise you'll see a lot of slantedness in the following text.

• When beginning the proof of a theorem, type "\proofbegin" (with no period following it) instead of "*Proof.*". For example,

```
\proofbegin It is clear that ...
```

(But use \dproofbegin if the preceding paragraph ended with a display.) At the *end* of the last paragraph of a proof, type the following ritual:

```
\quad\blackslug
⟨empty line to end the paragraph⟩
\yyskip
```

This typesets a "█" and leaves extra space before the paragraph that follows. The same ritual is used also at the end of the last step of an algorithm.

• Speaking of the steps of algorithms, each step is a separate paragraph. At the beginning of that paragraph the instructions

```
\algstep ⟨step number⟩.␣[⟨description of step⟩]
```

should be typed. For example, the following comes from page 2 of Volume 1:

```
\algstep E1. [Find remainder.] Divide $m$ by $n$ and let $r$
be the remainder.\xskip (We will have $0≤r<n$.)

\algstep E2. [Is it zero?] If $r=0$, the algorithm
terminates; $n$ is the answer.

\algstep E3. [Interchange.] Set $m←n$, $n←r$, and go back
to step E1.\quad\blackslug

\yyskip Of course, Euclid did not present his algorithm in
just this manner. The above format illustrates the style
in which all of the algorithms throughout this book will
be presented.
```

• Within a paragraph, type "\xskip" before and after parenthesized sentences. (For example, there is an \xskip in the paragraph you're now reading, and in algstep E1 above.)

• Sometimes the author wants to insert extra space between paragraphs of a section, in order to indicate a slight change of topic. For this you type "\yskip" just before the new paragraph. (The space corresponding to \yskip turns out to be just half the space corresponding to \yyskip.)

Another use of \yskip sometimes occurs when paragraphs appear in series, with "a)" inserted in place of the indentation in the first paragraph, "b)" in the next, and so on. For this you type "\yskip\textindent{a)}". Also add the control sequence "\hang" if the entire paragraph (except for the "a)") is to be indented. For example, the paragraph you are about to read next has been typeset with the instructions

```
\yskip\textindent{$\bullet$}Sections normally end ...
```

• Sections normally end with a group of exercises. At this point you type

```
\exbegin{EXERCISES}
```

or (in some cases) "\exbegin{EXERCISES---First Set}", etc. Then come the exercises, one by one, each starting a new paragraph. At the beginning of this paragraph you type

either   \exno ⟨number⟩.␣[⟨rating⟩]
or   \trexno ⟨number⟩.␣[⟨rating⟩]

where \trexno is used if the exercise is supposed to have a triangle in the margin. For example,

```
\exno 4. [M50] Prove that when $n$ is an integer, $n>2$, the
equation $x↑n+y↑n=z↑n$ has no solution in positive integers
$x$, $y$, $z$,
```

After the "[⟨rating⟩]" of an exercise there sometimes is a parenthesized descriptive title, or the name of the originator of the exercise. The descriptive title, if present, should be slanted; names should not. The closing right parenthesis should be preceded by a period and followed immediately by "\xskip" without any intervening space. For example (see *ACP* Volume 1, page 20):

```
\exno 14. [50] (R. W. Floyd.)\xskip Prepare a computer program ...
\trexno 15. [HM28] ({\sl Generalized induction.})\xskip The ...
```

If the exercise contains subparts (a), (b), etc., there are two cases: The subparts may be introduced by \textindents (as in the exercise 15 we were just looking at on

page 20 of Volume 1), or they may be embedded in a paragraph (as in exercise 29 on
page 26). The first case should be treated by making separate paragraphs introduced
by "\hang\textindent{a)}"; put \yskip before the first such paragraph, but not
before the others. In the second case, type "\xskip (a)" and "\xskip (b)", etc.,
where there is no space before the \xskip.

If the exercise contains a "hint" within a paragraph, you type "\xskip[{\sl
Hint:}␣]"; as usual, there should be no space before \xskip.

• Answers to the exercises appear at the back of the book; they are entered on a
separate file—e.g., v2ans.TEX for the answers of Volume 2. It is best to typeset the
answers for each individual section at the same time as you typeset the exercises for
that section, in order to ensure consistency. In the answer pages you say

> \ansbegin{⟨section number⟩}

just before the answers to the exercises for a particular section. Then each answer is
preceded by

> \ansno ⟨number⟩.␣

For example (reading from Volume 1, page 465),

> \ansbegin{1.1}
>
> \ansno 1. $t\leftarrow a$, $a\leftarrow b$, $b\leftarrow c$, $c\leftarrow d$, $d\leftarrow t$.
>
> \ansno 2. After the first time, ...

Now look at answer number 3 on that page of Volume 1; here you should *not* use
"\algbegin", since \algbegin is for algorithms in the text. By looking at the formal
definition of \algbegin in the later part of this appendix, you can see how to modify
it in order to handle this particular case, namely to type

> \ansno 3. {\bf Algorithm F }({\sl Euclid's
> algorithm\/}){\bf.}\xskip Given two positive ...

In still more complicated cases you may have to typeset the exercise number yourself
in connection with \halign. Then you use \anskip just before the answer, in order
to get the proper spacing between answers.

Sometimes one answer is given for two or more exercises. In this case you use
"\ansnos" instead of "\ansno". For example (please turn to page 599 of Volume 1),

> \ansnos 15, 16. $\rI1\eqv\.{P0}$, $\rI2\eqv\.{P1}$, ...

• This last example leads to the question of MIX programs, which make you work a bit harder. The word "MIX" should always be handled by typing the control sequence \MIX. This will set it in typewriter type, namely the fixed-width font used also for examples in this manual. (Remember to type "\MIX\ " when a blank space follows; it's the same problem as using the \TEX logo, see Chapter 3.)

When you want to typeset something else in typewriter type, use the abbreviation \tt; for example, \MIX is short for "{\tt MIX}". Or if typewriter type is being used in a math formula, you use the control sequence "\.", which comes in very handy. For example, "\.{P0}" in the excerpt from page 599 above yields the "P0" of the formula "rI1 ≡ P0". Another thing to keep in mind when doing formulas related to MIX is the fact that "rA", "rX", "rAX", "rI", and "rJ" are supposed to be in roman type, not italics; so you use the control sequences \rA, \rX, \rAX, \rI, \rJ. (The example above shows a typical use of "\rI".)

• For MIX programs themselves, further control sequences come into play. For example, let's continue with the example from page 599 of Volume 1:

```
{\yyskip\tabskip 25pt \mixthree{\!
D1@LD1@P0@\understep{D1.}\cr
@LD2@0,1(SIZE)\cr
@ENN6@0,2@$\.N←\.{SIZE(P0)}.$\cr
@INC2@0,1@$\.{P1}←\.{P0}+\.N$\cr
@LD5@0,2(TSIZE)\cr
@J5N@D4@To D4 if $\.{TAG(P1)}=\hbox{``$-$´´}$.\cr
\\D2@LD5@-1,1(TSIZE)@\understep{D2.}\cr
```

and so on, ending (on page 600) with

```
@ST6@-1,2(TSIZE)@$\.{SIZE(P1-1)}←\.N$,
    $\.{TAG(P1-1)}←\hbox{``$-$´´}$.\quad\blackslug\cr}}
```

Explanation: (i) "\tabskip 25pt" causes each line of the program to be indented 25 points. [For short programs, you can start with "$$\vbox{\mixthree{\!" and end with "\cr}}$$", if you want the program to be centered. But that would be a bad idea on such a long program, because it would disallow breaks between pages.]

(ii) "\mixthree{\!" is the way you begin MIX program format that has three columns of special code before the right-hand column; the right-hand column is typeset normally. Sometimes there are *four* special columns, as in the program on page 568; in this case the first column contains numbers in italics. The rule is to use \mixfour when there are four such columns. The first line on page 568, for example, would be typed

```
68⊗8H⊗CON⊗0⊗Zero constant for initialization\cr
```

provided that you are looking at the second edition of Volume 1—the first edition has a different line there, namely

```
65⊗0JMP⊗1F⊗\quad$\.{RLINK(U)}=\Lambda$.\cr   .
```

Sometimes, in fact, there are *five* special columns, as in the program on page 601; the fifth column contains centered math formulas, and for this you use \mixfive. (Incidentally, when a program turns out to be too wide for the normal page size, as this one does, it is typeset separately and reduced by the publisher's cameras.) At the other extreme, there sometimes are MIX programs with only two special columns; for example, to get the programs displayed at the bottom of page 242, you type

```
$$\vcenter{\mixtwo{LD1⊗I\cr LDA⊗L$↓0$,1\cr}}
\qquad\hbox{to, e.g.,}\qquad
\vcenter{\mixtwo{LD1⊗I\cr LDA⊗BASE(0:2)\cr
    STA⊗*+1(0:2)\cr LDA⊗*,1\cr}}\eqno(8)$$   .
```

(iii) When you type "\\" at the beginning of a line of a MIX program, using either \mixtwo or \mixthree or \mixfour or \mixfive, it signifies a desirable place to break the page if TₑX needs to make a break. The author will tell you where to put these.

(iv) "\understep" will underline a step description. This works nicely when the step doesn't involve any letters or symbols that go below the line; but otherwise you need to break the underline by brute force, discontinuing it so that it doesn't touch letters with descenders. For example, here is the proper way to type line 22 of the program on page 601 of Volume 1 (using \mixfive format):

```
22⊗R3⊗J3Z⊗DONE⊗1⊗\understep{R3. S}{\sl p\hskip-3pt}\!
\understep{\hskip3pt lit re\hskip 2.5pt}{\sl\hskip-2.5pt q}\!
\understep{uired?}\cr
```

The \hskipping brings the underlines partway under the *p* and *q*, making it look as if we have a special font with underlined symbols. This is messy in the manuscript, but it looks nice in the output; you get

22 R3   J3Z   DONE   1   *R3. Split required?*

(See also the examples in Chapter 18 of this manual—the boldface subheads were made with such underlining. The underlines actually drawn on page 601 of the second edition of Volume 1 are too low; the third edition—typeset by TₑX—will look much better!)

To sum up the last few paragraphs, we can say that MIX programs are indeed troublesome to typeset; but by using the control sequences \mixtwo, ..., \mixfive you can avoid almost all of the difficulty of changing in and out of typewriter type and lining up the columns. Incidentally, there is also another control sequence \mixans that you can use for answers like number 2 on pages 523 and 524. Instead of beginning that answer with "\ansno 2.", you type

```
\mixans 2. {⊗SHIFT⊗J5N⊗ADDRERROR\cr
⊗⊗DEC3⊗5\cr
   ⋮
⊗1H⊗SRC⊗1⊗\quad\blackslug\cr}
```

This works something like \mixthree, but each line begins with an additional ⊗.

• For quotations you type

```
\quoteformat{⟨first line⟩\cr
             ⟨second line⟩\cr
                ⋮
             ⟨last line⟩\cr
\author{⟨author information⟩}
```

For example, the quotation at the end of Chapter 2 (Volume 1, page 463) should be done this way (including a few small changes that will be made in the third edition):

```
\quoteformat{You will, I am sure, agree with me...that if page\cr
534 finds us only in the second chapter,\cr
the length of the first one must have been really intolerable.\cr}
\author{SHERLOCK HOLMES, in {\sl The Valley of Fear} (1888)}
```

Sans-serif 8-point fonts will automatically be used for quotations typed in this way. The quotation itself is automatically set in a slanted font, while the author information is automatically set in "roman"; you can vary these conventions if necessary by typing "\sl" or "\rm".

• To insert an illustration at the top of the next convenient page, type

```
\topinsert{\vskip ⟨height of the illustration plus a little white space⟩
\ctrline{\caption Fig.\ ⟨number⟩. ⟨text of the caption⟩}}
```

assuming that the caption fits on one line. This insertion usually goes into the manuscript just after the paragraph that first refers to this particular illustration. For example, the illustration in Volume 1, page 121, would be handled by typing

```
\topinsert{\vskip 5in
\ctrline{\caption Fig.\ 13. The \MIX\ computer.}}
```

• The following example (see Chapter 4 of this manual) shows how footnotes are treated:

```
... will never\footnote*{Well$\ldotsm$, hardly ever.} use the ...
```

• To get the heading "**Table 1**" centered on a line, type

```
\tablehead{Table 1}   .
```

For the table itself, it's best to let the author tell you exactly what he wants, since there are so many possibilities. The control sequence \9 gives a blank space equal to the width of a digit in the current roman font; this is occasionally useful when tables are being prepared.

• When you really get into typing the books, some things will occasionally arise that aren't covered here, but this might add a little spice to the task. The manuscript for Volume 2 of *ACP* (Second Edition) may be consulted for numerous examples of the recommended format.

Here now are the TeX language definitions that explain the meanings of all these new control sequences very precisely. All of the standard definitions at the beginning of Appendix B are used, up until the font specifications, and it is unnecessary to repeat them here. The remaining definitions are:

```
\def\mod{\<\,\mathbin{\char'155\char'157\char'144}\penalty900\<\,}
\def\modulo#1{\penalty0\;
  (\char'155\char'157\char'144\char'165\char'154\char'157\,\,\,#1)}
\def\deg{↑{\hbox{\hskip-1pt\:w\char5}}}
\:@←cmathx  \:a←cmr10   \:b←cmr9    \:c←cmr8
\:d←cmr7    \:e←cmr6    \:f←cmr5    \:g←cmi10
\:h←cmi9    \:i←cmi8    \:j←cmi7    \:k←cmi6
\:l←cmi5    \:m←cmsc10  \:n←cms10   \:o←cms9
\:p←cms8    \:q←cmb10   \:r←cmb9    \:s←cmb8
\:t←cmtt    \:u←cmsy10  \:v←cmsy9   \:w←cmsy8
\:x←cmsy7   \:y←cmsy6   \:z←cmsy5   \:;←cmtit1
\:<←cmssb   \:=←cmss12  \:>←cmss8   \:?←cmsss8
\hsize29pc \vsize45pc \maxdepth2pt \parindent19pt
\topbaseline10pt \parskip0pt plus1pt \lineskip1pt
\topskip24pt plus6pt minus10pt \botskip3pt plus6pt
```

```
\def\tenpoint{\baselineskip12pt
  \dispskip12pt plus3pt minus9pt
  \dispaskip0pt plus3pt \dispbskip7pt plus3pt minus4pt
  \def\rm{\:a} \def\sl{\:n} \def\bf{\:q} \def\it{\:g}
  \def\biglp{\mathopen{\vcenter{\hbox{\:@\char'0}}}}
  \def\bigrp{\mathclose{\vcenter{\hbox{\:@\char'1}}}}
  \mathrm adf \mathit gjl \mathsy uxz \rm}
\def\ninepoint{\baselineskip11pt
  \dispskip11pt plus3pt minus8pt
  \dispaskip0pt plus3pt \dispbskip6pt plus3pt minus3pt
  \def\rm{\:b} \def\sl{\:o} \def\bf{\:r} \def\it{\:h}
  \def\biglp{\mathopen{\hbox{\:a(}}}
  \def\bigrp{\mathclose{\hbox{\:a)}}}
  \mathrm bef \mathit hkl \mathsy vyz \rm}
\def\eightpoint{\baselineskip9pt
  \dispskip9pt plus3pt minus7pt
  \dispaskip0pt plus3pt \dispbskip5pt plus3pt minus2pt
  \def\rm{\:c} \def\sl{\:p} \def\bf{\:s} \def\it{\:i}
  \def\biglp{\mathopen{\hbox{\:a(}}}
  \def\bigrp{\mathclose{\hbox{\:a)}}}
  \mathrm cef \mathit ikl \mathsy wyz \rm}
\mathex @ \def\tt{\:t}
\def\bigglp{\mathopen{\vcenter{\hbox{\:@\char'22}}}}
\def\biggrp{\mathclose{\vcenter{\hbox{\:@\char'23}}}}
\def\bigglp{\mathopen{\vcenter{\hbox{\:@\char'40}}}}
\def\bigggrp{\mathclose{\vcenter{\hbox{\:@\char'41}}}}

\def\9{\hskip .5em}
\def\xskip{\hskip7pt plus3pt minus4pt}
\def\yskip{\penalty-50\vskip3pt plus3pt minus2pt}
\def\yyskip{\penalty-100\vskip6pt plus6pt minus4pt}
\def\sectionskip{\penalty-200\vskip24pt plus12pt minus6pt}

\def\textindent#1{\noindent
  \hbox to 19pt{\hskip0pt plus1000pt minus1000pt#1 }\!}
\def\hang{\hangindent19pt}


\def\tpage{F} \def\rhead{} \def\frstx{F} \def\csec{} \def\chd{}
\def\titlepage{\gdef\tpage{T}}
\def\runninglefthead#1{\gdef\rhead{\:m#1}}
```

```
\def\acpmark#1#2{\mark
  {\ifeven0{\hbox to .45 in{\:a\count0\hfill}\rhead\hfill\:a#2}
    \else{\:a\csec\hfill\:m#1\hbox to .45 in{\:a\hfill\count0}}}}
\def\runningrighthead#1 \section#2{\acpmark{\chd}{#2}
  \gdef\csec{#2} \gdef\chd{#1}}
\output{\baselineskip 0pt\lineskip0pt
  \vbox to 48pc{
    \if T\tpage{
      \gdef\tpage{F}
      \vskip24pt \page \vfill \ctrline{\:c\count0}}
    \else{\baselineskip12pt \null
      \hbox to size{\ifeven0{\topmark}\else{\botmark}}
      \null \page \vfill}}
  \advcount0}

\def\sectionbegin#1{\hbox{\:<#1}\penalty1000\vskip6pt plus3pt
  \acpmark{\chd}{\csec}\noindent\tenpoint\!}
\def\dimsectionbegin#1{\sectionskip
  \acpmark{\chd}{\csec}\noindent{\bf#1.}\tenpoint\xskip\!}
\def\subsectionbegin#1{\yyskip\noindent{\bf#1.}\tenpoint\xskip\!}
\def\algbegin#1(#2). {\yyskip\noindent
  {\bf #1}({\sl#2\/}){\bf.}\xskip}
\def\algstep #1. [#2]{\par\yskip
  \hang\textindent{\bf#1.}[#2]\xskip\!}
\def\thbegin#1. {\yyskip\noindent{\bf#1.}\xskip}
\def\proofbegin{\penalty25\vskip6pt plus12pt minus4pt
  \noindent{\sl Proof.}\xskip}
\def\dproofbegin{\penalty25\noindent{\sl Proof.}\xskip}
\def\exbegin#1{\sectionskip
  \hbox{\:<#1}\penalty1000\vskip8pt minus5pt
  \gdef\frstx{T}\ninepoint}
\def\ansbegin#1{\runningrighthead{ANSWERS TO EXERCISES}
  \section{#1}\sectionskip
  \hbox{\:<SECTION #1}\penalty1000\vskip8pt minus5pt
  \acpmark{\chd}{\csec}\gdef\frstx{T}\ninepoint}
\def\anskip{\par\if T\frstx{\gdef\frstx{F}}\else{\penalty-200}
  \vskip3pt plus3pt minus1pt}
\def\exno #1. [#2]{\anskip\textindent{\bf#1.}[{\it#2\/}]\hskip6pt}
\def\trexno #1. [#2]{\anskip\noindent\hbox to 19pt
  {\hskip-3.5pt\:@\char'170\hfill\bf#1. }[{\it#2\/}]\hskip6pt}
```

```
\def\ansno #1. {\anskip\textindent{\bf#1.}}
\def\ansnos #1,#2. {\anskip\textindent{\bf#1,}\hbox{\bf\!#2. }}
\def\quoteformat#1{\baselineskip11pt \def\rm{\:>} \def\sl{\:?}
  \vskip6pt plus2pt minus2pt {\sl\halign{\rjustline{##}\cr#1}}}
\def\author#1{\penalty1000\vskip6pt plus2pt minus2pt
  \rm\rjustline{---#1}\vskip8pt plus4pt minus2pt}
\def\tablehead#1{\ctrline{\:<#1}\ninepoint}
\def\caption Fig.\ #1.{\ninepoint{\bf Fig.\ #1.}\xskip\!}
\def\footnote#1#2{#1\botinsert{\hrule width5pc \vskip3pt
  \baselineskip9pt\hbox par size{\eightpoint#1#2}}}

\def\star{\hbox to 0pt{\hskip 0pt minus 100pt *}}
\def\blackslug{\hbox{\hskip1pt
    \vrule width4pt height6pt depth1.5pt \hskip1pt}}

\def\MIX{{\:t MIX}}
\def\.{\hbox{\:t#1}}
\def\rA{\hbox{\rm rA}} \def\rX{\hbox{\rm rX}}
\def\rAX{\hbox{\rm rAX}}
\def\rI{\hbox{\rm rI}} \def\rJ{\hbox{\rm rJ}}
\def\understep#1{$\underline{\hbox{\sl#1}}$}
\def\mixtwo#1{\ninepoint\def\\{\noalign{\penalty-200}}
  \halign{\lft{\:t##}\quad\tabskip0pt
    ⊗\lft{\:t##}\qquad⊗\lft{\rm##}\cr#1\\}}
\def\mixthree#1{\ninepoint\def\\{\noalign{\penalty-200}}
  \halign{\lft{\:t##}\quad\tabskip0pt
    ⊗\lft{\:t##}\quad⊗\lft{\:t##}\qquad⊗\lft{\rm##}\cr#1\\}}
\def\mixfour#1{\ninepoint\def\\{\noalign{\penalty-200}}
  \halign{\rt{\it##}\quad\tabskip0pt
    ⊗\lft{\:t##}\quad⊗\lft{\:t##}\quad
    ⊗\lft{\:t##}\quad⊗\lft{\rm##}\cr#1\\}}
\def\mixfive#1{\ninepoint\def\\{\noalign{\penalty-200}}
  \halign{\rt{\it##}\quad\tabskip0pt
    ⊗\lft{\:t##}\quad⊗\lft{\:t##}\quad
    ⊗\lft{\:t##}\quad⊗\ctr{$ ##$}\quad⊗\lft{\rm##}\cr#1\\}}
\def\mixans #1. #2{\def\\{\noalign{\penalty-200}}\anskip
  \halign{\hbox to 19pt{##}⊗\lft{\tt##}\quad
    ⊗\lft{\tt##}\quad⊗\lft{\tt##}\quad⊗\lft{\rm##}\cr
    {\hfill\bf #1. }#2}}
```

<F> Font tables

1. Standard "ascii" code. The American Standard Code for Information Interchange deals with characters that print and actions that don't. The following table of 128 codes shows "control" symbols for codes ´001 to ´032, since many computer terminals generate these symbols when the typist holds the control key down when typing a letter. These 26 codes also have other names not shown here; for example, ↑G (control-G) is also called BEL (ring the bell). It is rarely possible to transmit all 128 of these symbols from your terminal to a computer and vice versa—something strange usually happens to a few of them. But the most important ones get through.

	0	1	2	3	4	5	6	7
´000	NUL	↑A	↑B	↑C	↑D	↑E	↑F	↑G
´010	↑H	↑I	↑J	↑K	↑L	↑M	↑N	↑O
´020	↑P	↑Q	↑R	↑S	↑T	↑U	↑V	↑W
´030	↑X	↑Y	↑Z	ESC	FS	GS	RS	US
´040	SP	!	"	#	$	%	&	´
´050	(	)	*	+	,	−	.	/
´060	0	1	2	3	4	5	6	7
´070	8	9	:	;	<	=	>	?
´100	@	A	B	C	D	E	F	G
´110	H	I	J	K	L	M	N	O
´120	P	Q	R	S	T	U	V	W
´130	X	Y	Z	[	\	]	^	_
´140	`	a	b	c	d	e	f	g
´150	h	i	j	k	l	m	n	o
´160	p	q	r	s	t	u	v	w
´170	x	y	z	{	|	}	~	DEL

2. Stanford "SUAI" code. The following table of 128 codes (developed about 1965 at the Stanford Artificial Intelligence Laboratory) applies to numerous devices now used in the vicinity of Stanford University. For the most part it is ascii code but extended to include more printing characters. There's an unfortunate discrepancy, however, with respect to "}" ('175 in ascii, '176 at SUAI); also "~" ('176 in ascii, something like '032 at SUAI); also "^" ('136 in ascii, something like '004 at SUAI); and also "_" ('137 in ascii, '030 at SUAI). Essentially the same code is used at Carnegie-Mellon University and at the University of Southern California, but with '176 and '175 switched. At the Massachusetts Institute of Technology the code is somewhat the same but there are ten discrepancies: codes '010, '013, '030, '032, '033, '136, '137, '175, '176, '177 are respectively called BS, ↑, ←, ≠, ESC, ^, _, }, ~, DEL.

	0	1	2	3	4	5	6	7
'000	NUL	↓	α	β	∧	¬	ε	π
'010	λ	TAB	LF	VT	FF	CR	∞	∂
'020	⊂	⊃	∩	∪	∀	∃	⊗	↔
'030	_	→	∼	≠	≤	≥	≡	∨
'040	SP	!	"	#	$	%	&	'
'050	(	)	*	+	,	-	.	/
'000	0	1	2	3	4	5	6	7
'070	8	9	:	;	<	=	>	?
'100	@	A	B	C	D	E	F	G
'110	H	I	J	K	L	M	N	O
'120	P	Q	R	S	T	U	V	W
'130	X	Y	Z	[	\	]	↑	←
'140	`	a	b	c	d	e	f	g
'150	h	i	j	k	l	m	n	o
'160	p	q	r	s	t	u	v	w
'170	x	y	z	{	|	ALT	}	BS

3. TEX standard roman fonts. The following table of 128 codes shows the form TEX expects its fonts to have when you use the control sequences for accents and special foreign letters listed in Chapter 9, or when you use the control sequences for upper case Greek letters listed later in this appendix. (Actually TEX never addresses codes ´042, ´134, ´136, ´137, and ´173 to ´177 directly; they are accessed indirectly via ligature information stored within the font itself.) Codes ´043 and ´044 are undefined; special characters needed in particular jobs (e.g., inverted "?" and "!" for Spanish text) might be placed there. Note that there is agreement with ascii code on all of its printing characters except for #, $, @, \, ˆ, _, {, |, }, and ~, which TEX gets from its "symbol" fonts. The same codes are used for slanted roman fonts like cms10.

	0	1	2	3	4	5	6	7
´000	Γ	Δ	Θ	Λ	Ξ	Π	Σ	Υ
´010	Φ	Ψ	Ω	ı	ȷ	`	´	ˆ
´020	ˇ	˘	¯	··	~	ˍ	˝	˚
´030	¸	ˏ	⌢	ß	æ	œ	Æ	Œ
´040	ø	!	"	undefined	undefined	%	&	'
´050	(	)	*	+	,	-	.	/
´060	0	1	2	3	4	5	6	7
´070	8	9	:	;	<	=	>	?
´100	Ø	A	B	C	D	E	F	G
´110	H	I	J	K	L	M	N	O
´120	P	Q	R	S	T	U	V	W
´130	X	Y	Z	[	"	]	–	—
´140	'	a	b	c	d	e	f	g
´150	h	i	j	k	l	m	n	o
´160	p	q	r	s	t	u	v	w
´170	x	y	z	ff	fi	fl	ffi	ffl

4. TEX typewriter fonts. Fixed-width fonts such as the cmtt font shown below are sort of a cross between TEX roman and SUAI codes. All the accents and special characters of a TEX roman font are present except for \b, \l, \o, \ss, \H, and \O; and every ascii printing character is present. (SUAI code instead of ascii code is, however, used for the character "}", and TEX roman code is used for "~".) All SUAI characters that appear in these fonts appear in their SUAI positions, except for ∞, ~, ≤, ≥, and ⊥. (Furthermore you may prefer to use codes ´015 and ´016 in place of ´140 and ´047, as done in the examples of this manual.)

	0	1	2	3	4	5	6	7
´000	Γ	Δ	Θ	Λ	Ξ	Π	Σ	Υ
´010	Φ	Ψ	Ω	ı	ȷ	`	´	ˆ
´020	˜	˘	¯	¨	~	∞	⊗	•
´030	˙	→	≤	≥	æ	œ	Æ	Œ
´040	⊔	!	"	#	$	%	&	´
´050	(	)	*	+	,	−	.	/
´060	0	1	2	3	4	5	6	7
´070	8	9	:	;	<	=	>	?
´100	@	A	B	C	D	E	F	G
´110	H	I	J	K	L	M	N	O
´120	P	Q	R	S	T	U	V	W
´130	X	Y	Z	[	\	]	↑	←
´140	´	a	b	c	d	e	f	g
´150	h	i	j	k	l	m	n	o
´160	p	q	r	s	t	u	v	w
´170	x	y	z	{			⊥	}	´

5. TₑX standard italic fonts. The following table of 128 codes shows the form TₑX expects the italic (it) fonts to have in math mode, if you use the control sequences for lower case Greek letters, upper case italic Greek letters, and a few other special symbols listed later in this appendix. The same codes apply to text italic fonts like cmti10 and cmu10 (the "unslanted" italic font used in the running heads of this manual). Note that there is agreement with ascii code on all of its printing characters, except for the % sign and the ten symbols that are missing in TₑX roman fonts (see the previous page).

	0	1	2	3	4	5	6	7
´000	Γ	Δ	Θ	Λ	Ξ	Π	Σ	Υ
´010	Φ	Ψ	Ω	α	β	γ	δ	ϵ
´020	ς	η	θ	ι	κ	λ	μ	ν
´030	ξ	π	ρ	σ	τ	υ	ϕ	χ
´040	$\imath$	!	"	ℓ	$\wp$	∂	$\&$	'
´050	(	)	*	$+$	,	-	.	/
´060	0	1	2	3	4	5	6	7
´070	8	9	:	;	$<$	$=$	$>$	?
´100	$\jmath$	A	B	C	D	E	F	G
´110	H	I	J	K	L	M	N	O
´120	P	Q	R	S	T	U	V	W
´130	X	Y	Z	[	"	]	–	—
´140	'	a	b	c	d	e	f	g
´150	h	i	j	k	l	m	n	o
´160	p	q	r	s	t	u	v	w
´170	x	y	z	ψ	ω	φ	ϑ	ϖ

6. TEX standard symbol fonts. The following table of 128 codes shows the form TEX expects the symbol (sy) fonts to have in math mode, if you use the control sequences for various special symbols listed later in this appendix, or if you use special keys on your terminal in math mode as explained below in subsection 8. Several positions are undefined; they can be filled with any special characters that might be needed in a particular job.

	0	1	2	3	4	5	6	7
´000	—	·	×	*	\	∘	±	∓
´010	⊕	⊖	⊗	⊘	⊙	÷	⊤	•
´020	⊥	≡	⊆	⊇	≤	≥	≼	≽
´030	∼	≈	⊂	⊃	≠	≐	≺	≻
´040	←	→	↑	↓	↔	≪	≫	≃
´050	⇐	⇒	⇑	⇓	⇔	↖	↗	↦
´060	′	∞	∈	∉	∅	_	∠	undefined
´070	∀	∃	¬	ℵ	ℜ	ℑ	⊤	undefined
´100	∕	𝒜	ℬ	𝒞	𝒟	ℰ	ℱ	𝒢
´110	ℋ	ℐ	𝒥	𝒦	ℒ	ℳ	𝒩	𝒪
´120	𝒫	𝒬	ℛ	𝒮	𝒯	𝒰	𝒱	𝒲
´130	𝒳	𝒴	𝒵	∪	∩	⊎	∧	∨
´140	⊢	⊣	⌊	⌋	⌈	⌉	{	}
´150	⟨	⟩	|	‖	⟦	⟧	undefined	undefined
´160	√	♯	∇	∫	⊔	⊓	⊑	undefined
´170	§	†	‡	¶	@	©	£	$

7. T_EX standard extension fonts. The table of 128 codes on the next page shows the form T_EX expects the extension (`ex`) font to have in math mode, if you use variable delimiters or the control sequences for large operators listed later in this appendix.

Actually T_EX addresses most of these characters indirectly; for example, all left parentheses are addressed starting with character ´000, based on information stored in the font itself, and the font also tells T_EX that arbitrarily large left parentheses can be made from characters ´060 (top), ´102 (middle), ´100 (bottom). The only codes explicitly referred to by T_EX are ´000 to ´016, ´110, ´112, ´114, ´116, ´120 to ´127, and ´160. Thus, a font designer can move most of the other symbols if desired, subject only to the restriction that the code number of a large symbol be greater than the code numbers of its smaller variants. (If codes are changed, however, it may be necessary to change the definitions of control sequences like \bigglp in Appendix B.) It is expected that positions marked "undefined" in this chart will be filled with characters specially tailored to specific jobs; for example, character ´177 is used for the "dangerous bend" symbol in this manual, but it might not be present in all T_EX extension fonts.

	0	1	2	3	4	5	6	7
´000	(	)	[	]	⌊	⌋	⌈	⌉
´010	{	}	⟨	⟩	∣	∥	/	undefined
´020	(	)	(	)	[	]	⌊	⌋
´030	⌈	⌉	{	}	⟨	⟩	/	undefined
´040	(	)	[	]	⌊	⌋	⌈	⌉
´050	{	}	⟨	⟩	/	undefined	undefined	undefined
´060	(	)	⌈	⌉	⌊	⌋	∣	∣
´070	(	)	(	)	{	}	.	undefined
´100	\	/	∣	∣	undefined	undefined	⊔	⊔
´110	∮	∮	⊙	⊙	⊕	⊕	⊗	⊗
´120	∑	∏	∫	∪	∩	⊎	∧	∨
´130	∑	∏	∫	∪	∩	⊎	∧	∨
´140	undefined	undefined	undefined	undefined	undefined	undefined	undefined	undefined
´150	undefined	undefined	undefined	undefined	undefined	undefined	undefined	undefined
´160	√	√	√	√	√	∣	⌈	undefined
´170	▶	⌣	⌢	⌢	⌢	⌣	undefined	undefined

8. TEX math mode. When TEX is in math mode, it converts 7-bit codes into 9-bit codes according to the table below. Furthermore a "type" is associated with the 9-bit code, making (almost) a 12-bit code, since there are seven types (Ord, Op, Bin, Rel, Open, Close, Punct); see Chapter 18. This conversion is based on the SUAI code. For example, if you type "→" at Stanford (character ´031) the table below says that this is converted to Rel *441*, namely a mathematical "relation" found in the sy font as character ´041, and this is "→".

Not all of these 128 codes can appear in character files that are prepared with ordinary software, but the chart shows what would happen if they could. If people at MIT ever want to use TEX they will undoubtedly make changes to the internal table that TEX uses for this conversion, because of the ten discrepancies between MIT's code and the SUAI code. However, people at CMU or USC should have no trouble, since TEX uses this table only for characters classified as ⟨letter⟩ or ⟨otherchar⟩ (see Chapter 9).

	0	1	2	3	4	5	6	7
´000	Bin *401*	Rel *443*	Ord *213*	Ord *214*	Bin *536*	Ord *472*	Ord *217*	Ord *231*
´010	Ord *225*	Ord *215*	Ord *216*	Op *563*	Bin *406*	Bin *410*	Ord *461*	Ord *245*
´020	Rel *432*	Rel *433*	Bin *534*	Bin *533*	Ord *470*	Ord *471*	Bin *412*	Rel *444*
´030	Ord *465*	Rel *441*	Rel *430*	Rel *434*	Rel *424*	Rel *425*	Rel *421*	Bin *537*
´040	Ord *463*	Close *041*	Ord *541*	Ord *561*	Ord *577*	Ord *045*	Ord *046*	Close *047*
´050	Open *050*	Close *051*	Ord *052*	Bin *053*	Punct *054*	Bin *400*	Ord *056*	Ord *057*
´060	Ord *060*	Ord *061*	Ord *062*	Ord *063*	Ord *064*	Ord *065*	Ord *066*	Ord *067*
´070	Ord *070*	Ord *071*	Ord *072*	Punct *073*	Rel *074*	Rel *075*	Rel *076*	Close *077*
´100	Ord *574*	Ord *301*	Ord *302*	Ord *303*	Ord *304*	Ord *305*	Ord *306*	Ord *307*
´110	Ord *310*	Ord *311*	Ord *312*	Ord *313*	Ord *314*	Ord *315*	Ord *316*	Ord *317*
´120	Ord *320*	Ord *321*	Ord *322*	Ord *323*	Ord *324*	Ord *325*	Ord *326*	Ord *327*
´130	Ord *330*	Ord *331*	Ord *332*	Open *133*	Bin *404*	Close *135*	Rel *442*	Rel *440*
´140	Open *140*	Ord *341*	Ord *342*	Ord *343*	Ord *344*	Ord *345*	Ord *346*	Ord *347*
´150	Ord *350*	Ord *351*	Ord *352*	Ord *353*	Ord *354*	Ord *355*	Ord *356*	Ord *357*
´160	Ord *360*	Ord *361*	Ord *362*	Ord *363*	Ord *364*	Ord *365*	Ord *366*	Ord *367*
´170	Ord *370*	Ord *371*	Ord *372*	Open *546*	Ord *552*	Bin *405*	Close *547*	Bin *017*

9. Control sequences. The tables we have seen show all of the special symbols that appear in TEX's standard fonts. But the question remains, how can a person specify them on an ordinary keyboard? Well, you can always define your favorite control sequence in terms of the \char operation; and if you have a suitable keyboard you can type the symbols of SUAI code directly. TEX also recognizes the control sequences listed below, when in math mode.

(a) Lower case Greek letters:

α	\alpha	κ	\kappa	υ	\upsilon
β	\beta	λ	\lambda	ϕ	\phi
γ	\gamma	μ	\mu	χ	\chi
δ	\delta	ν	\nu	ψ	\psi
ϵ	\epsilon	ξ	\xi	ω	\omega
ζ	\zeta	π	\pi	φ	\varphi
η	\eta	ρ	\rho	ϑ	\vartheta
θ	\theta	σ	\sigma	ϖ	\varomega
ι	\iota	τ	\tau		

(b) Upper case Greek letters:

Γ	\Gamma	Σ	\Sigma	$\mathit{\Gamma}$	\Gammait	$\mathit{\Sigma}$	\Sigmait
Δ	\Delta	Υ	\Upsilon	$\mathit{\Delta}$	\Deltait	$\mathit{\Upsilon}$	\Upsilonit
Θ	\Theta	Φ	\Phi	$\mathit{\Theta}$	\Thetait	$\mathit{\Phi}$	\Phiit
Λ	\Lambda	Ψ	\Psi	$\mathit{\Lambda}$	\Lambdait	$\mathit{\Psi}$	\Psiit
Ξ	\Xi	Ω	\Omega	$\mathit{\Xi}$	\Xiit	$\mathit{\Omega}$	\Omegait
Π	\Pi			$\mathit{\Pi}$	\Piit		

(c) Script letters:

$\mathcal{A}$	\Ascr	$\mathcal{J}$	\Jscr	$\mathcal{S}$	\Sscr
$\mathcal{B}$	\Bscr	$\mathcal{K}$	\Kscr	$\mathcal{T}$	\Tscr
$\mathcal{C}$	\Cscr	$\mathcal{L}$	\Lscr	$\mathcal{U}$	\Uscr
$\mathcal{D}$	\Dscr	$\mathcal{M}$	\Mscr	$\mathcal{V}$	\Vscr
$\mathcal{E}$	\Escr	$\mathcal{N}$	\Nscr	$\mathcal{W}$	\Wscr
$\mathcal{F}$	\Fscr	$\mathcal{O}$	\Oscr	$\mathcal{X}$	\Xscr
$\mathcal{G}$	\Gscr	$\mathcal{P}$	\Pscr	$\mathcal{Y}$	\Yscr
$\mathcal{H}$	\Hscr	$\mathcal{Q}$	\Qscr	$\mathcal{Z}$	\Zscr
$\mathcal{I}$	\Iscr	$\mathcal{R}$	\Rscr	ℓ	\lscr

(d) Binary operators:

±	\pm	⊕	\oplus	∗	\ast
∓	\mp	⊖	\ominus	∘	\circ
×	\times	⊗	\otimes	•	\bullet
÷	\div	⊘	\odiv	⊤	\interc
\	\rslash	⊙	\odot	⊔	\lub
·	\cdot	⊎	\uplus	⊓	\glb

(e) Binary relations:

↑	\up	⊥	\perp	≺	\prec
↓	\down	⊢	\vdash	≼	\preceq
⇐	\←	⊣	\dashv	≻	\succ
⇒	\→	↦	\mapsto	≽	\succeq
⇑	\↑	|	\relv	⊑	\sqsub
⇓	\↓	‖	\relvv	≪	\lsls
⇔	\⇕	⊆	\subset	≫	\grgr
↰	\lsh	⊇	\supset	≃	\simeq
↱	\rsh	∈	\in	≈	\approx
		∉	\notin	≐	\doteq

You can also use the control sequence \not to negate or "cross out" most of the relations above. For example, the symbol "⊄" is really two symbols, obtained by typing "\not\subset". (Character ´100 in the symbol font has a width of zero, so it will overlap the following character.) But watch out: you should actually type "\mathrel{\not\subset}", in order to prevent TEX from breaking a line after \not. (See the definition of \neqv in Appendix B.)

(f) Brackets:

⌊	\lfloor	⌋	\rfloor
⌈	\lceil	⌉	\rceil
{	\{	}	\}
⟨	\langle	⟩	\rangle
⟦	\dleft	⟧	\dright
|	\leftv	|	\rightv
‖	\leftvv	‖	\rightvv

(g) "Large" operators (text and display styles):

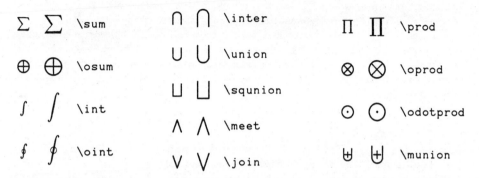

Σ ∑	\sum
⊕ ⊕	\osum
∫ ∫	\int
∮ ∮	\oint
∩ ⋂	\inter
∪ ⋃	\union
⊔ ⊔	\squnion
∧ ⋀	\meet
∨ ⋁	\join
Π ∏	\prod
⊗ ⊗	\oprod
⊙ ⊙	\odotprod
⊎ ⊎	\munion

(h) Miscellaneous math symbols:

ι	\iit	∞	\infty	∂	\partial
ȷ	\jit	∅	\emptyset	∇	\nabla
ℜ	\real	#	\#	∫	\smallint
ℑ	\imag	∥	|	√	\surd
ℵ	\aleph	∠	\angle	⊤	\top
℘	\wp	′	\prime	⊥	\bot

(i) Miscellaneous nonmath symbols (but allowed only in math mode):

§	\section	@	\@
†	\dag	©	\copyright
‡	\ddag	£	\sterling
¶	\P	$	\$

Some of the symbols in TeX's math fonts can be accessed directly only by using the SUAI-oriented conversions in subsection 8. For example, the only way to get a left arrow is by typing "$←$"; no built-in control sequence has been defined for it. If your keyboard doesn't have this symbol, the remedy is to define an appropriate new control sequence, such as

```
\def\from{\mathrel{\char´440}}  .
```

<H> Hyphenation

The conditions under which TₑX will try to hyphenate a word are discussed in Chapter 14. Now let's consider how hyphenation is actually accomplished.

It seems to be undesirable to look for the set of all possible places to hyphenate every given word. For one thing, the problem is extremely difficult, since the word "record" is supposed to be broken as "rec-ord" when it is a noun but "re-cord" when it is a verb. We might consider also the word "hyphenation" itself, which appears to be rather an exception:

$$\text{hy-phen-a-tion} \quad \text{vs.} \quad \text{con-cat-e-na-tion} \quad .$$

Why does the "n" go with the "a" in one case and not the other? Starting at letter a in the dictionary and trying to find rigorous rules for hyphenation without much knowledge, we come up against a-part vs. ap-er-ture, aph-o-rism vs. a-pha-sia, etc. It becomes clear that what we want is not an accurate but ponderously slow routine that consumes a lot of memory space and processing time; instead we want a set of hyphenation rules that are

      a) simple enough to explain in a couple of pages,

      b) almost always safe,

 and c) powerful enough that bad breaks due to missed hyphenations are very rare.

Point (c) means that a proofreader's job should be only negligibly more difficult than it would be if an intelligent human being were doing all of the hyphenations needed to typeset the same material.

So here are the rules TₑX uses (found with the help of Frank Liang):

1) Exception removal. If the first seven letters of the word appear in a small internal dictionary of words to be treated specially (about 350 words in all, see below), use the hyphenation found in that dictionary. Furthermore some of the entries in the dictionary specify looking at more than seven letters to make sure that the exception is real; e.g., "in-form-ant" wouldn't be distinguished from the unexceptional word "in-for-ma-tion" on the basis of seven letters alone. If the given word has seven letters or fewer and ends with "s", the word minus the s is also looked up. The dictionary contains nearly all the common English words for which the rules below would make an incorrect break, plus additional words that are common in computer science writing and whose breaks are not satisfactorily found by the rules.

2) Suffix removal. A permissible hyphen is inserted if the word ends with -able (preceded by e, h, i, k, l, o, u, v, w, x, y or nt or rt), -ary (preceded by ion or en), –cal, –cate (preceded by a vowel), –cial, –cious (unless preceded by s), –cient, –dent, –ful, –ize (preceded by l), –late (preceded by a vowel), –less, –ly, –ment, –ness, –nary (unless preceded by e or io), –ogy, –rapher, –raphy, –scious, –scope, –scopic, –sion, –sphere, –tal, –tial, –tion, –tion–al, –tive, –ture. Here a "vowel" is either a, e, i, o, u, or y; the other 20 letters are "consonants."

There is also a somewhat more complex rule for words ending with "ing": If ing is preceded by fewer than four letters, insert no permissible hyphens. Otherwise if ing is preceded by two identical consonants other than f, l, s, or z, break between them. Otherwise if it is preceded by a letter other than l, break the –ing. Otherwise if the letter before ling is b, c, d, f, g, k, p, t, or z, break before this letter (except break ck–ling if the word ends with ckling). Otherwise break –ing.

Furthermore the same suffix removal routine is applied to the residual word after having successfully found the suffixes –able, –ary, –ful, –ize, –less, –ly, –ment, and –ness. If the original word ends in s and no suffix was found, the final s is removed and the suffix routine is applied again. If the original word ends in ed the suffix routine is applied to the word with the final d removed, and (if that is unsuccessful) to the word with final ed removed.

Any suffixes found are effectively removed from the word, and not examined by rules 3 and 4. If the original word ends with e or s or ed, this final letter or pair of letters is also effectively removed.

3) Prefix removal. A permissible hyphen is inserted if the word begins with be– (followed by c, h, s, or w), com–, con–, dis– (unless followed by h or y), equi– (unless followed by v), equiv–, ex–, hand–, horse–, hy*per–, im–, in– (but use in*ter– or in*tro– if present), lex*i–, mac*ro–, math*e–, max*i–, min*i–, mul*ti–, non–, out–, over–, pseu*do–, quad–, semi–, some–, sub–, su*per–, there–, trans– (followed by a, f, g, l, or m), tri– (followed by a, f, or u), un*der–, un– (unless followed by der or i). Here an asterisk denotes a second permissible hyphen to be recognized, but only if the entire prefix appears.

After the prefixes dis–, im–, in–, non–, over–, un– have been recognized as stated, the prefix routine is entered again. Any prefixes found are effectively removed from the word, and not examined by rule 4.

4) Study of consonant pairs. In the remainder of the word, after suffixes and prefixes have been removed, we combine the letter pairs ch, gh, ph, sh, th, treating them as single consonants.

If the three-letter combination XYY is found, where X is a vowel and Y a consonant, break between the Y's, except if Y is l or s. In the latter case, break only if the following letter is a vowel and the word doesn't end "XYYer" or "XYYers".

If the three-letter combination Xck is found, where X is a vowel, break after the ck.

If the three-letter combination Xqu is found, where X is a vowel, break before the qu.

If the four-letter combination XYZW is found, where X and W are vowels and Y and Z are consonants, break between the consonants unless YZ is one of the following pairs:

bl, br, cl, cr, chl, chr, dg, dr, fl, fr, ght, gl, gr, kn, lk, lq, nch, nk, nx, phr, pl, pr, rk, sp, sq, tch, tr, thr, wh, wl, wn, wr.

Furthermore do not break between the consonants if the word ends with XYZer, XYZers, XYZage, XYZages, or XYZest, when YZ is one of the pairs

ft, ld, mp, nd, ng, ns, nt, rg, rm, rn, rt, st.

5) *Retaining short ends.* After applying rules 1, 2, 3, and 4, take back all "permissible" breaks that result in only one or two letters after the break, or that have only one letter before it, or that have only one letter between prefix and suffix. (Thus, for example, the suffix rule will break −ly, but this won't count in the final analysis; it does affect the hyphenation algorithm, however, since the suffixes in words like "rationally" will be found by repeated suffix removal.)

Also, take back any break leading to the syllable −e, −Xe, or −XYe, where X and Y are any two letters and where this e occurs at the end of the shortest subword on which suffix removal was tried in rule 2. (This rule avoids syllables with "silent e". For example, we do not wish to hyphenate rid−dle, proces−ses, was−teful, arran−gement, themsel−ves, lar−gely, and so on.) Similarly, final syllables of the form −Xed or −XYed (except −ized) are also disregarded.

Example of hyphenation:

su−per−califragilis−ticex−pialido−cious.

(This is a correct subset of the "official" syllabification specified by the coiners of this word, namely su−per−cal−i−frag−il−is−tic−ex−pi−al−i−do−cious.)

Now here's the dictionary of words that should be handled separately, as mentioned in rule 1. (When an asterisk appears, it means that this letter is checked too, in addition to the first seven letters.)

First, we include the following words since they are exceptions to the suffix rules:

```
(−able)   con−trol−lable eq−uable in−sa−tiable ne−go−tiable
          so−ciable turn−table un−con−trollable un−so−ciable
(−dent)   de−pend−ent in−de−pend−ent
```

```
(-ing)     any-thing bal-ding dar-ling dump-ling err-ing eve-ning
           every-thing far-thing found-ling ink-ling main-spring
           nest-ling off-spring play-thing sap-ling shoe-string
           sib-ling some-thing star-ling ster-ling un-err-ing
           up-swing weak-ling year-ling
(-ize)     civ-i-lize crys-tal-lize im-mo-bi-lize me-ta-bo-lize
           mo-bi-lize mo-nop-o-lize sta-bi-li*ze tan-ta-lize
           un-civ-i-lized
(-late)    pal-ate
(-ment)    in-clem-ent
(-ness)    bar-on-ess li-on-ess
(-ogy)     eu-logy ped-a-gogy
(-scious)  lus-cious
(-sphere)  at-mos-phere
(-tal)     met-al non-metal pet-al post-al rent-al
(-tion)    cat-ion
(-tive)    com-bat-ive
(-ture)    stat-ure
```

Exceptions to the prefix rules:

```
(be-)      beck-on bes-tial
(com-)     com-a-tose come-back co-me-dian comp-troller
(con-)     cone-flower co-nun-drum
(equi-)    equipped
(hand-)    handle-bar
(in-)      inch-worm ink-blot inn-keeper
(inter-)   in-te-rior
(mini-)    min-is-ter min-is-try
(non-)     none-the-less
(quad-)    qua-drille
(some-)    som-er-sault
(super-)   su-pe-rior
(un-)      u-na-nim-ity u-nan-i-mous unc-tuous
```

Exceptions to the consonant rules:

```
bt:  debt-or
ck:  ac-know-ledge
```

```
ct:  de-duct-i*ble ex-act-i-tude in-ex-act-i-tude
     pre-dict-*able re-spect-*able un-pre-dict-able vict-ual
dl:  needle-work idler
ff:  buff-er off-beat off-hand off-print off-shoot off-shore stiff-en
ft:  left-ist left-over lift-off
fth: soft-hearted
gg:  egg-nog egg-head
gn:  cognac for-eign-er vignette
gsh: hogs-head
ld:  child-ish eld-est gold-en hold-out hold-over hold-up
lf:  self-ish
ll:  bull-ish crest-fallen dis-till-*ery fall-out lull-aby
     roll-away sell-out wall-eye
lm:  psalm-ist
ls:  else-where false-hood
lt:  con-sult-ant volt-age
lv:  re-solv-able re-volv-er solv-able un-solv-able
mb:  beach-comber bomb-er climb-er plumb-er
mp:  damp-en damp-est
nch: clinch-er launch-er lunch-eon ranch-er trench-ant
nc:  an-nouncer bouncer fencer hence-forth mince-meat si-lencer
nd:  bind-ery bound-ary com-mend-*a-*t*ory de-pend-able
     ex-pend-able fiend-ish land-owner out-land-ish round-about
     send-off stand-out un-der-stand-able
ng:  change-over hang-out hang-over ha-rangue me-ringue
     orange-ade tongue venge-ance
ns:  sense-less
nt:  ac-count-ant ant-acid ant-eater count-ess per-cent-*age
     rep-re-sentative
nth: ant-hill pent-house
pt:  ac-cept-able ac-ceptor adapt-able adapt-er crypt-analysis
     in-ter-ru*p*t-*i*ble
qu:  an-tiq-uity ineq-uity iniq-uity liq-uefy liq-uid liq-ui-date
     liq-ui-da-tion liq-uor pre-req-ui-site req-ui-si-tion
     sub-sequence u-biq-ui-tous
rb:  ab-sorb-ent carb-on herbal im-per-turb-able
rch: arch-ery arch-an-gel re-search-er un-search-able
```

```
rd:   ac-cord-ance board-er chordal hard-en hard-est haz-ard-ous
      jeop-ard-ize re-corder stand-ard-ize stew-ard-ess yard-age
rf:   surf-er
rg:   morgue
rl:   curl-i-cue
rm:   af-firm-a*t*i*ve con-form-*ity de-form-ity in-form-a*nt
      non-con-form-ist
rn:   cav-ern-ous dis-cern-ible mod-ern-ize turn-about turn-over
      un-gov-ern-able west-ern-ize
rp:   harp-ist sharpen
rq:   torque
rs:   coars-en ir-re-vers-ible nurse-maid nurs-ery
      re-hears-al re-vers-ible wors-en
rt:   art-ist con-vert-ible court-yard fore-short-en heart-ache
      heart-ily short-en
rth:  apart-heid court-house earth-en-ware north-east north-ern
      port-hole
rv:   nerv-ous ob-serv-a*ble ob-server pre-serv-*a*t*i*ve serv-er
      serv-ice-able
sch:  pre-school
sc:   con-de-scend cre-scendo de-cre-scendo de-scend-ent de-scent
      pleb-i-scite re-scind sea-scape
sk:   askance snake-skin whisk-er
sl:   cole-slaw
sn:   rattle-snake
ss:   class-ify class-room cross-over dis-miss-al ex-press-*i*ble
      im-pass-able less-en pass-able toss-up un-class-i-fied
st:   ar-mi-stice astig-ma-tism astir astonish-ment blast-off
      by-stand-er candle-stick cast-away cast-off con-test-ant
      co-star de-test-able di-gest-ible east-ern ex-ist-ence
      fore-stall in-con-test-able in-di-ges*t-*i*ble
      in-ex-haust-ible life-style lime-stone live-stock mile-stone
      non-ex-ist-ent per-sist-ent pho-to-stat re-start-ed
      re-state-ment re-store shy-ster side-step smoke-stack
      sug-gest-*i*ble thermo-stat waste-bas-ket waste-land
sth:  mast-head post-hu-mous priest-hood
sw:   side-swipe
tt:   watt-meter
```

```
tw:   be-tween
tz:   kib-itzer
zz:   buzz-er
```

Of course, this is not a complete list of exceptions. But it does seem to cover all words that have a reasonably high chance of being mis-hyphenated in TEX's output, considering the fact that TEX usually finds a good way to break a paragraph without any hyphenation at all.

The following words have been also been included in the special dictionary, because they are common in the author's vocabulary, and because they need more hyphens than TEX would otherwise find:

```
al-go-rithm          es-tab-lish          prob-abil-ity
bib-li-og-raphy      gen-er-ator          prob-able
bi-no-mial           hap-hazard           pro-ce-dure
cen-ter              neg-li-gible         pub-li-ca-tion
com-put-a*bil-ity    pe-ri-odic           pub-lish
dec-la-ra-tion       poly-no-mial         re-place-ment
de-gree              pre-vious            when-ever
```

\<I\> Index

This index includes all control sequences known to TEX or defined in Appendix B, and it also lists error messages that are mentioned outside of Chapter 27.

<S> Special notes about using TₑX at Stanford

(1) The standard TₑX program that you get by typing "r tex" requires that fonts @, a, d, f, g, j, l, n, q, u, x, z, and ? be reserved for the fonts declared in Appendix B. (The reason is that the system program already has the font information for these fonts in its memory; this avoids making TₑX reload thirteen separate font information files each time.)

(2) The standard TₑX program produces output for the XGP. To produce output for the Alphatype (when it is available) we will use another program "texa".

(3) You can type "xgp" before a unit of measure, to avoid the expansion factor. For example, "\hsize 3 xgpin" gives 3×200 pixels, which equals 3 inches (more or less) on our XGP.

(4) The extension ".TEX" is assumed to apply to \input file names if you do not specify the extension. If TₑX can't find the file in your area, it tries system area [1,3] before giving up. (File basic.TEX is on this area.) Your output file will have the same name as the first file you \input, except that the extension will be changed to ".XGP" and the file will always be in your own area.

(5) The message "Warning: page limits exceeded!" is given when you try to output something below the place where the output page is cut, i.e., more than one xgp inch below the bottom of the box output by the \output routine.

(6) If a font you are using isn't on area [XGP,SYS], you must mention the area explicitly. TₑX ignores the extension on font file names; the XGP server will assume that the extension is ".FNT", and TₑX assumes that the font information is on another file with the extension ".TFX".

(7) Documentation for the TₑX processor appears in the file TEXSYS.SAI on area [TEX,DEK], and in several other files mentioned there.

(8) The implementation of TₑX is explicitly designed so that extensions can be written in SAIL and incorporated into your private version of the system. You write a module called TEXEXT.SAI and this replaces the dummy extension module that is ordinarily loaded with the TₑX processor.

<X> Recent extensions to TEX

Stop the presses! The following features were added to TEX just before this manual was printed:

1.   Several new ⟨dimenparam⟩s have joined \hsize, \vsize, \topbaseline, etc., namely \lineskiplimit, \mathsurround, and \varunit. By typing "\lineskiplimit ⟨dimen⟩" you specify a dimension p such that \lineskip glue is used as the interline glue if and only if $x - h - d < p$, in the notation of Chapter 15. By typing "\mathsurround ⟨dimen⟩" you specify an amount of blank space to be inserted at the left and right of any formula embedded in text (i.e., formulas delimited by $ and $). By typing "\varunit ⟨dimen⟩" you specify the current value of a variable-size unit; the code vu denotes such relative units in a ⟨dimen⟩ specification. For example, after you define "\varunit 2pt", a ⟨dimen⟩ of 7vu would stand for 14 points. When TEX begins, the values of \lineskiplimit, \mathsurround, and \varunit are 0pt, 0pt, and 1pt, respectively.

2.   There is a new option to \advcount: If you type "\advcount ⟨digit⟩ by ⟨number⟩", the specified counter is increased by the specified number. (When the "by" option is omitted, the counter is increased by plus-or-minus one as explained before.) For example, "\advcount0 by -\count1" subtracts counter 1 from counter 0.

3.   The control sequence \unskip can be used in horizontal mode (or restricted horizontal mode) to delete one glob of glue, if this glue was the last item added to the horizontal list. The main use of this is to remove an unwanted space that may have just appeared. For example, in a macro expansion the string "#1\unskip" denotes parameter #1 with a final blank space (or other glue) removed, if #1 ends with a blank space (or other glue).

4.   Typing "\uppercase{⟨token list⟩}" in horizontal mode will change all lower-case letters of the token list into upper case. (But not the letters of control sequences.) Similarly, "\lowercase{⟨token list⟩}" changes upper-case letters into lower case.

5.   Typing "\xdef⟨control sequence⟩{⟨result text⟩}" is just like "\gdef⟨control sequence⟩{⟨result text⟩}" except that definitions in the result text are expanded. For example, "\xdef\z{\z\y}" will append the current result text of macro \y to the current result text of macro \z. You can also use \xdef to expand \counts (as well as \topmarks, etc., in \output routines).

6.   The new control sequence \ifpos is analogous to \ifeven; the \else code is evaluated only if the specified counter is zero or negative. For example, you can use \ifpos to test if a counter is zero in the following way:

```
\def\neg#1{\setcount#1-\count#1}
\def\ifzero#1#2else#3{\ifpos#1{#3}\else{\neg#1
    \ifpos#1{\neg#1 #3}\else{\neg#1 #2}}}
```

7.   \chcode has been extended to give you the opportunity to change TEX's math mode conversion (Appendix F8). Type

$$\text{\chcode } \langle\text{ascii code plus } '200\rangle\leftarrow'\langle\text{type}\rangle\langle\text{char}\rangle$$

where ⟨type⟩ is 0, 1, 2, 3, 4, 5, 6 for Ord, Op, Bin, Rel, Open, Close, Punct, respectively, and ⟨char⟩ is the three-octal-digit code. For example, a colon (ascii code '072) is normally treated by TEX as Ord'072, according to Appendix F8. It turns out this is usually a mistake in computer science papers, it should rather be Rel'072 (treated as a relation box with respect to spacing in formulas, see Chapter 18.4). You can get this by typing "\chcode'272←'3072". Then formulas like "$x := x + 1$" and "$f : X \to Y$" will come out properly.

8.   Three new units of measure are allowed: wd⟨digit⟩, ht⟨digit⟩, dp⟨digit⟩, denoting the width, height, and depth of a saved box. For example, if you type "\save5\hbox{k}\hbox to 2wd5{}" you get an empty box that is twice the width of the letter k in the current font.

9.   You can use a single letter where TEX expects a ⟨number⟩; the result is the ascii code of that letter. For example, the definition of \max in Appendix B would now more properly be

```
\def\max{\mathop{\char m \char a \char x}}
```

This works only for letters (characters of type 11, see Chapter 7).

10.   The new control sequences \ifvmode, \ifhmode, \ifmmode (analogous to other \if's) select text based on the current mode.

11. The new control sequences \hfil, \hfilneg, \hss are short for \hskip 0pt plus 100000pt, \hskip 0pt plus −100000pt, \hskip 0pt plus 100000pt minus 100000pt, respectively, and they take less TEX memory space. The vertical analogs are \vfil, \vfilneg, and \vss.

Examples of use:

$$\text{\textbackslash vfil\textbackslash penalty0\textbackslash vfilneg}$$

specifies an optional page break, with a "short" page if the break occurs;

$$\text{\textbackslash penalty1000\textbackslash hfilneg\textbackslash⊔}$$

at the end of a paragraph will force the last line of the paragraph to be right justified (it cancels the paragraph-fill glue supplied automatically by TEX).

12. Control sequences of any length are now remembered in full; the seven-letter truncation mentioned in Chapter 2 no longer happens.

PART 3

METAFONT
a system for alphabet design

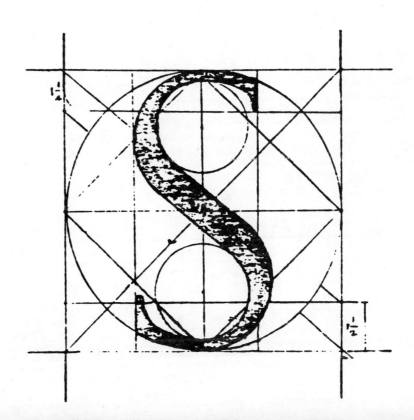

METAFONT
a system for alphabet design

G ENERATION OF TYPEFACES by mathematical means was first tried in the fifteenth century; it became popular in the sixteenth and seventeenth centuries; and it was abandoned (for good reason) during the eighteenth century. Perhaps the twentieth century will turn out to be the right time for this idea to make a comeback, now that mathematics has advanced and computers are able to do the calculations.

Modern printing equipment based on raster lines—in which metal "type" has been replaced by purely combinatorial patterns of zeros and ones that specify the desired position of ink in a discrete way—makes mathematics and computer science increasingly relevant to printing. We now have the ability to give a completely precise definition of letter shapes that will produce essentially equivalent results on all raster-based machines. Furthermore it is possible to define infinitely many styles of type at once; computers can "draw" new fonts of characters in seconds, so that a designer is able to perform valuable experiments that were previously unthinkable.

METAFONT is a system for the design of alphabets suited to raster-based devices that print or display text. The characters you are reading were all designed with METAFONT, in a completely precise way; and they were developed rather hastily by the author of the system, who is a rank amateur at such things. It seems clear that further work with METAFONT has the potential of producing typefaces of real beauty, so this manual has been written for people who would like to help advance the art of mathematical type design.

1

A METAFONT user writes a "program" for each letter or other symbol that is desired. Ideally the programs will be expressed in terms of variable parameters, so that a wide variety of typefaces can be obtained, simply by changing the parameters; but METAFONT can also be used to define a single solitary font, or even a single character, if anybody really wants to.

It is harder to write a METAFONT program than to draw a character with pen and ink, but once the program has been written you can easily "parameterize" it so that the letter shapes will adapt themselves to different specifications. And it is easier to write a METAFONT program than to draw a character ten times. Therefore METAFONT is usually used to provide an entire family of related fonts. By varying the programs and the parameters, you will be able to determine the most pleasing settings.

METAFONT programs are expressed in a declarative algebraic language that is rather different from ordinary computer languages, since it has been developed especially for the problems of type design. In this language you explain where the major components of a desired shape are located, and you specify how the shape is to be drawn using "pens" and "erasers." One of the advantages of METAFONT is that it provides a discipline according to which the principles of a particular alphabet design are stated explicitly—the underlying intelligence does not remain hidden in the mind of the designer, it is spelled out in the programs. Thus it is comparatively easy to obtain consistency where consistency is desirable, and to extend a font to new symbols that are compatible with the existing ones.

This manual is not a textbook about mathematics or about computers. But if you know the rudiments of those subjects (contemporary high school mathematics, together with the knowledge of how to use the text editor on your computer), you should be able to use METAFONT with little difficulty after reading what follows. Some parts of the manual are more obscure than others, however, since the author has tried to satisfy experienced METAFONTers as well as beginners and casual users with a single manual. Therefore a special symbol has been used to warn about esoterica: When you see the sign

at the beginning of a paragraph, watch out for a "dangerous bend" in the train of thought—don't read such a paragraph unless you need to. You will be able to use METAFONT reasonably well, even to design characters like the dangerous-bend symbol itself, without reading the fine print in such advanced sections.

Computer system manuals usually make dull reading, but take heart: This one contains JOKES every once in a while, so you might actually enjoy reading it. (Most of the jokes can only be appreciated properly if you understand a technical point that is being made, however—so read *carefully*.)

In order to help you internalize what you're reading, occasional EXERCISES are sprinkled through this manual. It is generally intended that every reader should try every exercise, except for the exercises that appear in the "dangerous bend" areas. If you can't solve the problem, you can always look at the answer pages at the end of the manual. But please, try first to solve it by yourself; then you'll learn more and you'll learn faster. Furthermore, if you think you do know the answer to an exercise, you should turn to the official answer (in Appendix A) and check it out just to make sure.

CONTENTS

<1> The basics

To define a shape using METAFONT, you don't draw it; you explain *how* to draw it. Explanation is generally harder than doing—for example, it's much easier to walk than to teach a robot how to walk—but the METAFONT language is intended to make the job of explanation relatively painless. Once you have explained how to draw some shape in a sufficiently general manner, the same explanation will work for related shapes, in different circumstances; so the time spent in formulating a precise explanation turns out to be worth it. The "META-" of "METAFONT" is meant to indicate the fact that a general explanation of how to draw a font of characters will transcend any particular set of drawings for those characters.

To explain how to draw a shape, we need a precise way to specify various key points of that shape. METAFONT uses standard Cartesian coordinates for this purpose [following René Descartes, whose revolutionary work *La géométrie* in 1637 marked the beginning of the application of algebraic methods to geometric problems]: The location of a point is defined by specifying its x coordinate, which is the number of units to the right of some reference point, and its y coordinate, which is the number of units upwards from the reference point.

For example, the six points shown in Fig. 1–1 have the following x and y coordinates:

$$(x_1, y_1) = (0, 100); \qquad (x_2, y_2) = (100, 100); \qquad (x_3, y_3) = (200, 100);$$
$$(x_4, y_4) = (0, \quad 0); \qquad (x_5, y_5) = (100, \quad 0); \qquad (x_6, y_6) = (200, \quad 0).$$

These six points will be used in several examples that follow.

All points in METAFONT programs are given an identifying number, which should be a positive integer (or zero). The x and y coordinates of each point are specified by so-called x-variables and y-variables; for example, "x_2" and "y_2" are the coordinates of point 2.

In a typical application of METAFONT, you prepare a rough sketch of the shape you plan to define, on a piece of graph paper, and you label the key points on that sketch with any convenient numbers. Then you write a METAFONT program that explains (i) how to figure out the coordinates of those key points, and (ii) how to draw the desired lines and curves between those points.

METAFONT programs for individual characters consist of a bunch of "statements" separated by semicolons and ending with a period. The most common

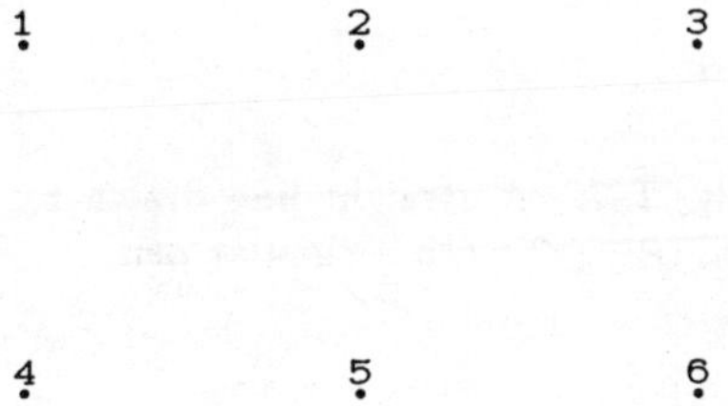

1 · 2 · 3 ·

Fig. 1–1. Six points that will be used in several examples of this chapter and the next.

4 · 5 · 6 ·

form of statement is an *equation* that expresses one or more algebraic relationships between variables. For example, consider the equations

$$x_1 = x_4 = y_4 = y_5 = y_6 = 0;$$
$$x_2 = x_5 = y_1 = y_2 = y_3 = 100;$$
$$x_3 = x_6 = 200;$$

these suffice to define the six points of Fig. 1–1.

Points are rarely specified in terms of fixed numbers like 100, however, since we will see later that this means a distance of 100 units on the square grid or "raster" that METAFONT works with. An alphabet defined in such absolute terms would come out looking very tiny on high-resolution machines but very large on machines with only a few raster units per inch. It is clearly better to write something like this:

$$x_1 = x_4 = 0; \quad x_2 = x_5 = d; \quad x_3 = x_6 = 2d;$$
$$y_1 = y_2 = y_3 = h; \quad y_4 = y_5 = y_6 = 0;$$

the auxiliary variables h and d, which we can assume have been defined at the very beginning of our METAFONT specifications, can readily be adjusted to give any desired scaling, without changing the rest of the program.

There are lots of other ways to specify the coordinates of those six points. For example, the equation "$x_3 = x_6 = 2d$" could have been replaced by "$x_3 = x_6 = x_2 + d$", or even by an implicit formula such as

$$x_3 - x_2 = x_6 - x_5 = x_2 - x_1.$$

The latter formula states that the horizontal distance from point 3 to point 2 is the same as from point 6 to point 5 and from point 2 to point 1. METAFONT

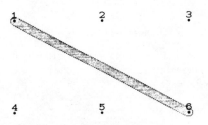

Fig. 1–2. A straight line drawn by METAFONT with a circular pen.

will solve such implicit equations as long as they remain linear; further details about equations are discussed in Chapter 5.

Of course there's no point in being able to define points unless there is something you can do with them. In particular, we want to be able to draw a straight line from one point to another. METAFONT uses "pens" to draw lines, and in our first examples we shall be using a circular pen that is nine raster units in diameter. We can write, for example,

cpen;   9 draw 1 . . 6;

these statements instruct METAFONT to take a circular pen ("cpen") of width 9 and to draw a straight line from point 1 to point 6, producing Fig. 1–2. We get to Fig. 1–3 after the subsequent statements

draw 2 . . 5;   draw 3 . . 4;

note that it is not necessary to respecify the "cpen" or the "9" when the pen does not change.

If Fig. 1–3 were to be scaled in such a way that 100 raster units came out exactly equal to the height of the letters in this paragraph, the character we have

Fig. 1–3. After two more lines we obtain a design something like the Union Jack.

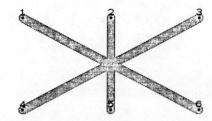

drawn would be "✕". Just for fun, let's try to typeset ten of them in a row: "✕✕✕✕✕✕✕✕✕✕". How easy it is to do this!*

The most important thing to notice about Fig. 1–3 is that the *center* of the pen goes from point to point when drawing a line. For example, points 1 and 6 do not appear at the edge of the line we have drawn from 1 to 6; they appear in the middle of the starting and stopping positions. In other words, we did not describe the boundary of the character, we described the pen motion. This makes it easy to do things like switch to a "boldface" ✕, namely to a ✕, merely by using a cpen of width 15 instead of width 9.

Pen widths are usually specified by so-called w-variables, which are somewhat analogous to x-variables and y-variables. For example, the normal procedure would be to define $w_1 = 9$ at the beginning of our program, then to write

$$\text{cpen;} \quad w_1 \text{ draw } 1 \mathinner{.\,.} 6; \quad \text{draw } 2 \mathinner{.\,.} 5; \quad \text{draw } 3 \mathinner{.\,.} 4;$$

by changing w_1 to 15 we would then get the boldface symbol without changing the rest of the program.

Since METAFONT draws things by describing the motion of a pen's center, it is desirable to have a way to specify the points so that the edge of the pen will be at a known place. For example, our character "✕" actually extends slightly below the baseline ($y = 0$) of normal lines of type, because the pen of width 9 extends 4 units below the baseline when the center of the pen is on the baseline. And the boldface ✕ goes down even further. The remedy for this is to define y_4 by using a special "bot" notation, e.g.,

$$\text{bot}_1 y_4 = 0,$$

which means that the bottom of the pen will be at 0 when the pen of width w_1 is at point 4. (The "1" in "bot$_1$" refers to the "1" in "w_1"; thus, the bot notation is meaningful only when the corresponding w-variable has a definite

---

*Now that authors have for the first time the power to invent new symbols with great ease, and to have those characters printed in their manuscripts on a wide variety of typesetting devices, we have to face the question of how much experimentation is desirable. Will font freaks abuse this toy by overdoing it? Is it wise to introduce new symbols by the thousands? Such questions are beyond the scope of this manual; but it is easy to imagine an epidemic of fontomania occurring, once people realize how much fun it is to design their own characters, and it may be necessary to perform fontal lobotomies.

value.) Similarly,

$$top_1 y_1 = 100$$

would say that the top of the pen will be at 100 when the pen of width w_1 is at point 1.

Using these ideas, we can revise our example program to obtain the following statements (assuming that h, d, and w_1 have already been defined and that the character's height and width have been set to h and $2d$, respectively):

$$x_1 = x_4 = 0; \quad x_2 = x_5 = d; \quad x_3 = x_6 = 2d;$$
$$y_1 = y_2 = y_3; \quad y_4 = y_5 = y_6;$$
$$top_1 y_1 = h; \quad bot_1 y_4 = 0;$$
$$cpen; \quad w_1 \ draw \ 1..6; \quad draw \ 2..5; \quad draw \ 3..4.$$

This program gives the characters ✳ and ✳ when $w_1 = 9$ and $w_1 = 15$, respectively; close inspection reveals that these characters just touch the baseline, and they are exactly as tall as an "h".

▶Exercise 1.1: Ten of the above characters will result in

note that adjacent characters join together, since the character width is $2d$, so that points 3 and 6 of one character coincide with points 1 and 4 of the next. Suppose that we actually wanted the characters to be completely confined to a rectangular box of width $2d$, so that adjacent characters would come just shy of touching (✕✕✕✕✕✕✕✕✕✕). Explain how to modify the example program above so that this would happen, assuming that METAFONT has operations "lft" and "rt" analogous to "top" and "bot".

<2> Curves

The sixteenth-century methods of mathematical type design failed because ruler and compass constructions were inadequate to express the nuances of good calligraphy. METAFONT attempts to get around this problem by using more powerful mathematical techniques: it provides automatic facilities for drawing "pleasing" curves, and this chapter explains how to use them.

The draw command introduced in Chapter 1 will produce curved lines, instead of straight lines, when it is given a list of more than two points. For example, let's go back to the six points of Fig. 1–1 and consider the effect of

cpen;   9 draw 5..4..1..3..6..5;

this produces a closed curve from point 5 to point 4 to point 1 to point 3 to point 6 to point 5, as shown in Fig. 2–1.

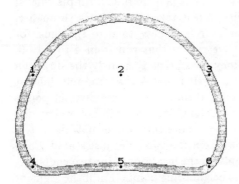

Fig. 2–1. A curve that passes through five of the six example points.

The bean-shaped path of Fig. 2–1 isn't bad looking, but it might not be the curve we had in mind. Indeed, if the draw command had been "draw 4..1..3" instead of the more complicated example above, we would have gotten the curve of Fig. 2–2, which is almost surely not what anybody wants. Something went wrong here, so it is important to get a clear idea of how METAFONT actually decides what curves to draw.

Fig. 2–2. If you don't understand how METAFONT draws curves, you might get ungraceful shapes.

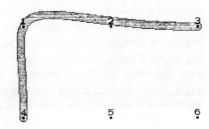

METAFONT's rules are (fortunately) quite simple. The curve between two points z_1 and z_2 depends only on four things:

$$\text{the location of } z_1 = (x_1, y_1);$$
$$\text{the location of } z_2 = (x_2, y_2);$$
$$\text{the angle of the curve at } z_1;$$
$$\text{the angle of the curve at } z_2;$$

Once these four things are given, METAFONT knows what curve it will draw.

But how are the angles at z_1 and z_2 chosen? Again there is a simple rule: If the curve goes from z_0 to z_1 to z_2, the direction it takes as it passes through z_1 is the same as the direction of the arc of a *circle* from z_0 to z_1 to z_2. Thus, for example, since both Figs. 2–1 and 2–2 have curves that run from 4 to 1 to 3, both curves have the same direction as they pass point 1, namely the direction of the circle determined by points 4, 1, and 3. (It is well known and not difficult to prove that there is a unique circle passing through any three distinct points z_0, z_1, and z_2, unless these points lie on a straight line. We will not worry just now about the exceptional cases when the points are collinear or not distinct.)

An important *locality property* follows from the two rules just stated: Each segment of a METAFONT curve depends only on the locations of the two endpoints of that segment and the locations of its two neighboring points. For if the segment runs from z_1 to z_2, and if the previous point is z_0 and the next point is z_3, the angle at z_1 is determined by z_0, z_1, and z_2, while the angle at z_2 is determined by z_1, z_2, and z_3. Other parts of the curve will have no effect; thus you can fix up any segments you don't like without harming the segments you do like.

So far we have discussed what the curve depends on, but not what the curve really is. METAFONT's curves satisfy an *invariance property* in addition to their locality property, in the following sense: Shifting a curve to the left or right, or up or down, does not change its shape, and rotation doesn't change the shape either. Furthermore if all coordinates are multiplied by some factor, the curve simply grows or shrinks by that factor. (In mathematical terms, using complex variable notation, the curve through points $\alpha z_1 + \beta, \ldots, \alpha z_n + \beta$ is equal to α times the curve through points $z_1, \ldots, z_n$, plus β.) Therefore we need only describe the curve from z_1 to z_2 when $z_1 = (x_1, y_1) = (0, 0)$ and $z_2 = (x_2, y_2) = (150, 0)$, say, and when the curve leaves z_1 at a given angle θ and enters z_2 at a given angle ϕ with respect to the horizontal. These special curves will produce all other METAFONT curves if we shift them, rotate them, and expand or contract them.

Fig. 2–3. Examples of **METAFONT**'s standard curves, leaving point 1 at an angle of 60° from the horizontal and entering point 2 at various multiples of 30°.

Fig. 2–3 shows typical curves that leave z_1 at an angle of 60°, coming in to point z_2 at angles of 120°, 90°, 60°, 30°, and 0°. When both angles are 60°, the curve is essentially the arc of a circle; when one angle is 60° and the other is 30°, the curve is essentially a quarter-ellipse. (**METAFONT**'s circles and ellipses aren't absolutely perfect, since they are approximated by cubic curves, but the error is much too small to be perceived.) At other angles the curves in Fig. 2–3 are less familiar mathematical objects, but at least they have a reasonable shape.

Fig. 2–4 shows several more curves that leave z_1 at 60°; but this time the curves have been forced to come into z_2 from *below* the horizontal, at angles of —30°, —60°, —90°, and —120°. Most of these curves (with the possible exception of the —60° one) are rather arbitrary, so you are taking a chance if you expect **METAFONT** to change directions so drastically.

Now let's return to the problem of Fig. 2–2; why did **METAFONT** choose such an ugly curve when commanded to "draw 4..1..3"? The answer is that no angle was specified for the curve at its beginning point 4 or at its ending point 3; so **METAFONT** used the directions from 4 to 1 and from 1 to 3, in order to be consistent with the two-point (straight line) case. In other words, the failure occurred because we didn't give **METAFONT** a clue about how the curve should

Fig. 2–4. Examples of **METAFONT**'s standard curves, when the outgoing and incoming angles have opposite signs.

be started and stopped. *When drawing curved lines, it is almost always desirable to specify the beginning and ending angles somehow,* otherwise METAFONT will be forced to choose directions that have little probability of success.

There are two main ways to specify directions at the endpoints. One way is to supply "hidden points" to the draw command, as in the following example:

$$\text{draw } (5\,..)4\,..\,1\,..\,3(\,..\,6).$$

The "$(5\,..)$" means that METAFONT is to imagine a curve that emanates from point 5, but the drawing doesn't actually begin until point 4; similarly, the "$(\,..\,6)$" means that the curve will stop at point 3 but act like it was going on to point 6. In this way METAFONT will select the same directions at points 4 and 3 that were chosen for the curve of Fig. 2–1 ("draw $5\,..\,4\,..\,1\,..\,3\,..\,6\,..\,5$"), so the result will be to reproduce the segment of Fig. 2–1 that runs from 4 to 1 to 3.

The second way to specify a curve's directions is considerably more flexible: You simply state what direction is desired. Let's consider another problem, in order to illustrate this technique. Suppose we wish to draw a beautiful heart shape. One approach is to start with a definite idea of what the heart should look like, then try to get METAFONT to agree; i.e., we want METAFONT to produce a drawing that matches the given idea. Since candy shops probably represent the ultimate authority about the proper shape a heart should take, the author purchased a box of chocolates on Feb. 14, 1979, and traced the outline of the box's shape onto a piece of graph paper (after appropriately disposing of the box's contents). In this way the following points were found to lie on an authentic heart:

$$x_1 = 100;\quad y_1 = 162;$$
$$x_2 = 200 - x_8 = 140;\quad y_2 = y_8 = 178;$$
$$x_3 = 200 - x_7 = 185;\quad y_3 = y_7 = 125;$$
$$x_4 = 200 - x_6 = 161;\quad y_4 = y_6 = 57;$$
$$x_5 = 100;\quad y_5 = 0;$$

see Fig. 2–5.

The naive way to ask METAFONT for the required drawing would be

$$\text{cpen;}\quad 9\ \text{draw } 1\,..\,2\,..\,3\,..\,4\,..\,5;\quad \text{draw } 5\,..\,6\,..\,7\,..\,8\,..\,1;$$

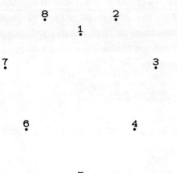

Fig. 2–5. Eight points to be used in
the design of a "heart."

but we don't expect this to be very successful, since it fails to specify proper
directions at the endpoints. In fact, it produces the lumpy shape of Fig. 2–6,
something one would hardly wish to leave in San Francisco. METAFONT will
certainly have to do better than that.

Fig. 2–6. The heart will look diseased
if you repeat the mistake of Fig. 2–2.

So now we come to the second way of providing the desired angles. By taking
a ruler, and drawing a straight line on the graph paper in the direction that the
correct heart shape takes at point 1, it is possible to specify the desired direction
by counting squares. The author found that the correct line goes 40 units upwards

when it goes 50 units to the right, so the direction at point 1 is specified by the numbers 50 and 40. At point 5 the corresponding line is not so steep, it goes down only 36 units per 50 units to the left; the direction in this case is specified by the numbers —50 and —36. METAFONT will adopt these directions if they are placed in braces following the names of the points:

$$\text{draw } 1\{50, 40\} \ldots 2 \ldots 3 \ldots 4 \ldots 5\{-50, -36\};$$

this does the right half of the heart, and the left-hand portion is similar, namely

$$\text{draw } 5\{-50, 36\} \ldots 6 \ldots 7 \ldots 8 \ldots 1\{50, -40\}.$$

When you give explicit directions in this way, any positive multiple of the direction is satisfactory; "$\{5, 4\}$" means the same thing as "$\{50, 40\}$", and you could even say "$\{1, 0.8\}$". However, the signs of these numbers must not be changed; "$\{-50, -36\}$" is emphatically *not* the same as "$\{50, 36\}$", since the former means that the curve is coming to the point from the upper right while the latter means that it is coming from the lower left. If the direction at point 5 had been specified as $\{50, 36\}$, METAFONT would dutifully have drawn something that comes from point 4, hooks around, and enters point 5 from the lower left; the result is best not shown here. On the other hand the right-hand portion of the curve could equally well have been drawn in reverse order,

$$\text{draw } 5\{50, 36\} \ldots 4 \ldots 3 \ldots 2 \ldots 1\{-50, -40\};$$

the signs are now reversed. A minus sign in the x part of a direction (the first part) means in general that the curve is going left, a plus sign means that it is going right, and zero means that it is going vertically. A minus sign in the y part (the second part) means that the curve is going down, a plus sign means that it is going up, and zero means that it is going horizontally.

The two draw commands above give explicit directions at the endpoints, while taking METAFONT's standard directions at the interior points 2, 3, 4 and 6, 7, 8. Unfortunately the result (Fig. 2–7) is still not quite right, the transition from 2 to 3 to 4 being somewhat disheartening. What we would like is to bring the curve a little to the right, between 2 and 3, and a little to the left between 3 and 4.

Fig. 2–7. Correction of the error leads to a better shape, but still further improvement is desirable.

One remedy that immediately springs to mind is to add more points. After all, there's no obvious reason why exactly eight points should be the right number to define this shape. It is a simple matter to look at the correct curve on the graph paper and to add two more points where Fig. 2–7 is in error, say

$$x_9 = 200 - x_{10} = 181; \quad y_9 = y_{10} = 97;$$

we can incorporate the new points by saying

draw 1{50, 40}..2..3..9..4..5{−50, −36};

draw 1{−50, 40}..8..7..10..6..5{50, −36}.

The result in Fig. 2–8 is now satisfactory.

Fig. 2–8. A satisfactory design can be obtained by inserting two extra points.

But there is a better way, and a user of METAFONT should be encouraged to avoid introducing new points whenever possible. The improvement comes when we realize how points 2 and 3 were actually selected in the first place: point 2 is the topmost point, where the heart shape reaches its maximum y coordinate, while point 3 is the rightmost point, where the maximum x coordinate is achieved. Thus we know the correct directions at these points: the curve is horizontal at 2 and vertical at 3. METAFONT allows curve directions to be specified at all points, not only at the endpoints, hence the improved solution is to say

$$\text{draw } 1\{50, 40\} . . 2\{1, 0\} . . 3\{0, -1\} . . 4 . . 5\{-50, -36\};$$
$$\text{draw } 1\{-50, 40\} . . 8\{-1, 0\} . . 7\{0, -1\} . . 6 . . 5\{50, -36\}.$$

This leads to Fig. 2–9, which is quite suitable for one's true valentine.

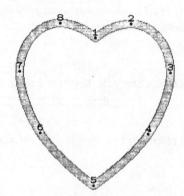

Fig. 2–9. Instead of specifying additional points, it is better to specify where the curve is travelling horizontally and vertically.

The success of this direction-specification approach suggests in fact that we might be better off with even *fewer* points. What would happen if we tried to get by with only four points instead of eight? Fig. 2–10 is the result of the commands

$$\text{draw } 1\{50, 40\} . . 3\{0, -1\} . . 5\{-50, -36\};$$
$$\text{draw } 1\{-50, 40\} . . 7\{0, -1\} . . 5\{50, -36\}.$$

It turns out that this curve doesn't come up high enough for point 2, but point 4 is very close. Thus points 2 and 8 should stay, but points 4 and 6 can be eliminated;

the candy makers probably wanted point 4 to be slightly to the left.*

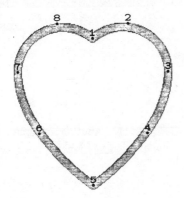

Fig. 2–10. This heart was drawn using only four of the eight given data points, specifying the desired directions at points 1 and 5 and specifying that the curve be vertical at points 7 and 3.

It isn't clear what will turn out to be the best strategy for cajoling META-FONT into drawing the shapes that its users have in mind; only time will tell. However, one further example will help to reveal how points should be chosen when attempting to draw curves: Let us consider the *shoemaker's problem*. The author made a tracing on graph paper of the sole of one of his left shoes, and this led to the following data:

$$x_1 = \ 77; \ y_1 = 322; \quad x_2 = 132; \ y_2 = 220; \quad x_3 = 117; \ y_3 = 150;$$
$$x_4 = 120; \ y_4 = 100; \quad x_5 = 131; \ y_5 = \ 55; \quad x_6 = \ 95; \ y_6 = \ \ 2;$$
$$x_7 = \ 48; \ y_7 = \ 60; \quad x_8 = \ 38; \ y_8 = 140; \quad x_9 = \ 20; \ y_9 = 200;$$

see Fig. 2–11.

---

*Another hypothesis is that the direction at point 5 isn't quite right in the author's data (since the box was in fact crumpled at point 5).

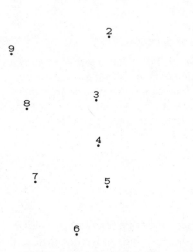

Fig. 2–11.   Another example, based on the shape of a shoe.

Since the sole's boundary is a closed curve without sharp corners, it is natural to try to get METAFONT to draw it with a single draw command, using hidden points:

$$\text{draw } (9\,.\,.)1\,.\,.\,2\,.\,.\,3\,.\,.\,4\,.\,.\,5\,.\,.\,6\,.\,.\,7\,.\,.\,8\,.\,.\,9\,.\,.\,1(\,.\,.\,2).$$

But the result is a disaster (Fig. 2–12a); the author's feet are somewhat ungainly, but not so gnarled as that. The reason for this failure is what we alluded to in connection with Fig. 2–4. METAFONT needs help when you want the curve to change directions.

Imagine that you are driving along a curved highway; sometimes you are turning left, sometimes you are turning right, and you are at a so-called *inflection point* when you are momentarily going straight. The biggest problem in Fig. 2–12a occurs between 2 and 3, when the shoe sole has an inflection point but there is no corresponding data point. Let's add one:

$$x_{10} = 125; \quad y_{10} = 184;$$

in general it is a good idea to include inflection points and to specify the desired direction of the curve at such points.

It turns out that all ten data points in this example are either inflection points or places where the curve travels horizontally or vertically. So the best way to draw the shoe sole is probably to specify directions at each point:

$$draw\ 1\{1,0\}\mathinner{\ldotp\ldotp}2\{0,-1\}\mathinner{\ldotp\ldotp}10\{-25,-60\}\mathinner{\ldotp\ldotp}3\{0,-1\}\mathinner{\ldotp\ldotp}4\{18,-60\}$$
$$\mathinner{\ldotp\ldotp}5\{0,-1\}\mathinner{\ldotp\ldotp}6\{-1,0\}\mathinner{\ldotp\ldotp}7\{0,1\}\mathinner{\ldotp\ldotp}8\{-30,60\}\mathinner{\ldotp\ldotp}9\{0,1\}\mathinner{\ldotp\ldotp}1\{1,0\}.$$

The result in Fig. 2–12b does indeed capture the author's sole.

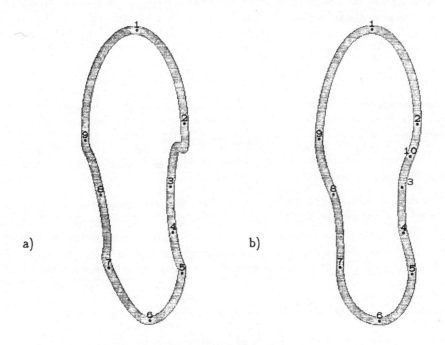

a)   b)

Fig. 2-12. METAFONT has difficulty changing from left turns to right turns; the remedy is to specify the proper direction at points of inflection.

Note that when all of the directions are specified explicitly as in this example, the draw command could have been split up into individual segments:

$$\text{draw } 1\{1, 0\} \mathbin{..} 2\{0, -1\};$$
$$\text{draw } 2\{0, -1\} \mathbin{..} 10\{-25, -60\};$$
$$\vdots$$
$$\text{draw } 9\{0, 1\} \mathbin{..} 1\{1, 0\};$$

the result would have been just the same.

Here is how **METAFONT** chooses the angle at point z_1 when the direction has not been explicitly given, for a curve from z_0 to z_1 to z_2: Let $z_k = (x_k, y_k)$, $\Delta x_k = x_{k+1} - x_k$, $\Delta y_k = y_{k+1} - y_k$, and $|\Delta z_k|^2 = (\Delta x_k)^2 + (\Delta y_k)^2$. Then if $|\Delta z_0|^2 = 0$ (i.e., if $z_0 = z_1$), the direction is $\{\Delta x_1, \Delta y_1\}$ (i.e., the direction from z_1 to z_2). If $|\Delta z_1|^2 = 0$ (i.e., if $z_1 = z_2$), the direction is $\{\Delta x_0, \Delta y_0\}$ (i.e., the direction from z_0 to z_1). Otherwise the direction is

$$\{\Delta x_0 \,/\, |\Delta z_0|^2 + \Delta x_1 \,/\, |\Delta z_1|^2, \ \Delta y_0 \,/\, |\Delta z_0|^2 + \Delta y_1 \,/\, |\Delta z_1|^2\},$$

which corresponds to the direction of the circle through z_0, z_1, z_2 if these points aren't collinear. The direction computed by these rules turns out to be $\{0, 0\}$ when $z_0 = z_2$; in this degenerate case it is arbitrarily changed to $\{1, 0\}$. When drawing a curve from z_1 to z_2 to $\cdots$ to z_n, **METAFONT** will set $z_0 = z_1$ if no hidden point is given at the beginning, and $z_{n+1} = z_n$ if no hidden point is given at the end; thus, each point of the curve has a predecessor and a successor.

▶Exercise 2.1: According to the rules in the preceding paragraph, what curve do you get from the command "draw $1 \mathbin{..} 2 \mathbin{..} 2 \mathbin{..} 3$"?

The actual curve drawn between $z_1 = (x_1, y_1)$ and $z_2 = (x_2, y_2)$, when the starting direction makes an angle θ and the ending direction makes an angle ϕ with respect to the straight line from z_1 to z_2, can be defined in the language of complex variables by the formula

$$z(t) = z_1 + (3t^2 - 2t^3)(z_2 - z_1) + r \cdot t(1-t)^2 \delta_1 - s \cdot t^2(1-t)\delta_2, \quad \text{for } 0 \le t \le 1.$$

Here r and s are special quantities explained below, while δ_1 and δ_2 are the specified directions of the curve at z_1 and z_2, normalized so that $|\delta_1| = |\delta_2| = |z_2 - z_1|$, namely

$$\delta_1 = e^{i\theta}(z_2 - z_1), \qquad \delta_2 = e^{-i\phi}(z_2 - z_1).$$

Whenever r and s are positive real numbers, the stated formula for $z(t)$ defines a curve having the specified directions at z_1 and z_2; conversely, all curves from z_1 to z_2 that have the specified directions, and that have degree 3 or less as a polynomial in t, can be put into this form for some r and s. We shall call r and s the "velocities" at z_1 and z_2, since a large value of r means that the direction remains approximately equal to δ_1 for a long time after the curve leaves z_1 and a large value of s means that the direction is approximately δ_2 for a long time before the curve reaches z_2. A small velocity means that the curve may be taking a sharp turn at z_1 or z_2, since the directions δ_1 or δ_2 will have comparatively little influence. METAFONT chooses velocities by the following formulas:

$$r = \left| \frac{2 \sin \phi}{(1 + |\cos \psi|) \sin \psi} \right|, \qquad s = \left| \frac{2 \sin \theta}{(1 + |\cos \psi|) \sin \psi} \right|, \qquad \psi = \frac{\theta + \phi}{2},$$

provided that ψ is not too near zero; otherwise the velocities are taken to be $r = s = 2$. These velocity formulas are rather arbitrary, but they have been chosen so that excellent approximations to circles and ellipses are obtained in the cases $\theta = \phi$ and $\theta + \phi = 90°$. Furthermore the formulas have at least one nice mathematical property, namely the fact that they keep the curve "in bounds": If θ and ϕ are nonnegative, the curve from z_1 to z_2 will lie entirely between or on the lines $z_1 + t\delta_1$ and $z_1 + t(z_2 - z_1)$ and entirely between or on the lines $z_2 - t\delta_2$ and $z_2 - t(z_2 - z_1)$ (for $t \geq 0$).

Actually the velocities r and s are adjusted so that they aren't too large or too small; METAFONT's standard mode of operation will ensure that $0.5 \leq r, s \leq 4$. (Small values of r and s usually make the curve turn too sharply at z_1 or z_2, while large values usually make it wander erratically.) In the cases corresponding to Figs. 2–3 and 2–4, for example, we have $\theta = 60°$ and the following values of ϕ, r, and s according to the formulas above:

ϕ	r	s	ϕ	r	s	ϕ	r	s
120°	1.7321	1.7321	30°	0.8284	1.4349	−60°	2.0000	2.0000
90°	1.6448	1.4245	0°	0.0000	1.8564	−90°	3.9307	3.4041
60°	1.3333	1.3333	−30°	1.9653	3.4041	−120°	1.8564	1.8564

When $\phi = 0°$ the value of r was raised by METAFONT to 0.5, otherwise the curve would have been a straight line from z_1 to z_2 (not having the correct direction at z_1). METAFONT also gave the message "Sharp turn suppressed between points 1 and 2 (r = .0000)" when it drew the curve for $\phi = 0°$.

There is a way to change METAFONT's velocity thresholds by altering maxvr, minvr, maxvs, and/or minvs, as explained in Chapter 9. For example, the commands "minvr 0.0; minvs 0.0" will allow arbitrarily sharp turns. This can be useful in certain circumstances, when it is desirable to ensure that the curves stay in bounds as explained above. Furthermore you can set r and s to any desired value (in case you don't like METAFONT's choice) by making maxvr and minvr be the desired r and by making maxvs and minvs the desired s.

▶Exercise 2.2: According to these rules, what curve do you get from the sequence of commands "minvr 0.0; minvs 0.0; draw 1..2..3"?

<3> Pens and erasers

Our examples so far have drawn straight lines and curved lines using pens shaped like circles. As you might suspect, METAFONT also has access to several other kinds of scriveners' tools. A METAFONT user's program is supposed to select the particular type of pen needed, and this will be the so-called current pen type until another one is specified. The current pen type might be

cpen, "circular pen," as in our previous examples;
hpen, "horizontal pen," having a fixed height and varying width;
vpen, "vertical pen," having a fixed width and varying height;
lpen, "left pen," a rectangle at the left of the current position;
rpen, "right pen," a rectangle at the right of the current position;
spen, "special pen," a specially defined elliptical shape;
epen, "explicit pen," a fairly arbitrary shape.

Chapter 1 discussed briefly the fact that pen sizes are generally expressed in terms of METAFONT's w-variables, namely the variables named w_0, w_1, w_2, etc. The command "w_4 draw 1..2..3" will, for example, draw a curve using the size-w_4 pen or eraser of the current type.

Pens of types cpen, hpen, and vpen are ellipses whose axes run horizontally and vertically. The rules by which METAFONT creates a size-w pen of these types are simple:

A cpen of size w has height w and width w;
an hpen of size w has height h_0 and width w;
a vpen of size w has height w and width v_0.

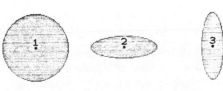

Fig. 3–1. Circular pen, horizontal pen, vertical pen.

Here h_0 and v_0 are the current values of METAFONT parameters called hpenht and vpenwd. For example, consider Fig. 3–1, which was drawn with the following METAFONT program:

$$x_1 = 0; \quad x_2 = 100; \quad x_3 = 200; \quad y_1 = y_2 = y_3 = 0;$$
hpenht 25; vpenwd 25;
cpen; 75 draw 1; hpen; 75 draw 2; vpen; 75 draw 3.

(Note that draw can be used for single points as well as for lines.) The effect of such oval-shaped pens is illustrated in Fig. 3–2a, which shows the shoe sole of Chapter 2 drawn with an hpen, and in Fig. 3–2b, which shows Chapter 2's heart shape drawn with a vpen. In both cases the variable pen size was 9 and the fixed sizes (h_0 and v_0) were 3.

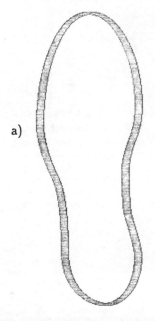

a)

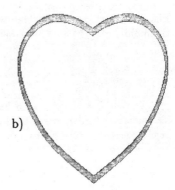

b)

Fig. 3–2. The example shapes of Chapter 2, drawn with a horizontal pen (a) and with a vertical pen (b).

Erasers can be used to "clean off the ink" in unwanted sections of previously drawn lines. Any pen can be converted to an eraser by simply putting the symbol "#" after its name; for example, "cpen#" specifies a circular eraser.

The rectangular-shaped pens lpen and rpen are most often used as erasers, since their shapes are convenient for typical cleanup operations. An lpen of size w is a rectangle w units wide and h_0 units high, lying to the left of the point being drawn and centered vertically with respect to this point. An rpen of size w is similar, but it lies just to the *right* of the point being drawn. For example, Fig. 3–3 shows the result of the METAFONT program

$$x_1 = 0; \quad x_2 = 100; \quad x_3 = 200; \quad y_1 = y_2 = y_3 = 0;$$
hpenht 25;
cpen;   150 draw 2;
lpen#;   35 draw 3;
rpen#;   35 draw 1.

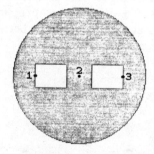

Fig. 3–3. Rectangular erasers used in the middle of a large circular pen.

The ellipses you get with hpen and vpen have both horizontal and vertical symmetry. In order to get ellipses that are tilted obliquely, you can construct special pens (type spen). The general form of an spen definition is slightly complicated but not hopelessly so: you say

$$\text{spen}(a, b, c, x_0, y_0, x_0', y_0')$$

(optionally followed by "#" if you want an eraser instead of a pen), and the result is a pen or eraser consisting of all points (ξ, η) such that

$$a(\xi - x_0)^2 + b(\xi - x_0)(\eta - y_0) + c(\eta - y_0)^2 \leq 1.$$

Fig. 3–4. An oblique pen gives this splendid valentine.

When later drawing with this pen at point (x, y), it is offset so that it actually is placed at $(x - x'_0, y - y'_0)$. The main parameters a, b, c of spen must satisfy the condition

$$b^2 < 4ac.$$

Furthermore, they had better be pretty small numbers, or the pen will be too small to be seen. When drawing with an spen (e.g., w_3 draw $1 . . 2$), its "size" (i.e., w_3) is ignored.

For simplicity let us consider first the case $x_0 = y_0 = x'_0 = y'_0 = 0$; these parameters are generally used only for fine tuning when the discreteness of the raster is considered. Here is a plug-in formula for generating a pen of height h and width w that has been rotated counterclockwise by an angle of θ degrees: Use spen$(a, b, c, 0, 0, 0, 0)$ where

$$a = 4\left(\frac{\cos^2\theta}{w^2} + \frac{\sin^2\theta}{h^2}\right), \qquad b = (4\sin 2\theta)\left(\frac{1}{w^2} - \frac{1}{h^2}\right), \qquad c = 4\left(\frac{\sin^2\theta}{w^2} + \frac{\cos^2\theta}{h^2}\right).$$

(When h or w are small, however, you may have to play with this formula a bit in order to avoid the effects of roundoff errors.) Fig. 3–4 shows what happens when such a pen is applied to the heart shape, using $w = 9$, $h = 3$, and an angle of $30°$.

The quantities a, b, c, x_0, y_0, x'_0, y'_0 are real numbers, but the discreteness of the raster implies that METAFONT's pen is actually the set of all *integer* points (ξ, η) satisfying $a(\xi - x_0)^2 + b(\xi - x_0)(\eta - y_0) + c(\eta - y_0)^2 \leq 1$. Therefore it is important for METAFONT to define its cpens, hpens, and vpens carefully in such a way that they have the correct relation to the curve being drawn. Consider, for example, a cpen of size 7, which looks like this when enlarged:

To "plot a point" with this pen at (x, y), when x and y are real numbers, METAFONT first rounds to the nearest integer point (x', y') and then blackens the pixels in locations $(x' + \xi, y' + \eta)$ where ξ and η run through the 37 square dots of the pen image:

$$(-1, 3), (0, 3), (1, 3), (-2, 2), (-1, 2), \ldots, (1, -2), (2, -2), (-1, -3), (0, -3), (1, -3).$$

This works fine because it gives three dots above and below and to the left and right of (x', y'); the pen has width 7 as desired. But now consider the problem of a cpen whose width is an even number, say 4. The desired pattern of dots is

and this shape can't be centered at an integer point (x', y') since none of its dots is the center. METAFONT's remedy is to consider that the pen shape is actually centered at $(\frac{1}{2}, \frac{1}{2})$; to plot a point with this pen at (x, y), when x and y are real numbers, the idea is to round the *shifted* point $(x - \frac{1}{2}, y - \frac{1}{2})$ to the nearest integer coordinates (x', y'), and then to blacken pixels $(x' + \xi, y' + \eta)$ for the appropriate values of (ξ, η):

$$(0, 2), (1, 2), (-1, 1), (0, 1), (1, 1), (2, 1), (-1, 0), (0, 0), (1, 0), (2, 0), (0, -1), (1, -1).$$

The net effect when drawing a curve is to have a pen of width 4 that is centered on that curve.

A further complication arises from the need to make sure that exactly the right number of integer points will satisfy the elliptical relation, since the discretized pen should occupy precisely w columns and h rows, for any given positive integers w and h. Let $\delta(n)$ be 0 when n is odd and $\delta(n) = \frac{1}{2}$ when n is even; then METAFONT's discrete pen of width w and height h is defined by $\mathrm{spen}\big(a, 0, c, \delta(w), \delta(h), \delta(w), \delta(h)\big)$ where

$$a = \frac{4}{(1 + f^2)w^2}, \qquad c = \frac{4}{(1 + f^2)h^2}, \qquad f = \max\left(\frac{2\delta(w)}{w}, \frac{2\delta(h)}{h}\right).$$

The most general pen or eraser shape you can get with **METAFONT** comes from an epen specification, which has the form

$$\text{epen } (l_k, r_k)(l_{k-1}, r_{k-1}) \ldots (l_0, r_0).(l_{-1}, r_{-1}) \ldots (l_{-m}, r_{-m})$$

(followed by "#" if you want it to be an eraser). This denotes a pen positioned at $(0,0)$ containing all integer points (ξ, η) for $l_\eta \leq \xi \leq r_\eta$ and $k \geq \eta \geq -m$; each l_η and r_η should be an integer, with $l_\eta \leq r_\eta$. If there are no points with $\eta < 0$, the ".$(l_{-1}, r_{-1}) \ldots (l_{-m}, r_{-m})$" part of this specification is omitted; on the other hand if $m > 0$ there should no space between the period and "(l_{-1}, r_{-1})".

Fig. 3–5 shows an example in which epen has been used to define an eraser in the shape of an isosceles triangle, 5 units high and 9 units wide. The illustration was generated by a rather simple **METAFONT** program:

$$x_1 = 0; \quad y_1 = -20; \quad x_2 = 50; \quad y_2 = 0; \quad x_3 = 100; \quad y_3 = 20;$$
cpen; 150 draw 2;
epen $(0,0)(-1,1)(-2,2)(-3,3)(-4,4)\#$;
draw $1 \ldots 3$.

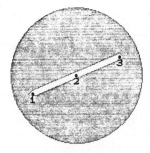

Fig. 3–5. A straight line "drawn" with a triangular eraser.

When **METAFONT** draws with an epen, it ignores the pen size, just as when it is using an spen. However, you can set epenxfactor and epenyfactor to a value greater than 1.0 if you wish to enlarge all of your epens (or to a value less than 1.0 if you wish to shrink them). The expansion or shrinkage occurs by epenxfactor in the horizontal dimension and by epenyfactor in the vertical dimension. Two other parameters epenxcorr and epenycorr can be set to nonzero values x'_0 and y'_0 if you wish to replace (x, y) by $(x - x'_0, y - y'_0)$ before rounding and plotting with an epen. It should prove interesting to create alphabets whose letters have been drawn with normal pen motions but with abnormal epen shapes (triangles, diamonds, teardrops, and so on).

▶Exercise 3.1: Explain how to specify an lpen of width 7 and height 5 using an epen. (When such a pen is "plotted" at point (x', y'), it whitens pixels $(x' + \xi, y' + \eta)$ for $-7 \leq \xi \leq -1$ and $-2 \leq \eta \leq +2$.)

Chapter 1 mentioned notations such as "$\mathrm{bot}_1 y_4$", meaning the y-coordinate of the bottom of a pen of size w_1 when the pen itself is positioned at y_4. These notations top_i, bot_i, lft_i, and rt_i always refer to the current pen type, and to size w_i (a w-variable that must have a known value). For example, you can't say "$\mathrm{bot}_1 y_4$" unless the value of w_1 has been defined earlier. If $w_1 = 9$ and the current type is cpen or vpen, "$\mathrm{bot}_1 y_4$" is equivalent to "$y_4 - 4$".

▶Exercise 3.2: Describe in words the difference between the shapes that would be drawn by the following two METAFONT programs (without typing them into the computer):

Program 1. $x_1 = y_1 = 0$; hpenht 25; $w_1 = 75$; hpen; w_1 draw 1.
Program 2. $x_1 = y_1 = y_2 = y_3 = 0$; $w_0 = 25$; $w_1 = 75$; cpen;
$\qquad\qquad$ $\mathrm{lft}_1 x_1 = \mathrm{lft}_0 x_2$; $\mathrm{rt}_1 x_1 = \mathrm{rt}_0 x_3$; w_0 draw 2 .. 3.

The following table gives the amount of offset produced by top, bot, lft, and rt with respect to a pen of size w, when w is a positive integer:

	cpen	hpen	vpen	lpen	rpen	spen, epen
top	$(w-1)/2$	$(h_0-1)/2$	$(w-1)/2$	$(h_0-1)/2$	$(h_0-1)/2$	$y_{\max} - y'_0$
bot	$(1-w)/2$	$(1-h_0)/2$	$(1-w)/2$	$(1-h_0)/2$	$(1-h_0)/2$	$y_{\min} - y'_0$
lft	$(1-w)/2$	$(1-w)/2$	$(1-v_0)/2$	$-w$	1	$x_{\min} - x'_0$
rt	$(w-1)/2$	$(w-1)/2$	$(v_0-1)/2$	-1	w	$x_{\max} - x'_0$

For spen and epen, the quantities $x_{\min}$, $x_{\max}$, $y_{\min}$, $y_{\max}$ denote the extremes of ξ and η in the discrete pen, while x'_0 and y'_0 denote the offsets subtracted from the coordinates before rounding and plotting. Note that pens of type cpen, hpen, vpen, lpen, rpen always have the property that

$$\mathrm{top}_i \mathrm{bot}_i y = y;$$

in other words $y_1 = \mathrm{top}_i y_2$ if and only if $y_2 = \mathrm{bot}_i y_1$. Similarly, the operations lft and rt are inverses of each other, for types cpen, hpen, vpen.

<4> Running METAFONT

It is high time now for you to stop reading and start playing with the computer, since METAFONT is an interactive system that is best learned by trial and error. (In fact, one of the nicest things about computer graphics is that your errors are often more interesting than your "successes.")

The instructions in this chapter refer to the initial implementation of META-FONT with Datadisc terminals at Stanford's Artificial Intelligence Laboratory; similar rules will presumably hold if METAFONT has been transported to other environments. The first thing to do (assuming that you are logged in) is to tell the monitor

```
    r  mf⟨carriage-return⟩
```

(meaning Run METAFONT). After METAFONT has been loaded into the machine, it will type "*"; this means it wants you to instruct it about what to do.

The second thing to do is type

```
    proofmode; drawdisplay;
```

and hit ⟨carriage-return⟩ again. The proofmode command instructs METAFONT that you want to print hard-copy proofs of the characters you are generating. (Such proofsheets will contain enlarged versions of the characters together with labeled points, as in the illustrations of this manual.) The drawdisplay command instructs METAFONT to display the current state of what has been drawn, after every draw command.

Before doing anything else, you might as well make an intentional error, so that you won't be quite so frightened later on when METAFONT detects unintentional ones. Type

```
    error; another error;
```

from now on the ⟨carriage-return⟩s at the end of lines will usually not be mentioned. METAFONT will try to figure out what you had in mind by typing this funny line, but pretty soon it will discover that the statements make no sense. The word "error" has no special meaning in the language, so METAFONT assumes that it is the name of one of your variables. Under this assumption, you might be typing a statement like "error = 5". But in fact you typed ";" after "error", and that doesn't obey the rules of METAFONT's language, so you get the following response:

```
! +1.0000 error + .0000
! Missing = sign, command flushed.
(*) error;
          another error;
↑
```

The "! Missing = sign" tells you what METAFONT thought was wrong about your statement; "command flushed" means that the statement has been ignored (the error didn't hurt anything); and "1.0000 error + .0000" is the algebraic value of the incomplete equation (in case you're interested). The "(*)" means that METAFONT was reading a line that you typed directly at your terminal, not a line from some file. The position where the error was detected is indicated by the fact that "another error;" appears on a separate line—this second line contains text that METAFONT hasn't looked at yet.

The "↑" means that METAFONT wants you to respond to the error message, but since you haven't used METAFONT before you don't know how to respond. Type "?" (no ⟨carriage-return⟩ is needed) and it will say

```
Type <cr> to continue, <lf> to flash error messages,
    1 or ... or 9 to ignore the next 1 to 9 tokens of input,
    i or I to insert something, x or X to quit.
```

OK, these are your options. If you type a digit (1 to 9) or the letter "i", you get the ability to change what METAFONT will read next; but these features are primarily of interest when METAFONT is processing input from a file, so we shall discuss them later. The best thing to do at this point is type ⟨carriage-return⟩ ("<cr>"), since ⟨line-feed⟩ ("<lf>") would not give you a chance to stop and correct any future error messages.

As you might have guessed, another error will now be detected. But you probably didn't guess what kind of error you were making, unless you've read Chapter 5. METAFONT believes that "another error" is wrong because "another" and "error" are the names of variables, and you are trying to multiply these variables together (as if you had written "another*error" or "another.error"—

multiplication signs need not be used in METAFONT formulas). But it is illegal to multiply two variables together unless at least one of them has previously been given an explicit value, as we shall see in Chapter 5, hence the error message is

```
! +1.0000 another + .0000
! Undefined factor, replaced by .1.0000.
(*) error; another error;
```

(The undefined value of "another" has been replaced by 1.0000 and the machine plans to continue evaluating the algebraic expression when you restart.) Hit ⟨carriage-return⟩ again. And again.

Now you are once more prompted with "∗" and we can proceed to do some real METAFONTing. For our first trick, let's try to produce the heart shape of Fig. 2–9, but without using points 4 and 6. Type the following four lines one at a time (without error, please):

```
x1=100; y1=162;
x2=200-x8=140; y2=y8=178;
x3=200-x7=185; y3=y7=125;
x5=100; y5=0;
```

don't forget the semicolons after each equation. Note that subscripted variables like x_2 are typed simply as "x2"; this works with w-variables, x-variables, y-variables, and with constructions like $bot_1 y_4$ (which would be typed "bot1y4").

At this point you might want to see if METAFONT was really smart enough to figure out the value of x_8 from the equation 200−x8=140. So type "x8;" and hit ⟨carriage-return⟩. This produces an error message we've seen before, namely

```
! +60.0000
! Missing = sign, command flushed.
(*) x8;
```

but it also reports the value of the incomplete equation x_8, namely 60 (as it should be). In this way you can use METAFONT as a handy on-line computer in case you've misplaced your pocket calculator; try typing "sqrt 2;" and see what happens. (Whoops, type ⟨carriage-return⟩ first, to get out of error-recovery mode.)

In the midst of all these digressions about errors, we have been trying to draw a heart shape; and in fact, we have made progress, since the shape is almost ready to be drawn. Type

```
vpenwd 3; vpen; 9 draw 1{50,40}..2{1,0};
```

you should now see a blip on your screen. Believe it or not, that's the arc from point 1 to point 2. The whole heart will appear after you type two more lines,

```
draw 2{1,0}..3{0,-1}..5{-50,-36};
draw 1{-50,40}..8{-1,0}..7{0,-1}..5{50,-36};
```

right?

Notice that the key points (x_i, y_i) in the heart figure don't appear on your screen (although they will appear in your proof copy). The following statements will draw some thin auxiliary lines so that you can identify points 2, 3, 7, and 8:

```
w0=1; cpen; w0 draw 2..5; draw 8..5; draw 3..7;
```

in general, some guidelines like this can be incorporated into your drawings while you are designing characters, thereby providing convenient reference points as you work on line. The example alphabet routines described in Appendix E include background grids to facilitate the design process.

Now the heart shape is complete; type a period ("`.`") and hit ⟨carriage-return⟩. (The period could also have been substituted for the semicolon at the end of your previous statement.) At this point—or perhaps we should say "at this period"— METAFONT prepares the proof copy of what has been drawn, since proofmode was requested; then it gets ready for another drawing. All of the x-variables and y-variables that have been defined so far now become undefined again; but the w-variables (and any other variables, if there had been any) retain their values. The picture of a heart remains on your screen, but it will vanish when the result of the next draw command is displayed.

You can test the fact that w_0 is still equal to 1 by typing

```
w0=1;
```

METAFONT will respond "`Redundant equation.`" You can also try typing

```
5w0=6;
```

METAFONT will respond "Inconsistent equation." (If you really want to change w_0 you can say, for example,

```
new w0; 5w0=6;
```

then w_0 will become 1.2, which will be rounded to 1 if it is used as a pen size. Things like this will be explained later in more detail.)

At this point you know enough about METAFONT to try a few experiments on your own. Perhaps you would like to play with it before finishing this run. Just remember to type semicolons after each statement, except that the last statement of any particular drawing should be followed by a period. The statements you know about so far are (i) equations, (ii) pen type specifications, (iii) **draw**.

When you're all done, type "end" and METAFONT should stop. Afterwards something like ".r xgpsyn;mfput.xgp/L" will show up on your terminal. Hit ⟨carriage-return⟩ and your proof sheets will be printed on the XGP printer.

After each run a record of what you typed and what error messages were issued will appear on your file errors.tmp; you can read this file to remind yourself about any errors that you would like to avoid next time.

That finishes Experiment Number One. Are you ready for Number Two? If not, now's a good time to take a break and put this manual down for a while.

Experiment Number Two should be fun, since you will learn (a) how to create a new "font of type" that can be used in printing future documents, and (b) how to get METAFONT to read from a file instead of from the terminal. The font to be created consists of seven characters,

$$a = \diagdown \quad b = \diagup \quad c = \diagdown \quad d = \diagup \quad e = \diagdown \quad f = \diagup \quad z = \langle\text{blank}\rangle,$$

each of which is 10 points square (in printers' units). We shall name the font DRAGON, since it can be used to typeset so-called "dragon curves" [cf. C. Davis and D. E. Knuth, *J. Recreational Math.* **3** (1970), 66–81, 133–149; see also D. E. Knuth and J. C. Knuth, *J. Recreational Math.* **6** (1973), 165–167]. For example, the text in Fig. 4–1 can be used with your font to produce Fig. 4–2, which is a dragon curve of order 9. Another thing you can do with DRAGON is (i) make a border of "dada...da\par" at the top of a page; then (ii) type any number of pairs of lines having the form "cxx...xb\par" followed by "dxx...xa\par", where the x's represent any random mixture of e's and f's, all of these lines having the same length as the first line; then (iii) finish up with the line "cbcb...cb\par". (Try it!)

```
\:b←dragon[⟨your file area⟩]            dfbzdfeffbcbzdadfbcbzdadfbcb\par
\baselineskip 0pt \lineskip 0pt        ceadeeefeazzzcefeazzzcefea\par
zzzzzdazzda\par                        dfefefefffadadefffadadefffadada\par
zzzzdfbzdfb\par                        cbceebceebceefeeefeeebceebceefea\par
zzzzceadeeada\par                      zzdfbzdfbzdffffeffffffbzdfbzdffbcb\par
zzzzdfebcbcfb\par                      zzcbzzcbzzcbceefeeefazcbzzcbca\par
zdazcfeazzzca\par                      zzzzzzzzzzzzdfefefefbzzzzzzzzdfa\par
dfbzdbcbzzzdb\par                      zzzzzzzzdazcfeeebceazzzzzzzzcfea\par
ceadeazzzzcb\par                       zzzzzzzzdfbzdfefbzdfbzzzzdzzdbcb\par
dfefefa\par                            zzzzzzzzceadeeefazcbzzzzzzcadea\par
cbceefea\par                           zzzzzzzzdfefefefbzzzzzzzzzzcbcb\par
zzdffbcb\par                           zzzzzzzzcbceebcea\par
zzcbca\par                             zzzzzzzzzzzdfbzdfb\par
zzzzdfadadazzzzdadazzzzdada\par        zzzzzzzzzzzcbzzcb\par
zdazcfeeefeazzzcefeazzzcefea\par       \vfill\end
```

Fig. 4–1. The TEX typesetting system will produce the famous "dragon curve" from this input, if you create the Dragon Font described in this chapter.

In order to get ready for Experiment Number Two, prepare a file called DRAGON.MF that contains the following data:

```
"The Dragon Font, created by ⟨your name⟩";
fntmode; % this causes a font for the XGP to be produced
tfxmode; % this causes a TEX information file to be produced
titletrace; % this prints out quoted strings when they occur
points=10; % change this if you want a different size font
pixels=3.6; % raster units per point for TEX on the XGP
w0=pixels+1; % pen size is one point plus one raster unit
cpen; maxht top0 points.pixels. % tallest output in raster units
⟨begin new file page⟩
"a: From W to S";
input drag; charcode `a;
w0 draw 4{1,0}..3{0,-1}.
⟨begin new file page⟩
"b: From W to N";
input drag; charcode `b;
w0 draw 4{1,0}..1{0,1}.
⟨begin new file page⟩
"c: From N to E";
input drag; charcode `c;
w0 draw 1{0,-1}..2{1,0}.
⟨begin new file page⟩
"d: From S to E";
input drag; charcode `d;
w0 draw 3{0,1}..2{1,0}.
```

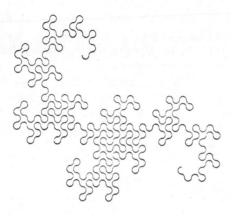

Fig. 4–2. Dragon curve of order 9, typeset by Fig. 4–1 (and reduced in size).

```
⟨begin new file page⟩
"e: From W to S and from N to E";
input drag; charcode `e;
w0 draw 4{1,0}..3{0,-1}; draw 1{0,-1}..2{1,0}.
⟨begin new file page⟩
"f: From W to N and from S to E";
input drag; charcode `f;
```
▶Exercise 4.1: Figure out what belongs here ...
```
⟨begin new file page⟩
"z: Blank";
input drag; charcode `z.
```

(Material beginning with the symbol "%" is ignored by METAFONT, up to the end of a line; such comments often provide useful documentation.) Let us hope that you don't think preparing this longish file was a drag, because there is yet one other file that needs to be created, a shortish one called DRAG.MF containing the following:

```
% Common routine for the DRAGON characters
y1=x2=points.pixels;
x1=x3=y2=y4=1/2 y1;
y3=x4=0;
error; 2.0 intentional errors to be removed later;
cpen;
charht points; charwd points; chardp 0; chardw round x2;
```

METAFONT is asked to read this file seven times by the commands "input drag" in DRAGON.MF, since DRAG.MF contains information that is useful for all seven characters. The charht, charwd, and chardp commands on the bottom line are for TEX's benefit, telling the character's height, width, and depth in units of points. The chardw command gives the character's approximate width in raster units. It is more interesting to draw the characters than to supply such information, but the information is necessary when a font is being made.

OK, now you're ready for the real action to take place. Type "r mf" to the operating system; and when you get the "∗", type "input dragon". The following data should soon appear on your screen:

```
(dragon.mf 1 2 3
a: From W to S... (drag.mf 1 2
! + 1.0000 error + .0000
! Missing = sign, command flushed.
p.2,1.5 error;
                2.0 intentional errors to be removed later;
↑
```

(If something else shows up, you might have forgotten a semicolon or made some other typing mistake. Chapter 10 contains a complete list of error messages in case you find METAFONT's remarks inscrutable.) The screen data shown above means that METAFONT has begun to read file DRAGON.MF; in fact it has gotten up to page 3 and passed the quoted statement "a: From W to S". Then it began to read DRAG.MF, where an error was encountered on page 2, line 5.[*]

We inserted an intentional error into file DRAG.MF in order to get used to error correction when METAFONT is reading from a file. Type "3" now, just to see what happens. When you type a digit from 1 to 9 in response to an error, METAFONT will delete this many so-called tokens from the input. In this case the result after deleting three tokens is

```
p.2,1.5 error; 2.0 intentional errors
                                    to be removed later;
↑
```

---

[*]Page numbers are one higher on Stanford's system than they might be at other places, since the system text editor supplies a directory page called page 1.

so you can see that the constant "2.0" is considered to be a single token (not three), and that "intentional" and "errors" were the other two tokens deleted. Generally speaking, a token is a variable name or a constant or a special character like a semicolon. (Furthermore the two dots in a command like "draw 1..2" count as a single token.)

At this point it would be a good idea for you to type "e". This tells META-FONT that you wish to terminate the present run and that you wish to make a correction at the current place in the current file. Soon after typing "e" you will find that the system text editor has started, and the cursor shows that you are positioned at page 2, line 5 of DRAG.MF, the place where the error was detected. Delete this offending line from the file and exit from the editor.

Are you continuing to follow these instructions faithfully? Please stick to the job just a little longer, then you'll be on your own. The next thing you should do is type "r mf" again; then type

```
input mumble
```

(and ⟨carriage-return⟩). This will produce yet another error message, but it is useful for you to learn how to recover from the wrong-file-name error since some people don't feel that METAFONT's recovery procedure is completely obvious. What you should do in response to

```
! Lookup failed on file mumble.mf.
(*) input mumble
              ↑
```

is (a) type "i" (meaning that you want to insert something into what METAFONT is reading), then (b) type "dragon" (the correct file name). This ought to work.

Now you might think everything will go smoothly, but the author has planned one more instructive error for you. The message that you get is

```
! Input page ended while scanning "a: From W to S".
p.3,l.2 input drag
                    ; charcode 'a;
```

Actually this isn't an error, it's just a warning that an error may have occurred, since normal usage of METAFONT will not end a file in the middle of processing a character. We have used the short DRAG file in this example to avoid repeating four lines of code in seven places, but in practice it is better to accomplish this by using subroutines (which we haven't learned yet) or by copying the four lines into the DRAGON file seven times using the system text editor. Since the file ended before "a: From W to S" was finished, METAFONT has issued a warning that an error might have occurred. To recover, you can either (a) hit the line-feed key now (so that METAFONT won't stop on future errors the next six times this happens), or (b) type "i" and then type "no pagewarning;" this suppresses the warning messages at the end of file pages. (If a no pagewarning command had been included near the beginning of your DRAGON.MF file, METAFONT would not have stopped to give you this message in the first place.)

Finally METAFONT will finish reading the last page of DRAGON.MF; it puts a ")" on your screen when this happens. You can now type "end" and the program will stop. If you have carefully followed the above instructions, METAFONT's closing words to you will be

```
Images written on DRAGON.FNT
TEX information written on DRAGON.TFX
```

so you will be able to use DRAGON as a font with your next TEX manuscript.

Note that the process of preparing a complete font is very much like the task of writing a medium-size computer program or technical paper. It takes a little while to get a correct computer file set up, and you have to dot the i's and cross the t's (perhaps literally); but once you have reached this point it is fairly easy to make changes and to develop bigger and better things.

▶Exercise 4.2: Since this was a long chapter, you should go outside now and get some *real* exercise.

<5> Variables, expressions, and equations

The examples we have seen so far give some idea of what METAFONT can do in simple cases, but in fact METAFONT knows a lot more mathematics than the above examples imply. In this chapter we shall discuss exactly what types of things are allowed in METAFONT equations.

The basic components of an equation are *variables* and *constants*, both of which take real numbers as values—they need not be integers. Since the rules for constants are simplest, we shall discuss them first. A constant usually has one of the forms

⟨digit string⟩   or   ⟨digit string⟩.⟨digit string⟩   or   .⟨digit string⟩

denoting a number in decimal notation. (A ⟨digit string⟩ is a sequence of one or more of the ten characters 0, 1, ..., 9.) Or the constant may have one of the above forms preceded by an apostrophe, in which case it represents a number in octal notation. For example, "´100" is the same as "64"; "´10.4" is the same as "8.5"; etc. One further form of constant is possible: A *reverse apostrophe* (i.e., a single open-quote mark) followed by any character denotes the 7-bit code for that character. For example, "`a" is the same as "´141". This notation was used to identify the **charcodes**, i.e., the font positions of the characters, in the DRAGON example of Chapter 4.

A variable is specified in METAFONT programs by typing its so-called ⟨identifier⟩, which is a sequence of one or more of the 26 letters a, b, ..., z, with upper-case and lower-case letters considered equivalent. However, the *first* letter must not be "w", "x", or "y", since these are reserved for the subscripted variables of METAFONT. Furthermore some letter strings like top and draw have a special meaning that precludes their being used as variables; all such "reserved words" are listed in boldface type in the index to this manual (Appendix I).

A variable may also have the form w⟨digit string⟩, x⟨digit string⟩, or y⟨digit string⟩, in which case it is said to be a *w*-variable (intended for pen widths), an *x*-variable (intended for *x* coordinates of points), or a *y*-variable (intended for *y* coordinates of points). We sometimes use the term *wxy*-variable to stand for any variable of one of these three types. Note that variables x3 and y3 are related to each other because they are the coordinates of point 3; but they have no connection to variable w3. In the examples of this manual we often use the notation x_3 and w_3 for what would actually be typed "x3" and "w3".

⚗ Actually a wxy-variable can have the slightly more general form $w\langle\text{index}\rangle$, $x\langle\text{index}\rangle$, or $y\langle\text{index}\rangle$, where $\langle\text{index}\rangle$ is either a digit string or the name of an index parameter to a subroutine, as we shall see in Chapter 8. Thus "xj" and "yj" stand for the coordinates of point j, inside of a subroutine having j as an index parameter; typographic conventions like x_j and $\text{top}_i y_j$ are used for what would actually be typed as "xj" and "top i yj".

It is important to keep in mind that variable names are composed of letters only, unless they are wxy-variables. You can't have variables called "s1" and "s2", METAFONT will think you are talking about s times 1 and s times 2. One way out is to use roman numerals like "si" and "sii".

Stanford's current implementation of METAFONT will not distinguish two different identifiers that begin with the same seven letters, unless they have different lengths; other implementations may be even more fussy, requiring for example that the first six letters be distinct. Therefore, although you are allowed to invent long descriptive names for variables, don't try to use distinct names like "heightofa" and "heightofb" in the same program.

No spaces should appear within the name of a variable or a constant; otherwise METAFONT may get confused. For example, "al pha" would look like two variables, and the period in "3. 14" would look like a period instead of a decimal point following the 3.

At the beginning of a METAFONT program, variables have no values; they get values by appearing in *equations*. It takes ten equations to define the values of ten variables, and if you have given only nine equations it might turn out that none of the ten variables has a known value. For example, if the equations are

$$x_0 = x_1 = x_2 = x_3 = x_4 = x_5 = x_6 = x_7 = x_8 = x_9$$

(which counts as nine equations, since there are nine $=$ signs), we don't know what any of the x's is. However, a further equation like

$$x_0 + x_1 = 1$$

will cause METAFONT to deduce that all ten of these variables are equal to $\frac{1}{2}$.

METAFONT always determines the values of as many variables as possible, based on the equations it has seen so far. For example, consider the two equations

$$y_1 + y_2 + y_3 = 3;$$
$$y_1 - y_2 - y_3 = 1;$$

METAFONT will deduce (correctly) that $y_1 = 2$, but all it will know about y_2 and y_3 is that $y_2 + y_3 = 1$. At any point in a program a variable is said to be "known" or "unknown," depending on whether or not its value can be deduced uniquely from the equations that have been stated so far.* Sometimes you will have to be sure that a certain variable is known; for example, when drawing a curve, the x- and y-variables for all points on that curve must be known.

You might wonder how METAFONT keeps its knowledge up-to-date based on the partial information it receives from miscellaneous equations. The details aren't really very important when you use the language, but they may help in understanding some error messages. If there are n variables and if m equations have appeared so far, METAFONT will classify $n - m$ of the unknown variables as "independent." The other m variables are expressed as linear combinations of the independent ones; if this linear combination has a constant value, the variable is "known", otherwise it is called "dependent." Every new equation, say the $(m + 1)$st, can be rewritten in the form

$$c_0 + c_1 v_1 + \cdots + c_{n-m} v_{n-m} = 0$$

where the c's are constants and $v_1, \ldots, v_{n-m}$ are the independent variables. If $c_k = 0$ for all $k > 0$, the new equation is rejected; it is either redundant (if $c_0 = 0$) or inconsistent (if $c_0 \neq 0$). Otherwise one of the variables v_k having maximum $|c_k|$ is selected. This variable ceases to be independent and the equation is used to express it in terms of the remaining independent variables $v_1, \ldots, v_{k-1}, v_{k+1}, \ldots, v_{n-m}$; several of the dependent variables might now become known.

You can experiment with METAFONT's equation-solving mechanism by typing "eqtrace;" near the beginning of your program. This causes the interpreter to tell you the values of all variables when they become known. Another way to experiment is to use the fact that METAFONT types out the value of an expression when there is no equals sign in a statement. For example, after "y1+y2+y3=3; y1−y2−y3=1;" you can type "y1; y2; y3;"—the result will be three harmless error messages in which you learn that $y_1 = 2$ and that y_2 and y_3 respectively have the current values "$-y_3 + 1.000$" and "y_3". (In other words, METAFONT has chosen to make y_2 dependent and y_3 independent.)

---

*This feature makes METAFONT different from most other computer languages; it tends to make your programs "declarative" more than "imperative" in that you say what relationships you want to achieve instead of how you want to compute the values that achieve them.

From variables and constants you can build up more complicated formulas called *expressions*. In order to state the rules for expressions clearly and completely, we shall discuss them in a rather formal manner. In order to state them in an understandable way, we shall also discuss informal examples.

Expressions come in several flavors, depending on how complicated they are and how they interact with their environment. A *primary* expression is, in a sense, a basic building block; it is one of the following things:

- a variable (whether known or unknown).

- a constant.

- nrand, denoting a random real number with the normal distribution, having mean 0 and standard deviation 1.

- sqrt ⟨term⟩, denoting the square root of the value of the term (e.g., sqrt .09 = .3). The term must have a known value.

- cosd ⟨term⟩, denoting the cosine of the value of the term in degrees (e.g., cosd 60 = .5). The term must have a known value.

- sind ⟨term⟩, denoting the sine of the value of the term in degrees (e.g., sind 30 = .5). The term must have a known value.

- round ⟨term⟩, denoting the value of the term rounded to the nearest integer; an integer plus .5 is rounded upwards (e.g., round 3.14 = 3.0; round 1.5 = 2.0; round (−1.5) = −1.0). The term must have a known value.

- good⟨index⟩⟨term⟩, denoting the value of the term rounded to the nearest "good" value, depending on the value of w_i (see Chapter 7), where i is the value of the ⟨index⟩. The term must have a known value.

- lft⟨index⟩⟨term⟩, rt⟨index⟩⟨term⟩, top⟨index⟩⟨term⟩, or bot⟨index⟩⟨term⟩, denoting the value of the term plus or minus a correction based on the current pen and the value of w_i (see Chapter 3), where i is the value of the ⟨index⟩. The term need not have a known value.

- an expression enclosed in parentheses, denoting the value of the expression as a unit in a larger expression. For example, we will see that "2(u+v)" means something different from "2u+v", but the latter denotes exactly the same thing as "(2u)+v".

In these rules "⟨index⟩" means either a ⟨digit string⟩, representing an integer subscript, or the name of an index parameter to a subroutine (see Chapter 8); "⟨term⟩" means an expression of the second flavor, which we shall describe next.

A *term* expression is, in a sense, a building block for sums; it is somewhat like a primary but it also includes products and quotients. Formally speaking, a term is a primary followed by zero or more occurrences of the following things as many times as possible in a given context:

- *⟨primary⟩ or .⟨primary⟩ or simply ⟨primary⟩, denoting the product of the value of the term so far and the value of the primary. (At least one of these factors must have a known value; i.e., you can't say "alpha*beta" when alpha's value is unknown unless beta's value is known. When multiplication is indicated by ".", no space should appear after the dot, and the primary should not be a decimal constant.

- /⟨primary⟩, denoting the value of the term so far divided by the value of the primary. (The primary must have a known value and it must not be zero.)

- [⟨expression₁⟩,⟨expression₂⟩], denoting $v_1 + a(v_2 - v_1)$, where a is the value of the term so far, v_1 is the value of the first expression, and v_2 is the value of the second. (Either the value of a or the value of $v_2 - v_1$ must be known.)

For example, "a*b/c" is a term meaning a times b divided by c. One can also write it as "a.b/c" or "a b/c"; the space between "a" and "b" is essential in the last example, since "ab/c" means the quotient of variable ab by variable c. Note also that "a/b*c" has the same meaning as "(a/b)*c", not "a/(b*c)". Some computer languages treat this expression one way and some treat it the other way, but METAFONT prefers the former for two reasons: (i) Division in METAFONT is most often used when dividing an integer by an integer, and cases like "2/3 c" are very common. It is desirable to avoid parentheses in such common cases. (ii) This rule is easily remembered, since terms are consistently evaluated from left to right in all cases.

The construction ⟨term⟩[⟨expression₁⟩,⟨expression₂⟩] deserves special discussion since it is an operation that occurs frequently in font design but there is no existing notation for it in traditional mathematics. In general, "$a[u, v]$" means "a of the way from u to v"; thus "2/3[x1,x2]" means the value obtained by starting at x_1 and going two-thirds of the distance between x_1 and x_2. If $x_1 = 100$ and $x_2 = 160$, this is 140; if $x_1 = 160$ and $x_2 = 100$ it is 120.

▶Exercise 5.1: What is the value of $0[x_1, x_2]$? Of $3/2[x_1, x_2]$? How would you express the value of the point midway between x_1 and x_2, using this notation?

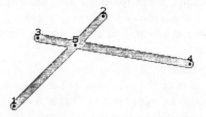

Fig. 5–1. The coordinates of point 5 can be readily calculated from those of points 1, 2, 3, and 4, using METAFONT equations.

One of the interesting applications of the bracket notation is to find the point (x_5, y_5) where the line from (x_1, y_1) to (x_2, y_2) intersects the line from (x_3, y_3) to (x_4, y_4), assuming that points 1, 2, 3, and 4 are already known (see Fig. 5–1). The following equations can be written, involving two variables *alpha* and *beta* that are not used elsewhere:

$$x_5 = alpha\,[x_1, x_2] = beta\,[x_3, x_4];$$
$$y_5 = alpha\,[y_1, y_2] = beta\,[y_3, y_4];$$

METAFONT will solve for *alpha*, *beta*, x_5, and y_5. The reasoning behind these equations is that there is some fraction α such that x_5 is α of the way from x_1 to x_2 and y_5 is α of the way from y_1 to y_2; similarly there is some fraction relating x_5 to x_3 and x_4 as y_5 is related to y_3 and y_4. We don't care what α and β are; but it doesn't hurt to ask METAFONT to compute more values than we really need, as long as it also computes the desired values x_5 and y_5. (Note: If you are applying this trick more than once, it is necessary to say "new alpha,beta"; this allows you to reuse the same auxiliary variables *alpha* and *beta* in each place. See Chapter 9 for the rules of new.)

Finally we come to expressions of the third flavor: *general* expressions. These consist of a term followed by zero or more occurrences of "+ ⟨term⟩" or "– ⟨term⟩", meaning to add or subtract the value of the term following the plus or minus sign to or from the value of the expression so far. A general expression can also begin with a plus sign or a minus sign, in which case we interpret it as if it had been preceded by the constant zero. (For example, the expression "$-2y_1 + 3y_2$" means the same thing as "$0 - 2y_1 + 3y_2$", which means, "Take zero, then subtract twice the value of y_1, then add three times the value of y_2.") Like terms, general expressions are evaluated from left to right.

Readers familiar with BNF notation may appreciate the following summary of the syntactic rules for **METAFONT** variables, expressions, and equations:

⟨digit⟩ ← 0 | 1 | 2 | 3 | 4 | 5 | 6 | 7 | 8 | 9
⟨digit string⟩ ← ⟨digit⟩ | ⟨digit string⟩⟨digit⟩
⟨non wxy⟩ ← a | b | c | d | e | f | g | h | i | j | k | l | m | n | o | p | q | r | s | t | u | v | z
⟨wxy⟩ ← w | x | y
⟨letter⟩ ← ⟨non wxy⟩ | ⟨wxy⟩
⟨identifier⟩ ← ⟨non wxy⟩ | ⟨identifier⟩⟨letter⟩
⟨index⟩ ← ⟨digit string⟩ | ⟨identifier⟩
⟨variable⟩ ← ⟨identifier⟩ | ⟨wxy⟩⟨index⟩
⟨radix⟩ ← ´ | ⟨empty⟩
⟨constant⟩ ← ⟨radix⟩⟨digit string⟩ | ⟨radix⟩⟨digit string⟩ . ⟨digit string⟩ |
                          ⟨radix⟩ . ⟨digit string⟩ | `⟨any character you can type⟩
⟨unary operator⟩ ← sqrt | cosd | sind | round | good⟨index⟩ | ⟨direction⟩⟨index⟩
⟨direction⟩ ← lft | rt | top | bot
⟨primary⟩ ← ⟨variable⟩ | ⟨constant⟩ | nrand | ⟨unary operator⟩⟨term⟩ | (⟨expression⟩)
⟨multiplication or division sign⟩ ← * | . | ⟨empty⟩ | /
⟨term⟩ ← ⟨primary⟩ | ⟨term⟩⟨multiplication or division sign⟩⟨primary⟩ |
                          ⟨term⟩[⟨expression⟩, ⟨expression⟩]
⟨addition or subtraction sign⟩ ← + | −
⟨expression⟩ ← ⟨term⟩ | ⟨addition or subtraction sign⟩⟨term⟩ |
                          ⟨expression⟩⟨addition or subtraction sign⟩⟨term⟩
⟨equation statement⟩ ← ⟨expression⟩ = ⟨expression⟩ |
                          ⟨equation statement⟩ = ⟨expression⟩

Before we close this discussion of expressions, a few things deserve special emphasis:

1) Blank spaces, ⟨tab⟩s, and ⟨carriage-return⟩s usually have no effect on a META-FONT program except for the fact that they may not appear within identifiers, constants, or file names, and the fact that they give a special meaning to each "." that they follow. A character that has no special meaning in the METAFONT language (e.g., "?" or "$" or "↓") is treated as if it were a blank space. (Of course, blank spaces and other characters do represent themselves when they immediately follow a ` mark or when they appear between quotes in titles.)

2) The symbol "." must be used carefully when not quoted, since METAFONT interprets it in four different ways depending on the immediate context:

i) If "." is followed by a blank space (or ⟨tab⟩ or ⟨carriage-return⟩), it denotes a period or "full stop" (the end of a METAFONT routine or subroutine).

ii) If "." is followed by a digit (0 to 9), it denotes a decimal point.

iii) If "." is followed by another ".", it denotes the ".." symbol in a draw (or ddraw) command.

iv) Otherwise "." denotes multiplication.

3) You don't need parentheses in expressions like "round $2z$" or "sqrt u/v". (Most computer languages require you to write "round$(2z)$" and "sqrt(u/v)" and even "sqrt(2)".)

▶Exercise 5.2: Does "sqrt x1+x2" mean the same as (a) "(sqrt x1)+x2"? (b) "sqrt(x1+x2)"? (c) "sqrt x1(+x2)"?

<6> Filling in between curves

Letter forms in modern alphabets are based primarily on the calligraphy of fine penmen in bygone ages; but they have gone through a long evolution so that a great many letters are quite different from what you would get using a fixed pen. Furthermore, real pens and brushes change their shape depending on how hard you press and on what direction you are moving, as you write or paint. Therefore METAFONT has provisions for producing shapes in which the pen seems to vary its proportions as it moves.

The basic way to accomplish such special effects is to use the ddraw (double draw) command, which is like draw but you specify two curves instead of one. When you say

$$w_5 \text{ ddraw } 1..2..3..4, 5..6..7..8$$

(for example), the effect is essentially to take the current pen of size w_5 and to draw the two curves $1..2..3..4$ and $5..6..7..8$, then to fill in the space between them. This filling-in process is achieved by drawing interpolating curves that are equally spaced between the corresponding pairs of points 1 and 5, 2 and 6, 3 and 7, 4 and 8.

Both curves in a ddraw command are specified exactly as in draw commands, with optional directions included in braces at each point, and with optional hidden points in parentheses at the beginning or end; the only proviso is that both curves must have exactly the same number of points (not counting hidden ones). You can say "ddraw 1, 2" (which turns out to be equivalent to "draw 1..2" since there is only one point in each "curve"), but you can't say "ddraw 1..2(..3), 4..5..6" (since that's a two-point curve with a three-point one).

Suppose, for example, that you wish to fill in the heart shape discussed in Chapter 2. Assuming that the points have been defined as in that chapter, and assuming that cpen has been selected, the following commands can be issued to METAFONT:

$$x_9 = \tfrac{1}{3}[x_1, x_3]; \quad y_9 = \tfrac{1}{3}[y_1, y_5];$$
9 ddraw 1{50, 40}..2{1, 0}..3{0, −1}..4..5{−50, −36}, 9..9..9..9..9;
ddraw 1{−50, 40}..8{−1, 0}..7{0, −1}..6..5{50, −36}, 9..9..9..9..9.

The outside boundary of the resulting shape will be precisely that of Fig. 2–9, while the interior will be solid black. Fig. 6–1 indicates how METAFONT actually does this, by showing the set of paths that a cpen of diameter 9 would take to fill in the middle; these paths are illustrated with a cpen of diameter 1 so that gaps are apparent.

Fig. 6–1. The heart shape (or any other shape) can be filled in by "double drawing."

There was, of course, no need for the example program above to define point 9 as it did; the two ddraw commands would have worked equally well if "9..9..9..9..9" had been replaced by "1..1..1..1..1" or "1..1..5..5..5" or a host of other possibilities. The off-center point 9 was merely chosen to give a nice-looking illustration that shows a bit more of how METAFONT draws curves.

▶Exercise 6.1: On the other hand, the command

$$9 \text{ ddraw } 1\{50, 40\} \ldots 2\{1, 0\} \ldots 3\{0, -1\} \ldots 4 \ldots 5\{-50, -36\},$$
$$1\{-50, 40\} \ldots 8\{-1, 0\} \ldots 7\{0, -1\} \ldots 6 \ldots 5\{50, -36\}$$

does *not* draw a filled-in heart shape, although it might seem at first that it should. Why doesn't it?

More precisely, suppose ddraw is given two curves that run through the points $(z_1, z_2, \ldots, z_n)$ and $(\hat{z}_1, \hat{z}_2, \ldots, \hat{z}_n)$. The two curves $z(t)$ and $\hat{z}(t)$ are computed as usual, then the curves $(k/m)[z(t), \hat{z}(t)]$ are drawn for $0 \le k \le m$, where m is computed in such a way that the interior is probably (but not always) filled in by this means. Finally, straight lines are drawn from z_1 to $\hat{z}_1$ and from z_n to $\hat{z}_n$. The value of m is determined as follows: For each j between 1 and n we compute $\Delta x_j = x_j - \hat{x}_j$ and $\Delta y_j = y_j - \hat{y}_j$ and m_j, where m_j depends on the current pen type and size w according to the formulas

cpen, spen, epen	hpen	vpen	lpen, rpen

$$\frac{\sqrt{\Delta x^2 + \Delta y^2}}{w} \qquad \sqrt{\left(\frac{\Delta x_j}{w}\right)^2 + \left(\frac{\Delta y_j}{h_0}\right)^2} \qquad \sqrt{\left(\frac{\Delta x_j}{v_0}\right)^2 + \left(\frac{\Delta y_j}{w}\right)^2} \qquad \max\left(\left|\frac{\Delta x}{w}\right|, \left|\frac{\Delta y}{h_0}\right|\right).$$

It follows that $\lceil m_j + 1 \rceil$ equally-spaced pen images between z_j and $\hat{z}_j$ would touch each other, making a connected set, if we weren't rounding to a discrete raster. (This is the only case where the "current size" is relevant for pens of type spen and epen; you should specify a size small enough that fill-in would occur properly if the pen were a cpen instead, but not so small that the filling-in takes extremely long.) The actual value of m is defined to be

$$\lfloor s \max(m_1, \ldots, m_n) \rfloor + 1$$

where s is a "safety factor" that is normally equal to 2. You can change the safety factor by saying "safetyfactor 2.5", for example, if it turns out that 2.0 isn't safe enough, but actually you won't ever need to do this unless the curves are quite unusual.

▶Exercise 6.2: How do you think the author produced Fig. 6–1, using a single ddraw command? (It was necessary to fool METAFONT into drawing curves that didn't really fill in the interior.)

Fig. 6–2 is another example of **ddraw**, a sort of calligraphic effect produced with the following program:

$$x_1 = 5; \quad y_1 = 10; \quad x_2 = 300; \quad y_2 = -5;$$
$$x_3 = 0; \quad y_3 = 0; \quad x_4 = 298; \quad y_4 = 10;$$
$$\textbf{cpen}; \quad 9 \textbf{ ddraw } 1\{x_2 - x_1, 2(y_2 - y_1)\} .. 2\{1, 0\},$$
$$3\{1, 0\} .. 4\{x_4 - x_3, 2(y_4 - y_3)\}.$$

In this case the two **ddrawn** lines actually cross each other.

Fig. 6–2. Typical effect obtainable with ddraw.

METAFONT also provides a mechanism for dynamically varying the pen width while drawing lines or curves, using a generalized draw command. For example, you can say

$$\textbf{hpen}; \quad \textbf{draw } |w_0|1 .. |w_1|2 .. |w_0|3$$

and METAFONT will draw a curve from point 1 to point 2 to point 3, starting with an hpen of size w_0 but changing the size gradually to w_1 and than back to w_0 again. You can also specify directions for the curve after the point specifications in the usual way, for example by saying

$$\textbf{draw } |w_0|1\{1, 0\} .. |w_1|2\{0, 1\} .. |w_0|3\{1, 0\};$$

but we shall ignore this fact in order to simplify the following discussion. The general rule for **draw** is that you can specify a pen size enclosed in "|" signs just *before* giving a point number, and you can specify a curve direction enclosed in "{" and "}" just *after* giving a point number. (See Figs. 8–1 and 8–2 in Chapter 8 for examples of this feature.)

If you don't specify a new pen size at a point, the pen size from the previous point is used; if you don't specify a new pen size at the *first* point, the so-called "current pen size" is used. The current pen size is set to zero whenever a new pen type is specified, and it is changed to the value of any expression that appears immediately before **draw** or **ddraw**; it is not changed by values in "|" signs within a **draw** command. Thus, for example, consider the commands

$$9 \text{ draw } 1 .. |5|2 .. 3; \quad \text{draw } 4 .. |8|5;$$

the pen size at point 1 is 9, at points 2 and 3 it is 5, at point 4 it is 9 again, at point 5 it is 8, and after these two statements the current pen size is still 9.

Important note: This generalized version of **draw** is allowed only when the pen is of type **hpen**, **vpen**, **lpen**, or **rpen**; you can't vary the size of a **cpen**, and it doesn't make sense to vary the size of an **spen** or **epen**. Furthermore the changing of pen widths is illegal in **ddraw** commands; in fact, as explained below, METAFONT actually implements variable-width **draw** commands by reducing them to **ddraw**.

The pen width varies smoothly according to a cubic spline function $w(t)$ analogous to the functions $x(t)$ and $y(t)$ used to control pen motion. Suppose we are drawing a curve from z_1 to z_2 to $\cdots$ to z_n, and let z_0 and z_{n+1} be the hidden points at the beginning and end of the path, where $z_0 = z_1$ and/or $z_{n+1} = z_n$ if hidden points were not specified. Similarly we will have pen sizes $s_0, s_1, \ldots, s_n, s_{n+1}$; if all the pen sizes are equal, the **draw** command proceeds as described in Chapter 2, otherwise we have to define the variation in pen size. First the derivatives $(s'_1, \ldots, s'_n)$, which express the rates of change in pen width as the curve passes points $(z_1, \ldots, z_n)$, are determined as follows: If no explicit pen size was given at z_j, or if a "#" appears just before the second "|" of a size specification at that point, we let $s'_j = 0$. (The # mark signifies stable pen size in the vicinity of that point. For example,

$$\text{draw } |s\#|1 .. 2 .. |2/3[s,t]|3 .. |t\#|4 .. 5$$

will draw a curve with pen size s between points 1 and 2, and pen size t between points 4 and 5; the pen size will be stable at points 1, 2, 4, and 5, and it will vary between points 2 and 4 in such a way that 2/3 of the change occurs between points 2 and 3.) Otherwise let $\Delta s_j = s_{j+1} - s_j$; then $s'_j = \Delta s_j$ if $\Delta z_{j-1} = 0$, otherwise $s'_j = \Delta s_{j-1}$ if $\Delta z_j = 0$, otherwise

$$s'_j = \left(\Delta s_{j-1}/|\Delta z_{j-1}|^2 + \Delta s_j/|\Delta z_j|^2 \right) \big/ \left(1/|\Delta z_{j-1}|^2 + 1/|\Delta z_j|^2 \right).$$

The pen size $s_j(t)$, as the curve $z(t)$ of Chapter 2 is drawn from z_j to z_{j+1} for $0 \leq t \leq 1$, is defined by the formula

$$s_j(t) = s_j + (3t^2 - 2t^3)\Delta s_j + t(1-t)^2 s'_j - t^2(1-t) s'_{j+1}.$$

When the pen size varies, a **draw** command is essentially reduced to **ddraw** in the following way: First the functions $s(t)$, $x(t)$, $y(t)$ describing pen size and pen motion are determined as described above. The minimum pen size, i.e., $\hat{s} = \min(s_1, \ldots, s_n)$, is also determined. A pen of size $\hat{s}$ will now be used to fill in the curve with the method of **ddraw**; the two curves $\bigl(x(t), y(t)\bigr)$ and $\bigl(\hat{x}(t), \hat{y}(t)\bigr)$ between which **ddraw**ing will take place are defined as follows, depending on the pen type:

	hpen	vpen	lpen	rpen
$x(t) \leftarrow$	$x(t) - \frac{1}{2}\bigl(s(t)-\hat{s}\bigr)$	$x(t)$	$x(t)$	$x(t)$
$y(t) \leftarrow$	$y(t)$	$y(t) - \frac{1}{2}\bigl(s(t)-\hat{s}\bigr)$	$y(t)$	$y(t)$
$\hat{x}(t) \leftarrow$	$x(t) + \frac{1}{2}\bigl(s(t)-\hat{s}\bigr)$	$x(t)$	$x(t) - \bigl(s(t)-\hat{s}\bigr)$	$x(t) + s(t) - \hat{s}$
$\hat{y}(t) \leftarrow$	$y(t)$	$y(t) + \frac{1}{2}\bigl(s(t)-\hat{s}\bigr)$	$y(t)$	$y(t)$

If the pen motion is being transformed by means of **trxx**, **trxy**, **incx**, **tryx**, **tryy**, or **incy** (see Chapter 9), the transformation applies to the original computation of $x(t)$ and $y(t)$ but not to the corrections by $s(t) - \hat{s}$ being applied here. In other words, transformations apply to the paths taken by pens, not to the pen shapes; you can use **ddraw** but not **draw** to get the effect of a rotated **hpen**.

<7> Discreteness and discretion

METAFONT does all of its drawing on a finite grid whose square pixels are either black or white; it does not actually draw continuous curves, it deals only with approximations to such curves. Such discreteness is not a severe limitation if the resolution is fine enough, i.e., if there are sufficiently many pixels per square unit, since physical properties of ink will smooth out the rough edges when material is printed. In fact, the human eye is itself composed of discrete receptors. However, the results of METAFONT might not look very good when the resolution is coarse, unless you are careful about how things are rounded to the raster. The purpose of this chapter is to explain the principles of "discreet rounding," i.e., tasteful application of mathematics so that the METAFONT output will look satisfactory even when the resolution is coarse.

The rest of this chapter is marked with dangerous bend signs, since a novice user of METAFONT will not wish to worry about such things. However, an expert METAFONTer will take care to round things properly even when preparing high-resolution fonts, since the subtle refinements we are about to discuss will improve the quality of the output when it is viewed with discerning eyes.

Chapter 3 mentioned the fact that pens are digitized before curves are drawn. This is important when low resolution is considered, otherwise vertical lines that would be 3.4 raster units wide (say) if drawn to infinite precision would be rounded sometimes to 3 units wide, sometimes to 4 units wide, depending on where they happen to fall. This looks bad, so METAFONT resolves the problem by drawing with a pen that is always 3 units wide or always 4 units wide.

Chapter 3 also hinted at METAFONT's method of drawing a curve $(x(t), y(t))$ as t varies, namely (a) to subtract offsets x'_0 and y'_0 from the x and y coordinates, depending on the pen being used, thereby compensating for the fact that the pen shape might be shifted by a non-integer amount with respect to the raster; then (b) to round $(x(t) - x'_0, y(t) - y'_0)$ to a sequence of integer points (x, y); and finally (c) for each integer point (x, y) at which the curve is to be "plotted," the pixels $(x + \xi, y + \eta)$ are made either black or white, depending on whether a pen or eraser is involved, for all integer points (ξ, η) in the pen shape.

Actually METAFONT does operation (c) at higher speeds than this description would imply, since it knows if it has reached (x, y) from an adjacent point, in which case most of the pixels $(x + \xi, y + \eta)$ are already known to be black or white. For example, when moving a pen one step upwards, only its top edge needs to be painted. METAFONT also gains speed by combining several horizontal and vertical steps into a single step.

What Chapter 3 failed to describe was how METAFONT chooses the sequence of points (x, y) that are to represent the curve $(x(t), y(t))$. The rule is essentially this: The integer point (x, y) is plotted if and only if the curve $(x(t) - x'_0, y(t) - y'_0)$ passes through the diamond-shaped region whose four corner points are

$$(x, y + \tfrac{1}{2})$$

$$(x - \tfrac{1}{2}, y) \qquad (x + \tfrac{1}{2}, y).$$

$$(x, y - \tfrac{1}{2})$$

This rule implies that if the curve is travelling in a basically horizontal direction (with x changing more rapidly than y), there is exactly one point plotted in each column, while if it is going in a basically vertical direction (with y changing more rapidly than x), there is one point plotted in each row. Furthermore the rule leads to proper behavior at the endpoints: If a curve is broken up into two segments, for example by inserting intermediate points in a **draw** command, you won't be plotting spurious points where the two curves join. (*Exception:* If an entire draw command has been processed but no point was plotted, because for example the command was trying to draw a tiny circle whose coordinates were all very close to $(a + \frac{1}{2}, b + \frac{1}{2})$ for some integers a and b, METAFONT will plot one point, obtained by rounding the first specified point z_1 to integer coordinates. Each draw therefore plots at least once.)

The diamond rule for plotting curves is ambiguous in one respect: It doesn't say what happens on the boundary of the diamond. For example, if a horizontal or nearly horizontal curve happens to pass exactly through the point $(x, y + \frac{1}{2})$, when x and y are integers, will METAFONT plot $(x, y + 1)$ or (x, y)? The answer is, sometimes $(x + 1, y)$ and sometimes (x, y), depending on the curve being drawn. The reason is that this behavior is what you want, although you may not realize it at first. If the same decision were made each time, independent of the path, the result would be undesirable because the curves would turn out to be unsymmetrical: the left half of an 'o' might look slightly different from the right half, and the top half might look different from the bottom. Therefore METAFONT's rounding rule is such that reflection symmetries are preserved:

a) If m is an integer then point (x, y) is plotted for the curve $(x(t), y(t))$ if and only if $(m - x, y)$ is plotted for the curve $(m - x(t), y(t))$.

b) If n is an integer then point (x, y) is plotted for the curve $(x(t), y(t))$ if and only if $(x, n - y)$ is plotted for the curve $(x(t), n - y(t))$.

(The only exceptions occur when it is essentially impossible to satisfy the conditions, namely when the curve $(x(t), y(t))$ in (a) is a vertical line with $x(t) = $ constant $=$ integer $+ \frac{1}{2}$, or similarly when the curve $(x(t), y(t))$ in (b) is a horizontal line with $y(t) = $ constant $=$ integer $+ \frac{1}{2}$.) In other words, you can almost always ensure symmetry of the rounding operation if you simply make the curve symmetric with respect to an integer. The precise rounding rule used by METAFONT will not be explained here, since only the symmetry principle above is important in practice. Symmetry is achieved by internally converting every curve to subintervals such that some subset of the transformations $x(t) \rightarrow -x(t)$, $y(t) \rightarrow -y(t)$, $x(t) \leftrightarrow y(t)$ produces a curve satisfying $0 \leq y'(t) \leq x'(t)$ throughout each subinterval. A particular rounding rule is used for curves satisfying $0 \leq y'(t) \leq x'(t)$, then the rounded points are untransformed again.

There is an analogous kind of symmetry that METAFONT cannot guarantee: The result of "draw $1..2..3$" might not be precisely the same as the result of "draw $3..2..1$", since the rounding might be slightly different when a curve is being drawn in the opposite direction.

The fact that METAFONT's rounding rule preserves certain symmetries is helpful in practice, yet it must be remembered that some asymmetry is inherent in the fact that rounding does take place. The curve $(x(t), y(t))$ will not, in general, look just like the curve $(x(t) + \frac{1}{3}, y(t) + \frac{1}{3})$, say, after rounding; so the question arises, do some

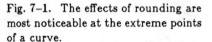

Fig. 7–1. The effects of rounding are most noticeable at the extreme points of a curve.

curves look much better than others? The answer is yes, but the only really critical places seem to be where the curve reaches a horizontal or vertical extreme (when it is travelling straight up or down, or when it is perfectly horizontal, if only for an instant). When a curve turns a corner in such places, its outside edge may look too flat after rounding (even when the resolution is fairly good), unless the turning point is selected appropriately. For example, Fig. 7–1 shows three curves plotted with an hpen of width 9, when the hpenht is 3. Each of the three curves is essentially the same, starting at $(x + 10, 50)$ with a slope of $\{-1, -1\}$, then coming down and left to points $(x, 0)$ where the direction is $\{0, -1\}$, then going down and right to point $(x + 10, -50)$ where the slope is $\{+1, -1\}$. The only difference is that $x = 0$ (an integer) in the lefthand curve; $x = 50.4999$ (almost halfway after an integer) in the middle curve; and $x = 100.5001$ (almost halfway before an integer) in the right-hand curve. The middle curve has an unfortunate glitch at $y = 0$, and the righthand curve looks too flat near $y = 0$.

We can conclude that a curve going from right to left and back again has a good position with respect to the raster if its extreme point occurs at an integer, when an hpen with an *odd* width is being used. The reason is that an integer point is halfway between the places where rounding makes an abrupt transition, so no obvious anomalies will appear. Similarly we get a good position for hpens of *even* width when the extreme point occurs at an integer plus $\frac{1}{2}$, since an offset of $\frac{1}{2}$ is subtracted before rounding. Both of these cases can be summed up in one rule, that a good case for rounding occurs if the left (or right) edge of the pen is an integer at the extreme point. Thus, one can get good results by computing an approximate value l for the left edge of the pen and writing the equation

$$\mathbf{lft}_i\, x_j = \mathbf{round}\, l;$$

here w_i is the pen width and x_j is the x coordinate of the extreme point. Another way to achieve the same objective is to compute an approximate value c for the center of the pen at its extreme point and then to write

$$x_j = \mathbf{good}_i\, c;$$

the good function produces the nearest integer to c if the pen width (round w_i) is odd, otherwise it yields the nearest point to c having the form integer $+ \frac{1}{2}$. Appendix E contains examples that show how round and good can be used to enhance the appearance of letter shapes.

<8> Subroutines

When you sit down and try to design the lower case letters a to z, you will probably discover that most letters have features in common with other ones; for example, consider the relations between l and h, h and n, n and m, n and u. You will therefore wish that different characters could share common portions of METfl-FONT programs, with only minor variations made when these common portions are used in different places, so that you can avoid inconsistencies and tedious repetitions. Well, you are in luck: Common operations need to be programmed only once, and the way to do this is much better than the "input drag" solution used in Chapter 4. *Subroutines* are the answer to your problem.

Subroutines are one level of complexity up from the simplest uses of METfl-FONT, however, so the rest of this chapter is marked off with dangerous bend signs. You should try to play around with the rest of METflFONT for at least a little while before you dive into the subroutine world. (Remember when you were learning other programming languages? Your first few programs probably did not involve subroutines or macros.) On the other hand, subroutines aren't completely mysterious, and you will be quite ready to read on as soon as you have gotten some METflFONT experience under your belt.

A subroutine begins with the reserved word subroutine and ends with a period. More precisely, a subroutine has the form

subroutine ⟨identifier⟩⟨arguments⟩: ⟨statement list⟩.

Here the ⟨identifier⟩ is the name of the subroutine; if that identifier has previously been used to stand for a variable or another subroutine, its old meaning is forgotten. The ⟨arguments⟩ represent special kinds of variables that correspond to any changeable parameters that this subroutine will have when it is called into action by a main routine or by another subroutine.

Arguments to a subroutine can be of two kinds, "var" and "index"; the var kind represent real values, while the index kind represent subscripts. An example should make this clear, so let's take a look at the "*darc*" subroutine of Appendix E, used to draw an elliptical double-arc such as the left half or the right half of the letter "o":

subroutine *darc*(index i, index j, var *maxwidth*):

$x_1 = x_5 = x_i$; $x_2 = x_4 = 1/sqrttwo\,[x_i, x_j]$; $x_3 = x_j$;

$y_1 = y_i$; $y_5 = y_j$; $y_3 = \frac{1}{2}[y_i, y_j]$;

$y_2 = 1/sqrttwo\,[y_3, y_i]$; $y_4 = 1/sqrttwo\,[y_3, y_j]$;

hpen;   draw $|w_0|1\{x_3 - x_1, 0\}..|\frac{2}{3}[w_0, maxwidth]|2\{x_3 - x_1, y_3 - y_1\}..$
$\qquad\qquad |maxwidth\#|3\{0, y_3 - y_1\}..$
$\qquad\qquad |\frac{2}{3}[w_0, maxwidth]|4\{x_5 - x_3, y_5 - y_3\}..|w_0|5\{x_5 - x_3, 0\}.$

(Constructions like "$\frac{1}{2}[y_i, y_j]$" would really be typed "1/2[yi,yj]"; it seems best to use special conventions when typesetting **METRFONT** programs in order to make them as readable as possible.) This particular subroutine deserves careful study, because it is a "real" example that illustrates most of **METRFONT**'s conventions about subroutines in general. Therefore it will be explained rather slowly and carefully in the following paragraphs.

In other parts of a **METRFONT** program containing the above subroutine, a statement like

$$\text{call } darc(6, 7, w_9)$$

will invoke *darc* with parameters $i = 6$, $j = 7$, *maxwidth* $= w_9$. The effect of *darc* in general is that a half-ellipse will be drawn starting at point (x_i, y_i) with an hpen of size w_0; this arc will proceed to point $(x_j, \frac{1}{2}[y_i, y_j])$ with the pen's width having grown to size *maxwidth*, then it will finish at point (x_i, y_j) where the pen once again will come back to size w_0. The subroutine will work when $x_i < x_j$ as well as when $x_i > x_j$, and when $y_i < y_j$ as well as when $y_i > y_j$.

The most important thing to remember about **METRFONT** subroutines is that each routine and each subroutine has its own x- or y-variables. When *darc* refers to x_1 it is NOT the same as the x_1 in the routine or subroutine that is calling *darc*; all x-variables and y-variables have a strictly local significance. (This is similar to the fact that x-variables and y-variables disappear at the end of each routine that defines a single character, i.e., they disappear when a period is reached; cf. the DRAGON example of Chapter 4.) The values of arguments (like i and j and *maxwidth*) are also local to a particular subroutine. On the other hand, w-variables and variables named by identifiers are *global*; they can be defined in one routine or subroutine and used in another. Thus, when *darc* refers to w_0 and to *sqrttwo*, these variables should have values that were defined before *darc* was called.

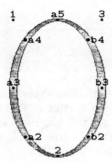

Fig. 8–1. This shape was drawn by calling the *darc* subroutine twice. Points labeled 1, 2, 3 were defined in the main routine; points whose labels begin with "a" were defined in the first call of *darc*; and points whose labels begin with "b" were defined in the second call.

A subroutine is able to refer to x-variables and y-variables of its caller by means of index arguments. For example, suppose that *darc* has been called with $i = 6$; when it refers to x_i, this means x_6 in the calling routine, it doesn't mean x_6 local to *darc*. On the other hand a reference to w_i denotes the unique variable w_6.

Since subroutines and their calling routines often have their own points x_1 and y_1, it is desirable to have some method of naming points meaningfully on the illustrations produced by proofmode and in METAFONT's error messages. Lower case letters may be specified for this purpose in call statements. For example, consider the following routine that uses *darc* twice:

$x_1 = 0$; $y_1 = y_3 = 150$; $x_2 = 50$; $y_2 = 0$; $x_3 = 100$;
sqrttwo $=$ *sqrt2*; $w_0 = 3$; $w_1 = 9$;
call `a *darc*$(2, 1, w_1)$;
call `b *darc*$(2, 3, w_1)$.

Fig. 8–1 shows the result together with the point labels. Here "1" denotes point (x_1, y_1) of the main routine, namely point $(0, 150)$; it doesn't happen to have been used directly for any of the curves drawn, but its coordinates x_1 and y_1 were used separately in *darc*'s calculations. The point labeled "a5" is point 5 inside the first call of *darc*, since the code `a was included in this call statement. Similarly, points whose name begins with "b" are the points defined in the second call. Points a1, b1, and b5 do not appear with these labels in Fig. 8–1, since they coincide with points that were already labeled.

All the clues needed to understand *darc* have now been given; please study that subroutine again now until you fully understand it. Incidentally, if the value of variable *sqrttwo* is made smaller than $\sqrt{2} = 1.4142$, the *darc* subroutine will draw a "superellipse" that opens wider than a normal ellipse does; this effect is occasionally desirable in font design. (Cf. Fig. 8–2.)

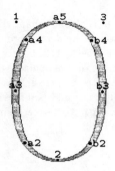

Fig. 8–2. This shape was drawn by the same routine as Fig. 8–1, except that *sqrttwo* has been set equal to 1.319507911 (the value $2^{2/5}$ recommended by Piet Hein).

The argument list in a subroutine definition is either empty or it is a list of one or more "var ⟨identifier⟩" or "index ⟨identifier⟩" entries enclosed in parentheses and separated either by commas or by ") (" pairs. (Subroutine *darc*'s definition might have begun

$$\text{subroutine } \textit{darc}(\text{index } i)(\text{index } j)(\text{var } \textit{maxwidth}):$$

some people prefer this syntax.) Formally speaking, we have the following BNF definition:

⟨arguments⟩ ← ⟨empty⟩ | (⟨argument list⟩)
⟨argument list⟩ ← ⟨argument⟩ | ⟨argument list⟩, ⟨argument⟩
                            | ⟨argument list⟩)(⟨argument⟩
⟨argument⟩ ← var ⟨identifier⟩ | index ⟨identifier⟩

A **call** command has a similar format. The parameters in a **call** must agree in number and kind with the arguments in the corresponding subroutine definition.

▶Exercise 8.1: Write a subroutine that will draw Fig. 2–3 when it is called by the following driver program:

$$x_1 = y_1 = y_2 = 0; \quad x_2 = 150;$$

call *curve*(60, 120, 1, 2);

call *curve*(60, 90, 1, 2);

call *curve*(60, 60, 1, 2);

call *curve*(60, 30, 1, 2);

call *curve*(60, 0, 1, 2).

⚠ Another example—this one contrived—should further clarify the general idea of index arguments. Consider the program

> subroutine sub(index i):
> ...;   call `a $subsub(i, 1)$;   ....
> subroutine $subsub$(index i, index j):
> ...;   draw $i..j..2$;   ....
> call `b $sub(3)$.

Can you figure out what points the "draw $i..j..2$" command refers to in *subsub*, before the answer is revealed in the next sentence of this paragraph? Answer (don't peek): inside *sub*, "i" refers to point 3 of the main routine and "1" refers to local point b1; therefore inside *subsub*, "i" and "j" refer to 3 and b1, while "2" refers to local point ba2. (Note the concatenation of labels since *subsub* is being used as a sub-subroutine.) If for some reason *subsub* forgot to define its local variable x_2, you would get the error message "Variable xba2 is undefined" at the time "draw $i..j..2$" was being interpreted.

⚠ This example reveals two other things about subroutines: (1) It is permissible for different subroutines to have arguments with the same name. In fact, the name of an argument may also be identical to the name of a global variable or even to the name of another subroutine; that identifier refers to the appropriate argument, within the subroutine being defined, but it reverts to its global meaning when the subroutine definition ends. (2) It is permissible to call subroutines that have not yet been defined. (Note that "call `a *subsub*" appeared in the program before *subsub* was known to be the name of a subroutine.) In fact, it is even permissible for a subroutine to call itself, if you are careful to avoid infinite recursion, provided that the subroutine has no arguments (see below). However, when a call is actually being interpreted, the called subroutine definition must already have appeared. It is easy to understand this rule if you understand how subroutines are actually implemented: When METAFONT sees a subroutine definition, it stores away the text for future use; then when a call statement appears, the text of the subroutine is fed through METAFONT's reading mechanism in place of the text of the call.

⚠ Since the previous paragraph mentions the possibility of recursion, an alert reader will have guessed that METAFONT has the capability of interpreting statements *conditionally*, i.e., performing certain computations only if certain relations hold. Yes, alert reader, there is an if statement. It has two general forms,

> if ⟨relation⟩: ⟨statement list⟩; fi

or   if ⟨relation⟩: ⟨statement list₁⟩; else: ⟨statement list₂⟩; fi where the first is treated like the second but with ⟨statement list$_2$⟩ empty. A ⟨relation⟩ has the form

$$\langle \text{expression}_1 \rangle \; \langle \text{relop} \rangle \; \langle \text{expression}_2 \rangle$$

where ⟨relop⟩ is one of the six relational operator symbols $=$, $<$, $>$, $\neq$, $\leq$, $\geq$. The meaning of an if statement is that ⟨statement list$_1$⟩ is interpreted if the relation is true, ⟨statement list$_2$⟩ is interpreted if the relation is false, and the error message "Indeterminate relation" results if the relation cannot be decided due to unknown variables. The relation "$z = z$" is known to be true whether z is known or not, but the relation "$z > 0$" is indeterminate unless z is known. *N.B.: Don't forget the* fi *that closes the* if.

When a subroutine is called, the current pen type and current pen size are remembered so that they can be restored when the subroutine is finished. The "control bits" described in Chapter 9, governing tracing and output modes, are also saved and restored across calls. The subroutine must specify a new current pen type and current pen size before it draws any curves or uses some other operation that depends on the current pen type, since METAFONT considers the pen type to be undefined upon entry to a subroutine. This restriction tends to catch careless errors; you can override it, if necessary, by saying "no penreset".

Let us close this chapter with an example of a recursive subroutine. Devotees of structured programming who have the conventional misunderstanding of that term will rejoice in the fact that METAFONT has no go to statement; but such people might not be so happy about the fact that there is no while statement either. In the comparatively few cases where iterations are desirable in font design, there is no reason to despair, since iteration is easy to achieve via recursion (even when we must live with METAFONT's restriction that recursive procedures cannot have arguments). The following subroutine draws an indeterminate number of straight vertical lines, from point $(a + kd, b)$ to point $(a + kd, c)$ for $k = 0, 1, \ldots$, as long as $a + kd \leq t$.

```
subroutine for (var a, var b, var c, var d, var t):
new aa, bb, cc, dd, tt;
aa = a;   bb = b;   cc = c;   dd = d;   tt = t;
call `a loop.

subroutine loop:
if aa ≤ tt: x₁ = x₂ = aa; y₁ = bb; y₂ = cc;
            cpen; w₀ draw 1 .. 2;
            x₃ = aa + dd; new aa; aa = x₃;
            call `b loop;
fi.
```

Note the use of new to emulate an operation that would be written "aa := aa + dd" in more conventional programming languages.

▶Exercise 8.2: Continuing this example, suppose that the main routine is "proofmode; $w_0 = 3$; call $\check{~}$c $for\,(0, 0, 100, 50, 150)$." What labels would appear on the eight points between which the four vertical lines are drawn?

<9> Summary of the language

A METAFONT program consists of sections, each of which is terminated by a period. (This period is followed immediately by a ⟨carriage-return⟩ or by a blank space, as explained in Chapter 5, so that it is readily distinguishable from a decimal points or a multiplication signs or the ".." of a draw or ddraw command.) The period that terminates the final section is followed by the word "end"; this terminates the program.

The x-variables and y-variables of each section are "local" to that section, in the sense that x_1 (say) in one section has no relation to x_1 in another; but the other variables are shared by all sections. Within a section, you write one or more "statements" separated by semicolons.

A typical METAFONT program starts out with a section in which you define important variables that will be used for all the characters you intend to generate, followed by sections for any subroutines you wish to define, followed by sections that draw each character. This order of sections is not absolutely necessary, but it is suitable for most purposes.

Appendix E contains examples of complete METAFONT programs used to define characters in the "Computer Modern" family of fonts designed by the author for use in his books *The Art of Computer Programming*. Basic META-FONT setups for designing new characters or modifying the designs of existing ones, as well as for producing new fonts with particular settings of the variable parameters, are described in that appendix.

The present chapter is intended to serve as a concise and precise summary of all of METAFONT's features. We have discussed most of these things already, but there are also a few more bells and whistles that you may want to use. The idea is now to get it all together.

As stated above, a **METAFONT** program has the general form

$$\langle section_1 \rangle \langle section_2 \rangle \ldots \langle section_m \rangle \text{ end}$$

where each $\langle section \rangle$ is either a subroutine definition or has the form of a $\langle statement\ list \rangle$ followed by a period, namely

$$\langle statement_1 \rangle; \ \langle statement_2 \rangle; \ \ldots; \ \langle statement_n \rangle.$$

The main question remaining is therefore, "What is a $\langle statement \rangle$?" The various kinds of statements are enumerated below, with a bullet symbol (•) in front of each kind.

- $\langle empty \rangle$ A null statement.

One of the things you can do with **METAFONT** is nothing. The null statement does this.

- $\langle equation \rangle$ An equation between variables.

Equations, which consist of two or more $\langle expression \rangle$s separated by "$=$" signs, are discussed thoroughly in Chapter 5. Each equals sign leads to the elimination of one independent variable, since an expression can be reduced to a linear combination of independent variables, unless the equation is redundant or inconsistent with respect to previous equations. The purpose of equations is to state the relationships you wish the variables of your program to satisfy; you must give enough equations so that **META-FONT** can solve them uniquely, obtaining known values for all variables that it needs to know.

- new $\langle variable\ list \rangle$ Undefines variables.

A $\langle variable\ list \rangle$ consists of one or more variable names separated by commas; for example, you can say "new *alpha*, *beta*, x_3, y_2". Sometimes you will have used equations to define the value of some variable that you now wish to redefine. By listing this variable in a new statement, its old value becomes forgotten. (You should do this only when the variable has a known value, or when it is already new and you are just trying to be safe—e.g., in a subroutine when the variable is to be used for temporary storage.)

- $\langle pen\ name \rangle \langle optional\ \# \rangle$ Specifies the current pen or eraser type.

At the beginning of each routine or subroutine, the current pen type is undefined, and you must define it before drawing anything or using an expression like top that requires knowledge of the pen type. The $\langle pen\ name \rangle$ statement defines the current pen type, and changes the pen to an eraser if a "#" appears. It also resets the current pen size to zero; this is a useless pen size, so you should probably specify a useful value on the next draw or ddraw command. Allowable pen names are cpen, hpen, vpen, lpen, rpen, spen, and epen, as described in Chapter 3. An spen or epen should be further specified, according to the rules in that chapter. However, if you wish the spen or epen to have the same specs as the most recent one that METAFONT has generated as it was interpreting your program, you can omit the specification and simply say "spen" or "epen".

- ⟨drawing command⟩   Draws a line or curve.

The general format of a ⟨drawing command⟩ is either

$$\langle expression\rangle \textbf{ draw } \langle path\rangle$$

or $$\langle expression\rangle \textbf{ ddraw } \langle path_1\rangle, \langle path_2\rangle$$

where the ⟨expression⟩ represents the new pen size; this can be omitted if the current pen size is to be used. The rules for draw and ddraw are explained in Chapters 2 and 6, so we shall merely summarize here the precise rules for a ⟨path⟩. In general a ⟨path⟩ has the form

$$\langle hidden\ beginning\rangle\langle point_1\rangle .. \langle point_2\rangle .. \cdots .. \langle point_n\rangle\langle hidden\ ending\rangle$$

for some $n \geq 1$, where the two paths in ddraw must have the same length n. The ⟨hidden beginning⟩ is either empty, representing a copy of ⟨point$_1$⟩, or it has the form "$(\langle point_0\rangle ..)$"; the ⟨hidden ending⟩ is either empty, representing a copy of ⟨point$_n$⟩, or it has the form "$(.. \langle point_{n+1}\rangle)$". The form of a ⟨point⟩ is

$$\langle optional\ pen\ size\rangle\langle index\rangle\langle optional\ direction\rangle$$

where ⟨optional pen size⟩ is either empty (meaning to use the pen size at the previous point, or to use the current pen size if this is the first point) or it has one of the two forms

$$|\langle expression\rangle| \text{or} |\langle expression\rangle\#|.$$

The ⟨expression⟩ denotes the desired pen size at the point; the # denotes stable pen size in the point's neighborhood, otherwise the pen size will change at a rate determined as explained in Chapter 6. A # is implied when the ⟨optional pen size⟩ is empty. The ⟨optional pen size⟩ *must* be empty for all points in the paths of a ddraw command. The ⟨optional direction⟩ is either empty (meaning to let METAFONT choose the direction in its standard way, as explained in Chapter 2), or it has the form

$$\{\langle expression_1\rangle, \langle expression_2\rangle\}.$$

In this case, if x is the value of ⟨expression$_1$⟩ and y the value of ⟨expression$_2$⟩, the curve will move toward a position that is x units to the right and y units upwards, when it passes the current point.

- "⟨any desired title⟩"   Names the font or the character being drawn.

(Not allowed in subroutines. The title can be any string of characters other than quote marks or ⟨carriage-return⟩s.) This statement has several effects: (i) The first time METAFONT interprets a title statement, it saves the string you have specified as the so-called main title that will appear in the computer file if you generate a font. (ii) If you are in titletrace mode, the title will be printed on your screen, as a sort of progress report. (iii) The title will appear on the proofsheet output if the current routine is used to draw a character in proof mode. (iv) A warning message will be printed (mentioning this title) if METAFONT scans the end of a file page before the current section ends, unless you are in no pagewarning mode.

- ⟨conditional statement⟩   Chooses between alternative programs.

A construction like

> if ⟨relation⟩: ⟨statement₁⟩; ⟨statement₂⟩; else: ⟨statement₃⟩; ⟨statement₄⟩; fi

will interpret ⟨statement₁⟩ and ⟨statement₂⟩ if the relation is true, ⟨statement₃⟩ and ⟨statement₄⟩ if the relation is false. Chapter 8 gives the general rules.

- **call** ⟨optional letter⟩⟨subroutine name⟩⟨parameters⟩   Invokes a subroutine.

The ⟨optional letter⟩ is either empty or an expression of the form "`⟨lower case letter⟩"; the ⟨subroutine name⟩ is the identifier of a subroutine that has already been defined; and the ⟨parameters⟩ part is either empty, or it is a parenthesized list of ⟨expression⟩s to be substituted for var arguments, and/or ⟨index⟩es to be substituted for index arguments, separated by commas or ")(" pairs. The parameters must be in the same order as the corresponding arguments, and there must be exactly as many parameters as arguments.

- ⟨parameter name⟩⟨expression⟩   Defines a METAFONT parameter.

A parameter statement like this is used to communicate values that METAFONT occasionally needs for its work. The parameters have "default" values when METAFONT begins; but once you change a parameter with an explicit parameter statement, its former value is forgotten. The value of the ⟨expression⟩ must be known at the time this statement is interpreted. Here is a list of the parameter names understood by the present implementation of METAFONT:

> trxx, trxy, incx, tryx, tryy, incy are used to rotate, translate, and/or expand or shrink the curves that METAFONT draws. After computing the functions $x(t)$ and $y(t)$ according to the rules described in Chapters 2 and 6, the actual curve that will be plotted—before subtracting the offsets x'_0 and y'_0 and before rounding, and before reducing variable-size draw to ddraw—is

$$(a_{xx}x(t) + a_{xy}y(t) + a_x, \, a_{yx}x(t) + a_{yy}y(t) + a_y),$$

where α_{xx}, α_{xy}, α_x, α_{yx}, α_{yy}, α_y are the respective current values of the six parameters stated. (The default values are, of course, trxx 1; trxy 0; incx 0; tryx 0; tryy 1; incy 0.) By setting trxy to 0.15, your drawings will be *slanted to the right as in the letters you are now reading*; those letters were made with the same METAFONT programs that generated the unslanted letters you are now reading, changing only the setting of trxy. The six transformation parameters do not affect the size or shape of pens, only the locations of their motions.

charwd, charht, chardp, charic are used to specify the width, height, depth, and italic correction for a character, in units of printers' points. These parameters are zero by default, and they are reset to zero at the end of every routine when a character is output. The parameters are used when preparing a font information file to be used by TEX; they do not affect the actual appearance of a character in a font.

epenxfactor and epenyfactor (normally 1.0) are used to enlarge or smallify the dimensions of an epen when an explicit pen is specified. These parameters should change in proportion to the number of pixels per inch when you are designing fonts for a variety of machines.

epenxcorr and epenycorr (normally 0.0) are used as the offsets x'_0 and y'_0 when an explicit pen (epen) is specified.

safetyfactor (normally 2.0) is used to govern the number of curves plotted by ddraw when it is filling in between two curves (see Chapter 6).

minvr, maxvr, minvs, maxvs (normally 0.5, 4.0, 0.5, 4.0) are used as velocity thresholds when computing the spline curves corresponding to a path, as explained in Chapter 2.

The following parameters are rounded to the nearest integer before METAFONT uses them:

hpenht and vpenwd (normally 1) are used to specify the height of each hpen and the width of each vpen. It is best to adjust these infrequently, since METAFONT has to recompute its accumulated pen information when they are reset.

nseed (normally set to a value based on the time of day, so that it will be different every time you run METAFONT) is used to start the pseudo-random number generator that produces the values of nrand. By setting nseed to a particular integer at the beginning of your program—any integer will do—you can guarantee that the same sequence of nrand values will occur each time the program is run.

maxht specifies the height (in pixels) of the tallest character in a font being generated for the XGP. This parameter, which is initially zero, must be set before the first character of the font has been output.

charcode is used to specify the 7-bit number of a character being output to a font. This parameter has the invalid value —1 when METAFONT begins, and it is reset to —1 after each character is output. No character will be output unless the charcode parameter has been set to a number between 0 and 127, inclusive, and it should be distinct from the numbers of other characters output.

chardw specifies the current character's width (in pixels), when a font is being produced for the XGP printer; this information is also used when preparing font information for TEX to use with the XGP. Like charwd, this parameter is zero for each character until you set it explicitly. There is no automatic connection between charwd and chardw.

crsbreak specifies the y coordinate at which a tall character will be broken into two pieces when preparing it for an Alphatype CRS font; the upper piece will contain raster positions for rows $\geq y$, the lower piece will contain rows $< y$. This parameter is normally set to an essentially infinite value, which is restored when a character is output, so that no characters will be broken unless a crsbreak has been explicitly specified.

dumplength (normally 1000) is the number of characters before "ETC" that will be displayed in error messages when METAFONT stops in the middle of a subroutine. If you make an error in a long subroutine, you may need to increase this parameter in order to see where the error occurred.

dumpwindow (normally 32) is the maximum number of characters displayed on each line of an error message when identifying the current program location.

- ⟨control code⟩   Sets a "control bit."

- no ⟨control code⟩   Unsets a "control bit."

These statements are used to turn on or turn off certain actions that METAFONT is capable of doing. METAFONT maintains a so-called control word, a set of bits that govern whether or not certain optional actions are taken; after a subroutine call, this control word is restored to the state it had before entering the subroutine. Initially the bits for modtrace, pagewarning, and penreset are turned on, all the others are off. Here is a list of the control codes understood by the present implementation of METAFONT:

eqtrace causes METAFONT to tell you what values are defined by your equations.

titletrace causes METAFONT to print title statements when they are encountered.

calltrace causes **METAFONT** to print the name of a subroutine and its parameter values, whenever a subroutine is called, and also to print the name of a subroutine whenever the call is completed.

drawtrace causes **METAFONT** to print out numeric specifications of the paths in draw or ddraw commands.

plottrace causes **METAFONT** to print lots of detailed information: "$|w|$" when generating a new pen of size w; "(x, y)" when plotting raster point (x, y); "$(x_1:x_2, y)$" when plotting a horizontal sequence of raster points from (x_1, y) to (x_2, y); "$(x, y_1:y_2)$" when plotting a vertical sequence of raster points from (x, y_1) to (x, y_2).

modtrace causes **METAFONT** to tell you whenever it changes the "velocities" r or s when computing cubic curves.

pause causes **METAFONT** to show each line of a text file that is being input, just before that line is scanned. This gives you a chance to edit the line before hitting ⟨carriage-return⟩, after which **METAFONT** will scan the edited line. If you want to get out of this mode, insert "no pause;" on the line as you are editing it.

drawdisplay causes **METAFONT** to display the raster after completing each draw or ddraw command. (The present implementation allows this only when you are running **METAFONT** from a Datadisc terminal.)

chardisplay causes **METAFONT** to display the raster after completing each section. (The present implementation allows this only when you are running **METAFONT** from a Datadisc terminal.)

pagewarning causes **METAFONT** to give a warning message whenever a file page ends inside a subroutine definition or a section containing a title statement.

penreset causes **METAFONT** to undefine the current pen whenever a subroutine call begins.

proofmode causes **METAFONT** to output a file of proofsheets containing the raster images of each character for which proofmode was in effect at the end of the section. These proof figures contain point labels for all points that lie in the "active" rectangle, i.e., in the smallest rectangle containing all pixels affected by the draw and ddraw commands for the current character, provided that the points became known when **proofmode** was on. Thus you can suppress all the points and labels if you turn off **proofmode** until just before finishing the section. (A point becomes known when both its x- and y-coordinates are known; if **proofmode** is on at that moment, the point's location (x, y) is recorded for proofing, after modifying (x, y) by the transformation parameters trxx ... incy currently in force and rounding to the nearest integer.)

fntmode causes **METAFONT** to output a file of font images in the format required by the XGP hardware and software.

crsmode causes **METAFONT** to output a file of font images in the format required by the Alphatype CRS hardware and software. It is illegal to use both fntmode and crsmode in the same program; and it is also ridiculous to do so, since the CRS has more than 26 times the resolution of the XGP.

chrmode causes **METAFONT** to output a text file of font images in the form of asterisks, dots, and spaces. (Such files can be edited with the system text editor, and there are auxiliary programs to convert font files into and out of this text format.)

tfxmode causes **METAFONT** to output a file of information that TEX needs for typesetting whenever it uses a font.

- varchar ⟨expression list⟩   Specifies a built-up character.
- charlist ⟨expression list⟩   Specifies a series of characters.
- texinfo ⟨expression list⟩   Specifies TEX font parameters.
- lig ⟨lig instruction list⟩   Specifies ligature/kerning information.

These four kinds of statements are relevant for tfxmode only, since they provide detailed information to TEX. See Appendix F for a detailed explanation.

- invisible ⟨expression$_1$⟩, ⟨expression$_2$⟩   Preempts a label position.

(Ignored except in proofmode.) The command "invisible x, y" makes **METAFONT** think that a point with coordinates (x, y) is going to be labeled, while in fact it may not be. The purpose is to cause **METAFONT** to choose a nicer place for other point labels, since they will now avoid the vicinity of (x, y), thereby sprucing up proof mode output in certain cases. For example, Fig. 2–3 of this manual was produced using "invisible $x_1, y_1 + 1$; invisible $x_2, y_2 + 1$;" this kept the labels 1 and 2 from appearing above points 1 and 2, where they would have interfered with the illustration. In general, **METAFONT** places labels on points by using a fairly simple-minded scheme: From top to bottom and right to left, the label is put either above the point, or to the left, or to the right, or below, or off in the right margin, whichever of these possibilities is first found to be feasible (with respect to the set of all points to be labeled, all invisible points, and all labels placed so far). Note that the label positions do not depend on the raster image, only on the locations of the visible and invisible points.

That completes the list of **METAFONT** statements. You might wonder why input was not in this list, since input was used several times in the example of Chapter 4. The reason is that input is not officially part of a ⟨statement⟩; it has the effect of redirecting METAFONT's eyes to a different file, even in the middle of some other statement. Chapter 4 used the construction

input ⟨file name⟩;

but this semicolon was unnecessary—METAFONT just executed a null statement after the input was complete. A ⟨file name⟩ in the current implement of META-FONT is any sequence of letters, digits, periods, and/or brackets, so a semicolon is one way to terminate a file name specification. Another way is to type a space or a ⟨carriage-return⟩.

So that's how METAFONT gets input; how does it decide where to put the output? Answer: It chooses an output file name as explained below, and uses the respective extensions .FNT, .ANT, .XGP, .CHR, .TFX for output produced by fntmode, crsmode, proofmode, chrmode, tfxmode. The output file name is the name of the first file you input, unless METAFONT has to output something before there has been any input from a file. In the latter case, the output file name is "mfput".

<10> Recovery from errors

OK, everything you need to know about METAFONT has been explained—unless you happen to be fallible.

If you don't plan to make any errors, don't bother to read this chapter. Otherwise you might find it helpful to make use of some of the ways METAFONT tries to pinpoint bugs in your routines.

In the trial runs you did when reading Chapter 4, you learned the general form of error messages, and you also learned the various ways you can respond to METAFONT's complaints. With practice, you will be able to correct most errors "on line," as soon as METAFONT has detected them, by inserting and deleting a few things. On the other hand, some errors are more devastating than others; one error might cause some other perfectly valid construction to be loused up. Furthermore, METAFONT doesn't always diagnose your errors correctly, since the number of ways to misunderstand the rules is vast, and since METAFONT is a rather simple-minded computer program that doesn't readily comprehend what you have in mind. In fact, there will be times when you and METAFONT disagree about something that you feel makes perfectly good sense. This chapter tries to help avoid a breakdown in communication by presenting METAFONT's viewpoint. Though it may seem like madness, there's method in 't.

By looking at the input context that follows an error message, you can often tell what METAFONT would read next if you were to proceed by hitting ⟨carriage-return⟩. For example, here is a slightly more complex error message than we encountered in Chapter 4, since it involves a subroutine call:

```
! Extra code at end of command will be flushed.
<subroutine> dot: x1 = y1 = a; cpen w3
                                         draw 1.
p.3,1.9 call dot;
.                       new a;
↑
```

In this case the error has occurred in the middle of subroutine *dot*, where a semicolon was forgotten after the pen name cpen. The next tokens that METAFONT will read are "draw" and "1" and then the period ending the subroutine call, after which METAFONT will read "new *a*;" and proceed to line 10 of page 3 of the current input file. Each pair of lines between the "!" line and the "↑" line of an error message shows where METAFONT is currently reading at some level of input; in this example there are two levels, one in the subroutine and one outside in page 3 of the file.

The best way to proceed after this particular error is to type "i" (for insertion), then (after getting prompted by "*") to type "; w3". This inserts the missing semicolon and reinserts the w_3 specification that METAFONT is flushing away, so that the program will proceed as if no error had occurred. In general, it is usually wise to recover from errors that say "command flushed" by inserting a semicolon and as many tokens as needed to provide the desired next statement, after deleting any tokens you don't wish METAFONT to read.

You can get more information about what METAFONT thinks it is doing by enabling the various kinds of tracing mentioned in Chapter 9 (calltrace, drawtrace, eqtrace, etc.).

Here is a complete list of the messages you might get from METAFONT, presented in alphabetic order for reference purposes. Each message is followed by a brief explanation of the problem, from METAFONT's viewpoint, and of what will happen if you proceed by hitting ⟨carriage-return⟩. This should help you to decide whether or not to take any remedial action. (See also Appendix I for references to these error messages in other parts of the manual.)

! Bad path, command flushed.
The ⟨path⟩ in the current draw or ddraw command does not follow the syntactic rules stated in Chapter 9. Proceed, and METAFONT will ignore all tokens up to the next semicolon or period.

! Boundary too long.
The current character was too complex to be drawn by the Alphatype CRS hardware. Perhaps it would have been okay if you had chopped it into two parts using crsbreak. Proceed; the character will not appear in the font output.

! Character '⟨octal code⟩ goes over the top (⟨constant⟩ > ⟨constant⟩).
You didn't specify a large enough maxht. Proceed, and the top rows of the current character will be erased.

! Character too tall.
The current character covers more than 1023 consecutive rows of the raster, so it exceeds the hardware capacity of the Alphatype CRS. You need to break it into two pieces using crsbreak. Proceed, and a partly erased character will be output.

! Comma substituted here.
A missing "," has been substituted for the most recently scanned token. Proceed, after possibly deleting and/or inserting some tokens to make the remaining expression read as you intended it to.

! Curve out of range.
The current draw or ddraw command has requested METAFONT to plot a point whose x-coordinate or y-coordinate is too large or too small. Proceed; the remainder of the current drawing will be omitted. (It is possible to increase METAFONT's drawing range by recompiling the system with different values of its internal parameters called xrastmin, xrastmax, yrastmin, yrastmax.)

! Curve too wild.
The current curve $(x(t), y(t))$ being drawn undergoes extremely fast changes for small increments in t; are you trying to break METAFONT's plotting routine? Proceed, and the remainder of the current drawing will be omitted.

! Division by 0.
The expression METAFONT is currently evaluating specifies a division by zero. Proceed, and the division will be bypassed.

! Duplicate charcode: '⟨octal code⟩.
Two routines have specified the same character code. Proceed, and the previous character will be overlaid by the present one.

! Duplicate ligature/charlist entry, command flushed.
It is illegal to specify two ligature labels for the same character code, or to include a character in a charlist when there is a ligature label for it. Proceed, and METAFONT will ignore all tokens up to the next semicolon or period.

! Empty pen specification.
The spen or epen you have specified contains no points. Proceed, and METAFONT will substitute a one-point pen.

! epenxfactor must be positive (1.0 assumed).
The value of epenxfactor cannot be zero or negative. Proceed, and METAFONT will reset it to 1.0 while making the current epen.

! epenyfactor must be positive (1.0 assumed).
The value of epenyfactor cannot be zero or negative. Proceed, and METAFONT will reset it to 1.0 while making the current epen.

! Extra code at end of command will be flushed.
METAFONT has read and interpreted a ⟨statement⟩, so it expected to find a semicolon or period as the next token. This expectation was not realized. Proceed, and METAFONT will ignore all tokens up to the next semicolon or period.

! hpen height too small, set to 1.
You shouldn't specify a setting of hpenht that is less than 0.5. Proceed, and its value will be set to 1.

! Illegal pen size (⟨constant⟩).
The pen size you have specified is either too large or too small. Proceed, and METAFONT will use size 1 instead.

! Image lost since charcode not specified.
Your program drew something, but no information was output for that character since you failed to specify any charcode for it. Proceed.

! Improper call, command flushed.
There are extraneous tokens following the current call statement (e.g., you may be supplying too many parameters). Proceed; the call statement and all tokens up to the next semicolon or period will be ignored.

! Improper charlist entry, command flushed.
Your charlist doesn't follow the rules stated in Appendix F. Proceed, and METAFONT will ignore all tokens up to the next semicolon or period.

! Improper index argument, command flushed.
You have just tried to call a subroutine having an index argument, but the parameter you are supplying isn't an ⟨index⟩. Proceed; the call statement and all tokens up to the next semicolon or period will be ignored.

! Improper index specification.
An ⟨index⟩ was supposed to have been here (either a digit string or the name of an index argument in a subroutine), for example after the word top. Proceed, and METAFONT will act as if the index were "0".

! Improper ligature/kern entry, command flushed.
The current ⟨lig instruction⟩ doesn't follow the rules stated in Appendix F. Proceed, and METAFONT will ignore all tokens up to the next semicolon or period.

! Improper name.
This token can't be made new (e.g., "new 5"). Proceed, and it will be ignored.

! Improper pen specs, command flushed.
You have not followed the rules of an spen or epen specification. Proceed, and META-FONT will ignore all tokens up to the next semicolon or period.

! Incompatible resolution.
You can't simultaneously select output in fntmode and crsmode.

! Inconsistent equation.
The equation just given does not jibe with information METAFONT already knows from previous equations. (If you can't understand why, try running your program again with eqtrace on.) Proceed, and the inconsistent equation will be ignored.

! Indeterminate relation.
METAFONT has just scanned "if ⟨relation⟩:" but it was impossible to decide whether the relation is true or false based on the equations given so far. To recover, insert and/or delete tokens so that the next thing METAFONT reads is a correct conditional statement (you must reinsert the "if" as well as a relation).

! Input page ended while scanning def of ⟨subroutine name⟩.
The end of a file page occurred between the beginning of a subroutine definition and the period ending that subroutine. (It is possible to suppress this message by putting METAFONT in no pagewarning mode.)

! Input page ended while scanning "⟨title⟩".
The end of a file page occurred between a quoted title statement and the period ending that routine; this may indicate an if not closed by fi, or some other anomaly, or it might not be an error at all. (It is possible to suppress this message by putting METAFONT in no pagewarning mode.)

! Ligature/kern table didn't end.
The final entry of your final ⟨lig instruction list⟩ was a continuation entry. Proceed, but don't be surprised if TEX blows up trying to use the font information produced on this run.

! Lookup failed on file ⟨filename⟩.

METAFONT can't find the file you indicated. Type "i" and insert the correct file name (followed by a ⟨carriage-return⟩). But be careful: You get only one more chance to get the file name right, otherwise **METAFONT** will decide not to input any file just now.

! METAFONT capacity exceeded, sorry [⟨size⟩=⟨number⟩].

This is a bad one. Some how you have stretched **METAFONT** beyond its finite limits. The thing that overflowed is indicated in brackets, together with its numerical value in the **METAFONT** implementation you are using. The following table shows the internal sizes that might have been exceeded:

epensize	number of (l, r) pairs in an epen specification;
maxpoints	number of points in a curve to be drawn;
memsize	memory above vmemsize used to store tokens;
names	number of bits used to represent subscripts;
namesize	memory used to store identifiers;
pmemsize	memory used to store information about pens and erasers;
proofmemsize	number of visible and invisible points for proof sheets;
stacksize	number of simultaneous input sources;
vmemsize	memory used to store variable values and many other things;
xpenmax	largest x-coordinate of a pen or eraser;
xpenmin	smallest x-coordinate of a pen or eraser;
xrastmax	maximum x-coordinate allowed when plotting;
ypenmax	largest y-coordinate of a pen or eraser;
ypenmin	smallest y-coordinate of a pen or eraser;
yrastmax	maximum y-coordinate allowed when plotting.

If your job is error-free, the remedy is to recompile the **METAFONT** system, increasing what overflowed. However, you may be able to think of a way to change your program so that it does not push **METAFONT** to extremes.

! Missing "(", command flushed.

You have just tried to call a subroutine without supplying enough parameters. Proceed; the call statement and all tokens up to the next semicolon or period will be ignored.

! Missing ",", command flushed.

The first ⟨path⟩ in the current ddraw command, or the first coordinate in the current invisible command, was not followed by a comma. Proceed, and **METAFONT** will ignore all tokens up to the next semicolon or period.

! Missing ":".

METAFONT has just scanned "if ⟨relation⟩" and the next token should have been a colon. To recover, insert and/or delete tokens so that the next thing **METAFONT** reads is a correct conditional statement (you must reinsert the "if" as well as a relation and a colon).

! Missing = sign, command flushed.
A METAFONT statement began with an expression, but the next token was neither "=" nor "draw" nor "ddraw". The value of this expression, in terms of independent variables, has been printed out on the line just preceding this error message. (See Chapter 4 for several examples.) Proceed, and METAFONT will ignore the expression and all tokens up to the next semicolon or period.

! Missing colon inserted.
There should have been a ":" after the word else; METAFONT has inserted one.

! Missing punctuation, command flushed.
You are trying to call a subroutine, but you didn't supply a comma or a right parenthesis after the current parameter. Proceed; the call statement and all tokens up to the next semicolon or period will be ignored.

! Missing relation.
METAFONT has just scanned "if ⟨expression⟩" and the next token should have been one of the six relation symbols ($<$, $>$, $=$, $\leq$, $\geq$, $\neq$). To recover, insert and/or delete tokens so that the next thing METAFONT reads is a correct conditional statement (you must reinsert the "if" and fix the relation).

! Negative chardw, replaced by 0.
The value of chardw must not be negative. Proceed; it has become 0.

! No parameter name.
The word "var" or "index" should be followed by an identifier that will be the name of the argument being specified. Proceed, and METAFONT will bypass the most recently scanned token and argument; you may want to insert another argument with the correct name.

! No pen defined.
You are trying to draw or ddraw, but the current pen type has not been defined. Proceed, and METAFONT will use cpen.

! No subroutine name, command flushed.
The word "subroutine" should be followed by an identifer that will be the name of the subroutine being defined. Proceed, and METAFONT will ignore all tokens up to the next semicolon or period.

! Paths don't match up, command flushed.
The two paths in the current ddraw command have unequal numbers of points. Proceed, and METAFONT will ignore all tokens up to the next semicolon or period.

`! Pen size too small (⟨constant⟩), replaced by 1.0.`
The pen size enclosed in "|" signs (within a variable-size draw command) should not
be less than 1.0. Proceed, and **METAFONT** will act as if it were 1.0.

`! Program ended while defining ⟨subroutine name⟩.`
Premature occurrence of the word end leads to a premature end.

`! Rectangle too wide.`
You have specified an lpen or rpen with too much width for **METAFONT**'s capacity.
Proceed, and **METAFONT** will cut the width to the maximum it can handle.

`! Recursive call not allowed, command flushed.`
You have just tried to call a subroutine having a parameter whose value is already
defined from another call not yet complete. (Recursion is allowed only with parameter-
less subroutines.) Proceed; the call statement and all tokens up to the next semicolon
or period will be ignored.

`! Redundant equation.`
The equation just given does not present any information that **METAFONT** didn't already know from previous equations. (If you can't understand why, try running your
program again with eqtrace on.) Proceed; no harm has been done.

`! Right bracket substituted here.`
A missing "]" has been substituted for the most recently scanned token. Proceed, after
possibly deleting and/or inserting some tokens to make the remaining expression read
as you intended it to.

`! Right parenthesis substituted here.`
A missing ")" has been substituted for the most recently scanned token. Proceed, after
possibly deleting and/or inserting some tokens to make the remaining expression read
as you intended it to.

`! Rounding of ⟨char dimension⟩ necessary, ⟨constant⟩ → ⟨constant⟩.`
The characters in the present font have too many distinct dimensions of the specified
type for TEX to handle. (For example, some versions of TEX will allow at most 16
different values of charht per font.) The specified approximation has been used; if
you want uniformity between different machines, you should redefine the dimensions
in accordance with TEX's limits.

`! Routine ended in skipped conditional text.`
Something is awry, since a period or end has occurred in the midst of part of your
program that is being skipped over (because it's in the unselected part of a conditional).
Proceed if you dare.

`Sharp turn suppressed between points ⟨point names⟩ (⟨velocity⟩)`
(This is not really an error message, it's a warning that you get when **modtrace** is in effect.) The curve **METAFONT** is about to draw would have had a sharp turn at one of the stated points (the first point if the "r" velocity is given, the second if the "s" velocity is given), because of the angles the curve is supposed to take between those two points. The velocity derived by **METAFONT**'s normal rules is below minvr or minvs, so **METAFONT** is suppressing the sharp turn by raising the velocity to the corresponding minimum value. (Cf. the latter part of Chapter 2 for further discussion.) This usually is a symptom of some problem in your program, although it may be perfectly all right.

`! Should be "(" or "," or ":" here.`
One of these three tokens is needed, since an argument list is being scanned; you should insert and/or delete tokens so that **METAFONT** sees the correct one, to get it back into synch.

`! Should say var or index here.`
The word "var" or "index" should have appeared at this point, to define the next subroutine argument. Proceed, and the most recently scanned token will be ignored.

`! String must end on the line where it begins.`
A quoted title cannot contain a ⟨carriage-return⟩; the title you supplied therefore seems to have ended without its closing """ mark. Proceed, and **METAFONT** will act as though the """ had been present here.

`! Subroutine definition should follow ".".`
A subroutine definition should not begin between a title statement and the period ending the corresponding routine. Proceed; **METAFONT** will define the subroutine and resume the routine, forgetting its title.

`! Subroutines can't be defined inside subroutines.`
Each subroutine should be a section unto itself. Proceed, and the word "subroutine" will be ignored; however, some other errors will probably show up unless you insert the text ". subroutine" now to recover from this error.

`! This can't happen.`
An internal consistency check has failed, causing **METAFONT** to be totally confused. Either you did something the author was unable to foresee, or somebody has been tampering with the **METAFONT** system programs.

`! Titles are ignored inside subroutines.`
You aren't supposed to have title statements in subroutines. Proceed, and this here one will be ignored.

```
! Too many different chardw values.
! Too many different charic/varchar values.
```
The TEX character information for the current font is too complex; TEX puts limits on the maximum number of distinct values of **chardw** and **charic/varchar** in any one font. (See Appendix F.)

```
! Too many ligatures, command flushed.
```
Your program is supplying more ligature/kern entries than TEX can tolerate in one font. (Some implementations of TEX have restricted capacity, but the present Stanford version allows 512, which should be plenty.) Proceed, and **METAFONT** will ignore all tokens up to the next semicolon or period.

```
! Too much texinfo, command flushed.
```
Your program is supplying more information parameters than TEX can understand. Proceed, and **METAFONT** will ignore all tokens up to the next semicolon or period.

```
! Undefined pen.
```
You are using a ⟨direction⟩ operation like top, but the current pen type has not been defined. Proceed, and **METAFONT** will ignore the ⟨direction⟩ operation.

```
! Undefined pen size.
```
The current pen size being supplied before the word **draw** or **ddraw** does not have a known value; its value in terms of independent variables has been printed out on the line just preceding this error message. Proceed, and the current pen size will retain its former value.

```
! Undefined ⟨something⟩, replaced by ⟨constant⟩.
```
The line before this error message shows the current value of the ⟨something⟩ that should have a definite value at this point, expressed as a linear combination of independent variables. The ⟨something⟩ might be any of the following:

character code	first ⟨expression⟩ in a ligature/kern instruction;
cosine	operand of **cosd**;
divisor	β in a term of the form α/β;
expression	entire ⟨expression⟩ whose value is needed;
factor	one factor of a product, when neither are defined;
goodee	operand of $\mathbf{good}_i$;
interval fraction	α in a term of the form $\alpha[\beta, \gamma]$;
root	operand of **sqrt**;
roundee	operand of **round**;
sine	operand of **sind**.

Proceed, and the computation will continue as though the ⟨something⟩ had the stated ⟨constant⟩ value.

`! Undefined subroutine, command flushed.`
You have just tried to call a subroutine that isn't currently defined. Proceed; the call statement and all tokens up to the next semicolon or period will be ignored.

`! Undefined size w⟨digit string⟩.`
Your program is using an operation like "top_6" when the corresponding w-variable (e.g., w_6) does not have a known value. Proceed, and the value will be assumed zero.

`! Unknown control code, command flushed.`
The word "no" must be followed by one of METAFONT's control codes. Proceed, and the tokens up to the next semicolon or period will be ignored.

`! Variable ⟨variable name⟩ never defined.`
The stated variable is about to become undefined (e.g., it is being made new, or it is an x-variable and a routine or subroutine is ending), but it has never gotten a fully known value. Thus, other variables might be depending on this one, because of equations that gave incomplete information. Proceed, and METAFONT will try to keep going. (If this variable is independent, it will essentially be replaced by 1.0 in the equations for all variables that depend on it.)

`! Variable x⟨point number⟩ is undefined, 0.0 assumed.`
METAFONT is about to carry out a draw or ddraw command, but the x-coordinate of this particular point does not have a known value. (The point number may be preceded by lower case letters if the point is defined within a subroutine, as explained in Chapter 8.) Proceed, and the drawing will take place using zero as the x coordinate.

`! Variable y⟨point number⟩ is undefined, 0.0 assumed.`
METAFONT is about to carry out a draw or ddraw command, but the y-coordinate of this particular point does not have a known value. (The point number may be preceded by lower case letters if the point is defined within a subroutine, as explained in Chapter 8.) Proceed, and the drawing will take place using zero as the y coordinate.

`Velocity reduced between points ⟨point name⟩ and ⟨point name⟩ (⟨velocity⟩)`
(This is not really an error message, it's a warning that you get when modtrace is in effect.) The curve METAFONT is about to draw would have had unusual behavior near one of the stated points (the first point if the "r" velocity is given, the second if the "s" velocity is given), because of the angles the curve is supposed to take between those two points. The velocity derived by METAFONT's normal rules is above maxvr or maxvs, so METAFONT is suppressing the wildness of the curve by lowering the velocity to the corresponding maximum value. (Cf. the latter part of Chapter 2 for further discussion.) This usually is a symptom of some problem in your program, although it may be perfectly all right.

`! vpen width too small, set to 1.`
You shouldn't specify a setting of vpenwd that is less than 0.5. Proceed, and its value
will be set to 1.

`! w-variable not followed by proper subscript.`
An identifier can't start with the letter w; thus you can't use a variable named `width`
except in a subroutine having an index parameter named `idth`. Proceed, and **META-
FONT** will act as though the offending w-variable were zero.

`! Whoops, you need a Datadisc for display modes.`
The **drawdisplay** and **chardisplay** control bits of **METAFONT** can be turned on only if
you are using it from a Datadisc terminal. Proceed, and these bits will be turned off.

`! x-variable not followed by proper subscript.`
An identifier can't start with the letter x; thus you can't use a variable named `xheight`
except in a subroutine having an index parameter named `height`. Proceed, and **META-
FONT** will act as though the offending x-variable were zero.

`! y-variable not followed by proper subscript.`
An identifier can't start with the letter y; thus you can't use a variable named `year`
except in a subroutine having an index parameter named `ear`. Proceed, and **METAFONT**
will act as though the offending y-variable were zero.

`! You can't begin a "primary" like that.`
At this point in your program, **METAFONT** is expecting to see a ⟨primary⟩, but the
token it has just scanned cannot be used at the beginning of a ⟨primary⟩ expression.
(Perhaps it is a reserved word that you intended to use as the name of a variable.)
Proceed, and **METAFONT** will pretend that the token it has just scanned was "0".

`! You can't begin a statement like that, command flushed.`
The token **METAFONT** has just read was supposed to be the first one of a ⟨statement⟩, but
no ⟨statement⟩ can possibly start with this particular token. Proceed, and **METAFONT**
will ignore all tokens up to the next semicolon or period.

`! You can't start an expression like that.`
At this point in your program, **METAFONT** is expecting to see an ⟨expression⟩, but the
token it has just scanned cannot be used at the beginning of an ⟨expression⟩. (Perhaps
it is a reserved word that you intended to use as the name of a variable.) Proceed, and
METAFONT will pretend that the token it has just scanned was a ⟨term⟩ of value zero.

`! You can't vary the pen size with ⟨pen type⟩.`
A **draw** command with varying sizes cannot be performed with a cpen, spen, or epen.
Proceed; the current drawing will be omitted.

<A> Answers to all the exercises

1.1: Replace the first line by "$x_1 = x_4$; $x_2 = x_5$; $x_3 = x_6$; $x_2 - x_1 = x_3 - x_2$; lft$_1 x_1 = 0$; rt$_1 x_3 = 2d - 2$;". (Adjacent characters will be separated by exactly one white pixel, not two, if the width of the character is $2d$ pixels, because a character of width $2d$ extends from column 0 to column $2d - 1$, inclusive.)

2.1: A straight line from point 1 to point 2, and another from point 2 to point 3.

2.2: The same "curve" as in exercise 2.1(!).

3.1: epen $(-7, -1)(-7, -1)(-7, -1).(-7, -1)(-7, -1)$; if the height were 4 instead of 5, the final "$(-7, -1)$" would be omitted and "epenycorr 0.5" would be used to center the pen vertically.

3.2: Program 1 yields an ellipse of width 75 and height 25, centered at the origin (i.e., at point $(0,0)$). Program 2 draws a shape of the same width and height—but it is composed of two semicircles of diameter 25 at the left and right, connected in the middle by a 25×50 rectangle.

4.1: `w0 draw 4{1,0}..1{0,1}; draw 3{0,1}..2{1,0}.`

4.2: Yes.

5.1: (a) x_1. (b) If x_1 is on one side of x_2, this point is on the opposite side, at a distance from x_2 that is half the distance from x_2 to x_1. (Imagine walking from x_1 toward x_2 at a constant speed that gets you there after one day; keep walking for a total of 3/2 days.) (c) $1/2[x_1, x_2]$. The formula $(x_1 + x_2)/2$ is one symbol shorter, but it is less descriptive once the bracket notation is understood.

5.2: (a) Yes. (b) No. (c) No (that one means $\sqrt{x_1 x_2}$).

6.1: The curve would be filled in between points 2 and 8, obliterating point 1, since 2 and 8 are corresponding points.

6.2: At least two ways will work. (a) By setting "**safetyfactor 0.22222**" and using "1 ddraw ...", the value of m is computed as if the pen size were 9 instead of 1. The safety factor must be reset to 2. (b) By using "epen $(0,0)$; 9 ddraw ..." you get the effect of a width-9 cpen but with an explicitly defined pen that blackens only one pixel at each point. Similarly an spen could be used.

8.1: subroutine *curve*(var *theta*, var *phi*, index i, index j):
cpen; 1 draw $i\{\text{cosd } theta, \text{sind } theta\} .. j\{\text{cosd } phi, -\text{sind } phi\}$.

8.2: ca1, ca2, cab1, cab2, cabb1, cabb2, cabbb1, cabbb2. (The value of xca3 is the same as that of xcab1, but no point is labeled ca3 since yca3 is never defined.)

<E> Example of a font definition

The alphabets used to typeset this manual belong to the "Computer Modern" family of fonts developed by the author at the same time as METAFONT itself was taking shape. Further experience will doubtless suggest many improvements, and in fact the design of Computer Modern is still far from finished. The purpose of this appendix is to illustrate what the author has learned so far about the task of designing a fairly complete alphabet, so that you can get an idea of why he finds it such a pleasant undertaking.

A complete font design is, of course, a complex system, so there are several levels at which one might understand it and use it—depending on how much of the "black box" is being opened. At the outermost level, all of the details can be left alone and we simply generate a particular font. For example, there is a file called "cmr10.mf", and when METAFONT is applied to that file it will produce the "Computer Modern Roman 10 point" font. Another file "cmsss8.mf" produces "Computer Modern Slanted Sans Serif 8 point," and so on. But if we actually look into files like cmr10.mf and cmsss8.mf, we find that they are quite short; they merely set up the values of certain parameters and input the file "roman.mf", which contains the actual METAFONT programs for individual leters. Therefore it is easy to make up a customized font for a particular application, simply by setting up new values of those parameters and inputting roman.mf ourselves.

At a still deeper level, we can also look at the file roman.mf, which consists of 128 short programs for the individual character shapes (followed by ligature and kerning definitions). These short programs are fairly independent, and they aren't completely inscrutable; it isn't difficult to substitute a new routine or two for characters that we wish to modify, since the programs make use of some fairly flexible subroutines that appear in file cmbase.mf.

At the deepest level, we could also fiddle with the subroutine definitions in cmbase.mf—and of course that would essentially amount to the creation of a new family of fonts.

In this appendix we shall study the Computer Modern fonts by working our way in from the outermost level. File cmr10.mf looks like this:

"Computer Modern Roman 10 point";

$ph = \frac{250}{36};$ $px = \frac{160}{36};$ $pe = \frac{90}{36};$ $pd = \frac{70}{36};$

$pb = \frac{20}{36};$ $po = \frac{4}{36};$ $ps = \frac{20}{36};$ $pa = .5(ph - pd);$

$$pw = \tfrac{9}{36}; \quad pwi = \tfrac{27}{36}; \quad pwii = \tfrac{32}{36}; \quad pwiii = \tfrac{36}{36};$$
$$pwiv = \tfrac{32}{36}; \quad pwv = \tfrac{38}{36}; \quad aspect = 1.0;$$
$$pu = \tfrac{20}{36}; \quad lcs = 1.075; \quad ucs = 1.7; \quad sc = 0;$$
$$slant = 0; \quad sqrttwo = \text{sqrt } 2; \quad fixwidth = 0;$$
$$halfd = 0; \quad varg = 0.$$
input cmbase; call *fontbegin*;
input roman;
end.

In other words, the file sets up a lot of parameters and then it does "input roman" to create the font.

We can obtain a great variety of related fonts by setting these parameters in different ways, once we know what they mean; and here's what they mean:

By convention, all of the parameters whose name begins with "p" are in units of printers' points. First come eight parameters covering important vertical dimensions:

ph is the h-height, the distance from the baseline to the top of an "h".

px is the x-height, the distance from the baseline to the top of an "x".

pe is the e-height, the distance from the baseline to the bar of an "e".

pd is the descender depth, the distance from the baseline to the bottom of a "p".

pb is the border height; characters extend as much as $ph + pb$ above the baseline and $pd + pb$ below it.

po is the amount of overshoot for optical adjustments at sharp corners; e.g., "A" is this much taller than "B".

ps is the vertical distance at which serif bracketing is tangent to the stems.

pa is the axis height, the distance from the baseline to the point where mathematical symbols like "$+$" and "$=$" have vertical symmetry.

Then there are seven parameters affecting the pen sizes:

pw is the hairline width, used in the thinnest parts of letters.

pwi is the stem width, used for the vertical strokes in an "h".

pwii is the curve width, used in an "o" at its widest point.

pwiii is the dot width, the diameter of the dot on an "i".

pwiv is the upper-case stem width, used for the vertical strokes in an "H".

pwv is the upper-case curve width, used in an "O" at its widest point.

aspect is the ratio of a hairline pen's width to its height.

Next come four parameters concerning horizontal dimensions:

pu is the unit width, 1/18 of an em.

lcs is the amount by which serifs of lower-case letters project from the stems, in units of *pu*.

ucs is the amount by which serifs of upper-case letters project from the stems, in units of *pu*.

sc is the serif correction in units of *pu*; each letter specifies multiples of *sc* by which its width is to be decreased at the left and the right.

Finally we have miscellaneous parameters that control special effects:

slant is the amount of additional increase in x per unit increase in y, used to slant letters either *forwards* or ꓭꓕꓲꓵꓪꓲꓭꓢ.

sqrttwo is used to control the ellipticity of the bowls of letters, as explained in Chapter 8.

halfd is nonzero if certain characters like "," are to descend only half as far as lower-case letters do.

varg is nonzero if the simple "ɡ" shape is to replace the classical "g".

File `cms10.mf` ("Computer Modern Slanted 10 point") is exactly the same as file `cmr10.mf`, except for its title and the fact that *slant* = 0.15. Similarly, the settings of parameters in file `cmb10.mf` ("Computer Modern Bold 10 point") are nearly identical to those of `cmr10.mf`, except that the pens are bigger:

$$pw = \tfrac{15}{36}; \quad pwi = \tfrac{40}{36}; \quad pwii = \tfrac{45}{36}; \quad pwiii = \tfrac{50}{36};$$
$$pwiv = \tfrac{50}{36}; \quad pwv = \tfrac{50}{36};$$

furthermore serifs are shorter (*lcs* = .85, *ucs* = 1.5).

File `cmr5.mf` generates 5-point type, but it is not simply obtained by halving the parameters of cmr10. The eight vertical dimensions *ph*, *px*, ..., *pa* are exactly half as large as before, but the pen sizes and the horizontal dimensions get smaller at different rates so as to enhance the readability of such tiny letters. The following settings are used:

$$pw = \tfrac{7}{36}, \qquad pwi = \tfrac{15}{36}, \qquad pwii = \tfrac{18}{36};$$
$$pwiii = \tfrac{20}{36}, \qquad pwiv = \tfrac{19}{36}, \qquad pwv = \tfrac{20}{36};$$
$$pu = \tfrac{25}{72}, \qquad lcs = 0.92, \qquad ucs = 1.32.$$

Two more examples should suffice to illustrate the variation of these parameters. **The bold sans-serif font used in this sentence and in the chapter headings of this manual is called "Computer Modern Sans Serif 10 point Bold Extended" (cmssb).** It uses the same vertical dimensions and miscellaneous settings as cmr10, and gets its other characteristics from the following parameter values:

$$pw = pwi = pwii = pwiii = \tfrac{37}{36};$$
$$pwiv = pwv = \tfrac{42}{36}; \qquad aspect = \tfrac{37}{23};$$
$$pu = \tfrac{22}{36}; \qquad lcs = ucs = 0; \qquad sc = \tfrac{9}{22}.$$

`To get the typewriter font "cmtt" used in this sentence, set`

$$ph = \tfrac{210}{36}; \qquad px = \tfrac{150}{36}; \qquad pe = \tfrac{75}{36}; \qquad pd = \tfrac{80}{36};$$
$$pb = \tfrac{30}{36}; \qquad po = 0; \qquad ps = 0; \qquad pa = \tfrac{85}{36};$$
$$pw = pwi = pwii = pwiv = pwv = \tfrac{20}{36};$$
$$pwiii = \tfrac{30}{30}; \qquad aspect = 1.0;$$
$$pu = \tfrac{23}{36}; \qquad lcs = \tfrac{8}{23}; \qquad ucs = \tfrac{19}{23}; \qquad sc = 0;$$
$$slant = 0; \qquad sqrttwo = \text{sqrt}\,2; \qquad fixwidth = 1;$$
$$halfd = 1; \qquad varg = 0.$$

By making stranger settings of the parameters you can also get strange fonts like this.

The programs for Computer Modern can be used in several ways. The general procedure is to run METAFONT and type

`mode = ⟨mode number⟩; input ⟨font name⟩;`

the routines will act differently depending on the specified mode. At present mode 0 generates proof sheets and shows the letters as they are being drawn,

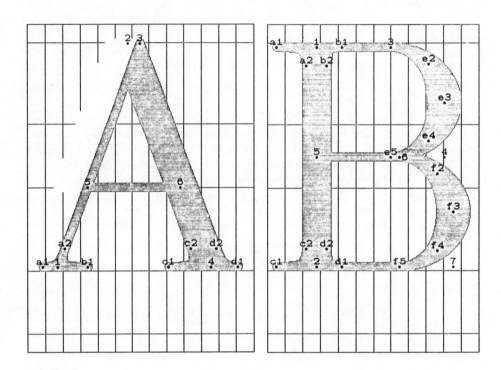

Fig. E–1. Two characters of font cmr10, as they appear when drawn with "mode 0". The horizontal guidelines indicate the h-height, x-height, e-height, and the depth of descenders in this font. The vertical guidelines are one "unit" apart, where there are 18 such units to an em.

with a resolution of 36 pixels per point; mode 1 generates a font for the XGP with a resolution of 3.6 pixels per point, displaying the letters on a Datadisc just after they are drawn; and mode 2 generates a font for the CRS with a resolution of 73.7973 pixels per point, displaying the titles of the letters as they are being drawn. In mode 0 the letters appear on a background grid as shown in Fig. E–1, so that you can see the settings of the parameters in a convenient way.

Actually mode 0 is rarely used with an entire font like cmr10, it is generally used to test out new characters. In that case you can make up a file called "test.mf" containing the characters you wish to try, and simply input the system file "proof.mf", which has the following form:

> $mode = 0$; input cmbase;
>
> $ph = \frac{250}{36}$;   ...⟨set up for cmr10⟩...;   call *fontbegin*.
>
> input test;
>
> new pw, ...⟨set up for cmb10⟩...;   call *fontbegin*.
>
> input test;
>
> new pw, ...⟨set up for cmssb⟩...;   call *fontbegin*.
>
> input test;
>
> new ph, ...⟨set up for cmtt⟩...;   call *fontbegin*.
>
> input test;
>
> new ph, ...⟨set up for cmsss8⟩...;   call *fontbegin*.
>
> input test;
>
> end.

Thus, it runs your test file against five different settings of the parameters.

Let's go one level deeper and take a look at the programs for individual letters; examples appear in Figs. E–2 and E–3 later in this appendix. Such programs are expressed in terms of variables something like the parameters we have been discussing, but the variables are slightly different since the letters are to be drawn on a raster and we need to work in raster units instead of printers' points. The point-oriented variables ph, px, pe, etc., have corresponding raster-oriented variables, satisfying the approximate relation

$$\langle \text{raster-oriented variable} \rangle \approx pixels \cdot \langle \text{point-oriented variable} \rangle,$$

where $pixels$ is the number of pixels per point. This relation is only approximate, not exact, because the raster-oriented variables have been rounded to values that help to provide satisfactory discretization of the characters. As explained in Chapter 7, good designs are written with discreteness in mind, although METAFONT tries to do the right thing automatically when it can.

There are seven raster-oriented variables corresponding to seven of the eight pixel-oriented vertical dimensions, namely

$$h \leftrightarrow ph, \ c \leftrightarrow px, \ e \leftrightarrow pe, \ d \leftrightarrow pd, \ b \leftrightarrow pb, \ o \leftrightarrow po, \ a \leftrightarrow pa;$$

in other words, we just drop the "p", except in the case of "px" (since a variable can't be named "x"). Fortunately the height of a "c" is the same as the height of an "x", so we can use the term c-height in place of the traditional term x-height. The baseline of each character is row 0, so the bottom pixel of a letter like "h" has y-coordinate 0. The top pixel of an "h" is in row h, which is always an integer. (Note that there are actually $h + 1$ occupied rows, not h, although h is called the h-height.) The top pixel of a "c" is in row c, and the bottom pixel of the descender letters (g,j,p,q,y) appears in row $-d$. All three of these variables (h, c, d) are integers, and so is the overshoot variable o (which is used as a correction to h, c, or d in certain cases). Variable e is either an integer or an integer plus $\frac{1}{2}$, whichever is better for a pen of the hpen height, since the bar of an "e" is drawn with an hpen and its y-coordinate is e. Variable b is an integer calculated in such a way that tall characters can run up to row $h + b$ and deep characters can descend to row $-d - b$; more precisely, it is the smallest integer such that $h + d + 2b + 1$ rows of the raster occupy a vertical distance that exceeds or equals the true point size $ph + pd + 2pb$.

The pen sizes in Computer Modern programs for individual letters are generally expressed in terms of the following variables, each of which has a positive integer value intended to approximate the "true" infinite-resolution value (and slightly increased in order to look right on the output device):

> w_0, the hairline width;
> w_1, the stem width;
> w_2, the curve width;
> w_3, the dot diameter;
> w_4, the upper-case stem width;
> w_5, the upper-case curve width;
> w_6, the hairline height;
> w_7, the stem height;
> w_8, the upper-case stem height.

Note that the last three of these variables have no "p-variable" equivalent; they satisfy the approximate relation

$$w_0/w_6 \approx w_1/w_7 \approx w_4/w_8 \approx aspect.$$

The hpenht is w_6 and the vpenwd is w_0. Thus, an hpen of size w_0 is equivalent to a vpen of size w_6; we may call it the "hairline pen" for the font.

In the horizontal dimension, the Computer Modern programs make frequent use of variable u, the approximate unit width when there are 18 units to an em. The width of a character is expressed in terms of units (e.g., an "h" is $10u$ wide, unless there is a serif correction $sc \neq 0$), and key positions can be specified as a certain number of units from the left (e.g., the stems of an "h" are centered at $2.5u$ and $7.5u$). The vertical guidelines in Fig. E–1 indicate the unit spacing for a 13-unit-wide "A" and a 12-unit-wide "B".

If the character is t units wide, variable u has been calculated so that t times u is an integer r, the rightmost column of the character. (The value of u itself is usually not an integer, nor need t be an integer.) Just as a character typically occupies rows 0 through h, inclusive, in the vertical direction, we use columns 0 through r inclusive in the horizontal direction, although most characters leave white space at the left and right boundaries. The integer r is calculated so that $r + 2$ is the nearest integer to the character's true width ($t \cdot pu \cdot pixels$); the reason for this extra "$+ 2$" is that low-resolution devices should keep a blank column (column $r + 1$) between adjacent characters. However, it is best for conceptual purposes to think of r as the character's actual width, and to think of "$r - 2.5u$" as a point $2\frac{1}{2}$ units from the right edge, etc.

We're ready now to look more closely at a program for the upper-case letter "A" (Fig. E–2). The first line of that program simply gives the title that will appear on proof sheets, or possibly on the terminal when the character is being drawn. Then comes a call to the *charbegin* subroutine, with seven parameters: the character code, the width of the character in units, the multiples of sc that are to be trimmed from the left and right, and the character's height, depth, and italic correction. These last three parameters must be in absolute units of printers' points, hence ph (not h) is used here for the height.

The next few lines give eight equations to define the locations of points 1, 2, 3, and 4. First point 1 is positioned so that, using an hpen of size w_0 (the hairline pen), the pen's left edge will be 1.5 units from the left edge of the character, and the bottom will be on the baseline. Similarly point 4 is placed so that the pen's right edge will be 1.5 units from the right edge of the character and the bottom will be on the baseline, where this time the pen is an hpen of size w_5. (The upper-case curve width w_5 is used here in preference to the stem width w_4, since a diagonal stroke tends to decrease the effective pen width.) The positioning of points 2 and 3 is more interesting: the idea is that we want to draw a line from 2 to 4 with an hpen of width w_5, and another from 3 to 1 with an hpen of width w_0. First we define y_2 and y_3 so that the top occurs at the h-height h, plus the "overshoot" o that gives this letter a touch of class. Then we state that $x_3 - x_1 = x_4 - x_2$, so that the two diagonal strokes will have the same slopes (the same amount of change in the x direction). Finally we stipulate that $\mathrm{rt}_5 x_2 = \mathrm{rt}_0 x_3$, so that the line from 2 to 4 will have the same top right boundary as the line from 1 to 3. These equations give METAFONT enough information to determine points 2 and 3 uniquely.

After drawing the right diagonal stroke, we need to erase part of the stem line at

```
"The letter A";
call charbegin(`A, 13, 2, 2, ph, 0, 0);
hpen;
lft_0 x_1 = round 1.5u;   bot_0 y_1 = 0;
rt_5 x_4 = round(r − 1.5u);   bot_5 y_4 = 0;
top_0 y_3 = top_5 y_2 = h + o;
x_3 − x_1 = x_4 − x_2;   rt_5 x_2 = rt_0 x_3;
w_5 draw 2..4;                              % right diagonal stroke
y_5 = y_6 = e;
x_5 − 1 = (y_5 − y_1)/(y_3 − y_1)[x_1, x_3];
x_6 + 1 = (y_6 − y_4)/(y_2 − y_4)[x_4, x_2];
w_0 draw 5..6;                              % bar line
lpen#;   w_5 draw 3..5;            % erase excess at upper left
hpen;   w_0 draw 3..1;             % left diagonal stroke
if ucs ≠ 0:
call `a serif(1, 0, 3, −.5ucs);
call `b serif(1, 0, 3, +ucs);              % left serifs
call `c serif(4, 5, 2, −ucs);
call `d serif(4, 5, 2, +.5ucs);            % right serifs
fi.
```

Fig. E–2. A METAFONT program for upper-case "A".

the top, where it protrudes to the left of the left stroke (which is thinner). Before erasing anything, however, we may as well draw the bar line. Computer Modern fonts place this line at the e-height, the same level as the bar line in an "e", hence $y_5 = y_6 = e$. The calculation of x_5 and x_6 is slightly trickier; x_5 lies between x_1 and x_3, and the ratio of its distance is the same as the same as the ratio of $y_5 − y_1$ to $y_3 − y_1$. The equation "$x_5 = (y_5 − y_1)/(y_3 − y_1)[x_1, x_3]$" would almost surely work to define a suitable point; but the program actually uses $x_5 − 1$ instead of x_5, just to be absolutely safe against weird possibilities of rounding that might cause the bar line to stick out at the left. (It doesn't hurt to start a line one pixel to the right of a point that lies on another line.)

Now the lpen# is used to erase unwanted black pixels, changing them back to white. Actually this erases more than we wanted to get rid of, since it has a rectangular shape and we are erasing at an angle; but that doesn't matter, because the left diagonal stroke blackens all the necessary pixels. (Note that the eraser has also done away with part of the guidelines in Fig. E–1.)

Finally the serif subroutine is used to attach fancy serifs at points 1 and 4; these

```
"The letter B";
call charbegin(`B, 12, 2, 0, ph, 0, ph·slant − 2pu);
hpen;
lft₄x₁ = lft₄x₂ = round 2u;   top₄y₁ = h;   bot₄y₂ = 0;
w₄ draw 1 .. 2;                                        % stem
if ucs ≠ 0: call `a serif(1, 4, 2, −ucs); call `b serif(1, 4, 2, .5ucs);   % upper serif
     call `c serif(2, 4, 1, −ucs); call `d serif(2, 4, 1, .5ucs);   % lower serif
fi;
x₃ = ½[2u, r];   y₃ = y₁;
rt₅x₄ = round(r − u);   y₄ = good₀ ½h;
w₀ draw 1 .. 3;                                        % upper bar line
call `e darc(3, 4, w₅);                                % upper counter
x₅ = x₁;   x₆ = x₃ + ½u;   y₄ = y₅ = y₆;
rt₅x₇ = round(r − ½u);   bot₅y₇ = 0;
w₀ draw 5 .. 6;                                        % middle bar line
call `f darc(6, 7, w₅);                                % lower counter
x₈ = x₆;   y₈ = y₇;   w₀ draw 2 .. 8.                  % lower bar line
```

```
"The letter B";
call charbegin(`B, 12, 2, 0, ph, 0, ph·slant − 2pu);
hpen;
```

$\text{lft}_4 x_1 = \text{lft}_4 x_2 = \text{round } 2u;$ $\text{top}_4 y_1 = h;$ $\text{bot}_4 y_2 = 0;$

w_4 draw $1 .. 2;$ % stem

if $ucs \neq 0$: call `a $serif(1, 4, 2, -ucs);$ call `b $serif(1, 4, 2, .5ucs);$ % upper serif

     call `c $serif(2, 4, 1, -ucs);$ call `d $serif(2, 4, 1, .5ucs);$ % lower serif

fi;

$x_3 = \frac{1}{2}[2u, r];$ $y_3 = y_1;$

$\text{rt}_5 x_4 = \text{round}(r - u);$ $y_4 = \text{good}_0 \frac{1}{2}h;$

w_0 draw $1 .. 3;$ % upper bar line

call `e $darc(3, 4, w_5);$ % upper counter

$x_5 = x_1;$ $x_6 = x_3 + \frac{1}{2}u;$ $y_4 = y_5 = y_6;$

$\text{rt}_5 x_7 = \text{round}(r - \frac{1}{2}u);$ $\text{bot}_5 y_7 = 0;$

w_0 draw $5 .. 6;$ % middle bar line

call `f $darc(6, 7, w_5);$ % lower counter

$x_8 = x_6;$ $y_8 = y_7;$ w_0 draw $2 .. 8.$ % lower bar line

Fig. E–3. A METAFONT program for upper-case "B".

serifs extend .5ucs units outwards and ucs units inwards. Details of this subroutine appear below.

Once you understand this program for "A", you will have no trouble writing programs for "V" and "v", as well as for the Greek letter "Λ"; and you will be well on your way to having a "W" too. Similarly, the code for "B" in Fig. E–3, which is presented here without further comment, leads to "D" and "P" with little further ado.

We shall now plunge into the deepest level, the subroutines in cmbase.mf that take care of nasty details. Four of the most important subroutines are given here, as examples of how this level operates; the four subroutines (*fontbegin*, *charbegin*, *serif*, and *darc*) suffice to do everything required by the programs for "A" and "B".

$eps = .000314159;$ % a very small random positive number

if $mode = 0$: proofmode; drawdisplay; $pixels = 36;$ $blacker = 0;$

else: if $mode = 1$: fntmode; tfxmode; chardisplay; $pixels = 3.6;$ $blacker = 1.2;$

        else: crsmode; tfxmode; titletrace; $pixels = 73.7973;$ $blacker = 1;$

        fi;

fi;

```
subroutine fontbegin:                          % Initialize before making a font:
no eqtrace;                                % Turn off tracing within this subroutine.
new typesize;                                    % the vertical size of the font
new cf;                          % conversion factor, approximately equal to pixels
new h, d, c, e, o, b, s, a;                        % raster-oriented vertical dimensions
w₀ = round(pixels·pw + blacker);
w₁ = round(pixels·pwi + blacker);
w₂ = round(pixels·pwii + blacker);
w₃ = round(pixels·pwiii + blacker);
w₄ = round(pixels·pwiv + blacker);
w₅ = round(pixels·pwv + blacker);
w₆ = round(pixels·pw/aspect + blacker);
w₇ = round(pixels·pwi/aspect + blacker);
w₈ = round(pixels·pwiv/aspect + blacker);
hpenht w₆;   vpenwd w₀;

typesize = ph + pd + 2pb;    cf·typesize = pixels·typesize − 1;
h = round cf·ph;    d = round cf·pd;    c = round cf·px;
o = round cf·po;    s = cf·ps;    a = .5 round 2cf·pa;
b = −round(.5(h + d − typesize·pixels));
hpen;   e = good₀ cf·pe;

maxht h + b;
trxy slant;
if mode ≠ 0: texinfo slant, 6pu, 3pu, 3pu, px, 18pu, 2pu;
fi.
```

```
subroutine charbegin(var charno)                     % seven-bit character code
              (var charuw)                       % character width in units
          (var lftcorr, var rtcorr)           % serif-oriented corrections in units
(var charh, var chard, var chari):        % charht, chardp, charic values in points
no eqtrace; no calltrace;                     % Shut off tracing in this subroutine.
new uw;                                  % the correct character width in units
new r;                                    % raster-oriented character width
new u;                                      % raster-oriented design unit
new tu;                                   % unmodified raster-oriented unit
new italcorr;                                       % italic correction
if chari ≥ 0: italcorr = chari; else: italcorr = 0;
fi;
charcode charno; charht charh; chardp chard; charic italcorr;
tu = pu·pixels;
```

if *fixwidth* = 0: $r + 2$ = round *charuw*·*tu*;
      uw = *charuw* − *sc*·(*lftcorr* + *rtcorr*);
else: $r + 2$ = round((9 + *sc*·(*lftcorr* + *rtcorr*))·*tu*);
      uw = 9;
fi;
u·*charuw* = *r*; charwd *uw*·*pu*; chardw *uw*·*tu*;
incx round(−*sc*·*lftcorr*·*tu*);
if *mode* = 0: call *box*(round *sc*·*lftcorr*·*tu*);
fi.

subroutine *box*(var *offset*):　　　　　% Draw guildelines and box around a character:
no drawtrace; no proofmode;
new *topp*, *bott*, *left*, *right*, *pos*;
topp = *h* + *b*;　　*bott* = −*d* − *b*;
left = *offset*;　　*right* = *offset* + *u*·*uw*;
$x_1 = x_3 = x_5 = x_7 = x_9 = x_{11} = x_{13} = x_{15} = x_{17}$ = *left*;
$x_2 = x_4 = x_6 = x_8 = x_{10} = x_{12} = x_{14} = x_{16} = x_{18}$ = *right*;
$y_1 = y_2 = 0$;　　cpen;　　1 draw 1..2;　　　　　　　　　% baseline
$y_3 = y_4 = e$;　　draw 3..4;　　　　　　　　　　　　　　% e-height
$y_5 = y_6 = c$;　　draw 5..6;　　　　　　　　　　　　　　% x-height
$y_7 = y_8 = h$;　　draw 7..8;　　　　　　　　　　　　　　% h-height
$y_9 = y_{10} = topp$;　　draw 9..10;　　　　　　　　　% top of character
$y_{11} = y_{12} = −d$;　　draw 11..12;　　　　　　　% descender line
$y_{13} = y_{14} = bott$;　　draw 13..14;　　　　　　% bottom of character
trxy 0;　　　　　　　　　　　　　　　% Temporarily turn off the slant.
$y_{15} = y_{16} = topp$;　　$y_{17} = y_{18} = bott$;
draw 15..17;　　draw 16..18;　　　　　　　% left and right edges
if *italcorr* > 0: $x_{19} = x_{20}$ = *right* + *italcorr*·*pixels*;
      $y_{19} = topp$;　　$y_{20} = 0$;　　draw 19..20;　　　% show italic correction
fi;
trxy *slant*;　　　　　　　　　% Restore slanted transformation
pos = 0;　　call *unitlines*.　　　　% Draw the unit guidelines.

subroutine *unitlines*:　　　　　　% Recursive subroutine to draw guidelines:
$x_1 = x_2 = pos$; $y_1 = topp$; $y_2 = bott$; cpen;
if *pos* ≥ *left*: 1 draw 1..2;
fi;
new *pos*; *pos* = $x_1 + u$;
if *pos* ≤ *right*: call *unitlines*;
fi.

subroutine *serif* (index i)   % point where serif appears
             (index k)   % w-variable for stem line
             (index j)   % another point on the stem line
             (var sl):   % serif length

$y_1 = y_i$;
if $y_i < y_j$: $y_2 = y_i + s$;   else: $y_2 = y_i - s$;
fi;
hpen;
if $sl < 0$: $\text{lft}_0 x_1 = \text{lft}_k x_i + sl \cdot u - eps$;
       $\text{lft}_0 x_2 = \text{lft}_k (y_2 - y_i)/(y_j - y_i)[x_i, x_j]$;
else: $\text{rt}_0 x_1 = \text{rt}_k x_i + sl \cdot u + eps$;
       $\text{rt}_0 x_2 = \text{rt}_k (y_2 - y_i)/(y_j - y_i)[x_i, x_j]$;
fi;
no proofmode;
$x_3 = \frac{1}{3}[x_1 - sl \cdot u, \frac{1}{2}[x_1, x_2]]$; $y_3 = \frac{1}{3}[y_i, \frac{1}{2}[y_1, y_2]]$;
minvr 0; minvs 0;
w_0 ddraw $1\{x_i - x_1, 0\} . . 3 . . 2\{x_j - x_i, y_j - y_i\}$, $1 . . 1 . . i$;
minvr 0.5; minvs 0.5.

subroutine *darc* (index i)   % starting point
             (index j)   % opposite corner point
          (var *maxwidth*):   % the pen grows from w_0 to this size

$x_5 = x_i$; $x_2 = x_4 = 1/sqrttwo\,[x_i, x_j]$; $x_3 = x_j$;
$y_5 = y_j$; $y_3 = \frac{1}{2}[y_i, y_j]$;
$y_2 = 1/sqrttwo\,[y_3, y_i]$; $y_4 = 1/sqrttwo\,[y_3, y_j]$;
hpen;   draw $|w_0|i\{x_3 - x_i, 0\} . . |\frac{2}{3}[w_0, maxwidth]|2\{x_3 - x_i, y_3 - y_i\} . .$
           $|maxwidth\,\#|3\{0, y_3 - y_i\} . .$
           $|\frac{2}{3}[w_0, maxwidth]|4\{x_5 - x_3, y_5 - y_3\} . . |w_0|5\{x_5 - x_3, 0\}$.

<F> Font information for TEX

The TEX typesetting system assumes that some "intelligence" has been built into the fonts it uses. In other words, information stored with TEX's fonts has an important effect on TEX's behavior. This has two consequences for people who use TEX: (a) Typesetting is more flexible, since fewer conventions are frozen into the computer program. (b) Font designers have to work a little harder, since they have to tell TEX what to do. The purpose of this appendix is to explain how you, as a font designer, can cope with (b) in order to achieve spectacular success with (a). (You should of course be somewhat familiar with TEX if you expect to provide it with the best information.)

In the first place, TEX needs to know how big a box each character is supposed to occupy, since TEX is based on the primitive concepts of boxes and glue. When it typesets a word like "box", it places the first letter "b" in such a way that the METAFONT pixel whose x and y coordinates are $(0, 0)$ will appear on the baseline of the current horizontal line being typeset, at the left edge of the "b" box. The second letter "o" is placed in a second box adjacent to the first one, so it is obvious that we must tell TEX how wide to make the "b". In fact, TEX also learns how tall the "b" box should be; this affects the placement of accents, if you wish to write "b̄ōx̃", and it also avoids overlap with unusual constructions in an adjacent line.

A total of four dimensions is given for each character of a font to be used by TEX, in units of printers' points:

charwd, the width of the box containing the character.

charht, the height (above the baseline) of the box containing the character.

chardp, the depth (below the baseline) of the box containing the character.

charic, the "italic correction". This amount is added to the width of the box (at the righthand side) in two cases: (a) When a TEX user specifies an italic correction ("\/") immediately following this character, in horizontal mode. (b) Whenever this character is used in math mode, unless it has a subscript but no superscript. (For example, the italic correction is applied to P in the formulas $P(x)$ and P^2, but not in the formula P_n.)

If you don't specify one or more of these four dimensions, METAFONT assumes that you intended any missing dimensions to be zero. For example, the italic correction for most letters in non-slanted fonts is zero, so you needn't say anything about it.

It is important to note the difference between charwd (the width of the character box) and chardw (the character's device width, discussed in Chapter 9). The former is given in units of points, and it affects TEX's positioning of text, while the latter is an integer number of pixels that has no influence on the appearance of TEX output. The purpose of chardw is merely to compress the data that TEX transmits to a typesetting machine; for example, TEX needn't specify where to put the "o" following a "b", in the common case that the typesetting device will figure the correct position by its knowledge of the approximate size chardw. Furthermore chardw is the width of the character if for some reason you are (shudder) typesetting something without using TEX.

The next kind of information that TEX wants is concerned with pairs of adjacent characters within a font, namely the data about ligatures and kerning. For example, TEX moves the "x" slightly closer to the "o" in the word "box", because of information stored in the font you are now reading. Otherwise (if the three boxes had simply been placed next to each other according to their charwd) the word would have been "box", which looks slightly less attractive. Similarly there is a difference between "difference" and "difference", because the font tells TEX to substitute the ligature "ff" when there are two f's in a row.

Ligature and kerning information is specified by giving TEX short programs to follow. For example, the font you are now reading includes the following programs (among others):

$$\text{lig } `f: `i = `174, `f = `173, `l = `175;$$
$$\text{lig } `173: `i = `176, `l = `177;$$
$$\text{lig } `V: `F: `A \text{ kern } -2.5ru,$$
$$`X: `K: `O \text{ kern } -.5ru, `C \text{ kern } -.5ru,$$
$$`G \text{ kern } -.5ru, `Q \text{ kern } -.5ru;$$

information like this can appear anywhere in a METAFONT program after tfxmode has been specified. Both ligatures and kerns are introduced by the keyword lig, and this example can be paraphrased as follows:

Dear TEX, when you are typesetting an "f" with this font, and when the following character also belongs to this font, do this: If the following character is an "i", change the "f" to character code octal 174 [namely "fi"] and delete the "i"; if it is an "f" or "l", similarly change the pair of characters to octal 173 ["ff"] or 175 ["fl"]. When you are typesetting character code 173 ['ff'] and the next character is an "i" or "l", change to codes 176 ["ffi"] or 177 ["ffl"]. When you are typesetting a "V" or an "F" and the next character is an "A" in this font, delete 2.5ru of space before the "A". [Variable ru has been defined elsewhere in the program to be $\frac{1}{18}$ of a quad, i.e., $\frac{10}{18}$ of a point in 10-point type.] If the next character is "O" or "C" or "G" or "Q", delete $\frac{1}{2}ru$ of space between the letters. These last four instructions apply after "X" and "K" as well as after "V" and "F".

The general form of ligature/kerning statements is

lig ⟨lig instruction list⟩

where ⟨lig instruction list⟩ is a list of one or more ⟨lig instruction⟩s. There are three kinds of ⟨lig instruction⟩s, which may appear intermixed in any order:

1) Labels, having the form "⟨expression⟩:". The ⟨expression⟩ is usually a constant, as in our examples above; it denotes a character code, which is rounded to an integer that should be between 0 and 127 (octal *177*). At most one label should appear for each character code. The label means that the ligature/kerning program for the specified character starts here. Note that the program for characters `X and `K in our example starts in the middle of the program for characters `V and `F, while the latter two letters have identical programs; this device saves space inside TEX, and it also saves time since TEX has fewer instructions to load with the fonts.

2) Ligature replacements, having the form "⟨expression₁⟩ = ⟨expression₂⟩". Both ⟨expression⟩s are rounded to integers that should be between 0 and 127; they are usually constants. The meaning is that if the current character is followed by the character whose code is ⟨expression₁⟩, this pair is replaced by the character whose code is ⟨expression₂⟩.

3) Kern specifications, having the form "⟨expression₁⟩ **kern** ⟨expression₂⟩". The first expression is usually constant; it is rounded to an integer that should lie between 0 and 127. The second expression is usually negative, but it need not be. The meaning is that if the current character is followed by the character whose code is ⟨expression₁⟩, in the same font, additional spacing of ⟨expression₂⟩ points is inserted between the two.

Instructions of types (2) and (3) must be followed by commas, unless they are the final instruction of the ⟨lig instruction list⟩; labels, on the other hand, are never followed by commas.

We have said that the ligature/kerning program for each character starts at the corresponding label, but where does that program stop? Answer: It stops at the end of the ⟨lig instruction list⟩ containing the label, unless the last ⟨lig instruction⟩ of that list is a label, or unless that last ⟨lig instruction⟩ is followed by a comma. In the latter cases, the ligature/kerning program continues into the next ⟨lig instruction list⟩ that **METAFONT** interprets. Thus you can use **METAFONT**'s subroutines and/or conditional statements to generate intricate patterns of ligature/kerning instructions, if you really want to.

Caution: Novices often go overboard on kerning; restraint is desirable. It usually works out best to kern by at most half of what looks right to you at first, since kerning should not be noticeable by its presence (only by its absence). Kerning that looks right in a logo often interrupts the rhythm of reading when it appears in other textual material.

The remaining information that TEX needs in a text font can be provided by the command

texinfo ⟨expression list⟩

where the ⟨expression list⟩ is a list of seven ⟨expression⟩s separated by commas. The seven ⟨expression⟩s should contain the following data, in order:

1) "slant". The change in x coordinate per unit change in y coordinate when TEX is raising or lowering an accent character.

2) "space". The amount of space (in points) between words when using this font.

3) "stretch". The amount of stretchability (in points) between words when using this font, according to TEX's notion of glue. (This is the maximum amount of additional space that would look tolerable.)

4) "shrink". The maximum amount of shrinkage (in points) between words when using this font, according to TEX's notion of glue.

5) "xheight". The height of characters (in points) for which accents are correctly situated. An accented character has the accent raised by the difference between its charht and this value.

6) "quad". The width of one em unit (in points) when using this font.

7) "extraspace". The amount of additional space inserted after periods when using this font. (Strictly speaking, it is the amount added to "space" when TEX's "space factor" exceeds 2.)

The DRAGON example of Chapter 4 gave no texinfo, so all seven of these parameters were set to zero in that font.

If your font is for use in TEX math mode, as a mathsy or a mathex font, you need to specify still more information. Otherwise, you can stop reading this appendix, right now.

Math symbols fonts (mathsy) require more texinfo. In fact, you can give several texinfo commands in a single METAFONT program, and their ⟨expression list⟩s can contain more then or fewer than seven ⟨expression⟩s; each texinfo appends one or more values to the TEX information. The total number of parameters TEX uses in a mathsy font is 22, and they must consist of the first six above and the following additional ones in order:

7) "math space". If this is not zero, it denotes the amount of space in points that will be used for all nonzero space (except \quad) in math formulas: thin spaces, thick spaces, control spaces, and op spaces, whenever these are nonzero according to TEX's rules. The parameter is generally zero unless TEX is outputting to a fixed-width device like a typewriter or line printer.

8) "num1". Amount to raise baseline of numerators in display styles.

9) "num2". Amount to raise baseline of numerators in non-display styles, except for "\atop".

10) "num3". Amount to raise baseline of numerators in non-display \atop styles.

11) "denom1". Amount to lower baseline of denominators in display styles.

12) "denom2". Amount to lower baseline of denominators in non-display styles.

13) "sup1". Amount to raise baseline of superscripts in unmodified display style.

14) "sup2". Amount to raise baseline of superscripts in unmodified non-display styles.

15) "sup3". Amount to raise baseline of superscripts in modified styles.

16) "sub1". Amount to lower baseline of subscripts if superscript is absent.

17) "sub2". Amount to lower baseline of subscripts if superscript is present.

18) "supdrop". Amount below top of large box to place baseline if the box has a superscript in this size.

19) "subdrop". Amount below bottom of large box to place baseline if the box has a subscript in this size.

20) "delim1". Size of \comb delimiters in display styles.

21) "delim2". Size of \comb delimiters in non-display styles.

22) "axisheight". Height of fraction lines above the baseline. (This is usually midway between the two bars of an $=$ sign.)

Similarly, a mathex font requires 13 items of texinfo, namely the standard first seven and the following additional things in order:

8) "defaultrulethickness". The thickness of \over and \overline bars.

9) "bigopspacing1". The minimum glue space above a large displayed operator.

10) "bigopspacing2". The minimum glue space below a large displayed operator.

11) "bigopspacing3". The minimum distance between a limit's baseline and a large displayed operator, when the limit is above the operator.

12) "bigopspacing4". The minimum distance between a limit's baseline and a large displayed operator, when the limit is below the operator.

13) "bigopspacing5". The extra glue placed above and below displayed limits, effectively enlarging the corresponding boxes.

If you supply fewer than 22 items of texinfo for a mathsy font, or fewer than 13 for a mathex font, TEX will probably do very strange and undesirable things. So don't.

Still more information is needed in mathex fonts. In the first place, the italic correction for symbols used as \mathops (e.g., summation and integral signs) has a special significance: If it is zero, the limits for this operator will be centered above and below the operator. If it is nonzero, the limits will be set immediately to the right, with the lower limit shifted left by the amount of charic. (A TEX user writes \limitswitch to reverse these conventions; when limits are set above and below the operator, the upper limit is charic points to the right of the lower limit.)

Another difference for mathex fonts is the provision of "built up" symbols that can get arbitrarily large. Such symbols are manufactured from up to four pieces, including a mandatory extension part and optional top, middle and bottom parts. For example, the left brace at the left of this paragraph has all four pieces, while the norm symbol at the right is made up solely of extension pieces. Similarly, floor and ceiling brackets (⌊ ⌋ and ⌈ ⌉) are built up from the same components as regular brackets, but without top or bottom, respectively. TEX makes the smallest symbol meeting a given size constraint, using zero or more copies of the extension component. If there is a middle, the same number of extension components will appear above and below.

Suppose c is the 7-bit code representing a built-up character. TEX requires the following conventions: (1) The charht field for code c must be zero, and there must be no ligature program for c. (2) The command

varchar ⟨expression₁⟩, ⟨expression₂⟩, ⟨expression₃⟩, ⟨expression₄⟩

is given for c in lieu of a charic command, where the four ⟨expression⟩s stand respectively for the character codes of the top, middle, bottom, and extension components. These codes should be zero if the component doesn't exist, otherwise they should round to numbers between 1 and 127. For example, the left brace symbol in font cmathx has been defined by "varchar ´070, ´074, ´072, ´076". (Code c itself need not be any of these four.) (3) The charwd of the extension component is taken to be the charwd of the entire built-up symbol.

One final kind of information appears in mathex fonts, namely the lists that tie related characters together in increasing order of their size. For example, all of the left parentheses in cmathx have been specified by the command

charlist ´000, ´020, ´022, ´040, ´060, 0.

(Cf. Table 7 of Appendix F in the TEX manual.) When TEX needs a variable-size left parenthesis, it looks first at character ´000, then (if this is too small) at ´020, and so on, until either finding one that is large enough or reaching ´060 (the end of the list). The zero following ´060 indicates that ´060 is a built-up symbol that can grow arbitrarily large. If the last entry of a charlist is not zero, this symbol is not of the built-up variety, and it is used by TEX whether or not it is large enough. For example, the slash symbols in cmathx are specified by "charlist ´016, ´036, ´054", the latter being the largest slash present. A charlist in general consists of ⟨expression⟩s (usually constants) that are in increasing order except that the last one may be zero. The nonzero ⟨expression⟩s should round to integer character codes between 1 and 127. None of these characters should have a ligature/kern program, since TEX stores the charlist information in the same place that is usually used for ligatures and kerns.

The charlist for square root symbols should start at character position ´160 in a mathex font. These symbols should be designed so that they look right when a horizontal rule of the default rule thickness is placed with its upper left corner coinciding with the upper right corner of the character box.

<I> Index

This index shows all of METAFONT's "reserved words" in boldface type, and it also lists error messages that are mentioned outside of Chapter 10.

About the Author

Donald E. Knuth is Professor of Computer Science and Professor of Electrical Engineering at Stanford University. He has in the past served as Guest Professor of Mathematics, University of Oslo; Staff Mathematician, Institute for Defense Analysis—Communications Research Division; Associate Professor of Mathematics, California Institute of Technology; and Consultant, Burroughs Corporation, Pasadena, California.

His honors and awards include a Guggenheim fellowship; membership in the American Academy of Arts and Sciences and the National Academy of Sciences; the Grace Murray Hopper award and the Alan M. Turing award of the Association for Computing Machinery; the Lester R. Ford Award of the Mathematical Association of America; the Distinguished Alumni award of the California Institute of Technology; and he is the first holder of the Fletcher Jones professorship in computer science, the first endowed chair in computer science at Stanford.

Dr. Knuth is the author of *The Art of Computer Programming: Volume 1, Fundamental Algorithms; Volume 2, Semi-Numerical Algorithms;* and *Volume 3, Sorting and Searching*—the first three of a projected series of seven. Each has received universal acclaim. Among his other publications is perhaps the world's only mathematical novelette, *Surreal Numbers*.

T_EX Users' Group

The American Mathematical Society has an advisory Standing Committee on Composition Technology. Currently the Society contemplates the addition of a T_EX capability to its other typesetting facilities. In addition, the committee is investigating the development of a T_EX-based system to permit authors of papers for AMS (and eventually other) journals to "typeset" their papers themselves on their own institutions' computer systems. Because of this expected involvement with T_EX, the AMS has a natural interest in seeing the development of a strong and healthy T_EX users' group for such purposes as overseeing the certification of and the distribution of information on implementations of the T_EX system, their maintenance and upward-compatible enhancements. The above committee announces its readiness to help in the initial organization of such a users' group. If you feel you might be interested either in belonging to such a group or in receiving information from it, please fill out and return one of the attached reply forms.

Please fill out and return this sheet to the American Mathematical Society if you have an interest in participating in a TEX users' group.

Date _____

Name _____

Title _____

Institution _____

Mailing address _____

_____

Phone _____

How do you plan to make use of TEX? _____

_____

_____

To what kind of computing equipment do you have access? _____

_____

_____

Is TEX presently running on that equipment? If not, when will TEX probably be installed?

_____

_____

_____

Please fill out and return this sheet to the American Mathematical Society if you have an interest in participating in a TEX users' group.

Date _____

Name _____

Title _____

Institution _____

Mailing address _____

_____

Phone _____

How do you plan to make use of TEX? _____

_____

_____

To what kind of computing equipment do you have access? _____

_____

_____

Is TEX presently running on that equipment? If not, when will TEX probably be installed?

_____

_____

_____

BUSINESS REPLY MAIL

FIRST CLASS PERMIT NO. 3356 PROVIDENCE, R. I.

POSTAGE WILL BE PAID BY ADDRESSEE

AMERICAN MATHEMATICAL SOCIETY

P.O. Box 6248

Providence, Rhode Island 02940

BUSINESS REPLY MAIL

FIRST CLASS PERMIT NO. 3356 PROVIDENCE, R. I.

POSTAGE WILL BE PAID BY ADDRESSEE

AMERICAN MATHEMATICAL SOCIETY

P.O. Box 6248

Providence, Rhode Island 02940